BR 560 .P86 S33 2000
Schantz, Mar'
Piety in Prc

P9-ARY-477

DATE DUE

JUL 0 5 2001			

DEMCO 38-297

NEW ENGLAND INSTITUTE
OF TECHNOLOGY
LEARNING RESOURCES CENTER

PIETY IN PROVIDENCE

PIETY IN PROVIDENCE

CLASS DIMENSIONS OF RELIGIOUS EXPERIENCE IN ANTEBELLUM RHODE ISLAND

Mark S. Schantz

Cornell University Press ITHACA AND LONDON

NEW ENGLAND INSTITUTE
OF TECHNOLOGY
LEARNING RESOURCES CENTER

5|01   # 43784686

Copyright © 2000 by Cornell University

All rights reserved. Except for brief quotations in a review, this book, or parts
thereof, must not be reproduced in any form without permission in writing
from the publisher. For information, address Cornell University Press,
Sage House, 512 East State Street, Ithaca, New York 14850.

First published 2000 by Cornell University Press

Library of Congress Cataloging-in-Publication Data

Schantz, Mark S. (Mark Saunders), b. 1955
    Piety in Providence : class dimensions of religious experience in antebellum Rhode
    Island / Mark S. Schantz.
        p.   cm.
    Includes bibliographical references and index.
    ISBN 0-8014-2952-8
    1. Providence (R.I.)—Church history—19th century.   2. Religion and social
    status—Rhode Island—Providence—History—19th century.   I. Title.

BR560.P86 S33 2000
274.5′2081—dc21   00-022674

Printed in the United States of America

Cornell University Press strives to use environmentally responsible suppliers and
materials to the fullest extent possible in the publishing of its books. Such materials
include vegetable-based, low-VOC inks, and acid-free papers that are recycled,
totally chlorine-free, or partly composed of nonwood fibers. Books that bear
the logo of the FSC (Forest Stewardship Council) use paper taken from forests
that have been inspected and certified as meeting the highest standards for
environmental and social responsibility. For further information, visit our website
at www.cornellpress.cornell.edu.

Cloth printing   10   9   8   7   6   5   4   3   2   1

FSC FSC Trademark © 1996 Forest Stewardship Council A.C.
        SW-COC-098

FOR MY PARENTS
AND MY BROTHER

Contents

Tables

Acknowledgments

Any fair rendering of all of those who have helped me with this book would yield another volume at least as long as this one. I owe debts, first, to my graduate school mentors at Emory University, Jonathan Prude, Jim Roark, and Brooks Holifield, who guided the project in its earlier incarnations. A Charlotte W. Newcombe Grant from the Woodrow Wilson National Fellowship Foundation, a Frances Hiatt Fellowship from the American Antiquarian Society, and an award from the Colonial Dames in the State of Georgia made it possible to complete the manuscript in its first form. Since that time a Hendrix College Faculty Project Grant awarded in 1993 and a Summer Stipend awarded by the National Endowment for the Humanities in 1995 have supported me as I completed this book.

Numerous librarians and archivists also shared their expertise and enthusiasm for this project. At the Rhode Island Historical Society, Harold Kemble, Carol Hagglund, Cindy Bendroth, and Richard D. Stattler proved invaluable in steering me to sources and in helping me to track down leads. Mark Brown and his superb staff at the John Hay Library of Brown University proved to be unflinchingly helpful and efficient. The fine librarians at the John Carter Brown Library, also at Brown University, pointed me toward valuable sources in their collections. At the American Antiquarian Society, John Hench, Nancy Burkett, Joanne D. Chaison, and Marie Lamoureux made my visits there enormously productive and enjoyable. Dave Maslyn and his staff guided me with unparalleled skill through the sources of the Episcopal Church held by the University of Rhode Island. And Phyllis Silva at the Rhode Island State Archives gave me free reign to search their holdings and enabled me to find rare gems, including Seth Luther's 1823 petition for debt relief.

Individual congregations graciously opened their records for me, trusting me with their treasures. This was an act of faith on their part, which I hope this book in some small way justifies. I want to thank the members of First Baptist Church for their permission to cite from their extraordinary records. At Beneficent Congregational Church I want to thank Ralph Barlow (who was pastor during my many visits) and Nancy Russell; they both bent over backward to allow me access to church records tucked away in their vault. Nancy Russell, especially, made valiant contributions to my work by giving up some of her Saturdays in order to open the church vault for me. I also want to thank Trinity United Methodist Church, St. Joseph's Church, St. Patrick's Church, and the Cathedral Church of SS. Peter and Paul for allowing me to examine their records. While I labored in archives and in church basements, Mrs. Eleanore Monahon provided me with a room in her wonderful home and shared with me much sagely wisdom about the history of Providence. Rob Emlen and Joyce Botelho at the John Nicholas Brown Center for American Civilization also provided me with lodgings and never flagged as sources of encouragement for this project.

I am deeply grateful to all those friends and associates who read part or all of this book over the years. Among a group of intrepid and incisive commentators, Susan Juster, Teresa Murphy, Ken Fones-Wolf, and Jama Lazerow deserve pride of place. Their insights are responsible for a large measure of what is worthy here. J. Stanley Lemons of Rhode Island College, who knows more about First Baptist Church than anyone I know, read the entire manuscript and saved me from a number of errors. Carl Gersuny of the University of Rhode Island shared his enthusiasm and deep knowledge of Seth Luther by telephone and by letter. Gary Kornblith lavished me with advice regarding the Providence Association of Mechanics and Manufacturers and shared with me his computer listing of that organization's membership for the entire antebellum era. As the pages that follow testify, that proved to be resource I turned to often. My colleagues at Hendrix College, especially Ian King, Tim Maxwell, Jay Barth, Stella Čapek, Karen Gaul, Allison Shutt, James Jennings, Garrett McAinsh, and David Larson, also deserve their due. They have borne my struggle with this book with an easy forbearance and have intuited in a most uncanny fashion when to ask about it and when to keep their silence. My students, too, have cheerfully nudged the project along, assuring me that they really do want to read it. Friends from around the country, including Mart Stewart, John Rodrigue, Steve and Martha Goodson, Martha Sledge, Steven Hornsby, James Miller, Mary-Margaret Johnston-Miller, and Susan McGrath are probably more glad than I am that this book is finally completed. They have all been more generous with their encouragement than anyone has a right to expect. Martha Sledge went far beyond the call of duty by crafting the index. At Cornell University Press, I owe a great debt to senior manuscript editor Teresa Jesionowski and to John LeRoy, who combed through the manuscript looking for grammatical scandals and stylistic infelicities. Both of them have made this a better book. Peter Agree, my editor, has carried this manuscript forward with wisdom, gusto, and a watchful eye for my panicky e-mail messages. And although there are a good many words here, none of them can adequately thank my wife, Nancy Ellen Barr. She has lived with this project for as long as I have, and that alone should merit the highest praise. She has helped to format computer discs and allowed me to discuss the nuances of pew auctioning on long walks when other subjects might well have been introduced. Her faith in me and her gentleness of spirit made it possible for me to finish this book, when it could have finished me.

MARK S. SCHANTZ

Conway, Arkansas

PIETY IN PROVIDENCE

Introduction

First Baptist Church in Providence, Rhode Island, nourished the lives of two men who could not have cut a sharper contrast. One was Seth Luther. An itinerant preacher and labor spokesman, he maintained a membership in the church from 1815 to 1824, when he was excommunicated for "disorderly walking." It may have been the time he served behind prison walls for bankruptcy that helped him discover words for his deep opposition to the culture of greed he witnessed in the hustling world of Jacksonian America. And when he did speak, he proclaimed his message in the prophetic language of evangelical Christianity. "Avarice," he thundered in an 1833 oration, "manufactures drunkards, chains and lashes the slave, and crowds down and oppresses the poor, the friendless, and the destitute: it is the father of *all crime* from the days of Adam until the present time."[1] Such a statement could never have escaped the mouth of Francis Wayland, another communicant of Baptist heritage. Called to serve as president of Brown University in 1826, he glided easily in circles that included men such as Nicholas Brown, a lion of the merchant and manufacturing elite. What Luther called avarice, Wayland knew as the pursuit of wholesome and godly industry. In his weighty 1837 discourse on political economy, he intoned that a man must "be allowed to gain all that he can; and 2nd. That having gained all he can, he be allowed to use it as he will."[2] Seth Luther and Francis Wayland, Baptists alike, articulated understandings of the gospel that tugged them in opposite directions.

[1] Seth Luther, *An Address to the Working Men of New England, on the State of Education, and on the Condition of the Producing Classes in Europe and America* (New York, 1833), 7.
[2] Francis Wayland, *The Elements of Political Economy* (New York, 1837), 111.

1

This book had its origins in an effort to comprehend how Seth Luther and Francis Wayland, men who (we have been told) shared the common cup of evangelical Christianity, could have construed their Baptist heritage in such powerfully contrasting ways. The search for an answer to this question led me to an investigation of the religious, social, and cultural history of the city that they both inhabited for a large portion of their lives: Providence, Rhode Island. What began as an investigation of two prominent Baptists quickly expanded to become a study of a city, and then an even wider project whose focus was the intricate relationship between social class and religious culture in the antebellum Northeast. The city of Providence—a locus of great religious diversity, originating in Roger Williams's vision of "soul liberty," and one of the centers of the market revolution in southern New England, evidenced by the creation of the nation's first cotton spinning mill in nearby Pawtucket—proved an excellent location in which to conduct such a study.

The central argument of this book is that religious culture played a decisive role in the process of class formation in antebellum Providence, Rhode Island. Evangelical Christianity was not the possession of a single social class or constituency in the industrializing Northeast. It served simultaneously to bolster the rising power of the American bourgeoisie and to create an alternative religious culture that fueled opposition to that power. Social and labor historians have tended to see religious culture in this era as *either* a source of legitimating power for the nation's entrepreneurial interests *or*, in fewer cases, as a source of resistance to those interests.[3] In some sense both interpretations are right. The problem is that we rarely see both sides of the story, the perspective of both classes, unfolding in the same place over the same period, and are thus robbed of seeing the complex dynamic of religious culture and social class.[4] The narrative constructed here attempts

---

[3] Classic works that emphasize evangelical Christianity's power in legitimating entrepreneurial interests include Paul E. Johnson, *A Shopkeeper's Millennium: Society and Revivals in Rochester, New York, 1815–1837* (New York, 1978), and Anthony F. C. Wallace, *Rockdale: The Growth of an American Village in the Early Industrial Revolution* (New York, 1978). Christianity's power in shaping and sustaining market values is also a major theme in Charles Sellers, *The Market Revolution: Jacksonian America, 1815–1846* (New York, 1991). Among recent works that stress evangelical Christianity's importance for laborers in challenging the interests of employers, see Teresa Anne Murphy, *Ten Hours' Labor: Religion, Reform, and Gender in Early New England* (Ithaca, 1992); Jama Lazerow, *Religion and the Working Class in Antebellum America* (Washington, D.C., 1995); and William R. Sutton, *Journeymen for Jesus: Evangelical Artisans Confront Capitalism in Jacksonian Baltimore* (University Park, Pa., 1998).

[4] In their book *The Kingdom of Matthias: A Story of Sex and Salvation in Nineteenth-Century America* (New York, 1994), Paul Johnson and Sean Wilentz have focused on the conflict between the religious perspective of middle-class Finneyite reformers and that of plebeian street preachers,

to show how in one city, Providence, the bifurcation of religious culture shaped both the emerging class of merchants and manufacturers and the plebeian members of that community. In this book I argue that entrepreneurs and industrialists, on the one hand, and workers and plebeians, on the other, both understood themselves in religious terms and that religious culture therefore could not help but shape their sense of identity and their actions. I seek to treat all parties as whole people to whom concerns of the spirit mattered, and mattered deeply.

This narrative of evangelical Christianity, an interpretation that takes seriously profound divisions and cracks within what some historians have called the "United Evangelical Front," is at odds with the dominant picture sketched by more traditional church historians. Given H. Richard Niebuhr's landmark work, *The Social Sources of Denominationalism* (1929), the reticence of more recent historians of religion to address the economic and social divides within nineteenth-century Christianity is puzzling.[5] Unlike Niebuhr, they have presented an essentially harmonious picture of early American religious history, downplaying the reality of class conflict and insisting instead upon the pervasively democratic features of Christianity in the new republic.[6] Even studies that endow "popular religion" with unmistakable importance sometimes unfold as if they did not take seriously the outpouring of scholarly work on labor and social history in the past two decades.[7] Although we are learning more and more about popular religion in the early republic, those insights often remain segregated from the work being done by historians of American labor and social life.[8] Here, on the contrary, I give serious consideration to the fractures in nineteenth-century evangelical

---

but we need to learn more about how such class tensions played themselves out in individual congregations.

[5] H. Richard Niebuhr, *The Social Sources of Denominationalism* (1929; reprint, Gloucester, Mass., 1987).

[6] See here especially Nathan O. Hatch, *The Democratization of American Christianity* (New Haven, 1989). Hatch's work makes a marvelous contribution to our understanding of religious culture in this era and has more to say about class relationships in the antebellum era, I think, than the author fully acknowledges. See, for instance, his remark that "the Great Awakening delineated the fault line of class within American Christianity" (226). This insight, which appears in a concluding section of his book titled "Redefining the Second Great Awakening: A Note on the Study of Christianity in the Early Republic," begs for further elaboration.

[7] See Jon Butler, *Awash in a Sea of Faith: Christianizing the American People* (Cambridge, Mass., 1990). Like Hatch, Butler has made a signal contribution to our comprehension of religious life in this period, but he fails to take the notion of class seriously (although he refers to it in passing in numerous passages—see, for examples, 235, 255, 256, 279, and passim).

[8] An exception to this general trend is Teresa Murphy's chapter on "Popular Religion" in *Ten Hours' Labor*.

culture, and I question the wisdom of characterizing it as "a single evangelical tradition."[9]

The story begins in late-eighteenth-century Providence with an exploration of religious community in the decades before the great revival
of 1820. In Chapter 1, I contend that the religious culture of this era embodied elements of a conservative social ethos, one that was profoundly
hierarchical but that also made room for a wide range of residents within
Providence congregations. I chart the breakdown of this inclusive religious culture in Chapters 2 and 3. First in the mill villages of the Rhode
Island countryside and then in Providence itself during the revival of 1820,
plebeian residents (especially Freewill Baptists, Methodists, and Universalists) began to carve out their own religious institutions. The bifurcation
of Providence religious life was now underway. In Chapters 4 and 5, I trace
the contours of the bourgeois and plebeian religious cultures that evolved
in Providence during the decades that followed the revival of 1820. Here I
show how Francis Wayland and Seth Luther became key spokesmen for
their respective religious cultures. I explore, as well, the intersection of
gender and class in antebellum religious culture. In ways that scholars have
not fully appreciated, Protestant bourgeois religious culture remained under the firm control of men, which impels us to modify the assumption that
the faith of the propertied classes in the Jacksonian North was being "feminized."[10] Plebeian religious culture, by contrast, retained strong elements
that might be considered feminine. Aside from the important roles played
by female preachers in the factory villages of the Rhode Island countryside,
even urban street preachers (such as Seth Luther) displayed in their penchant for "disorderly" behavior, features that respectable churchgoers had
come to identify as peculiarly female sins.[11] In Chapter 6 we see how these
two religious cultures collided in the crucible of the Dorr Rebellion of
1842—Rhode Island's "taste of civil war"—which arose from a major dispute over property qualifications for voting. Chapter 7 serves as a denoue-
ment. Although Providence's bourgeois Protestants came out of the Dorr
Rebellion more robust than ever, they simultaneously wrestled with a per-
sistent sense that their own material prosperity sapped the vitality of their

[9] The phrase is from William E. Gienapp, "The Myth of Class in Jacksonian America," *Journal
of Policy History* 6 (1994): 246.
[10] See Ann Douglas, *The Feminization of American Culture* (New York, 1977), and Jane Tompkins,
Sensational Designs: The Cultural Work of American Fiction, 1790–1860 (New York, 1985),
122–146, for a more nuanced discussion of the political ramifications of the idea of
sentimentality.
[11] On these points see Susan Juster, *Disorderly Women: Sexual Politics and Evangelicalism in Revolutionary New England* (Ithaca, 1994).

faith. They also remade their vision of religious community, fracturing the older commitment to inclusivity and validating a more exclusive and individualistic understanding of congregational life.

The concept of class invoked in this essay leans heavily on the idea of culture.[12] I am deeply indebted to the work of scholars such as Lawrence Levine, Richard Bushman, and John F. Kasson, who have explored the process of what Levine has termed "cultural bifurcation" in the nineteenth century.[13] In a sense, this book applies some of their insights to the evolution of antebellum religious life. One need not subscribe to Charles Sellers's lapidary dichotomy of "Moderate Light" Arminians versus "New Light" antinomians to come to an appreciation of the bifurcated quality of religious life in the early republic.[14] At the same time, I have tried to work with a notion of class that is not severed from the economic and social structures in which individuals lived and worked. Thus, in tracing the emergence of bourgeois and plebeian churches I pay close attention to the realities of wealth (as evidenced in town tax lists) and occupation (as derived from city directories) as well as to patterns of pewholding and the characteristics of religious experience. In taking wealth, occupation, and religion seriously, I have offered what I hope will be a more expansive vision of what social class meant in antebellum America. I have tried, especially, to avoid treating religious culture as the simple product of "deeper" social and economic forces. While this methodology may not be as theoretically tidy as one would hope, weighing economic, social, and religious factors together has the advantage of treating the people of this era as whole human beings, who lived

[12] Like dozens of other students of antebellum America, I have been deeply influenced by the work of E. P. Thompson, especially his *The Making of the English Working Class* (New York, 1963) and his numerous essays, especially *Customs in Common: Studies in Traditional Popular Culture* (New York, 1993). For a critical engagement of the Thompsonian legacy see, among other treatments, Harvey J. Kaye and Keith McClelland, *E. P. Thompson: Critical Perspectives* (Philadelphia, 1990), and Michael D. Bess, "E. P. Thompson: The Historian as Activist," *American Historical Review* 98 (1993): 19–38.

[13] The phrase "cultural bifurcation" is from Lawrence W. Levine, *Highbrow/Lowbrow: The Emergence of Cultural Hierarchy in America* (Cambridge, Mass., 1988), 81; see also John F. Kasson, *Rudeness & Civility: Manners in Nineteenth-Century Urban America* (New York, 1990), and Richard L. Bushman, *The Refinement of America: Persons, Houses, Cities* (New York, 1992). See also the conceptual framework employed by Mary Kupiec Cayton in "Who Were the Evangelicals? Conservative and Liberal Identity in the Unitarian Controversy in Boston, 1804–1833," *Journal of Social History* 31 (1997): 85–107. She describes the battle between militant Congregational insurgents and the Unitarian establishment there as a "clash of two divergent cultures" (86).

[14] See Sellers, *Market Revolution*, passim. This dichotomy has been challenged by Richard J. Carwardine in his essay "'Antinomians' *and* 'Arminians': Methodists and the Market Revolution," in Melvyn Stokes and Stephen Conway, eds., *The Market Revolution in America: Social, Political, and Religious Expressions, 1800–1880* (Charlottesville, 1996), 282–307.

in this world but who simultaneously kept on eye on their eternal home in the next one.

It must be admitted, however, that the concept of class itself has been besieged by its critics in recent years.[15] Living in a postmodern age, in which all metahistorical categories are viewed with a skeptical eye, this must inevitably be the case. Even scholars who have attempted to revitalize the concept of class by nudging it in a more linguistically oriented direction have been hammered by their colleagues who perceive that they have abandoned the materialist roots necessary to any notion of class relations in the first place.[16] More narrowly understood, the battle over class conflict thrives in studies of the Jacksonian era. The appearance in 1991 of Charles Sellers's synthesis, *The Market Revolution,* sparked substantial controversy and debate over the degree to which American society had become polarized during the era of the Second Party System. Some critics have not been persuaded by Sellers's insistence that American society in this era must be understood, fundamentally, as a struggle over the coming of the market economy. In a withering critique of Sellers's book, William Gienapp, for instance, has made a strong case for the position that to posit the existence of class in antebellum America is, essentially, to construct a "myth" that bears little resemblance to what we know of the social and political history of the period.[17]

While the concept of class clearly cannot be a category of universal explanatory power in early America, it may yet have vitality. People of the early nineteenth century spent much time and energy discussing the various social classes they saw in their society. As Martin J. Burke has eloquently argued in *The Conundrum of Class,* Americans throughout the early nineteenth century debated the meaning of class among themselves, wondering especially if the interests among classes were reconcilable in the new nation.[18] It is difficult to read the political rhetoric of the era—Andrew Jackson's 1837 farewell address, for example—without recognizing that the people who lived during this age knew their society was rent by profound social

[15] See, for example, William M. Reddy's chapter "The Crisis of the Class Concept in Historical Research," in his *Money and Liberty in Modern Europe: A Critique of Historical Understanding* (New York, 1987), 1–33. See also John R. Hall, ed., *Reworking Class* (Ithaca, 1997).

[16] See, for instance, Gareth Stedman Jones, *Languages of Class: Studies in English Working Class History, 1832–1982* (Cambridge, 1983), and the response by Bryan D. Palmer, *Descent into Discourse: The Reification of Language and the Writing of Social History* (Philadelphia, 1990), esp. 128–133.

[17] Gienapp, "Myth of Class," 232–259. This essay appeared a part of a larger forum on Charles Sellers's *The Market Revolution.*

[18] Martin J. Burke, *The Conundrum of Class: Public Discourse on the Social Order in America* (Chicago, 1995), 1–132.

divisions. While they did not create a consensus with respect to the precise constituencies of these classes, they nevertheless spoke of their society in terms that identified powerful colliding interests. Moreover, an exploration of religious life in the early nineteenth century may enrich, rather than diminish, our understanding of class. Take, for instance, the view afforded by a pew plat from an evangelical church of the era.[19] Here, laid out for all to observe, were ranks of pews, each with its assigned price and rent, that would be put up for public auction. Other than town tax lists, we have no more powerful evidence of the fact that Americans divided themselves up with scrupulous attention to matters of wealth and power.

Blending the study of religious culture and social class helps us to make sense of the conflicting social ethics of Seth Luther and Francis Wayland. As Baptists and as Providence residents, they shared not only a common religious heritage but the same secular community. But without an appreciation of the social and economic contexts in which they lived and worked, we cannot grasp how important their theological differences were or why they developed such divergent visions in the first place. And without an understanding of their religious convictions, we can scarcely see how they interpreted and acted upon the material circumstances of their lives. The book that follows is an attempt to comprehend both their world and the faith that enabled them to navigate it.

---

[19] An example of such a pew plat may be found in Chapter 4 below.

1

"As Members of One Great Family"

Church and Society in Early National Providence, 1790–1820

Although Americans of the Revolutionary Age looked warily on any scheme that would tax them, the members of First Baptist Church in Providence, Rhode Island, showed no hesitation in pressing home their prerogatives on precisely this point. On January 26, 1797, they decided to investigate the behavior of one of their own, Benjamin Knowles. They wanted Knowles to attend the next meeting of the church to "assign his reasons for not paying his Tax for support of our poor agreeably to the Vote of this church."[1] Since 1792, when the congregation had formally and unanimously created a fund for "the support of the poor and other necessary expenses of the Church," they had kept a sharp eye on the needs of their less prosperous members.[2] References to specific acts of charity and gestures of kindness toward "the Indigent members of this Church" pervade the records maintained by the congregation during this decade.[3] Knowles appears to have been among only a tiny handful of members who refused to acknowledge the church's commitment to its poor. He also failed to respond to the entreaties of the church committee members who visited him. After repeated attempts to coax him to appear before them, the

---

[1] Record Book, First Baptist Church, January 26, 1797, Manuscript Collection, Rhode Island Historical Society, hereafter cited as RIHS.

[2] Record Book, First Baptist Church, October 4, 1792.

[3] Record Book, First Baptist Church; see, for example, meetings of March 29, 1792; November 24, 1796; and November 22, 1798, when the church voted funds designed to support specific members undergoing financial or medical hardships.

congregation voted without dissent to "exclude Brother Knowles from their communion."[4]

In excluding Benjamin Knowles, the members of First Baptist Church simultaneously pronounced their vision of religious community. They insisted upon a broadly inclusive conception of church membership, one that found a place for the impoverished among its ranks. Rather than being siphoned off into separate institutions such as "reform" homes or "free churches" as they would be during the 1850s, poor members possessed a legitimate claim to worship with the most affluent citizens of the town. The language of the church records is unambiguous and revealing on this point. Minutes recording the congregation's dealings with the poor speak of "our poor" or the "Indigent members of this Church," showing that the congregation did not regard them as alien or in need of special redemption but as full participants in the life of faith.[5] Far from excluding the impoverished, the members of First Baptist Church moved against a communicant who refused to acknowledge his duty to support the poor.

The capacious understanding of religious community evinced by the Baptists found expression in four key ways throughout early national Providence. First, the pervasiveness of religion served to knit together a wide range of residents and nurtured a variety of civic groups and reform movements. Second, pewholding patterns within individual congregations reveal that members of the merchant elite heard sermons alongside humble mechanics. Third, the round of church meetings and disciplinary cases, too, attest to the inclusive character of religious life in this period. And, finally, the sermons articulated by Providence clergy, while celebrating individual industry and accomplishment, stressed the communal value of labor rather than the headlong pursuit of wealth. In all these ways, the religious life of Providence proved to be remarkably elastic, embracing all manner of the town's residents.

To say that the religious culture of the town was essentially inclusive should not blind us to the reality of the power relations that governed that community. At the apex of Providence society stood a cluster of merchant princes and aspiring manufacturers, the top 5 percent of whom controlled nearly 50 percent of the assessed property in town.[6] Turning their eyes from the coast to the hinterland, these men tied their futures to the fledgling

---

[4] Record Book, First Baptist Church, December 26, 1799. A report made to the church on October 25, 1798, indicated that "the Tax assessed for the poor of the Church is Collected from all the Members Except four."

[5] For instances of such language see the church meetings listed in the preceding notes.

[6] See Gary J. Kornblith, "'Cementing the Mechanic Interest': Origins of the Providence Association of Mechanics and Manufacturers," *Journal of the Early Republic* 8 (1988): 365.

textile industry.[7] This economic elite demonstrated its power in church as well. The rise of public pew auctioning, a critical development of the period, marked the expansion of the market revolution into church sanctuaries and publicly expressed the boundaries of wealth in powerful and precise terms. Providence residents, too, grappled to understand the reconfiguration of gender relations in the postrevolutionary era. Disciplinary cases and the practices of church governance reveal that the "age of democratic revolutions" was not so democratic for Providence women.[8] Like their other northern neighbors, the white citizens of Providence also failed to deliver on the revolutionary promise of equality for African Americans.[9] By 1822, African-American men suffered at the hands of a new law that disenfranchised them by defining "freemen" as white.[10] Although they might be welcomed as members, blacks were relegated to secondary status in the predominantly white churches they attended, ascending to balconies to peer down upon white worshippers. Inclusivity did not necessarily bring with it social equality or democratic process.

In important respects, despite the "radicalism" of the revolutionary era, Providence remained a place in which a conservative, eighteenth-century ethos continued to pulse.[11] In politics, Providence residents backed a powerful and orderly national government, embraced the Federalists, and held slight regard for the more democratic "Country" party that sought to block Rhode Island's entrance into the Union.[12] In economics it was merchant capital, controlled by members of the eighteenth-century elite, that launched Rhode Islanders into the industrial age. Even as these merchants

---

[7] The classic accounts of the expansion of the Providence economy in the early national period are Lynne Withey, *Urban Growth in Colonial Rhode Island: Newport and Providence in the Eighteenth Century* (Albany, 1984), 91–112, and Peter J. Coleman's magisterial *The Transformation of Rhode Island, 1790–1860* (Providence, 1963). Developments in the countryside are analyzed in Daniel P. Jones, *The Economic and Social Transformation of Rural Rhode Island, 1780–1850* (Boston, 1992).

[8] Susan Juster, *Disorderly Women: Sexual Politics and Evangelicalism in Revolutionary New England* (Ithaca, 1994), 108–144.

[9] Gary B. Nash, *Race and Revolution* (Madison, Wisc., 1990), especially 25–52.

[10] Robert J. Cottrol, *The Afro-Yankees: Providence's Black Community in the Antebellum Era* (Westport, Conn., 1982), 42, on "the erosion of black rights in the early nineteenth century."

[11] A compelling case for the radical changes wrought by the American Revolution is argued by Gordon S. Wood, *The Radicalism of the American Revolution* (New York, 1992).

[12] Kornblith, "'Cementing the Mechanic Interest,'" 385–386, and David Hackett Fischer, *The Revolution of American Conservatism: The Federalist Party in the Era of Jeffersonian Democracy* (New York, 1965), 277–284. With the exception of the Jeffersonian landslide of 1804, Rhode Islanders voted Federalist in 1796, 1800, 1808, and 1812. See Arthur M. Schlesinger, Jr., ed., *History of American Presidential Elections 1789–1968* (New York, 1971), 1:98, 140–141, 156, 182, 296.

became manufacturers, they rebuffed more modern corporate forms of business organization, adhering instead to the model of the joint-stock company and the family partnerships and alliances they already knew.[13] These men and their families could be glimpsed at the Providence theater, where "liveried servants entered the circles, bearing trays laden with wines and sherbets, and served them to their masters and mistresses."[14] In dispensing charity, the Providence Female Society for the Relief of Indigent Women and Children continued the eighteenth-century practice of binding out impoverished children to learn a trade.[15] Tradition, too, abided in the dynamic of race relations. Despite Rhode Island's gradual emancipation act of 1784, "the majority of blacks in 1790 lived in white-headed households, performing the tasks that their former masters desired."[16] Not until 1810 would most African Americans live outside the reach of white-headed households.[17] Thus ancient notions of hierarchy, deference, and order endured alongside the newer forces of individualism, equality, and the market economy unleashed by the Revolution.

Providence's churches played a critical role in bringing together its residents during a time of wrenching change. A 1790 sketch of the city accorded paramount importance to three congregations on the east side of the "Great Salt River" that split the city geographically: St. John's Church (Episcopal), First Baptist Church, and First Congregational Church. The east side also boasted a Quaker meetinghouse, which was complemented by Beneficent Congregational Church on Weybosset Street on the west side of town. Taken together, these churches could accommodate most of Providence's six thousand residents.[18] The Baptist meetinghouse, for example, contained room for an estimated fourteen hundred persons, its size justified in part by the use of the building for Rhode Island College commencements.[19] An 1820 survey of the congregations in the town reveals that institutional religion kept pace with population growth. By then, Providence's twelve thousand citizens could also attend services at Second Baptist Church (also called Pine Street Church), at two new Congregational

---

[13] See Coleman, *Transformation of Rhode Island*, esp. ix, 81.

[14] Charles Blake, *An Historical Account of the Providence Stage, being a paper read before the Rhode Island Historical Society, October 25, 1860* (Providence, 1868), 75–76.

[15] See *The Constitution of the Providence Female Society, for the Relief of Indigent Women and Children* (Providence, 1801), 7.

[16] Cottrol, *Afro-Yankees*, 48.

[17] Ibid.

[18] For population figures see Coleman, *Transformation of Rhode Island*, 220.

[19] See John Hutchins Cady, *The Civic and Architectural Development of Providence, 1636–1950* (Providence, 1957), 50.

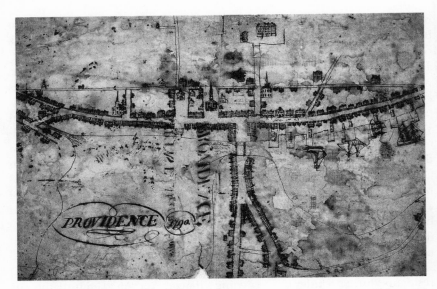

John Fitch's map of Providence, drawn in 1790, shows the spires of the city's three East Side churches: *left to right,* St. John's Episcopal Church, First Baptist Church, and First Congregational Church. Courtesy of The Rhode Island Historical Society, RHi (×3) 336.

churches, at small Methodist or Catholic communities, or at the newly formed African Union Meeting House.[20] Even before the fiery revival of 1820, the citizens of the town had forged a religious culture of diversity and strength. Timothy Dwight, the Federalist avatar and president of Yale, found himself enthralled by the force of these churches in shaping the lives of the town's residents. "The morals of Providence," he sang, "are probably superior to those of any other town in this state."[21]

Beyond the boundaries of meetinghouses, public political rituals took on a distinctly religious coloration. In August 1790, when President George Washington docked in Providence to celebrate the entrance of Rhode

[20] See Coleman, *Transformation of Rhode Island*, 220. The new Congregational churches were the Richmond Street Congregational Church, completed in 1807, and the Pacifick Congregational Church, gathered in 1814. On the first Richmond Street church building see Cady, *Civic and Architectural Development*, 75. On the Pacifick Congregational Church see *The Articles of Faith and the Covenant of Pacifick Congregational Church in Providence, 1814* (Providence, 1814).

[21] Timothy Dwight, *Travels in New England and New York*, ed. Barbara Miller Solomon with the assistance of Patricia M. King, 4 vols. (Cambridge, Mass., 1969), 2:17.

Island into the Union, he was greeted by the pealing of "Bells of the several Places of Worship." In the procession that followed, "The Reverend Clergy" of the town assumed an honored place, marching ahead of merchants, professionals, shopkeepers, and the artisans of the recently created Providence Association of Mechanics and Manufacturers.[22] Providence churchmen continued their involvement in politics by holding forth as featured speakers at annual Independence Day celebrations.[23] They also contributed to Washington's national canonization by preaching lavish sermons on the occasion of his death. "It is not expected that we should all be generals, presidents or rulers," announced Stephen Gano, minister of First Baptist Church, "but we should all be good citizens—peaceable, industrious, virtuous and faithful, in our several stations."[24] In Gano's hands, Washington emerged not only as a model citizen but as a model Christian as well, fulfilling the duties appropriate to his "station" in life.

The activities of reform associations underscored the prominent place of religion in the community. The Providence Society for the Abolition of the Slave Trade gathered for the first time in the Quaker meetinghouse on February 20, 1789.[25] Under the direction of Moses Brown, a prominent merchant and philanthropist, the members recognized that since "the Creator of Mankind" had designed all human beings, "it becomes them to consult and promote each other's happiness, as Members of One great Family." To put this belief into practice they thought it "incumbent on them to endeavor the Suppression of that unrighteous Commerce."[26] Evincing a dedication to put religious principle ahead of sheer profit, the Abolition Society supported federal efforts to enforce a 1794 ban on those facilitating the slave trade outside America.[27] Given the dominance of Rhode Island merchants in the slave trade, men who "held a virtual monopoly in that brand of commerce" in the postrevolutionary era, this was a bold stand

[22] *The Providence Gazette and Country Journal*, August 21, 1790, and broadside titled "Order of Procession to be Observed on the Arrival of the President of the United States," August 17, 1790, Graphics Department, RIHS.

[23] Jonathan Maxcy, *An Oration Delivered in the First Baptist Meeting-House in Providence, July 4th, a.d. 1795 at the celebration of the nineteenth anniversary of American Independence* (Providence, 1795); Asa Messer, *An Oration Delivered at Providence in the Baptist Meeting-House on the Fourth of July, 1803* (Providence, 1803); and James Wilson, *An Oration Delivered at Providence in the First Congregational Meeting-House, on the Fourth of July, 1804* (Providence, 1804), Brown University Library.

[24] Stephen Gano, *A Sermon on the Death of General George Washington; Delivered Lord's Day, January 5, 1800, before the Baptist Society, in Providence* (Providence, 1800), 16–17.

[25] Abolition Society Book, 1789–1827, meeting of January 29, 1789, Quaker Archives, RIHS.

[26] Ibid.

[27] Jay Coughtry, *The Notorious Triangle: Rhode Island and the African Slave Trade, 1700–1807* (Philadelphia, 1981), 206–220.

indeed.[28] Moses Brown provided the common link to another genre of religious reform. In 1814 he joined a group of other Providence "gentlemen" in establishing the Bible Society of the State of Rhode-Island and Providence Plantations. Harbinger of later and more concerted efforts to spread religious print in the city and state, the Bible Society intended to supply all citizens with a copy of the Scriptures. Its members agreed that worthy but impoverished families held "a strong claim upon the charity of the more opulent and prosperous."[29] Thus both the Abolition Society and the Bible Society rooted their reform efforts in a religious sensibility that connected the greater and lesser members of the social order.

Even civic groups formed under ostensibly secular auspices projected a strong spiritual dimension. The Providence Association of Mechanics and Manufacturers, formed in 1789 to promote "the Mechanic Interest," held meetings in Providence churches. In 1800, for example, the First Congregational Meeting-House served as the destination for the artisans' annual procession and meeting.[30] In 1803 the committee appointed to arrange the anniversary festivities again secured a church. This time they selected Beneficent Congregational Church "for the accommodation of the Association."[31] The association's selection of Beneficent Congregational Church was especially appropriate since the pastor there, James Wilson, had apprenticed as a cabinetmaker in Ireland before giving up his apron for clerical attire.[32] The association's custom of holding annual meetings in churches continued well into the 1820s, with Second Baptist Church and the Universalist Chapel hosting them in 1822 and 1826 respectively.[33] Moreover, the library that the association established for its members housed an extensive collection of religious titles. Here artisans could find classics such as Butler's *Analogy*, Bunyan's *Pilgrim's Progress*, and William Paley's *Natural Theology*. Given the hefty representation of mechanics among

[28] Coughtry, *Notorious Triangle*, 25.
[29] *A Statement Respecting the Bible Society of the State of Rhode Island and Providence Plantations; With an Appendix addressed to the Publick by the Board of Trustees* (Providence 1814), 8, Brown University Library.
[30] Records of the Providence Association of Mechanics and Manufacturers, vol. 2, 1794–1811, entry for April 14, 1800, RIHS.
[31] Records of the Providence Association of Mechanics and Manufacturers, entry for April 4, 1803.
[32] Arthur E. Wilson, *Paddy Wilson's Meeting-House in Providence Plantations, 1791–1839* (Boston, 1950), v and passim.
[33] See broadsides entitled, *Order of Performances at the Second Baptist Meeting House, on Monday, April 8th, 1822; In Commemoration of the 33rd Anniversary of the Association of Mechanicks and Manufacturers* and *Celebration at the Universalist Chapel. Order of Exercises at the Anniversary Meeting of the Providence Association of Mechanics and Manufacturers, April 10, 1826*, Harris Collection, Large Broadsides, Brown University Library.

the ranks of pewholders in the town's churches, it is little wonder that their organization revealed such a profoundly religious sensibility.[34]

Periods of religious awakening frequently punctuated the regular cycle of church meetings and community events. In 1790, 1805, 1812, and 1815, at least, discernible revivals rippled through the town. Accounts of these revivals indicate that they touched persons throughout the community— young and old, rich and poor, women and men, black residents and even Native Americans. In 1790 the Baptist minister Isaac Backus pointed to the miraculous work taking place among the faculty and students of Rhode Island College. Chief among the converts was Jonathan Maxcy, a young tutor who would become an ordained clergyman and prominent educator: in the course of his career he served as president of Rhode Island College, Union College in Schenectady, New York, and the University of South Carolina. Backus reported that when Maxcy "was alone in his chamber, under a clear sense of the justice of God in his condemnation, such light and love shined into his soul as struck his body to the floor, and he cried out, 'Glory! glory to God, for his free love!' "[35] In January 1806, in a report he filed in the *Massachusetts Baptist Missionary Magazine*, Stephen Gano identified a wider arena for the workings of the spirit. As over 150 new members joined his church, he noted converts of all kinds including "the poor," "the more opulent, as to this world," and even "a number with tawny skins."[36] In 1812 Gano reported with satisfaction that "several people of color have also participated in the riches of grace; and I have rejoiced in having the opportunity of going with them into the water, and burying them in baptism."[37] In 1815 David Benedict, a Baptist minister in nearby Pawtucket, observed an equally diverse group of converts, including "a number of persons of considerable standing in society." Moreover, he noticed the prominent role of female converts, describing one woman who "when she got into the street, she hardly knew how to spend time to go from one to another to tell them individually, but wanted some herald with a trumpet to sound it abroad."[38] At St. John's Church, rector Nathan B. Crocker himself embraced enthusiastic religion after a mysterious encounter with the works of Jonathan

---

[34] See *Catalogue of the Mechanics' and Apprentices' Library, Established by the Association of Mechanics and Manufacturers in Providence, R.I. 1821* (Providence, 1821), American Antiquarian Society Library, Worcester, Mass., hereafter cited as AAS.

[35] Quoted in William G. McLoughlin, ed., *The Diary of Isaac Backus*, 3 vols. (Providence, 1979), 3:1285.

[36] *Massachusetts Baptist Missionary Magazine* 1 (1806): 179–180.

[37] *Massachusetts Baptist Missionary Magazine* 3 (1813): 307.

[38] Benedict's account may be found in Joshua Bradley, A.M., *Accounts of Religious Revivals in Many Parts of the United States From 1815 to 1818, Collected from numerous Publications, and Letters from Persons of piety and correct information* (Albany, 1819), 49–53. See 49 and 52 for quotations.

Edwards.[39] In 1816 an amazed Asa Messer, then president of Rhode Island College, recorded the results. "Mr. Crocker," he wrote with astonishment, "has baptized one in the Providence *river;* and among his people, the Episcopalians, there is a very solemn engagedness."[40] That Episcopalians dared to immerse themselves in the icy waters of the Providence River testifies to the pervasive quality of enthusiastic religion within the town.

Waves of fresh converts spelled expansion for Providence churches. Between 1809 and 1816, three congregations erected new places of worship: Beneficent Congregational in 1809, St. John's Episcopal in 1811, and First Congregational in 1816. Although extraordinarily different in style, the three churches ranked among the most impressive buildings in the city. The new home of Beneficent Congregational Church, known as the "Round Top Church," eschewed a traditional steeple for a dome. The octagonal base of the building contained 150 pews as well as a ring of spacious balconies.[41] Across the river on the north end of Main Street, the members of St. John's Episcopal Church replaced the building in which they had worshipped since 1722. John Holden Greene, master carpenter and architect, brought his considerable skill and imagination to the task. Of Gothic design, the new church with its solid walls of Smithfield stone resembled a squat but ornate fortress. In decorating the interior of the church the members spared no expense. In 1816 the women of the congregation orchestrated a fund drive that produced nearly six hundred dollars for the purchase of a new chandelier.[42] In that same year, the members of First Congregational Church moved into their new building, also a John Holden Greene production. Perched on College Hill, its magnificent spire appeared even taller than the two hundred feet called for in the architect's drawings.[43] A trace of denominational rivalry may be detected in the design, as the steeple of First Baptist Church measured only 185 feet. From its already elevated position along Benefit Street, the First Congregational Church marked the high point of the Providence skyline.

All three churches relied on the same revolutionary method to finance their construction: the public auctioning of pews. Although the private ownership of pews dates from the colonial period, what was new in the early

[39] Richard Bache Duane, *Memorial of Nathan B. Crocker, D.D., late Rector of Saint John's Church, Providence* (Providence, 1866), 53–54.

[40] Asa Messer to William Rogers, D.D., of Philadelphia, April 13, 1816, Asa Messer Papers, Brown University Library.

[41] See Cady, *Civic and Architectural Development*, 73–75.

[42] See ibid., 74–76; "The Names of the Liberal donors to Purchase a Chandelier," St. John's Cathedral Records, box 1, Account Book, 1810–1819, 80–81, University of Rhode Island Archives, Kingston, Rhode Island.

[43] Cady, *Civic and Architectural Development*, 85–86.

nineteenth century was the practice of raising the total funds necessary for church construction from a public auction. In 1775, for example, the expense of raising the Baptist meetinghouse was covered in part by a public lottery for prizes and in part by private subscriptions, which did not necessarily consist of cash donations. Instead, members pledged their own labor and goods toward the process of construction.[44] As late as 1795, First Congregational Church, too, had conducted a lottery to raise funds for its new meetinghouse.[45] But during the opening decades of the nineteenth century, lotteries gave way to the auctioning of pews. Instead of relying on the work of artisans, pledged through the subscription procedure, churches hired these skilled craftsmen and paid them wages.[46] Churches thus emerged as employers within the labor market. Moreover, congregations developed intricate sets of rules that governed the trade in pews. Church committees made available lists of pew valuations prior to the sale so that perspective buyers might consider their options, judging the cost of a pew against the status it might bring them once purchased. At a set time and place, buyers tendered offers for their choices. Virtually anyone, regardless of personal religious convictions, could purchase a pew in a given church, provided that they observed the rules that governed the "society" of pewholders who actually owned the church building. During the bidding procedure, all perspective buyers needed to be aware of the pew taxes that would be assessed on their seats in the future, an amount usually reckoned as a percentage of the total valuation of the pew. Expensive pews meant higher taxes. As the society clerk or treasurer entered the name of each purchaser into a ledger book and completed the pew deed, methods of payment might be discussed. In 1816, First Congregational Church eased the major purchase of a pew with a graduated payment plan. Half of the total cost—that is, the pew valuation plus the actual amount bid for the seat—would be due in six months, with the balance due a year after that "with interest" from the date of purchase. If one added to

---

[44] See Norman M. Isham, *The Meeting House of the First Baptist Church in Providence, A History of the Fabric* (Providence, 1925), 28–29. On First Baptist Church see J. Stanley Lemons, *The First Baptist Church in America* (East Greenwich, R.I., 1988).

[45] On the lottery for First Congregational Church, see the *Providence Gazette*, August 1, 1795, which published a list of the prizes. Lotteries seem to have endured as means of financing churches where members were not wealthy enough to purchase pews. In 1822, for instance, a Freewill Baptist Church in Smithfield, Rhode Island, petitioned the General Assembly for the right to hold a lottery since the members wished "the pews therein to be free to all persons." See *Petitions to the Rhode Island General Assembly*, 50:13, Rhode Island State Archives, Providence.

[46] St. John's Cathedral Records, box 22, folder 173, Society History, December 21, 1810, University of Rhode Island Archives. This entry includes a list of carpenters to be retained "in employment and be allowed wages attached to their respective names."

these costs the expense of "pew furniture"—that is, cushions, foot stoves, hymn books, Bibles, etc.—the purchase of a pew represented a major investment.[47]

While at first glance the rise of public pew auctioning might seem only a matter of antiquarian fascination, it actually demands our careful scrutiny. For on a broad level, the practice of pew auctioning demonstrates in extraordinary fashion the linkages between religious culture and the market revolution in the early republic. Pew auctioning marked the visible and explicit appearance of market transactions in church sanctuaries. The sale of pews transformed what had previously been "sacred" space into the rationally organized "profane" domain of the market economy. Viewed from this perspective, the rise of pew auctioning contributed to the "desacralized cosmos" that, according to Mircea Eliade, typifies most modern societies.[48] While it could still function as the place in which communicants might experience the "mysterium tremendum," there could be little sense in which the church building remained a locus for the "wholly other."[49] Pews, like other goods, could simply be bought and sold, divorced in a profound sense from the substance of faith. By commodifying religious space, evangelical churches contributed to the "origins of unbelief" in American society.[50]

The public sale of pews delineated the boundaries of wealth and economic power in unprecedented ways. By tradition, New England's meetinghouses had been sat by town committees who considered not only the wealth but the social status, age, character, and even military service records of potential pewholders.[51] Pew auctioning compressed such distinctions by transforming one's place in church into a function of wealth alone. The only comparable ranking of the wealth of Providence citizens for this period can be found in the city's manuscript tax lists, and even here the assessments

[47] An especially detailed description of procedures for pew auctioning has survived in "Conditions of the Sale of Pews in the First Congregational Meeting-House, October, 1816," Benevolent Congregational Society Records, box 11, RIHS.

[48] Mircea Eliade, *The Sacred and the Profane: The Nature of Religion,* trans. Willard R. Trask (New York, 1959), esp. 13, 58–65. On the notion that the domain of the marketplace is rationally organized, see Max Weber, *The Protestant Ethic and the Spirit of Capitalism,* trans. Talcott Parsons (New York, 1958), 24 and passim.

[49] Rudolf Otto, *The Idea of the Holy: An Inquiry into the Non-rational Factor in the Idea of the Divine and Its Relation to the Rational,* trans. John W. Harvey (New York, 1923), 25–30.

[50] The rationalization of religious space described by pew auctioning meshes with the intellectual rationalization of Christian belief in antebellum America described by James Turner in *Without God, Without Creed: The Origins of Unbelief in America* (Baltimore, 1985).

[51] Robert J. Dinkin, "Seating the Meeting House in Early Massachusetts," *New England Quarterly* 43 (1970): 450–464.

The pew deed of Thomas P. Ives, a Providence merchant and manufacturer. Although the price Ives paid for this pew, $535, makes this pew deed an exceptional example, hundreds of Providence residents owned deeds similar to this one during the antebellum era. Courtesy of The Rhode Island Historical Society, RHi (x3) 8974.

of citizens were not made a matter of public ceremony. To view an early-nineteenth-century pew plat (a diagram of the interior of a church that typically showed pews, occupants, and valuations) is to glimpse the economic hierarchy of a community. It also provides a window on the emergence of nascent class distinctions in antebellum America. While there is no evidence that wealthy pewholders squared off against the less affluent on a regular basis, we can perceive the clear distinction between those who owned religious property (the pewholders) and those who did not. This distinction could be keenly experienced. William J. Brown, who left us an extraordinary account of Providence's African-American community, recalled that some black residents refused to attend church "because they said they were opposed to going to churches and sitting in pigeon holes."[52] While Brown's situation was surely compounded by his status as an African American, it is not difficult to imagine white plebeian residents feeling a similar resentment toward their social betters. The distinction between pewholders and non-pewholders, then, signified one of the earliest indications of class formation in antebellum Providence. To point to the crucial religious element in the process of class formation challenges the notion that religious culture was simply the reflection of a deeper and more fundamental material reality. As E. P. Thompson has reminded us, "class is a historical formation, and it does not occur only in ways prescribed as theoretically proper."[53]

Pew auctioning also underscored the highly gendered quality of religious life in the early republic. While it has become a commonplace observation that women constituted the majority of church members in antebellum America, this generalization should not lead us to the conclusion that women controlled evangelical congregations. In the first place, to the degree that pew auctioning reflected an exercise in public institution building, it highlighted male prerogatives. The construction of churches meshed with other manly work: the framing of governments and civic institutions in the postrevolutionary era.[54] Moreover, by privileging the monetary contributions of members rather than their spiritual zeal, pew auctioning served to underscore the power of men within their congregations. It is important to see that the move to pew auctioning took place at precisely the time in which Federalist theorists, such as Alexander Hamilton, redefined work in such a way that "only paid labor was comprehended as a part of the econ-

---

[52] William J. Brown, *The Life of William J. Brown, of Providence, R.I. With Personal Recollections of Incidents in Rhode Island* (Freeport, N.Y., 1971), 46.

[53] E. P. Thompson, "Eighteenth-Century English Society: Class Struggle without Class?" *Social History* 3 (1978): 150.

[54] Juster, *Disorderly Women*, 142–143.

omy."[55] This understanding of the masculine quality of true labor crept into the thinking of at least one Providence minister. Before the Providence Association of Mechanics and Manufacturers, Jonathan Maxcy explained that "labouring people are the security of a free nation. Those who live in idleness and effeminacy are not easily brought to laborious exertion."[56] Women's work, because it remained outside the cash nexus, was thus devalued both in discourses on political economy and within religious communities. Finally, the practice of pew auctioning blended with the emerging doctrine of "separate spheres," which designated the home as the proper station for women and the marketplace as the arena for competitive men.[57] The sale of pews clearly occupied the realm of the market rather than the domain of the home. While women may have been more likely to own the covenant than men, the public trade in pews served to remind them that men, quite literally, owned the church.

Given that pew auctioning inscribed the demarcations of social inequality in new and profound ways, what is striking about pewholding patterns before 1820 is their wide inclusivity. China merchants and textile investors, artisans and shopkeepers, humble mechanics and mariners, black residents, students, and even transients could find seats in Providence congregations. Most fundamentally, the distribution of wealth among the pewholders indicates the diversity of those who bought seats in the new churches. (See Table 1.) To be sure, especially at St. John's Episcopal and First Congregational churches, significant numbers of pewholders represented the top strata of wealth in the town. At St. John's, over 36 percent of the pewholders could be located among men assessed at more than fifty dollars in the tax rolls. Still more impressive, however, was the relatively even distribution of wealth in the middle ranges and in the clustering of pewholders who were assessed for twenty dollars or less. Those in the latter category represented 41 percent of the pewholders at Beneficent Congregational Church, 37 percent at First Congregational Church, and 31 percent of those who held places at the elite St. John's Church. Men of modest means could find places in any of the three new meetinghouses.

Committees charged with assigning pew valuations designed a wide range of options for perspective purchasers. (See Tables 2 and 3.) The best seats,

[55] Jeanne Boydston, *Home and Work: Housework, Wages, and the Ideology of Labor in the Early Republic* (New York, 1990), 45.

[56] Jonathan Maxcy, *An Oration Delivered Before the Providence Association of Mechanics and Manufacturers at Their Annual Election*, April 13, 1795 (Providence, 1795), 9, Brown University Library.

[57] Nancy F. Cott, *The Bonds of Womanhood: "Woman's Sphere" in New England, 1780–1835* (New Haven, 1977).

Table 1. Wealth distribution among early national pewholders

Tax Value in Dollars[a]	First Congregational Church, 1816		Beneficent Congregational Church, 1809		Saint John's Episcopal Church, 1811	
	Pewholders	%	Pewholders	%	Pewholders	%
501+	2	1.2	0	0	3	3.8
101–500	15	9.3	8	5.0	11	13.9
51–100	13	8.0	14	8.7	15	18.9
41–50	11	6.8	4	2.5	6	7.6
31–40	13	8.0	10	6.2	5	6.3
21–30	11	6.8	12	7.5	4	5.0
11–20	24	14.8	25	15.5	13	16.5
0–10	37	22.8	42	26.0	12	15.2
TOTAL LISTED	126	77.7	115	71.4	69	87.2
Pewholders not listed	36	22.3	46	28.6	10	12.8

Sources: Records of the Beneficent Congregational Church, Pewholders 1809–1811, Rhode Island Historical Society (RIHS); Benevolent Congregational Society Records, vol. 23, RIHS; St. John's Cathedral Records, box 13, folder 117, University of Rhode Island Archives; town tax lists for Providence for the years 1809, 1810, 1811, and 1816, RIHS.
[a] Based on total assessed town tax valuation (both real and personal) for pewholders in the year indicated. It should be noted that in this table and in all other tables where tax assessment information is provided that individual residents were worth far more in actual terms than their assessments might indicate. I was unable to uncover the exact formulas or methods that tax assessors used in assigning specific valuations, but it is clear that whatever method they employed could vastly understate the real value of Providence fortunes. Members of the merchant and manufacturing elite may well have been worth many thousands of dollars even if their assessed value was measured in the mere hundreds.

Table 2. Average pew valuations

Church	Overall average value	Ground floor	Balcony
Beneficent Congregational Church, 1809	$223.75	$247.77	$76.36
First Congregational Church, 1816	299.16	348.53	98.27
St. John's Episcopal Church, 1811	344.35	344.35	—

Sources: See Table 1.

of course, commanded handsome sums. First Congregational Church contained the most expensive pews in town, eight of them valued at an extraordinary seven hundred dollars each. At the same time, members could select balcony pews for as little as seventy-five dollars. St. John's, while not selling pews at exceptionally high prices, maintained the highest aver-

Table 3. Range of pew valuations

Church	Most expensive pew		Least expensive pew	
Beneficent Congregational Church, 1809	Ground floor	$430	Ground floor	$80
	Balcony	100	Balcony	65
First Congregational Church, 1816	Ground floor	700	Ground floor	100
	Balcony	125	Balcony	75
St. John's Episcopal Church, 1811	Ground floor	430	Ground floor	200
	Balcony	n.a.	Balcony	n.a.

Sources: See Table 1.

age valuation of some $345 per pew. Buyers might locate the best bargains among pews sold at the Beneficent Congregational Church, which sold some in its balcony for as low as sixty-five dollars. One could even occupy a pew without the expense of ownership. First Congregational and Beneficent Congregational made it possible for occupants to lease pews, for a modest rent plus the taxes levied on the pew's assessed value. Both churches also set aside pews, without cost, for "strangers" and "students." St. John's Church, too, sought to accord the less affluent a measure of status by reserving eight pews on the ground floor for "the Poor of the Church."[58] They also designated a committee "authorized to let out to any reputable people of color the three back pews in the north gallery of the church."[59] Churches proved themselves mindful of the reality of social inequality and sought to comprehend the civic order within their walls.

A survey of the Providence pewholders describes what might be termed a religious variation on the theme of the "Great Chain of Being."[60] The top link of the chain included members of the merchant and manufacturing elite. Typically they owned the prime pews, located front and center on the church floor—but not so close to the pulpit as to create a severe angle for observing the pastor at his work. The merchant princes also demonstrated a propensity to purchase multiple pews. At St. John's, for example, Thomas Halsey purchased two fine pews for a total of $1,035, including his auction bid. In 1809 at Beneficent Congregational Church, Benjamin Hoppin collected four pews with a combined valuation exceeding $1,400. The Butler clan, Samuel Butler and Samuel Butler Jr., approached Hoppin's total,

[58] "Pews on the first floor of St. John's Church in Providence unsold on the 11th of May, 1813," St. John's Cathedral Records, box 13, folder 118.
[59] Meeting of the Cathedral Society, December 27, 1811, St. John's Cathedral Records, box 7, folder 46.
[60] See Arthur O. Lovejoy, *The Great Chain of Being: A Study in the History of an Idea* (Cambridge, Mass., 1936).

amassing pews worth a total of $1,370 including the auction bids. Some grandees extended their eminence by purchasing pews in churches of different denominations. In 1811 Thomas P. Ives, Edward Carrington, Sullivan Dorr, Samuel G. Arnold, and Oliver Kane all bought into the new Episcopal Church. Kane made an impression on the church treasurer when he paid for his $420 seat in cash, an extraordinarily rare feat. By 1816 this coterie of the Providence elite threw their support to First Congregational Church as well. Without relinquishing their Episcopal pews, all of these men purchased pews in the new Congregational house of worship. Even Nicholas Brown, the great Baptist benefactor, transcended denominational boundaries by acquiring a pew in St. John's Church. Thus did the elite demonstrate the universal largesse expected of gentlemen of their rank.[61]

Patterns of elite pewholding also cemented business partnerships. Nicholas Brown's decision to purchase a pew in St. John's Church gave him a stake in the religious community of his financial colleague Thomas P. Ives, who also owned a pew there. In 1815, when Rhode Island entrepreneurs and manufacturers petitioned Congress for trade protection, the first three signers of the document—James Burrill Jr., Daniel Lyman, and Thomas Burgess—all held pews at First Congregational Church. Daniel Lyman's cotton manufacturing company included Sullivan Dorr, Jacob Dunnell, and Samuel Nightingale, who could also be located among the pewholders at First Congregational Church. Other signers of the 1815 petition, Philip Allen and George Jackson, represented the textile interests at St. John's Episcopal Church. At St. John's, the Lippitt clan also brought fellow pewholder George Jackson into their manufacturing concern. In 1814, five of the original ten partners in the Providence Dyeing, Bleaching and Calendering Company also owned pews at Beneficent Congregational Church. The religious culture of Providence nurtured the emerging textile industry that transformed the Rhode Island countryside.[62]

Below the circle of merchants and aspiring industrialists, artisans could be counted among the ranks of the city's pewholders. Even when measured by the relatively exclusive criteria of membership in the Providence Association of Mechanics and Manufacturers (PAMM), artisans made an impres-

---

[61] See sources listed for Table 1.

[62] Sources for the business associations listed are as follows: for 1815 cotton textile petitioners see *Cotton Manufacturers in Providence and Vicinity to the Honourable Senate and House of Representatives of the United States* (Providence, 1815), AAS; on the members of the Lyman Cotton Manufacturing Company see Shepley Papers, 11:5, RIHS; on the Lippitt Manufacturing Company see L. E. Rogers, *The Biographical Cyclopedia of Representative Men of Rhode Island* (Providence, 1881), 400; on the Providence Dyeing, Bleaching and Calendering Company see Welcome Arnold Greene, *The Providence Plantations for Two Hundred and Fifty Years* (Providence, 1886), 254.

Table 4. Summary of pewholders and members of the Providence Association of Mechanics and Manufacturers

Church	Pewholders	PAMM members	
		Number	% of pewholders
Beneficent Congregational Church, 1809	161	27	16.77
First Congregational Church, 1816	162	29	17.90
St. John's Episcopal Church, 1811	79	6	7.59
Totals	402	62	15.42

Sources: See Table 1; also a master list of the membership of the Providence Association of Mechanics and Manufacturers (PAMM), courtesy of Gary Kornblith.

sive show of strength in church. Sixty-two of the 402 total pewholders among all three new congregations maintained active memberships in PAMM, suggesting that master mechanics embraced Christianity as well as the traditions of artisan republicanism. (See Table 4.) The case of the housewright Daniel Hayford reveals that these artisans prized their participation in church affairs. A man sensible of his mechanic interest, he had joined PAMM in 1797 and maintained that affiliation until his death in 1834. Hayford's career, however, did not proceed smoothly. In February 1807, he petitioned the Rhode Island General Assembly for debt relief due to "a great variety of misfortunes." As required by law, Hayford included a list of his property along with his petition for relief. Aside from furniture and tools, he also recorded "one Third of a Pew in the Cong. Meeting House." We know that Hayford made use of his seat since he also included "one Large Bible & Four Hymn Books" among his worldly goods. The General Assembly granted Hayford's request for relief, and shortly thereafter his employment picture improved. In 1810 he joined John Holden Greene and a group of other craftsmen as employees of St. John's Episcopal Church. By 1816 he had collected the funds necessary to purchase a pew worth $150 in the newly constructed First Congregational Church. Although a bargain in comparison to other pews on the ground floor, Hayford's place reflected a measure of his modest prosperity, since in the old church he had owned only a portion of a pew. Hayford's career was that of an artisan of both considerable industry and tenacious religious conviction.[63]

[63] The sources used for the reconstruction of the Hayford case are: Gary Kornblith, comp., "Masterlist of Members of the Providence Association of Mechanics and Manufacturers" (unpublished listing in the possession of the author); debtor's petition in *Petitions to the Rhode Island General Assembly*, 37:43, Rhode Island State Archives; Society History, 1794–1810, St. John's Cathedral Records, box 22, folder 173; Benevolent Congregational Society Records, vol. 23.

In several respects, patterns of artisan pewholding diverged from those practiced by the Providence elite. Most obviously, they acquired less expensive seats than the entrepreneurs. Even important members of PAMM, such as John Howland, president of the association from 1824 to 1830 and a respected civic leader, settled for less expensive locations. Howland's pew carried a modest $125 valuation in 1816.[64] In addition, no artisan appears to have owned or leased more than a single pew. Rather, abiding by traditions of "cooperation and solidarity," some artisans shared the expenses of pew ownership.[65] At Beneficent Congregational Church, Nathaniel Cooke, a housewright, and Charles Hartshorn, a mason, both members of PAMM joined in the purchase of pew no. 36. At First Congregational Church, Moses Richardson and Josiah Whitaker, also association colleagues, shared in the costs of pew no. 23. Finally, whereas members of the merchant and manufacturing elite almost always held a pew in St. John's Episcopal Church—the locus of the highest average pew valuations in town—artisans rarely made an appearance there. (See Table 4.) Instead, they spread themselves rather evenly between the Beneficent Congregational Church, a community with strong evangelical traditions, and First Congregational Church, a body that would declare itself in the Unitarian fold during the 1820s.

Petty merchants, traders, and even sailors also sought pews in Providence churches. Consider the case, for instance, of Spooner Ruggles. A mariner who resided on South Main Street near the waterfront, Ruggles leased pew no. 89 in the First Congregational Church, appraised at $275. His choice of the seat went uncontested, and he consequently tendered no bid for the pew. Even so, the taxes on the pew would have tested his devotion, as Ruggles was assessed for only five dollars of property in the 1816 town tax list. As he listened to the Reverend Henry Edes deliver sermons, Ruggles might have been joined by the imposing China merchant Edward Carrington. The owner of a sumptuous mansion and a virtual armada of sailing vessels, Carrington claimed pew no. 5, valued at $700, to which he added an auction bid of $240. The prospect of the elegant Carrington and the seaman Ruggles participating in the same worship service speaks to the inclusive quality of religious culture in early national Providence.[66]

Women entered pew boxes, although they rarely owned them. In an era

[64] See Gary John Kornblith, "From Artisans to Businessmen: Master Mechanics in New England, 1789–1850" (Ph.D. diss., Princeton University, 1983), 239–258.
[65] Kornblith, "'Cementing the Mechanic Interest,'" 386.
[66] Benevolent Congregational Society Records, vol. 23; on Ruggles's identity see *Providence Directory* (Providence, 1824), 57. On Carrington's vessels see Edward Field, ed., *State of Rhode Island and Providence Plantations at the End of the Century: A History*, 3 vols. (Boston, 1902), 2:471–473.

in which husbands assumed the property rights of their wives, pew plats typically reveal a scattering of widows as the only women who purchased seats. This begs the question of how could women constitute the majority of church members if they owned almost none of the pews. The key here can be found in the distinction between church membership and pew ownership, a difference frequently overlooked by students of early American religious history.[67] Fundamentally, church membership required that applicant to pronounce a confession of faith and to assent to the doctrinal positions of the church as articulated in its covenant. Pew ownership demanded no such profession. Societies of pewholders did follow their own standards for sound moral conduct, but these did not require a statement of faith on the part of the applicant. Evidence reveals that women proved more willing to make professions of faith than men, while men tended to express their devotion through the purchase of a pew. Between 1805 and 1816, Henry Edes of First Congregational Church kept a meticulous accounting of the members who entered his flock.[68] He recorded precisely one hundred names, seventy-seven of whom were women. Fifty-one of these women shared kin linkages with the male pewholders of the church. Only fourteen of the pewholding men could be found as members on Henry Edes's list. Edes's figures suggest a pattern: women appear to have been responsible for professions of faith while their male kin purchased the pews. Thus women most often attended church in family pews owned by men, a practice that reinforced the authority of men as governors of family life. Simultaneously, however, family pews reveal the concern for inclusivity and order that characterized the religious culture of Providence in the early national period.

The regular round of church meetings and disciplinary cases, too, exposes the expansive reach of religious life. Since church membership involved a confession of faith rather than the ability to afford a seat, plebeian residents found it even more accessible than pew ownership. First Baptist Church records classified some members as "transient," suggesting that even permanent residence in the town was not a requirement for joining the congregation. Moreover, churches understood their obligations to the wider community to extend well beyond the circle of their own immediate membership. In November 1805, the members of First Baptist Church responded to a request for assistance from "the united Brethren in our Lord

---

[67] For a perceptive, and exceptional, treatment of this issue see Ann C. Rose, "Social Sources of Denominationalism Reconsidered: Post-Revolutionary Boston as a Case Study," *American Quarterly* 38 (1986): 250.
[68] "Members of the First Congregational Church, October 29th, 1821, at the time of the revision of the Covenant," First Congregational Church Records, vol. 17, RIHS.

Jesus Christ at the Factory in Warwick."[69] This marked one of the earliest manifestations of concern for the moral and spiritual welfare of factory workers, an issue that would command the keen attention of Rhode Island domestic missionaries during the 1820s and 1830s. Within Providence, too, Stephen Gano ministered to the despairing and dispossessed. His "Memorandum Book" for the years 1813–14 provides poignant glimpses of the pastoral care he provided for the poor. On August 6, 1814, he "Visited a poor sick Sailor this evening in great distress body & mind." Evidently committed to the mariner's cares, Gano performed the man's funeral ten days later. Entries such as "Funeral of black woman," and "Gave poor man .25c" and "Visited 2 very poor sick & distressed families to day" pepper Gano's journal of activities. Whether professing members or not, no citizen of the town stood outside the realm of Gano's benevolence.[70]

As the case of Benjamin Knowles at First Baptist Church makes clear, congregations committed themselves to the care of economically struggling members. Patience Borden, "a free woman of color" at that church, went well beyond the call of duty in assisting the needy of her church. A tombstone recording her death in April 1811 took note of the extraordinary sum of $230 that she had donated "as a fund for the relief of the Poor of Colour of that Church."[71] The communicants at Beneficent Congregational Church, too, had historically made support of the poor a clear priority. As early as 1769, they decided to distribute the burden of poor relief equally among all those able to pay.[72] And they raised significant sums for this purpose. In October 1774, for example, the church voted fifty dollars to "several" members who "stood in need of present assistance."[73] In addition, the church functioned as an advocate for poor members in obtaining civic relief from the Overseer of the Poor. Still, communicants did not intend to stand by while town officials took their time to act. They considered it "the Duty of the Church to administer Temporary relief to all such members and not to let them suffer."[74] Congregations found nothing unusual or sinful about the occasion of economic hardship.

Churches extended their humble members full voice in matters of governance and polity. On August 4, 1791, for instance, a gathering of some

[69] Record Book, First Baptist Church, November 3, 1805.

[70] Stephen Gano Memorandum Book, 1813–1814, entries for August 6, August 16, 1814; February 23, 1813; June 3, 1814; March 1, 1813; and passim, RIHS.

[71] Jamie Coughtry and Jay Coughtry, "Black Pauper Burial Records: Providence, Rhode Island, 1777–1831," *Rhode Island History* 44 (1985): illustration following 109.

[72] Record Book, Beneficent Congregational Church, October 30, 1769, Vault of Beneficent Congregational Church, Providence, Rhode Island.

[73] Record Book, Beneficent Congregational Church, October 11, 1774.

[74] Record Book, Beneficent Congregational Church, June 6, 1794.

sixty-nine members of the First Baptist Church convened to decide "Whether noncompliance with the imposition of hands shall be a bar to church membership or not."[75] The laying on of hands constituted a vital part of Baptist polity that the Six-Principle Baptists in the Rhode Island hinterland still guarded with jealousy.[76] In 1791, Providence Baptists considered whether they wanted to continue this practice or distinguish themselves from their rural neighbors. Almost unanimously the members voted to abolish the traditional practice, advancing what some in the countryside might have viewed as urbane pretensions. A diverse group had deliberated in order to reach this conclusion; "every member's name was written down and the voice of every member asked." Thirty-seven women and thirty-two men spoke out on the issue. Moreover, Membo Navy, William Caesar, and Cuff Hammond, all black members of the congregation, registered their opinions. Prominent tradesmen such as Joseph Martin, a glazier, and Daniel Martin, a carpenter, both of whom ranked in the top 6 percent of those assessed in the 1790 town tax list, offered their opinions. But so too did John Hill, a baker, and Samuel Gorham, a blacksmith, both of whom had been assessed for no property in the previous year's tax list. The vote thus rendered irrelevant distinctions of wealth, race, and gender. Indeed, Membo Navy, who voted with the majority, found herself in the position of prevailing over Joseph Martin and David Martin, both of whom wanted to continue the traditional practice. That her voice was accorded equal weight with the Martins' speaks to the extraordinarily inclusive and democratic character of Baptist governance in the 1790s.[77]

In matters of church discipline, congregations went to great lengths to reclaim sinful members.[78] Although churches certainly had to maintain their standards of membership (without which a profession of faith would cease to have meaning), they demonstrated a deep capacity to forgive and to reincorporate errant communicants. Some disciplinary actions took place over many years as congregations waited on evidence of true repentance from the guilty. In June 1804 Beneficent Congregational Church admonished James Hammon for utter incompetence in the conduct of his tanning business. In a lengthy list of charges, the church chastised him for not keeping account of his debts or credits and with making "erroneous statements"

---

[75] Record Book, First Baptist Church, August 4, 1791.

[76] Jones, *Economic and Social Transformation,* 17–27.

[77] Ann C. Rose found a similar pattern of plebeian participation among the Baptists in Boston during the postrevolutionary period. See "Social Sources of Denominationalism Reconsidered," 251.

[78] The cases considered here are from First Baptist Church and Beneficent Congregational Church. Comparable records from First Congregational Church and St. John's Episcopal Church have evidently not survived.

regarding the amount of his property. His "negligence" in business had resulted in "grate loss" not only to his creditors but had damaged his family
as well. Despite this litany of criticism, the church gave Hammon ample
opportunity to reform. In 1810, "after much labor" with the church, the
tanner "acknowledged his Faults and promised to fulfill his Covenant
obligations."[79] An even more lengthy restoration involved the case of
Prudence Sisco, a black woman at First Baptist Church. In May 1782 the congregation had withdrawn fellowship from her for the crime of "disorderly
walking." At the time of this action they stipulated that she could return if she
made "an acknowledgment of her fault." She complied. In April 1796, the
church verified her "apparent Repentance" and restored her to membership, observing that she had "for a long time left her place."[80] Such language
suggests that for fourteen years the members at First Baptist Church had
reserved for Prudence Sisco "her place" within the community of faith.

Nathaniel Fuller's tribulations at Beneficent Congregational Church describe an even more turbulent ordeal than the one experienced by Prudence Sisco. In September 1801 the church first sensed trouble with Fuller
and admonished him with respect to his "withdrawing your self from our
communion and not attending the meetings of this Church." Stung by the
accusations, Fuller appeared before the congregation in November and
"made Satisfaction" before them. But he could not stay out of trouble. In
June, 1804, the church cited Fuller for "his disorderly walk heretofore his
being admonished to order & Duty." Unsatisfied with Fuller's responses to
members who had talked with him about the charges, the church voted to
"withdraw their watch and care from him." Fuller resurfaced in the church's
records in December 1810, this time "in Consequence of a Report taken up
by the Church Committee against our brother Nathaniel Fuller of Immoral
Conduct with a young girl." The Church suspended him from taking communion and "forbid his publick improvement untill due Repentance and
Reformation was manifested." By July 1811, Fuller had provided evidence
of his transformation, and the congregation received him back into communion but remained cold to his proposal "to improve in publick," that is,
to preach before them. But in the end Fuller prevailed. In November 1812,
the church decided that "our brother Nathanael Fuller be Liberated from
the Suspension not to Exhort in meetings" and granted him permission to
"Pray and Speak in Meetings when desired." Chief among sinners,
Nathaniel Fuller eventually won the right to preach in public.[81]

[79] Record Book, Beneficent Congregational Church, September 17, 1804; March 7, 1810.
[80] Record Book, First Baptist Church, May 2, 1782, and April (no date given), 1796.
[81] Record Book, Beneficent Congregational Church, September 21, 1801; November 9, 1801;
June 27, 1804; December 24, 1810; July 19, 1811; November 23, 1812.

Beyond evincing a determination to forgive the truly repentant, church disciplinary cases reveal a commitment to the preservation of social order and harmony. In this sense the cases reveal a dedication to an organic understanding of religious community in which respect governed relations between those of different social rank. So did members of the Beneficent Congregational Church hear a complaint lodged by "Brother Calvin Dean against William Chace for abusing a aprintis of his brother." Having been confronted by the church on the matter, "brother Chace owned the accusation and acknowledged his fault."[82] Thus did the church send a signal that employers were to treat their humblest employees with decency. But neither did they countenance instances of assault on gentlemen. On August 25, 1808, First Baptist Church heard that "Brother John Whipple was engaged in quarreling and fighting with Wheeler Martin, Esq., in the street on Friday evening last."[83] They met the next day to look into the fracas and found Whipple still simmering. "He did not deny the charge brought against him," recorded the clerk; "he said he was sorry for what he had done, but said he should do so again if he should be in a passion as he was before." Unwilling to risk another fiery episode, the Baptists voted "to exclude Whipple from fellowship & communion."[84] In such ways did churches work to preserve peace among their communicants.

Cases involving drunkenness, a common church crime of the era, may also be understood in the context of efforts to cement social relationships. Church committees overlooked the moderate consumption of alcohol and focused their efforts on those who abused drink at the expense of their other Christian obligations. Hence First Baptist Church moved against Abigail Hopkins for "being guilty of the Sin of Drunkenness, and using profane language."[85] They also confronted William Givens, who, in response to the charge that he had been intoxicated, answered evasively that the accusation "may be so, and may not; without showing any Repentance for his conduct."[86] The members of Beneficent Congregational Church noticed that strong drink had so clouded Stephen Olney's judgment that he "thus Intoxicated himself even to the violation of an oath which he had declared he had solemnly taken."[87] They also cited Joseph Snow for having missed their regular meetings and also charged him "with expending larg Quantities of Spiritus Liquors in his family to the hurt of the

82 Record Book, Beneficent Congregational Church, October 16, 1809.
83 Record Book, First Baptist Church, August 25, 1808.
84 Record Book, First Baptist Church, August 26, 1808.
85 Record Book, First Baptist Church, October 27, 1796.
86 Record Book, First Baptist Church, September 1, 1794.
87 Record Book, Beneficent Congregational Church, May 10, 1799.

same."[88] Although the temperance issue might come to be used in the enforcement of industrial work discipline, as it was in 1827 when PAMM sought to eliminate drink from workplaces, this was not the case in early national Providence.[89] Rather, church committees thought that strong drink promoted foul and corrupting language, blurred sound thinking, and tore apart the fabric of domestic life.

Congregations also fought to keep themselves free from heresy. Given Rhode Island's heritage as a haven for religious outcasts, this could be a challenging task. Disciplinary cases reveal that both Beneficent Congregational Church and First Baptist Church faced particularly troublesome threats from the emerging Universalist movement in town. Foreshadowing developments that would lead to the establishment of a Universalist Chapel in the 1820s, these dissenters made their voices heard even in the 1790s. On April 23, 1798, Beneficent Congregational Church held a special meeting to deal with the pernicious "sentiment that all Mankind Shall finally and Ultimately be saved." The communicants held "that it is highly expedient . . . to discourage & put a stop to the progress of so dangerous a doctrine."[90] Dangerous as the doctrine was, it persuaded some in the Providence artisan community.[91] Solomon Serls at Beneficent Congregational, along with Samuel Gorham, Alpheus Billings, and James Westcott at First Baptist Church—all members of PAMM—found themselves excluded from their churches for adhering to their Universalist beliefs.[92] Hiram Hill, a carpenter and also a PAMM member, testified to the Universalist proclivities of Providence artisans. He had been apprenticed to master builder John Holden Greene and recalled that "Mr. Greene was a strong Universalist and I had embraced that belief soon after I went to live with him, used to attend the meetings very steadily."[93] Bennett Wheeler, a printer and another leading figure in the mechanic community, thought revivalists "were all *ignoramuses*" and purchased a pew in the First Universalist Church in

---

[88] Record Book, Beneficent Congregational Church, February 22, 1809.

[89] See "Special Meeting Called May 29, 1827," Records of the Providence Association of Mechanics and Manufacturers, RIHS.

[90] Record Book, Beneficent Congregational Church, April 23, 1798.

[91] On the appeal of Universalism among artisans see Ronald Schultz, "God and Workingmen: Popular Religion and the Formation of Philadelphia's Working Class, 1790–1830," in Ronald Hoffman and Peter J. Albert, eds., *Religion in a Revolutionary Age* (Charlottesville, 1994), 125–155.

[92] For these cases, see respectively Record Book, Beneficent Congregational Church, August 5, 1799 (for Serls); Record Book, First Baptist Church, June 26 and August 25, 1796 (for Gorham); June 3, June 26, and August 25, 1796; February 23 and March 23, 1797 (for Billings); and Record Book, First Baptist Church, April 27, 1797 (for Westcott).

[93] Hiram Hill, autobiography and diary, entry for November 20, 1822, RIHS.

1824 as soon as he could.[94] The rumblings of Universalist dissent could thus be detected among established Providence congregations.

Perhaps nothing spoke more loudly to the desire of Providence churches to maintain social harmony than disciplinary cases involving the charge of "disorderly walking." This term covered a multitude of sins but targeted especially those members who challenged the authority of the church in matters of worship or governance. When George Benson attempted to withdraw his membership from First Baptist Church following a bitter personal dispute, the congregation cited him as a "disorderly walker."[95] Since members could leave the church only by requesting their permission, Benson's self-pronounced retirement constituted a breach of church polity. Communicants who slighted or questioned the judgment of the church in disciplinary matters were also subject to the charge of disorderly conduct. When William Givens appeared to ridicule the committee responsible for looking into his intemperance, the church and pastor responded by condemning him as a "disorderly walker." First Baptist Church also found Jane Freeman, "a sister of color," disorderly after she "attempted to extenuate her conduct" regarding a report that a young stranger had been seen in her bed.[96] The Beneficent Congregational Church condemned more roundly one "Sister Hand" as a "disorderly Person" in light of her admission that she "never wanted to join this Church but joined to please her Husband."[97] In jealously guarding the procedures of church governance, devout members simultaneously proclaimed their adherence to an orderly life of faith.

But the lineaments of religious authority in early national Providence came to be defined in increasingly masculine terms. As we have already seen, pew auctioning served to dramatize the control of men over the sanctuary. Within church meetings, as well, men moved to solidify their power. Although congregations did not hold meetings that systematically prohibited women from participating in their common life, it is nonetheless the case that churches narrowed the opportunities for self-expression they had once offered women. In 1792, for example, when "Sister Jones" applied for membership at First Baptist Church, she asked that she "might be allowed to speak in publick when it was strongly impressed upon her mind." The

---

[94] Diary of Bennett H. Wheeler, including notes by his father beginning in 1776 and concluding with his son's remarks in 1863, entry for Sunday, June 16, 1806, RIHS. On Wheeler's participation in the Universalist Chapel see First Universalist Society Minutes, 1821–1839, RIHS.
[95] Record Book, First Baptist Church, May 27, June 27, July 25, and August 23, 1799, on the Benson case.
[96] Record Book, First Baptist Church, March 1, March 29, and May 3, 1810, on the Freeman case.
[97] Record Book, Beneficent Congregational Church, October 16, 1809.

congregation rejected her overture.[98] Moreover, the lively theological disputes that embroiled male communicants rarely involved women. The Universalist threat in Providence was almost exclusively a masculine affair, with only a single woman, Elizabeth Arnold, openly announcing such views.[99] The absence of female voices in matters of doctrinal affairs suggests the degree to which women's opinions had become marginalized. In cases involving sexual deviance and especially those touching on "disorderly" conduct, however, women found themselves particularly vulnerable.[100]

Still other evidence points toward the marginalization of women in congregational affairs. In 1793 Beneficent Congregational Church faced a crisis involving two ministers, Joseph Snow and James Wilson, both of whom wanted to lead the church. In a meeting held on May 2, the members came down squarely on Wilson's side, laying out a nine-article case against Joseph Snow for "neglects of the Dutys of your office."[101] In constructing these charges and in considering the case, church records do not distinguish between the contributions made by the male and female communicants. But slowly, over roughly a period of twenty years, the church limited the scope of female participation. In August 1814 Harriet Jones found herself before "a meeting of the male Members" to answer charges that she had been "Cohabitating with a Man other than her lawful husband."[102] In December 1815 Mehaley Dyer requested permission to move her membership from Beneficent Congregational Church to the "Methodist people in this Town." Again, a committee of "Brethren Unanimously voted to dismiss Sister Mehaley."[103] Thus, male communicants assumed the lead role in matters of church polity. A similar process took place at First Baptist Church. Recall the 1791 vote concerning the issue of the laying on of hands as a requirement for membership. When the issue surfaced again in 1808, men alone voted on the issue, the women of the church only confirming the decision the brethren had already reached. As Susan Juster observes, "women had been effectively disenfranchised from the Providence Baptist Church."[104]

But if the conception of manly citizenship, both within the new nation and within the church, diminished the participation of women in congregational governance, it did not prohibit them from launching institutions of

[98] Record Book, First Baptist Church, November 29, 1792, and January 3, 1793.
[99] Record Book, First Baptist Church, July 23 and August 25, 1802.
[100] Juster, *Disorderly Women*, 145–179.
[101] Record Book, Beneficent Congregational Church, May 2, 1793.
[102] Record Book, Beneficent Congregational Church, August 8, 1814.
[103] Record Book, Beneficent Congregational Church, December 20, 1815.
[104] Juster, *Disorderly Women*, 126.

their own making. In the Providence Female Society for the Relief of Indigent Women and Children (formed in 1801) and the Providence Female Tract Society (1815), women exercised primary authority. In this sense Providence women heralded the quest for religious independence, which was embraced, as we shall soon observe, by both rural factory workers and the plebeian residents of the city. As Lori D. Ginzburg has demonstrated, the ideology of "benevolent femininity" that animated reformers in the early nineteenth century simultaneously masked the "often considerable authority" that women commanded in carrying out acts of charity.[105] As one young Massachusetts woman confided to her diary after her conversion, "I made religion the principal business of my life."[106] Within the context of religious reform, women elected their own officers, collected and dispensed money and goods, organized meetings, and considered matters of public policy. While congregational life strictly defined did not offer women such opportunities, participation in charitable and missionary societies did.

The Providence Female Society organized principally young women of elite social standing. A glance over the record of its first list of subscribers reveals names such as Allen, Arnold, Bowen, Brown, Bridgham, Clark, Halsey, Ives and Nightingale, all members of Providence's leading merchant and manufacturing families.[107] Like women in other such benevolent societies, the Providence ladies took advantage of the status and prestige their families offered.[108] Mrs. John Innes Clark, wife of the prominent Federalist and merchant leader, served as the Society's first directress. The same issue of the *Providence Gazette* that announced her husband's appointment as president of the Providence Bank also publicized a meeting of the Providence Female Society at their home.[109] The presence of women like Mrs. Clark brought the charitable efforts of the society considerable visibility and panache. They also reveal that Providence women, like their elite husbands and fathers, shared a notion of religious duty that the rich had special obligations to care for the poor.

The Providence Female Society undertook an ambitious agenda of reform activities. They purchased materials, primarily cloth, to afford

---

[105] Lori D. Ginzburg, *Women and the Work of Benevolence: Morality, Politics, and Class in the Nineteenth-Century United States* (New Haven, 1990), 35; Margaret Morris Haviland, "Beyond Women's Sphere: Young Quaker Women and the Veil of Charity in Philadelphia, 1790–1810," *William and Mary Quarterly*, 3d ser., 51 (1994): 419–446.

[106] Quoted in Cott, *Bonds of Womanhood*, 139.

[107] See *Constitution of the Providence Female Society*, 9–12.

[108] Nancy A. Hewitt, *Women's Activism and Social Change: Rochester, New York, 1822–1872* (Ithaca, 1984), 50; Ann M. Boylan, "Women in Groups: An Analysis of Women's Benevolent Organizations in New York and Boston, 1797–1840," *Journal of American History* 71 (1984): 511.

[109] *Providence Gazette*, March 23, 1805.

employment for idle women. They put out children to learn a trade or service. They supplied the needy "with money to procure medicine and wood."[110] They also hoped to establish a home in which young girls would "be taught to read, write, sew, and perform every branch of domestic business."[111] While these women clearly accepted the contributions of male donors (in many cases family members), the Society managed the disbursement of these funds. They elected their own slate of officers, including a treasurer, and collected dues from the membership. Moreover, the ladies commanded sufficient community respect to be addressed by clergymen at special public meetings held in churches rather than private homes.[112] In such ways did women reclaim meetinghouses as their own. Still, for all they did, the women of the Providence Female Society couched their activities in rhetoric that belied their importance. "And it is hoped by a prudent management of their own little concerns," ventured the Society's first publication, "and by proper observations and reflections, they will in time be qualified to discharge the duties of office with honour to themselves and advantage to society."[113] This self-deprecating claim obscures the extensive work of the town's first female reform organization.

By 1815 the women of the Providence Female Tract Society (PFTS) moved the project of remaking society to a more expansive level. Although a handful of women who had launched the Providence Female Society also participated in the PFTS, the membership of the new group was both larger and more diverse. While the Providence Female Society had published a list of approximately seventy subscribers at its inception, the PFTS featured a list of nearly 470 contributors in its first annual report.[114] To be sure, members of merchant and manufacturing families were well represented in the ranks of the PFTS, but its extensive roster makes it impossible to conclude that only elite women could join. Indeed, whereas the Providence Female Society had requested its members to pay a three-dollar fee, the PFTS asked for only fifty-two cents. The new organization also outlined loftier goals. Rather than ministering to the needs of poor women and children only within city limits, the PFTS proposed to set up schools in the rural communities and factory villages that dotted the Rhode Island countryside.[115]

[110] *Constitution of the Providence Female Society*, 8.
[111] Ibid., 7.
[112] James Wilson, "A Sermon Preached Extempore before the Providence Female Charitable Society on October 5th, 1803, in the First Congregational Meeting House," RIHS.
[113] Ibid., 4.
[114] See *Constitution of the Providence Female Society*, 9–12; *The First Annual Report of the Providence Female Tract Society* (Providence, 1816), 14–18, Brown University Library.
[115] These activities will be considered in Chapter 2.

The women who forged the Providence Female Society and the Providence Female Tract Society claimed a measure of institutional control not accorded them in the churches in which they had professed their faith. One might speculate that religious reform in antebellum New England proved so enormously popular for women precisely because churches had so effectively limited their participation in congregational governance. Reform organizations promised women more spiritual independence than they could find in the very churches that had nurtured their faith in the first place. In the years to come, this inheritance of religious autonomy would give women a vantage point from which to enter debates on the morality of the factory system, to participate in distributing religious tracts, to address the plight of urban needlewomen and to engage in a host of other public and political activities. In creating the Providence Female Society and the Tract Society, the women of the city laid the foundations for their entrance into the civic life of the town.

The Providence clergy validated the expression of religious community evinced by both reform groups and their congregations. They held out a vision of an orderly Christian society in which the exertions of individuals blended harmoniously with the good of the whole. They insisted on the mutual dependence of the various ranks that constituted the social order and encouraged all persons to embrace their particular stations in life. They extolled benevolence as the highest virtue of civilized society. Theirs was a surprisingly sunny social ethic that did not yet fully articulate the gloomy doubts over the destructive effects of material prosperity that would plague churchmen in later generations. In considering the earthly pursuits of their communicants, the clergy sounded much more like their Puritan forbears than they did like apostles for the dawning industrial age. Resurrecting a Puritan theme, the Providence clergy embraced a version of what Stephen Innes has termed "communal capitalism," a social ethic that stressed that individual acquisitiveness must always be understood in a communal context and that "present profit" must never be preferred over the pursuit of "honest gain."[116] Rather than preaching an ethic of "Christian industrialism" that amounted to an apologia for the unbridled accumulation of wealth, the Providence clergy looked back to the ethics of an earlier era.[117] They validated the quest for prosperity that animated Providence merchants and manufacturers in the early national period, but they insisted that this endeavor be harnessed to a firm understanding that

---

[116] Stephen Innes, *Creating the Commonwealth: The Economic Culture of Puritan New England* (New York, 1995), esp. 75–76, 92, 114, 120, 126, 132, 192, 224, 236.
[117] For the content of "Christian industrialism" see Anthony F. C. Wallace, *Rockdale: The Growth of an American Village in the Early Industrial Revolution* (New York, 1980), 350–397.

the happiness of individuals can never be separated from the felicity of the community.

The ministers began with the assumption that all members of the social order were inextricably bound together. Of all Providence theologians, none spoke more eloquently on behalf of this organic conception of society than did Jonathan Maxcy. A revival convert, Baptist elder, and president of Rhode Island College (1792–1802), he possessed one of Providence's keenest minds. In delivering a July 4th oration in 1795, Maxcy reminded his listeners that they "must not consult and gratify private inclination at the expense of the public."[118] He observed that "the condition of men and their connexions and dependencies in civil society" entailed obligations that impinged upon the conduct of all.[119] "The lives and fortunes of all Americans are on board one vessel," he maintained, and "it is therefore the duty, interest and happiness of all to take care of it."[120] By 1802, in a sermon delivered before the Female Charitable Society, Maxcy had taken an even firmer position against veneration of the self. "Selfishness," he proclaimed, "is the source of all moral evil."[121] He went on to explain that the members of society "are so connected with each other, by mutual dependence, and the necessity of mutual aid, that the good of the individual is essentially involved in the good of the whole."[122] Maxcy yielded no quarter to those who attempted to stretch the social fabric to gratify their own interests at the expense of others. "If each individual pursues exclusively his own welfare," he held, "if he invariably makes this his highest object, he breaks asunder the bond of public union; and his conduct tends to introduce disorder and misery."[123] Thus did Maxcy identify and applaud the relationships of mutuality that cemented the social order.

Other ministers echoed Jonathan Maxcy's assertions. In his July 4th oration of 1803, Asa Messer, who followed Maxcy as president of Rhode Island College, offered an inspiring variation on the theme of orderly community life. Invoking the heritage of the classical republican tradition, he told his audience at the Baptist meetinghouse that "true virtue will bind men together, and give them all a common interest."[124] He insisted that living the

---

[118] Jonathan Maxcy, *An Oration Delivered in the Baptist Meeting-House in Providence, July 4, a.d. 1795, at the Celebration of the Nineteenth Anniversary of American Independence* (Providence, 1795), 10.

[119] Ibid.

[120] Ibid., 14.

[121] Jonathan Maxcy, *A Sermon Preached in the Baptist Meeting-House in Providence Before the Providence Female Society, September 21, 1802* (Providence, 1802), 5.

[122] Ibid.

[123] Ibid.

[124] Asa Messer, *An Oration Delivered at Providence in the Baptist Meeting-House on the Fourth of July, 1803* (Providence, 1803), 9.

virtuous life would teach men that "while they are laboring for the good of the whole, they are laboring for the good of themselves."[125] And while Messer certainly countenanced the value of industry and commerce, a position he made clear in a speech he delivered to PAMM, he did not smile on the unchecked gratification of individual ambition. To the contrary, he observed that "true virtue will induce each citizen to be satisfied with his proper station, and to be zealous for the order and concord which alone can give strength or respect to a nation."[126] James Wilson of Beneficent Congregational Church carried the logic of the well-ordered community to the level of national politics. In his July 4th address, delivered a year after Messer's, he observed that "our dangers are not, however, to be apprehended so much from abroad, as from and within ourselves; for our most formidable enemy is *disunion*."[127] Stephen Gano, too, thought that internal bickering, rather than the threat of foreign arms, represented the more serious threat to the new nation. In his litany of praise for George Washington, he argued that "without order and government, peace cannot long be maintained."[128] Providence churchmen thus recognized the critical importance of social order, both within their town and in the nation as a whole.

The only external danger worth considering was posed by the carnage unfolding in revolutionary France. Providence clergymen recoiled in horror at the rule of the Committee of Public Safety, the execution of Louis XVI, and the rise of the Directory. In 1799 Jonathan Maxcy ventured a particularly chilling view of the character of the republican revolutionaries. "These men discard," he claimed, "as the effects of superstition, all ancient institutions; and instead of adhering to an uniform order of things, delight in perpetual revolutions." Furthermore, "their system of rights, like their system of government, is metaphysic and fanatical."[129] James Wilson agreed. In 1804 he announced that he found himself "disgusted with the atrocities of *republican* France, now expiating her offenses under the iron yoke of an absolute despotism."[130] In such pronouncements the ministers made clear their commitment to a stable order that preserved "ancient institutions" and held in check the passions of revolution. Indeed, even Enos Hitchcock, a Congregational minister in Providence who campaigned as a chaplain with Washington's armies, could not quite break free of older traditions. In

---

[125] Ibid.

[126] Ibid.

[127] James Wilson, *An Oration, Delivered at Providence, in the First Congregational Meeting-House on the Fourth of July, 1804* (Providence, 1804), 12, Brown University Library.

[128] Gano, *A Sermon on the Death of General George Washington*, 9.

[129] Jonathan Maxcy, *An Oration Delivered in the First Congregational Meeting-House in Providence on the Fourth of July, 1799* (Providence, 1799), 5.

[130] Wilson, *Oration Delivered at Providence in the First Congregational Meeting-House*, 12.

1786 he spoke before a meeting of the Society of the Cincinnati in East-Greenwich, Rhode Island.[131] The Society of the Cincinnati, a fraternal and mutual support organization formed by officers of the Continental Army, had provided for the extension of membership to the sons of original members. Such provisions smacked of the hereditary form of government that Americans had recently rejected. Yet Hitchcock had no trouble in addressing the group and applauding their mission. With other Americans, and especially the Federalists of their day, Providence ministers viewed with some uneasiness the progress of democracy. As Stanley Elkins and Eric McKitrick have asserted, " 'Democracy' was not to emerge as a fully legitimate cultural value in America, commanding more or less universal approval, until the 1830s, with the appearance of a national system of mass political parties."[132] In holding to a vision of an organic social order, the clergy embraced an ethic that did not readily accept the changes unleashed by the age of democratic revolutions.

It would be a mistake, however, to conceive of the ministers' message as entirely conservative, let alone reactionary. For especially in speeches before PAMM, they sanctioned the pursuit of industry and commercial progress. Asa Messer himself, cardinal spokesman for the commonweal, purchased shares in a cotton spinning concern in Wrentham, Massachusetts.[133] But in championing material prosperity, the ministers clung to the central idea that all individual industry takes place in the context of community. Asa Messer spoke eloquently on this point. In his 1803 address to the mechanics, he divided human industry into agriculture, commerce, and the "mechanical arts."[134] All of these pursuits, according to Messer, were so inextricably linked that no single branch could prosper without the success of the other two. Farmers needed merchants to bring their goods to market. Merchants needed goods to trade. Merchants and farmers needed the wares produced by mechanics. Tipping his hat to Adam Smith's famous illustration of pin manufacture in *The Wealth of Nations*, Messer insisted that the "division of labour" held the key to the country's prosperity.[135] It also ensured that the fortunes of all would rise together in harmony. "The real interest of

---

[131] Enos Hitchcock, *A Discourse on the Causes of National Prosperity, Illustrated by Ancient and Modern History, exemplified in the late American Revolution. Addressed to the Society of the Cincinnati, in the State of Rhode Island at their annual Meeting at East-Greenwich, July 4, 1786* (Providence, n.d.).

[132] Stanley Elkins and Eric McKitrick, *The Age of Federalism: The Early American Republic, 1788–1800* (New York, 1993), 451.

[133] See Messer to Nathan Comstock, November 7, 1815, Asa Messer letterbooks, Brown University Library.

[134] Asa Messer, *An Oration Delivered Before the Providence Association of Mechanics and Manufacturers, at their Annual Election, April 11, 1803* (Providence, 1803), 4–10.

[135] Ibid., p. 10.

every part of the community," Messer exalted, "is happily blended with the interest of the whole."[136] Even when speaking to the mechanics, Messer insisted that "it not be imagined that, while we celebrate this anniversary, we patronize one class of citizens at the expence of another."[137] James Wilson, too, asserted that the purpose of human industry was not the accumulation of quick and easy profit. In his address to the artisans, Wilson inventoried the attributes necessary for business success and identified not only "Genius," "Application," "Perseverance," and "Capital" but "Honesty in Dealing" and "Moderation in Profits" as well.[138] Like Messer, Wilson also understood that the mechanical arts benefited other members of society. "You shall not only benefit yourselves," he explained to his audience, "your country shall rejoice, the husbandman seek your mart, and the merchant your commodities."[139] Rightly comprehended and correctly executed, human industry would redound to the benefit of all.

In 1795 Jonathan Maxcy underscored the communal dimensions of progress in the mechanical arts in his address to PAMM. Sounding a Lockean theme, Maxcy began his speech with a resounding affirmation of the importance of human labor in creating all value. He insisted that "labour is the only original source of wealth. Consequently it must add a real and permanent value to those materials on which it is bestowed."[140] But lest the artisans swell with inordinate pride, Maxcy reminded them of the key role played by merchants in expanding the demand for trade goods. "Encomiums too great," soared Maxcy, "cannot be lavished on Commerce. It enlarges the acquaintance of men, unites distant nations in affection; promotes the spirit of peace, and gradually cements the whole world into one family."[141] Notice that in enumerating the benefits of commerce, Maxcy sidestepped direct reference to material prosperity. Rather, he thought the links of trade would enlarge and enrich the human relationships that brought order and harmony to the world. Thus did Maxcy's vision of the widening market economy contain within it an implicit "humanitarian sensibility."[142] Moreover, he reminded the artisans that the fruits of their labor worked to the benefit of all: "Your exertions not only promote your own, but

---

[136] Ibid.

[137] Ibid., 3.

[138] James Wilson, *An Oration Delivered Before the Providence Association of Mechanics and Manufacturers, at their Annual Election, April 14, 1794* (Providence, 1794), 18–21, Brown University Library.

[139] Ibid., 26.

[140] Maxcy, *Oration Delivered Before the Providence Association of Mechanics and Manufacturers*, 8.

[141] Ibid., 8–9.

[142] See essays by Thomas L. Haskell in Thomas Bender, ed., *The Antislavery Debate: Capitalism and Abolitionism as a Problem in Historical Interpretation* (Berkeley, 1992), 107–160.

the interests of society."[143] Gary John Kornblith, a most careful student of PAMM, concludes that these artisans in the early national period held to the doctrine of "self-interest *collectively* understood."[144] The ministers who addressed them both reflected and shaped the belief that human industry be understood in the context of society at large and never be construed as simply a matter of private gain.

The clergy also insisted that those who had been blessed with material success owed special obligations to those who had less. In a sermon preached in 1803 before the Providence Female Charitable Society (the renamed Providence Female Society), James Wilson cast the "rich and affluent as being more especially called to the exercise of compassionate liberality in banishing want from the door."[145] He illustrated his point by telling the tale of one "Mr. Thornton of London, a merchant distinguished in his day for his extensive commerce."[146] According to Wilson, it had been Thornton's practice to set aside a portion of his earnings each year for the use of the poor. When an economic downturn placed Thornton's finances in jeopardy, he was advised by his cashier to abandon this charitable custom. Thornton refused. Going the extra mile, he doubled his donations to the impoverished, reasoning that if he had been hit hard, the poor must be suffering even more. Wilson again raised an illustration of genteel charity in his address to PAMM. He held up for imitation the model of "the aged Squire, possessed of ample wealth; he knows its value, he distributes it to the poor, who are his daily guests."[147] Given the policies Providence congregations put in place to support their impoverished members, they appear to have needed little prompting to implement James Wilson's admonitions.

But even in the postrevolutionary years, seams had begun to appear in the inclusive religious culture the citizens of the town had forged. For inclusivity did not necessarily endow the practice of religion with notions of equality and democracy, although, as we have observed, the churches made some gestures in that direction. Congregations certainly included places for plebeian residents, African Americans, and women, but these niches were clearly inferior to the places of honor assumed by the affluent men who owned pews in the church and therefore made the important decisions. The rise of public pew auctioning served notice on less affluent members that sheer financial muscle mattered in the disposal of church affairs. As

---

[143] Maxcy, *Oration Delivered Before the Providence Association of Mechanics and Manufacturers*, 15.
[144] Kornblith, "'Cementing the Mechanic Interest,'" 387.
[145] Wilson, "Sermon Preached Extempore Before the Providence Female Charitable Society," RIHS.
[146] Ibid.
[147] Wilson, *Oration Delivered Before the Providence Association of Mechanics and Manufacturers*, 20.

William J. Brown testified, African Americans did not enjoy their lofty vantage point in the balcony of First Baptist Church. Some artisans, such as those who followed the Universalists, also found themselves excluded from the formal religious life of the town. Providence women, especially those who joined the Baptists and Congregationalists, witnessed an erosion of the rights they had once enjoyed within their churches. The actions of Providence women, in forming the Providence Female Charitable Society and the Providence Female Tract Society, prefigured a wider quest by plebeian residents in search of their own religious terrain. First in the mill villages of the Rhode Island countryside and then within the city itself during the revival of 1820, plebeian residents struggled to establish their own religious institutions beyond the control of the merchant and manufacturing elite. The subordinate members of Providence's "One great Family" looked for opportunities to take in hand their own understandings of salvation.

2

"Brought into Liberty"
Religion in the Rhode Island Countryside, 1812–1837

On April 25, 1821, Stephen S. Wardwell traversed the twenty-six miles that separated Providence, Rhode Island, from the small mill village of Killingly, Connecticut. Fresh from his recent conversion at Beneficent Congregational Church the previous spring, the twenty-year-old Sunday school instructor arrived in time to lead a religious meeting that same evening. As his text, Wardwell selected the dramatic account of Goliath's challenge to the nation of Israel (1 Sam. 17). His message has not survived, but his choice of a text resonated among the villagers and operatives at a meeting he considered "well attended." In the confrontation between the authentically pious boy, David, and the powerful Philistine, Goliath, some mill hands may have glimpsed how the lowly could overcome the mighty.

Upon waking the following morning, Wardwell surveyed the terrain owned by the Davidson Manufacturing Company. He took special delight in the way two streams flowed together, just below the site of the factory. "After foaming and rolling over rugged rocks which God hath here made and which convey to the Spectator a proof of his omnipotence and power," he wrote, "they join together and again rapidly pour their streams over rocks below." When Wardwell inventoried the buildings belonging to the company, moreover, he commented on their relation to the rushing water. A three-story factory headed his list, complete with fifteen hundred spindles and separate rooms for carding and weaving. A gristmill, equipped with three stones, also made Wardwell's catalogue. "I think the miller stated," he recalled, "that he could with three stones in operation grind about 4 or 5 hundred bushels per day." Wardwell discovered, as well, a blacksmith's shop, "the bellow and sledge of which is moved by machinery acted upon by the water." A sawmill, too, stood close by, with the capacity to "saw about a thousand feet per day." Wardwell perceived in the manufacturing village evidence of God's power, revealed in the provision of the stream that set the entire hamlet in motion. He became so inspired by this "delightful situation" that he recorded his impressions in verse: "Go there, thou Atheist, and if you dare, / In those great wonders, say no God is there."[1]

Stephen S. Wardwell's missionary excursion to Killingly is significant because his trip evokes the intense interest that Providence residents took in the Rhode Island countryside in the opening decades of the nineteenth century. Beginning in 1790, with the involvement of Moses Brown and William Almy in Samuel Slater's cotton spinning mill in Pawtucket, Providence merchants and bankers proved decisive in fostering Rhode Island's textile industry. The Jeffersonian Embargo only opened wider avenues for the investment of Providence capital, contributing to what local residents called the "cotton mill fever." By 1815, one group of Providence investors estimated the number of rural mills surrounding the city to be one hundred and forty, "containing in actual operation more than 130,000 spindles."[2] Despite the resistance of rural folk to the incursion of turnpikes and mill dams, the threat of floods and fires to the mill buildings themselves, and the panic of 1819, the rural textile industry boomed.[3]

Missionaries followed in the wake of Providence investment capital. In 1815, the same year in which Providence investors chronicled their success, the formation of the Providence Female Tract Society (PFTS) marked the genesis of concerted missionary effort to reform the rural manufactories.[4] In 1825 the Providence-based Rhode Island Sunday School Union had joined the women of the city in making mill village reform a top priority. "The object of this association," the members stated at their 1827 gathering in First Baptist Church, "is to form Sunday Schools in every village, factory establishment and neighborhood within the limits of this state."[5] Denominational associations, too, wanted to improve religious life in the mill towns.

---

[1] Stephen S. Wardwell diary, April 25 and 26, 1821, Beneficent Congregational Church, Providence, Rhode Island.
[2] *Cotton Manufacturers in Providence and its vicinity to the Honourable Senate and House of Representatives of the United States* . . . (Providence, 1815), 3, American Antiquarian Society Library, Worcester, Mass. See also Peter J. Coleman, *The Transformation of Rhode Island, 1790–1860* (Providence, 1963), 86–87.
[3] The best account of the conflicts attending the emergence of market relations in the Rhode Island countryside is Daniel P. Jones, *The Economic and Social Transformation of Rural Rhode Island, 1780–1850* (Boston, 1992).
[4] *The First Annual Report of the Providence Female Tract Society* (Providence, 1816), Brown University Library.
[5] Reported in the *Rhode-Island Religious Messenger* 2 (1827): 6.

In 1830, the Baptist State Convention trumpeted the call for more missionaries "to engage in the labor of gathering in the multitudes with which our
factory villages abound."[6] Congregationalists from both Massachusetts and
Rhode Island sent scores of indefatigable missionaries to the mills. "Villages
exist, and are constantly springing into existence," lamented the Evangelical Consociation and Missionary Society of the Congregational Churches in
Rhode-Island, "where are congregated hundreds and thousands of children, youth and adults, to whom the gospel must be sent, or they have it
not."[7] Virtually hundreds of Providence residents, then, shared Stephen
Wardwell's fascination with the manufacturing villages that surrounded
their city.

Stephen Wardwell's missionary excursion is also important for its suggestion that mill village religion was the product of a complex series of
relationships between manufacturers, domestic missionaries, and factory
workers. This chapter explores those relationships and documents a fundamental shift in the initiative for religious life in the mill villages of
Rhode Island between the War of 1812 and the economic panic of
1837. Beginning as early as the 1790s, textile entrepreneurs advanced their
manufactories as instruments of moral and religious reform. Embodying
the conservative ethos that characterized the established churches of
Providence, manufacturers and mill owners championed religion in
essentially paternalistic terms. They argued for a religious life that would
enlighten their employees in matters of the spirit even as it created steady
and sober hands at their machines. In this project, the manufacturers
blended a genuine recognition of their civic responsibilities with a canny
understanding that a religious workforce portended greater productivity.
Yet, the manufacturers were limited in pursuit of religious reform by their
own dedication to a refined and genteel style of religion that set them apart
from their workers. By the 1820s and 1830s, they seemed less willing than
they had once been to put their financial resources toward the cause of
saving souls.

Domestic missionaries called the factory masters to task for retreating
from the ambitious claims about religious reform they had once sounded.
Beginning with the creation of the PFTS in 1815 domestic missionaries
from across the denominational spectrum took the initiative for reaching
out to the mill hands. Rather than perceiving mill villages as centers of spir-

---

[6] *Minutes of the Baptist Convention in the State of Rhode-Island and Vicinity, held with the First Baptist
Church in Providence, April 14, 1830* (Providence, n.d.), 4.
[7] *Proceedings of the Evangelical Consociation and Missionary Society of Congregational Churches in
Rhode-Island, June 1836* (Providence, 1836), 15.

itual reformation, domestic missionaries worried about the negative impact of factory work on the religious development of the workers. The missionaries also distributed religious tracts, helped to create networks of schools, and frequently joined with operatives to sustain these ventures. In all of this, women played central roles as both tract distributors and teachers. Buoyed by the powerful notion that women shared a special obligation to attend to the spiritual needs of society, Providence women imparted to mill village religion models of female leadership and initiative that stood in contrast to the paternal pretensions of mill owners and promoters. Compared to the profoundly masculine notions of church governance articulated in Providence congregations, mill village religion took on a distinctively feminine quality.

Factory workers joined with domestic missionaries in forging a system of schools beyond the direct control and supervision of manufacturers. These schools formed but one component in the creation of a distinctive plebeian religious culture. This plebeian religious culture celebrated an Arminian theological perspective (most evident among the Freewill Baptists and the Methodists), embraced itinerant and female preaching, acknowledged the validity of dreams, visions, and intense displays of emotion, and manifested a tenacious spirit of institutional independence. Overlapping with and adumbrating developments that would take place in Providence following the revival of 1820, workers and common folk created a religious culture of their own. In both countryside and city, the spiritual upheavals of the Second Great Awakening promised plebeian residents not the yoke of industrial discipline but independence through religious institutions of their own making. Religious enthusiasm, as one revival account put it, offered the means that "brought into liberty" the plain farmers and factory workers of the countryside.[8]

From the outset, Rhode Island's textile entrepreneurs attempted to blend industrial development and religious improvement in their mills. The opening of Samuel Slater's celebrated Sunday school in Pawtucket represented one of the earliest efforts to associate the cotton mills with the cause of religious reform.[9] Slater himself maintained a grim view of the virtues of rural society and advanced his manufactories as a means to bring backward country folk the advantages of civilization. "An exclusively pastoral or

[8] *Free-will Baptist Magazine* 1 (1827): 112–113, for an account of the revival at Swansecut factory village in Scituate.

[9] On the evolution of Slater's Sunday schools and related matters see Jonathan Prude, *The Coming of Industrial Order: Town and Factory Life in Rural Massachusetts, 1810–1860* (New York, 1983), 38–45, 110–116, 125.

agricultural nation," he insisted, "can never be formed into a polished or powerful community."[10] According to George S. White, Slater's comrade and biographer, mill villages would provide the means by which "the disorderly and vicious" would be "reclaimed, civilized and Christianized."[11] Regular employment alone, boasted the entrepreneurs, could work moral wonders. In 1815 Samuel Ogden, a skilled British workman and mill promoter, attempted to deflect charges that mill children were "deprived of the privileges of education" by boldly asserting that "a cotton factory is a school for the improvement of ingenuity and industry."[12] Some manufacturers went beyond Ogden's suggestion that cotton mills were schools by designing their manufactories to look like churches, thus further cementing the connection between industrial work and the godly life.[13]

Among entrepreneurs who sponsored religion in the countryside, John Slater and Zachariah Allen command special attention. For in their actions, we can illuminate both the scope and the limitations of the mill owners' interest in religious reform. Although these men differed in both temperament and approach, they shared an essentially conservative and paternalistic outlook. Both men also expressed a religious sensibility that emphasized refinement, emotional reserve, and gentility.[14] They preferred tasteful churches, accomplished in the Greek Revival or Gothic style, to the less polished meetinghouses of the Freewill Baptists or to the groves and glades of the Methodists. Whenever they could, they selected the company of educated missionaries (especially those trained at Harvard, Yale, or Brown) who could navigate their way through the nuances of church doctrine rather than the coarse preachers of the backcountry who appealed directly to the heart. Like other Congregationalists and Episcopalians of their day, Slater and Allen embraced what Richard Bushman has described as "the theology of taste."[15] They distrusted outbursts of emotional display, preferring

---

[10] Slater quoted in Louis McLane, *Report of the Secretary of the Treasury, 1832. Documents Relative to the Manufactures in the United States*, House Executive Documents, 22d Cong., 2d sess., Doc. 308, vol. 1 (Washington, D.C., 1833), 931.

[11] White quoted in Gary Kulik, Roger Parks, Theodore Z. Penn, eds., *The New England Mill Village, 1790–1860* (Cambridge, Mass., 1982), 345–346.

[12] Ogden quoted in Kulik et al., *New England Mill Village*, 312–313.

[13] See David Zonderman, *Aspirations and Anxieties: New England Workers and the Mechanized Factory System, 1815–1850* (New York, 1992), 84–85.

[14] See Richard L. Bushman, *The Refinement of America: Persons, Houses, Cities* (New York, 1992), esp. 313–352. See also Alan Taylor, *William Cooper's Town: Power and Persuasion on the Frontier of the Early American Republic* (New York, 1995). Like some early cotton manufacturers who hoped that religion would tame their industrial villages, William Cooper patronized "the more orthodox and conservative denominations committed to public decorum and a learned ministry" (349; but see 348–351 for an excellent summary of the genteel religious sensibility).

[15] Bushman, *Refinement of America*, 326–331.

instead modes of religious expression based on genteel equanimity. For men who esteemed decorum "there was a suspicion that the harsh rigor of religions like Methodism actually hardened the heart and made a person less Christian."[16] These predilections shaped the kinds of religious institutions these entrepreneurs were willing to sponsor.

During the spring and summer of 1806, John Slater (the brother of Samuel) created, virtually ex nihilo, the manufacturing center of Slatersville, in the northwestern corner of the state near the Massachusetts border. A man of "pluck and push," Slater signed a petition to the state legislature requesting permission to raise four thousand dollars by lottery for a meetinghouse.[17] Completed in 1808, the church provided a setting for religious services conducted by Congregationalists and Methodists and served the town as a schoolhouse. From the start, however, Slater and especially his wife Ruth, "a woman of strong personality, and the first lady of the place," favored the Congregationalists over the Methodists.[18] By 1816 the Slaters had tired of dealing with the more numerous Methodists and made the church an exclusively Congregational meetinghouse.[19] This move did not signal Slater's unconditional assent to the Congregationalists in all matters theological. For like the gentlemen who held multiple pews in Providence congregations, Slater spread his religious largesse beyond one denomination. In 1833 he purchased a seat in an Episcopalian church in Smithfield, Rhode Island.[20]

In bringing religious taste to his village, Slater collaborated closely with two intrepid Congregationalist missionaries, Ephraim Abbott and Daniel Waldo. Both Abbott and Waldo traveled for the Massachusetts Society for Promoting Christian Knowledge, a Congregationalist organization based in

---

[16] Ibid., 326.

[17] Rev. Albert Donnell, *Sermon Preached at the Ninetieth Anniversary of the Organization of the Congregational Church at Slatersville, Rhode Island, September 6, 1906* (Woonsocket, R.I., 1906), 11–12. The original petition, signed by Slater and forty-eight other men, stated that the funds would go "for the building of a Meeting House on a lot given by Seth Mowry to the second Baptist Society in the Town of Smithfield," indicating that the church originally had a connection to the Baptists. Original dated October 26, 1807, in *Petitions to the Rhode Island General Assembly,* 37:99, Rhode Island State Archives, Providence. On the creation of Slatersville generally see Walter A. Nebiker, *The History of North Smithfield* (North Smithfield, R.I., 1976), 68–82.

[18] Donnell, *Sermon Preached,* 13.

[19] On the shift of the Slatersville church into the Congregational fold see ibid., 12–17.

[20] Slater paid "One Hundred and Five Dollars" for "Pew Number Forty Five, in our Church, situate in Bernon Village in said Smithfield." The May 18, 1833, pew deed may be found in John Slater Papers, Manuscript Collection, Rhode Island Historical Society, hereafter cited as RIHS. On the Episcopalian identity of the St. James congregation see E. Richardson, *History of Woonsocket* (Woonsocket, R.I., 1876), 81.

Boston.[21] The journals these men kept, in part to provide a record of their activities with an eye toward obtaining renewed funding, provide wonderfully detailed glimpses into the religious life of Rhode Island's factory towns. They demonstrate in particular the degree to which all three men, Slater, Abbott, and Waldo, worked to establish a Congregational community at Slatersville in the midst of the troublesome Methodists. In November 1812, Abbott reported with satisfaction that John and Ruth Slater had snubbed the Methodist preacher "Mr. Moab Paine" by refusing to attend his services in the meetinghouse.[22] Moreover, Slater consistently sponsored Congregationalist preaching, helped to transport religious literature for the missionaries, provided them with lodging, and even sent "a bundle of cloth" to Mary Pearson, Abbott's fiancee.[23] Trained at Harvard and Yale respectively, Abbott and Waldo aimed to bring respectable and learned Congregationalism to the untutored mill hands of Slatersville.

The religious language Abbott and Waldo spoke betokened their dedication to a religion of sophistication and taste. Abbott sometimes referred to giving a sermon as preaching "a lecture" and was most concerned with the knowledge his hearers received during his discourse.[24] The best audiences were ones who evidenced "a seriousness in the attention with which they listened" or who had "been considerably decent in their deportment" on the Sabbath.[25] Waldo, too, insisted upon good order and right behavior as essential to the Christian life. In examining members for admission to the Congregationalist Church in Slatersville, Waldo reported that "we found their knowledge, & character, & religious views were such as to intitle them to the privileges of the gospel ordinances."[26] For Waldo, only candidates who manifested correct knowledge and proper character could be candidates for the rewards of Congregationalist membership. Disorderly worship, especially, earned Waldo's disapproval. He found scandalous the services of Native Americans in Charleston, Rhode Island, in which he found "male and female voices all speaking at once."[27] He deplored Methodist meetings

---

[21] Abbott's 1813 certificate of membership in the group may be found in the Ephraim Abbot Papers, American Antiquarian Society Library, Worcester, Mass. (Abbott's name is spelled with only one "t" in this collection.) A summary of Waldo's work appears in Donnell, *Sermon Preached*, 14–15.

[22] Ephraim Abbott diary, November 22, 1812, RIHS.

[23] On Abbott's relationship with Slater see also Abbott diary, October 12, 1812; and Abbott to Edward A. Pearson (Boston), November 29, 1812, Abbot Papers.

[24] Abbott diary, October 14, November 12, 1812.

[25] Abbott diary, October 11, 1812.

[26] Waldo diary, November 23, 1816, John Carter Brown Library, Brown University, hereafter cited as JCB.

[27] Daniel Waldo diary, April 12, 1818, Manuscripts, RIHS. See also Waldo diary, July 25, 1817, JCB, for another account of the "disorderly conduct of the Indians in their meetings."

in which "the women prayed & exhorted," taking comfort in Congregationalism because the women "never lead in religious services when the men are present."[28] Abbott and Waldo understood Congregationalism as a masculine faith in which right knowledge and proper conduct ruled.

During the 1830s Slatersville Congregationalists distinguished themselves in ways that would have pleased Ephraim Abbott and Daniel Waldo. In 1838 they constructed a beautiful, new Greek Revival church with fine Doric columns and a graceful spire. As was typical among New England Congregationalists after 1825, these churches began to replace the "barn-like structures with the pulpit on the long side and a door opposite, and as often as not lacking a tower and belfry."[29] Committing themselves to architectural good taste, the Congregationalists simultaneously reaffirmed their doctrinal distinctiveness. In 1839 the members published a revised set of their beliefs in which they stated their decided preference for baptism by sprinkling rather than immersion, and clung to the traditional Congregational formula that the church constituted a body of "visible saints."[30] So zealously did the members enforce the covenant of the church that the membership remained, by design, exclusive.[31]

Zachariah Allen's attitude toward mill village religion differed significantly from that of John Slater. Unlike Slater, who seems to have been tightly focused on his industrial pursuits, Allen took an interest in a tremendous variety of intellectual endeavors, publishing travel narratives such as *The Practical Tourist* and a scientific treatise, *Solar Light and Heat*. Among the most theoretically nimble of nineteenth-century industrialists, Allen conceptualized the moral function of the mill village itself differently from men like the Slaters and Samuel Ogden. According to his analysis, the task before the manufacturers was to preserve the rural quality of American manufacturing and thus avoid the creation of a permanent working class, the dangers of which he had observed in England. Congruent with Stephen Wardwell's rendering of the mill village at Killingly, Allen described his vision of the new industrial order in "essentially romantic terms."[32] He endorsed the idea that American mills ought to be operated by "the sons and daughters of respectable farmers." In his view, rural life was not flawed. Instead, the preservation of this rustic location for American industry would

---

[28] Waldo diary, August 9, 1818, RIHS.

[29] Bushman, *Refinement of America*, 338. See Nebiker, *History of North Smithfield*, 69, 73.

[30] *The Doctrinal Articles and Covenant of the Slatersville Congregational Church, Smithfield, R.I.* (Providence, 1839), 17, 19.

[31] Donnell, *Sermon Preached*, 16.

[32] Richard E. Greenwood, "Zachariah Allen and the Architecture of Industrial Paternalism," *Rhode Island History* 46 (1988): 121.

promote "the purity of those moral principles, without which neither nations nor individuals can become truly great and happy."[33]

Allen brought these convictions and his considerable skills in architecture to bear in the creation of his first mill village, Allendale, just north of Providence. Begun in 1822, the manufactory he designed continued to refine its organization well into the 1840s. A smaller project than Slatersville, Allen's manufactory boasted a total workforce of only 67 in 1832.[34] And to provide for his operatives' spiritual welfare, he constructed a small Gothic-style chapel on the northern edge of the mill pond. More unusual than the architecture, however, was Allen's decision to put the religious affiliation of the church up to a popular vote among the workers. As we have observed at Slatersville, the prevailing practice in Rhode Island mills reserved this choice for the owner. In Allendale, the operatives selected to connect themselves with the Baptists.[35] Allen's faith in the inherent goodness of country life and his adherence to republican principles influenced his decision to allow the workers to make this important choice for themselves.

The operatives' choice of the Baptists certainly cut against the grain of Allen's own religious sensibilities. Allen had been a longtime pewholder and member of the vestry at St. John's Episcopal Church in Providence. Still, even in the Episcopal Church, Allen lacked the conviction to make a full confession of faith before the congregation. A man of liberal religious beliefs and emotional restraint, he found it impossible to partake of communion with his fellow members until the revival of 1857–58.[36] Yet it would be a mistake to think of Zachariah Allen as a calculating entrepreneur devoid of sincere religious sentiments. The sheer beauty and spectacle of Episcopal worship captured his imagination. He found himself enchanted, for example, with a Christmas service at Providence's ornate Grace Church. "The gothic arches," he wrote, "lighted brightly by gas, and casting their shadows around, the reverberations of the chants & the peals of the organ, at one time sounding in thunder chimes & then faintly breaking the silence—the impressive discourse of the bishop,—all conspired to remind me of some of the sublime ceremonies of the cathedral churches in

---

[33] Zachariah Allen, *The Practical Tourist, or Sketches of the State of the Useful Arts, and Society, Scenery etc., in Great Britain, France and Holland*, vol. 1 (Providence, 1832), quotes on 154 and 155.

[34] Greenwood, "Zachariah Allen," 123.

[35] According to Richard Greenwood, it was Allen's custom here and at his Georgiaville mill village to allow his operatives the right to select the religious denomination of the chapel. See "Zachariah Allen," 126, 131. I am indebted to Professor J. Stanley Lemons of Rhode Island College for pointing out that the church at Allendale fell within the fold of the "regular" Baptists and was not part of the Freewill Baptist tradition as Greenwood points out.

[36] See Zachariah Allen diary for 1857–1858, RIHS.

Europe."[37] Although Allen preferred the Gothic to the Greek Revival style evidenced at Slatersville, both Allen and Slater could agree on a religious culture that emphasized refinement and taste.

While they may have dreamed of European cathedrals, evidence suggests that over time the entrepreneurs strayed from their earlier claims of social and religious responsibility. Beginning in the 1830s, when the Rhode Island textile industry entered what Peter Coleman has termed "the era of expansion," mill owners pumped millions of dollars into improving and enlarging their factories but could hardly scrape together the marginal sums needed to support churches, schools, and religion among their workers.[38] Several factors help to explain this behavior. As we have seen, the dedication of mill owners to a polished style of religious worship made them reluctant to embrace the enthusiastic services favored by their workers. Few mill owners cast themselves as evangelical crusaders. Zachariah Allen's aesthetic Episcopalianism gave pride of place to liturgy and architecture rather than to revivalism. John Slater's stolid Congregationalism did not capture the raw enthusiasm of his pesky Methodist adversaries. Moreover, the ideology of paternalism itself might have made them hesitant to fund reform groups over which they held no final authority. Finally, the behavior of the mill owners, especially in the 1830s and beyond, indicates that some of their earlier conservative notions of social responsibility were being supplanted by a more liberal understanding of their relationships with their employees. Rather than perceiving their workers as part of an organic community over whom they held authority and to whom they owed duties, mill owners began to see their workers as individuals in the marketplace to whom they owed no special spiritual obligations. The balance between the quest for individual profit and the claims of duty to community that had been so central to the economic ethic articulated by the clergy in early national Providence had begun to tilt. The lure of personal gain began to outweigh obligations to the whole.

Testimony from the religious reformers indicates clearly that they expected the entrepreneurs to make good on their earlier promises of paternal care at precisely the historical moment when the mill owners began to slough off that ideology. But having once voiced claims of paternal responsibility, the mill owners exposed themselves to criticism on exactly those terms. As late as 1836, George S. White, comrade to and biographer of Samuel Slater, admitted, "It is evidently an abuse to collect a mass of vicious population, and keep them in a state of ignorance and irreligion. When this

---

[37] Zachariah Allen diary, 2:62–63, entry for Christmas 1855, RIHS.
[38] Coleman, *Transformation of Rhode Island*, 119.

is done, the whole community have a right to complain."[39] And complain they did. Even Daniel Waldo, a Slater associate and ardent Congregationalist, deplored the lack of social responsibility he identified among some manufacturers. Upon visiting the Lippet manufactory, he discovered that the village's moral poverty began at the top. "I was afflicted on learning," he recalled, "that the agent & overseers of this Factory did not aid good morals & temperance by their example. The Sabbath is disregarded except as a day of visiting & amusement." Waldo broadened his critique of the situation in the village to include the leadership the management should have been exercising. "If the head is wrong in a family, village, or nation very little good can be done without correcting the source of influence. If those who give law to society, as it respects manners & morals, are full of blemishes," he argued, "the reformation of those under their influence is hopeless."[40] Daniel Waldo accepted the claims of paternal responsibility articulated by the mill owners and mobilized them in service of his critique.

In 1818, the women of the PFTS recalled the rhetoric of paternalism in comments targeting the wealthy members of society. In their *Third Annual Report*, the women reminded the community that "much remains to be done in Rhode Island" with respect to the task of moral reform. The members argued that "the object we conceive will be accomplished, when the rich among the people are excited to do that for themselves, and their poor, which the Society are now attempting to do for them."[41] And while the mill owners were not explicitly cited, it is clear that the women of the society were responding to the assertions of paternal responsibility voiced by the manufacturers. The women of the society had reason to worry about their financial situation. Between the years 1818 and 1824, their operating budget fell from $314.62 to $175.80.[42] Even a February 1828 appearance by Francis Wayland, at the Society's meeting in Providence's First Baptist meetinghouse produced a collection of only $108.[43] Moreover, the financial difficulties of the Society were well publicized in the Providence religious press. In 1821 the Providence *Religious Intelligencer* attempted to garner support for the organization by stressing its usefulness. "Will any reasonable

---

[39] George S. White, *Memoir of Samuel Slater, the Father of American Manufactures Connected with a History of the Rise and Progress of the Cotton Manufacture in England and America* (1836; reprint, New York, 1967), 116–117.

[40] Waldo diary, September 9, 1818, JCB.

[41] *The Third Annual Report of the Providence Female Tract Society* (Providence, 1818), 4, Brown University Library.

[42] Financial information on the Tract Society is from *Third Annual Report*, 5, and the Ninth Annual Report of the Society in the *Christian Monitor and Weekly Register* 1 (July 3, 1824).

[43] On Wayland's lecture see *Rhode-Island Religious Messenger* 2 (February 28, 1828): 187, and the Providence Female Tract Society Minutes, meeting of February 27, 1828, RIHS.

man," asked the publication, "pretend that the education of children is beneath attention, or will he maintain, in opposition to the plainest facts, that
in our country towns children are sufficiently instructed without the aid
of this Society?"[44] By 1823, when the society's resources proved even more
slender, the paper stated flatly, "The Society are now in want of funds to
enable them to continue their operations."[45] Indeed, the dramatic decline
in funding for the society resulted in its collapse by about 1830.

Although a better-heeled group, the Rhode Island Sunday School Union
(RISSU) complained that manufacturers could be more interested in the
organization's work. In 1830 an agent of the organization reported that "few
capitalists are willing to part with a portion of their treasures for the luxury
of doing good."[46] Such a statement regarding the entrepreneurs is extraordinary, given that some of Providence's leading businessmen could be
found among the board of directors of the RISSU.[47] But the missionaries
continued to ascribe at least partial blame to the industrialists for their
financial trials. In 1833 the RISSU's annual report cited the "neglect of
parents" as a major factor inhibiting their reform efforts in the mill villages,
but it also noted that "in some cases the avarice of those who run the mills"
was a problem to be overcome.[48] In its 1835 report, the members called the
entrepreneurs to task for not fulfilling their moral obligations. They directed an "appeal to those who, to a very great extent, control not only the
children, but above all others, can exert influence over parents. We refer to
the owners of the mills in the manufacturing villages."[49] Increasingly,
domestic missionaries found the paternalistic claims of the entrepreneurs
to ring hollow.

Even from the outset, domestic missionaries never seemed to accept fully
the mill owners' easy claims that factory villages would function as institu-

[44] *Religious Intelligencer* 1 (June 30, 1821): 22.

[45] *Religious Intelligencer and Evening Gazette* 3 (June 20, 1823): 18.

[46] *The Fifth Report of the Rhode-Island Sunday School Union, read at their Annual Meeting, held in
Providence on Wednesday Evening April 7, 1830* (Providence, 1830), 8.

[47] These men included the manufacturer Walter Paine, merchants Charles Dyer and
Alexander Jones, bank clerk Nathan Waterman, Jr., and the ubiquitous Stephen S. Wardwell.
On the identities of these men see *The Seventh Annual Report of the Rhode-Island Sunday School
Union, Auxiliary to the American Sunday School Union, Read at their Annual Meeting, held in
Providence, on Wednesday Evening, April 4, 1832* (Providence, 1832), 5; *The Providence Directory*
(Providence, 1832); and the 1832 Manuscript Town Tax List, RIHS.

[48] *The Eighth Report of the Rhode-Island Sunday School Union, Auxiliary to the American Sunday
School Union, Read at their Annual Meeting, Held in Providence, on Wednesday Evening, April 3, 1833*
(Providence, 1833), 13.

[49] *The Tenth Annual Report of the Rhode-Island Sunday School Union, Auxiliary to the American
Sunday School Union, Read at their Annual Meeting, Held in Providence, on April 1, 1835*
(Providence, 1835), 22.

tions of moral and religious uplift. While the missionaries sometimes condemned the entire countryside as backward, the rural manufactories consistently received the worst religious reviews. When Daniel Waldo visited the Natick Factory in February 1819, he learned that a sermon had not been preached in the village for six months. The people, he wrote sadly, "are in a most deplorable state of ignorance & stupidity."[50] At Capron's Mills, near Smithfield, Waldo may have learned why preachers sometimes avoided the manufacturing villages. A drunken man there disrupted one of Waldo's lessons—he "took hold of a large bible that lay before me & turned it round to read in it."[51] A missionary in the service of the Rhode Island Domestic Missionary Society, too, described scenes of religious horror at the mills near Woonsocket Falls: "A factory village of about 1,000 inhabitants where there was no preaching and not even a school house. The leading men were said to be Universalists—This village was a scene of moral desolation."[52] In the judgment of these missionaries, factory work appeared to erode rather than to edify the religious life of the operatives.

The women of the PFTS also denounced factory villages as moral trouble spots. From its inception, the society proposed to establish three Sunday schools "in such places as appeared most destitute of moral and religious advantages." Accordingly, two of the three schools were located in mill villages: one in Smithfield and "one in Coventry, in the vicinity of the Arkwright, Lippitt and Hope manufactories."[53] That these schools were established at all directly contradicted mill promoter Samuel Ogden's assertion that a cotton factory was a school in itself. The school teachers of the society discovered, as well, that the routine of factory labor impinged upon the time operatives had for education and religious exercises. Miss Lovina Goldthwait's report to the society implied that mill work contributed to the ignorance she found in "the vicinity of the Anthony, Stone, and Green Manufactories." A determined instructor, Miss Goldthwait made the best of her situation. The society commended her superior efforts and was especially pleased "that so large a number of children (139) at Coventry, who are now engaged in Factories, so as to preclude them from the advantages of education, should have received the benefits of instruction the last summer while the Factories had stopped, at the only period, perhaps, in their childhood when they may be at liberty to attend to it."[54] In the Washington factory

[50] Waldo diary, February 16, 1819, JCB.

[51] Waldo diary, April 24, 1818, RIHS.

[52] See "Religion in Rhode Island, 1828–1829," addressed to the "Gov. Sec. D.M.S.R.I.," 1–2, Brown University Library.

[53] *First Annual Report*, 22.

[54] *The Second Annual Report of the Providence Female Tract Society* (Providence, 1817), 5, Brown University Library.

village, too, the missionary working for the Rhode Island Domestic Missionary Society observed that mill hands were deprived of education. He wrote that "many children who work in the factories—cannot attend the week day schools and must obtain all their instruction from sabbath schools."[55] In such ways did the routine of factory labor contribute to moral decay and numbing ignorance.

The evidence from Rhode Island complicates historical interpretations that would cast religious reformers as unflinching advocates for a liberal and acquisitive capitalist society.[56] To be sure, the domestic missionaries occasionally articulated sentiments that would have earned them plaudits from mill owners. The PFTS, for example, aimed to teach workers and villagers "such habits of industry, temperance, and prudence, as will qualify them to be useful and respectable members of Society."[57] Moreover, some of the most substantial merchants in Providence also sat on the boards of religious reform groups. Josiah Chapin, a cotton factor and prominent Congregationalist lay leader, served in the 1830s as president of the Rhode Island Domestic Missionary Society, a group intimately involved in ministering to the mill villages.[58] Yet, entrepreneurial leadership of reform groups did not always blunt the harsh truths that missionaries communicated about religious life in the manufacturing districts. What the missionaries had to say went beyond broad, sentimental gestures against "materialism" in the abstract and included detailed remarks about the social relationships of industrial capitalism. They reported on specific conditions in specific mill villages at specific times. They worried about issues of morality, literacy, and salvation and, quite simply, did not swallow whole the basic premise that mill villages heralded the rise of an advanced civilization and a Christian republic.

To fill the moral and religious lacunae evident in the mill hamlets, the domestic missionaries launched a two-tiered reform effort. First, through the medium of the religious tract, they attempted to reach the unchurched with basic theological and moral truths. They also created and administered

[55] "Religion in Rhode Island," p. 20.

[56] See, among many influential works, Paul Boyer, *Urban Masses and Moral Order in America, 1820–1940* (Cambridge, Mass., 1978); Anthony F. C. Wallace, *Rockdale: The Growth of an American Village in the Early Industrial Revolution* (New York, 1980), 350–397; Charles Sellers, *The Market Revolution: Jacksonian America, 1815–1846* (New York, 1991), 211 and passim. Steven Mintz, in his survey of antebellum reformers, concedes that some of them longed for a "stable, orderly past," but he finally concludes that they "were nevertheless modernizers, promoting market values." See his *Moralists and Modernizers: America's Pre-Civil War Reformers* (Baltimore, 1995), xix.

[57] *First Annual Report*, 8.

[58] Chapin served as president from at least 1834 to 1841. See *Proceedings of the Evangelical Consociation and Missionary Society of the Congregational Churches in Rhode-Island* (Providence, 1834) and *Proceedings of the Evangelical Consociation and Home Missionary Society of Congregational Churches in Rhode Island* (Providence, 1841).

Sunday schools in dozens of the rural mill villages. Both the distribution of religious tracts and the creation of Sunday schools were designed by the missionaries with a plebeian constituency in mind. The religious tracts which the missionaries used had a tradition of readership among the English working class. The tracts carried by the American reformers were often reproductions of versions used in English Sunday schools in the late eighteenth and early nineteenth centuries. English favorites, such as Legh Richmond's tract *The Dairyman's Daughter*, and Hannah More's *The Shepherd of Salisbury Plain* and *'Tis All For the Best*, also achieved popularity in the Rhode Island countryside. The success of tracts among English workers shaped the decision of Providence reformers to distribute them among Rhode Island's first operatives.[59]

Domestic missionaries knew that religious tracts would reach their working-class audience. "This method of instruction is peculiarly calculated for the poor," commented the Providence *Religious Messenger*, "and is especially demanded by the poor of our extended population."[60] What made the tract such a powerful medium, these authors argued, was its brevity and the small cost involved to produce it. As one editor maintained, "A tract is short. In a little time it may be read, and its contents for meditation may be treasured in the mind."[61] Another writer declared, "A single penny gives it existence; it goes forth; it checks the swearer in the highway; it finds the farmer in his field; the mechanic at his bench."[62] Writers said that tracts possessed a mystical power to transform souls. The *Christian Monitor and Weekly Register* explained how the tract might work its miracles. These documents, it reported, "find their way to the poor man's cot. In the restlessness of inaction, his eye rests on the humble page; he begins with indifference to peruse it; his attention, as if by magick, is arrested, and the Holy Spirit leads him to the Saviour for pardon and grace."[63] In this account the tract, possessing a life of its own, works salvation "as if by magick" upon the reader. Like their seventeenth-century ancestors, nineteenth-century New Englanders continued to believe that religious books contained a palpable spiritual power.[64] The magical power of tracts also had a bearing on their use in the

---

[59] On the English origins of the tracts see Thomas Walter Laqueur, *Religion and Respectability: Sunday Schools and Working-Class Culture, 1780–1850* (New Haven, 1976), 15–16.

[60] *Religious Messenger* 1 (July 23, 1825): 13. On religious reading among common folk see especially David Paul Nord, "Religious Reading and Readers in Antebellum America," *Journal of the Early Republic* 15 (1995): 241–272.

[61] *Free-will Baptist Magazine* 2 (January 1829): 178.

[62] *Religious Messenger* 1 (January 21, 1826): 119.

[63] *Christian Monitor and Weekly Register* 1 (September 11, 1824).

[64] See David D. Hall, *Worlds of Wonder, Days of Judgment: Popular Religious Belief in Early New England* (New York, 1989), 23–27.

mill villages because the tract could work its moral reformation even after the distributor had moved on to other missionary ground. Workers, too, could carry tracts with them, moving from village to village and factory to factory, themselves becoming agents in the grand plan of salvation.

In the stories they told, the tracts celebrated the piety of humble farmers and peasants. The theme of the moral superiority of the poor figured prominently in the tracts, especially among those that circulated among the mill villages of Rhode Island. Gilbert Manson, of the Arkwright Factory in Coventry, communicated to the PFTS that these were precisely the type of tracts that would appeal to his workers. Although he considered his employees "in general a people who dislike all holy institutions," he suggested that titles such as *The Shepherd of Salisbury Plain*, *'Tis All For the Best*, and *The Dairyman's Daughter* could be used with success. His report to the society two months later suggests that the operatives gobbled up these selections and had "become anxious for more instruction."[65] These tracts, extolling the virtues of farming life in eighteenth-century England, seem strangely divorced from the world of factory labor in rural Rhode Island. They celebrated a conservative world of social stability, of squires and humble farmers, country parsons and pious daughters.[66] Moreover, in their original English context, these tracts were crafted to convince laborers that poverty was their divinely ordained lot in life. Hannah More's classic tract, *The Shepherd of Salisbury Plain*, makes this point explicitly. In conversation with a "gentlemen," the old shepherd exclaims, "I wonder all working men do not derive as great joy and delight as I do, in thinking how God has honored poverty."[67] Hardly the rhetoric of labor activism or of social revolution, the old shepherd's comments seem to signal satisfaction with his place in the divinely sanctioned social order.

Given the transparent intent of tracts to foster contentment with a mean existence, the question remains as to why operatives appear to have read and enjoyed them. In the first place, it is likely that factory workers took seriously the fate of their souls and looked to the tracts for spiritual truths. It is also likely that Rhode Island mill hands glimpsed meanings in the tracts that the mill owners and missionaries might have missed. Although designed to promote satisfaction with poverty, the tracts also contained a notion of divine justice that worked in favor of the poor. Such a perspective

---

[65] See Manson's letters of August 11, 1815; October 28, 1815, Providence Female Tract Society Manuscripts, RIHS, hereafter cited as PFTS MSS.
[66] Mark S. Schantz, "Religious Tracts, Evangelical Reform, and the Market Revolution in Antebellum America," *Journal of the Early Republic* 17 (1997): 425–466.
[67] Hannah More, *The Shepherd of Salisbury Plain*, no. 10 (New York, n.d.), 5. This tract, and other titles distributed in Rhode Island, was published by the American Tract Society.

is embedded in the storyline of the tract *'Tis All For the Best*. Mrs. Simpson, the long-suffering protagonist is eventually informed that the evil land-lord—known as her "old oppressor"—has suddenly died. Commenting on this reversal of fortune to her friend Betty, Mrs. Simpson warns, "You think I am good just now because I am prosperous. Success is no sure mark of God's favor."[68] The operatives, then, may have warmed to stories that located moral superiority among the poor and exposed the rich in society as sinners. Much already in the Scriptures, especially within the prophetic tradition, would have supported such a reading. To the extent that tracts were psalms of capitalist celebration, they provided entrepreneurs with much less substance than scholars have commonly assumed.

Despite the contention that tracts could work their magic independently, Sunday schools provided the usual context in which these texts were employed. In several important respects the institution of the Sunday school differed from the Baptist and Congregational missionary churches entrepreneurs sometimes supported. Doctrinally, the schools were multidenominational and did not require a profession of faith on the part of the student. Participating in Sunday schools did not require loyalty to a specific church building nor did it entail the purchase of a pew. Nor did poverty present a bar to participation. The PFTS, for example, initiated a program for "charity scholars," aimed at including even the most impoverished of mill village children.[69] The RISSU, too, provided materials free of cost and maintained libraries at each of its auxiliary schools. Like the tracts they often used as texts, the network of Sunday schools operated by the reformers accommodated mobility and poverty, two realities of working-class life.

The Sunday schools operated by the PFTS and the RISSU proved wildly popular among rural workers. As early as 1818, the PFTS employed eleven instructors and claimed to have enrolled over seven hundred students in its classes.[70] In 1820 the society even changed its name to the Providence Female Tract and School Society, to celebrate its emerging school system. As funding for the organization tightened in the late 1820s, the RISSU filled the gap left by the women of Providence. In 1830 it counted some thirty-two auxiliaries in its domain attended by nearly 4,100 students. And the Union conducted classes in some of Providence's established churches as well as the mill hamlets.[71] By 1838 the RISSU boasted nearly 160 affili-

---

[68] *'Tis All For the Best*, no. 11 (New York, n.d.), 13–14.
[69] On the support of "charity scholars" see *First Annual Report*, 22–23; *Third Annual Report*, 10–11; *The Fifth Annual Report of the Providence Female Tract and School Society* (Providence, 1820), 10, 12, 16; and PFTS MSS, September 28, 1822; December 15, 1825; March 3, 1826; May 15, 1826.
[70] *Third Annual Report*, 3.
[71] *Fifth Annual Report*, 5.

ated schools with about 12,000 scholars on the rolls.[72] With such success, it is not surprising that the members of the RISSU contended that their Sunday schools constituted a "radical reform in education, morals and religion."[73] Participation in the Sunday school movement thus connected Rhode Island's workers to the vast project of social redemption in which the evangelicals of the Benevolent Empire were engaged.

The active participation of the operatives themselves proved of central importance in the success of the missionary reform efforts. After 1818 especially, the reports of the PFTS are peppered with requests from "the people" to keep the school system in operation.[74] In November of 1819, for instance, the Society approved Miss Tillinghast's request to extend her school in Johnston through the winter months. "We are induced to this measure," reported the society, "by the request of the people & the uncommon progress of the children, most of whom are very poor and labor in the Factory."[75] In South Kingston, too, Susan Wakefield found support for her efforts. "Not only the children," she discovered, "but the people here became very much interested in the school & have often afforded me assistance."[76] The teachers of the PFTS commented repeatedly on the enthusiasm that their child operatives brought to their studies. One Miss Tuttle, who conducted a school in Smithfield, found that her students had been catching up on their homework during factory hours. Like any dedicated teacher, Miss Tuttle approved of this ordering of priorities. "My scholars did wonders," she reported. "I enquired when they learnt so much. They replied, that they set up their lessons before them while at work. I could not refrain from tears during recitation."[77] Miss Latham, who conducted the Smithfield school the year before noticed a similar pattern among her students. "Some of the larger boys," she explained, "who were scarcely seen to take a book before, were now seen working with one hand and holding a book in the other."[78] Some students evidently preferred learning their lessons to tending their machines.

In championing literacy among workers, the teachers of the PFTS and

---

[72] *The Thirteenth Annual Report of the Rhode-Island Sunday School Union, Auxiliary to the American Sunday School Union, Read at the Annual Meeting Held in Providence, Wednesday Evening, April 4, 1838* (Providence, 1838), 10.

[73] *The Eighth Annual Report of the Rhode-Island Sunday School Union, Auxiliary to the American Sunday School Union, Read at Their Annual Meeting held in Providence on Wednesday Evening, April 3, 1833* (Providence, 1833), 21.

[74] PFTS MSS, meetings of November 25, 1819; March 24, 1821; October 18, 1826.

[75] PFTS MSS, November 25, 1819.

[76] PFTS MSS, October 18, 1826.

[77] *Fifth Annual Report*, 6.

[78] *Third Annual Report*, 7.

RISSU pressed an issue that could put them at odds with mill owners. One incident in North Kingston suggests that factory agents moved to shut down a school operated by the PFTS. The young instructor had set up shop near the manufactory for the purpose of teaching the children to read during intermissions from work. This arrangement worked for about a month until the mill management suddenly cut the intermission period to thirty minutes. In the words of the reformers, the teacher "was compelled to relinquish" her school.[79] Miss Tillinghast, who operated a school "in the vicinity of the Lyman factory," nudged her students toward risky behavior when she admitted that the "little factory children took their lessons with them to the mill, that they might improve every leisure moment."[80] However much they might have spoken the language of paternal responsibility, it hardly seems likely that factory owners would have welcomed the sight of workers trudging to work with tracts, books, and Bibles in hand, ready to savor a moment of "leisure" in which to improve their souls.[81]

Factory workers also embraced the work of the RISSU. In 1832, for instance, the RISSU conducted schools in at least twenty manufacturing centers made up of some 1,628 students and 223 instructors. (See Table 5.) Given that the total number of children employed in the Rhode Island cotton industry in that year was 3,550, this level of operative participation is striking. (See Table 6.) There is no precise way of determining whether all the scholars in these villages were operatives, but the number of children employed in these villages seems to correspond roughly to the number of children enrolled in RISSU classes. (See Table 7.) Some mill children must also have been scattered among the other rural schools not specifically designated as belonging to manufacturing villages. Thus it is probable that as many as one-half of the youthful mill hands in the hinterland received training in a RISSU school. Like the records of the PFTS, the reports of the RISSU expose a rapport between the missionaries and the operatives. In 1830, for instance, the RISSU congratulated the "inhabitants of the Lippitt, Phoenix and Harris Villages, for their liberal donations, in support of the School."[82] The 1834 report of the RISSU also shows highly successful schools functioning in the manufacturing centers of Natick Village,

---

[79] *Fifth Annual Report,* 11.

[80] Ibid., 10.

[81] The Tract Society did report, however, that some factory agents continued to support their work even when children did "study while at work." See *Fifth Annual Report,* 8. For other illustrations of workplace conflict over reading see Zonderman, *Aspirations and Anxieties,* 30, 150, 159, 226, and Lucy Larcom, *A New England Girlhood, Outlined From Memory* (1889; reprint, Boston, 1986), 180–181.

[82] *Fifth Annual Report,* 18.

Table 5. Sunday schools in manufacturing villages, 1832

Manufactory	Teachers		Students	
	Male	Female	Male	Female
Lyman's Factory	2	10	21	32
Slatersville	6	19	47	117
Albion Mills	3	10	50	70
Lonsdale	1	3	15	15
Arkwright & Fiskville	12	13	64	64
Rockland	2	8	32	33
Belle Fonte	2	2	8	9
Lippett & Phoenix	15	10	100	100
Crompton Mills	6	8	70	85
Natick Union	3	9	30	70
Central Factory	3	3	35	36
Washington Village	5	10	54	56
East Greenwich	3	3	30	30
Bellville	4	4	35	35
Wakefield	13	9	70	70
Arnold's Factory	2	3	30	30
Reynold's Factory	2	5	20	20
Globe Factory	4	6	18	27
TOTAL	88	135	729	899

Sources: The Seventh Report of the Rhode-Island Sunday School Union, Auxiliary to the American Sunday School Union, Read at their Annual Meeting, held in Providence, on Wednesday Evening, April 4, 1832 (Providence, 1832), 33–35; Louis McLane, *Report of the Secretary of the Treasury, 1832. Documents Relative to the Manufactures in the United States*, House Executive Documents, 22d Cong., 2d sess., Doc. 308, vol. 1 (Washington, D.C., 1833), 927–976.

Table 6. Textile employees in Rhode Island, 1832

Type of manufacturing	Number of establishments	Employees		
		Men	Women	Children
Cotton	119	1,744	3,301	3,550
Woolen	22	150	124	106
Bleacheries	5	200	40	60
Print works	2	120	30	36
TOTAL	153	2,214	3,495	3,752

Sources: See Table 5.

Table 7. Sunday school members and child operatives, 1832

Manufactory	Total students	Total child operatives
Lyman's Factory	53	24
Slatersville	164	169
Albion Mills	120	120
Lonsdale	30	50
Arkwright & Fiskville	128	99
Rockland	65	41
Belle Fonte	17	13
Lippett & Phoenix	200	126
Crompton Mills	155	164
Natick Union	100	200
Bellville	70	36

Sources: See Table 5.

Arkwright, Fiskville, Hopkin's Mill, Slatersville, Crompton's Mills, and the Rockland Factories in Scituate. The school at Natick Village "has been so pleasing to the children, that the school-house has been crowded; and we have been obliged to divide the school and establish a new one, in order to accommodate all the little ones who came."[83]

The curriculum offered in the Sunday schools provides clues as to their enormous popularity. It blended subjects such as geography, history, and arithmetic with more explicitly religious materials. The RISSU, for instance, maintained libraries at each of its branch schools and carried a variety of "historical, biographical, narrative and other instructive books proper for juvenile libraries."[84] At the same time, Sunday school scholars enlisted their best efforts toward memorizing Bible verses, lines from Dr. Watt's *Divine Songs*, and passages from Brown's *Catechism.* The instructors of the schools recorded the triumphs of their students in recitation and memorization with great pride and mathematical precision. Susan Wakefield reported to the PFTS that at her school in South Kingston, "The number of verses of Scripture recited during the term were 4,472."[85] A RISSU instructor crowed from North Scituate that "one girl of thirteen years of age has repeated from the Bible and Hymn-book two thousand and ninety-seven verses." The enthusiastic teacher went on to explain the importance of such achievements of memory: "They are storing their minds with scripture facts and doctrines;

[83] *The Ninth Annual Report of the Rhode-Island Sunday School Union, Auxiliary to the American Sunday School Union, Read at Their Annual Meeting, held in Providence, on Wednesday Evening, April 2, 1834* (Providence, 1834), 12–15, quote on 12.

[84] *Fourth Annual Report,* 4.

[85] PFTS MSS, October 18, 1826.

and it would be strange if these should not have some influence on their future lives and conduct."[86] Memorization of religious texts constituted a specific form of religious devotion aimed at the transformation of the soul. In their extraordinary accomplishments, quantified in nearly every missionary report, the scholars and parents evidently felt a strong sense of self-esteem and empowerment.

In sharp contrast to the masculine notions of church governance that abided in Providence churches, women and men created and organized the tract and Sunday school network in rural Rhode Island. An extensive organization, the PFTS collected fifty-two cents from each of 469 female subscribers to inaugurate its work.[87] Initially, the women decided to hire three Brown University undergraduates to teach their schools while the women distributed tracts and handled issues of administration and finance. With the success of the school system, however, women began to take a leading role in conducting the schools. In 1818, the PFTS reported that it had "employed" seven "gentlemen" (they retained some students from Brown) and four "ladies" during the course of the year.[88] In the published reports of the society, however, the essays written by the female teachers received the largest consideration and often contained the most poignant accounts of scholarly progress and religious reformation. Women taught even more schools for the RISSU. In 1832 women outnumbered men 135 to 88 as instructors listed in the RISSU annual report (see Table 5). The RISSU differed significantly from the PFTS in that its administrative leadership was decidedly male. Nonetheless, women conducted the majority of its schools and claimed authority as its teachers.

At a number of levels, the work of female missionaries, tract distributors, and teachers challenged the ideology of paternalism evident among Providence congregations and among the mill owners of the countryside. When women stood in front of their Sunday schools, they embodied patterns of female leadership that overturned the assertion that entrepreneurs supervised the spiritual life of their employees. When female (and male) missionaries offered comments on the moral dangers of factory work, child labor, or the problem of illiteracy among workers, they also edged into the masculine domain of politics. As scholars are beginning increasingly to recognize, the overt political activism of women in Jacksonian America, even before the surge of interest in the years after the Seneca Falls Convention in 1848, has not received its due. We have known about female abolitionists and temperance reformers, but recent work on the early 1840s has pointed

[86] *Eighth Annual Report,* 13.
[87] Subscribers' list in *First Annual Report,* 14–18.
[88] *Third Annual Report,* 3.

to the critical involvement of Whig women within the competition of the emerging two-party system.[89] While they did not launch themselves directly into electoral politics in the 1820s or 1830s, Rhode Island women confronted issues of central concern regarding the political economy of their society. The issue of literacy among factory workers, for example, constituted a core issue for Rhode Island labor activists in the 1830s. Even before 1832, when the New England Association of Farmers, Mechanics and Other Workingmen took on the issue in their reports, domestic missionaries and female Sunday school teachers knew that it was a problem.[90] In offering their views on the morally damaging aspects of mill work, female missionaries explicitly questioned the arguments for industrialization that had been advanced by the mill owners themselves. By reflecting publicly on the moral and social impact of manufacturing, Rhode Island's domestic missionaries and Sunday school teachers entered one of the most fundamental political debates of Jacksonian America.

In pushing into the uncharted territory of reforming the world, women employed the idea that they had unique obligations for tending to religious life in the early republic. As Nancy Cott has argued, the notion of a "woman's sphere" that coalesced in New England in the opening decades of the nineteenth century contained within it the conviction that women, by nature, were ideally suited to religious pursuits. "In moral reform activities," Cott has written, "women took up (literally with a vengeance) the power that ministers had for decades told them they possessed."[91] Rhode Island missionaries, especially, used that religious leverage to address the problems they perceived in the factories of the countryside. Since most of the workers in Rhode Island's cotton manufactories were women and children (see Table 6), missionary women could make an especially strong case for their activism. For in tending to the needs of the dependent and the young, women simply extended the duties of the domestic hearth into the mill villages. And as we have observed, reports from PFTS and RISSU teachers highlighted their work with the "children" and the "little ones" who attended their classes. In such ways did the notion of a uniquely feminine spirituality translate into broader social activism outside the domestic sphere.

For all of their activism, the women who taught in the rural factories shared close personal and social ties with the rising industrial elite. Bonds

---

[89] See Elizabeth R. Varon, *We Mean to Be Counted: White Women and Politics in Antebellum Virginia* (Chapel Hill, 1998).

[90] *New England Artisan*, February 23, 1832.

[91] Nancy F. Cott, *The Bonds of Womanhood: Woman's Sphere in New England, 1780–1835* (New Haven, 1977), 153.

of kinship and church linked the teachers and subscribers of the PFTS, RISSU, and other reform associations with some of the biggest names in the Rhode Island textile business. For instance, among the PFTS subscribers in 1816 could be found Mrs. Samuel G. Arnold, Mrs. Edward Carrington, Mrs. John Innes Clarke, Mrs. Lydia Dorr, Mrs. Jacob Dunnell, Mrs. Bemjamin Hoppin, Mrs. Oliver Kane, Mrs. George Olney, and Mrs. George Weeden, all pewholders in Providence churches and key figures in the merchant and manufacturing community. These reformers were not marginal insurgents working at the fringes of respectable Providence society but were, in some cases, the wives and daughters of affluent entrepreneurs. Viewed from one perspective, these women might be seen as putting into practice the ideology of paternal care articulated by the manufacturing elite. As scholars have acknowledged, the creation of female moral reform groups and tract societies helped to organize and energize members of the aspiring bourgeoisie.[92]

During the 1820s and 1830s, Providence women had not closed ranks entirely with Providence men when it came to a full-scale endorsement of the new industrial order. To the degree that these elite Christian women questioned some of the basic assumptions of male industrial leaders, they limited the degree to which the Providence bourgeoisie could jell as a class. As we shall observe, throughout the 1830s and during the political controversy surrounding the Dorr Rebellion in 1842, affluent Providence women continued to aim occasional, but sharp, barbs against Rhode Island's industrial and political elite. Only during the 1850s did Providence women and men join forces in forging a new style of religious reform designed to keep the poor at arm's length.[93] But in the early decades of the nineteenth century, Providence women determined to take the gospel to factory operatives on their own ground. They saw these workers as human beings who could be brought to salvation rather than as social problems to be quarantined.

As reform efforts continued apace, the factory hands and farmers of rural Rhode Island crafted a religious culture of their own. In some cases, and especially in the creation of the Sunday school network, the interests of the workers and missionaries found happy coincidence. But the factory workers

---

[92] See Mary P. Ryan, *Cradle of the Middle Class: The Family in Oneida County, New York, 1790–1860* (New York, 1981); Christine Stansell, *City of Women: Sex and Class in New York, 1789–1860* (Urbana, 1987).

[93] See also Carol Smith-Rosenberg, "The Cross and the Pedestal: Women, Anti-Ritualism, and the Emergence of the American Bourgeoisie," in *Disorderly Conduct: Visions of Gender in Victorian America* (New York, 1985), 134; Lori D. Ginzburg, *Women and the Work of Benevolence: Morality, Politics, and Class in the Nineteenth-Century United States* (New Haven, 1990), 100.

of Rhode Island were interested in more than the school network and the benefits of literacy. They expressed a preference for the Freewill Baptists and Methodists, delighted in itinerant and female preaching, continued to trust in dreams, visions, and intense emotional display, and sought to retain control over their own churches. Alongside the decorous, refined religious tastes of the entrepreneurs swirled the more boisterous, rough religious life of workers and local farmers. What Alan Taylor, in his study of the Maine backcountry during the Revolutionary era, has called "the cultural divide between the visionary and the orthodox" might well be applied to the situation in the Rhode Island mill villages as well.[94] In both places, common farmers and workers embraced a religious culture at odds with the one favored by their "proprietors." Although Rhode Island possessed no state-supported church (as Massachusetts did until 1833), the "cultural divide" in the hinterland was nevertheless pronounced.

The wild diversity of religious life in the Rhode Island countryside provided an affront to refined religious culture. In 1812 Ephraim Abbott, the Harvard-trained Congregationalist missionary, wrote to Mary Pearson in Boston that "Religion in this state seems like a house divided against itself. Baptists, Methodists, & Friends are scattered here and there one, among a multitude of nothingarians."[95] The very disorderliness of religious loyalties among the rural folk he visited seemed to disturb Abbott almost as much as their resistance to mainline Congregationalism. Ephraim Abbott could have added to his inventory of religious diversity the Shakers, the Universalists, the "Christians," and Baptists of seemingly endless variety. Among the most popular among backcountry folk were the Six-Principle Baptists, prickly traditionalists who insisted on the laying-on of hands for church membership, disdained an educated and professional clergy, and looked with suspicion on anything that smacked of the missionary reform impulse. Moreover, as Daniel Jones has demonstrated, the Six-Principle Baptists formed an important part of a rural, subsistence culture that resisted the intrusions of turnpikes, banks, mill dams, and cotton factories.[96] Some backcountry folk hardly seemed to be Christians of any stripe, which confounded even further the Congregational desire for orderly Christianity. "The younger families," Abbott reported in the same letter to Mary Pearson, "are mostly without any religion, & professedly belong to no denomination. Some of those confess that they are sick of what are sometimes called the steady habits of R.I." In Abbott's view, godliness, the promotion of "steady habits," and the polity of Congregationalism formed part of a single, coher-

---

[94] Alan Taylor, *Liberty Men and Great Proprietors: The Revolutionary Settlement on the Maine Frontier, 1760–1820* (Chapel Hill, 1990), 148, and 123–153 generally.

[95] Ephraim Abbot to Mary Pearson, October 3, 1812, Abbot Papers.

[96] Jones, *Economic and Social Transformation*, 63–98.

ent perspective. The chaotic tenor that distinguished religious life in the backcountry formed a counterpoint to the stable and polished religious life prized by Congregationalist missionaries and entrepreneurs like John Slater.

Among the faiths contending for the allegiance of rural Rhode Islanders, and especially factory operatives, the Freewill Baptists and the Methodists proved particularly successful. During the first half of the nineteenth century, the Freewill Baptists, originally a sect from the New England hills, grew to become the fourth largest church in Rhode Island.[97] Although they were not drawn from those at the bottom of Rhode Island's economic order, the Freewill Baptists enjoyed immense popularity in the mill villages of the hinterland. The Methodists, too, garnered the support of Rhode Island's workers. Especially before 1833, when the trial of Methodist minister Ephraim Avery for the murder of a Sarah Maria Cornell, a young factory operative, temporarily tarnished the Methodists' image, camp meetings, class meetings, and love feasts percolated in factory villages throughout the state.[98] Indeed, the evidence produced at the trial, including the letters of Sarah Cornell, revealed the extraordinary appeal of Methodism among the first generation of Rhode Island's workers.[99]

Theologically, the Freewill Baptists and the Methodists shared a fundamentally Arminian perspective. Both denominations rejected the Calvinist idea of predestination, which held that God had already separated the saved from the damned and, thus, that the human will had little role to play in the process of salvation. Both Freewill Baptists and Methodists rehabilitated human volition in "the history of redemption," insisting that persons could freely accept Christ as their savior.[100] It is important to note that the particular kind of anti-Calvinism embraced by the Freewill Baptists and the Methodists was not rooted in cool-headed rationalism. These Baptists and Methodists did not share the view of the theologians who, laying the foundations for Unitarianism, believed that predestination was intellectually repugnant and that religion must be given a more reasonable basis. Unlike the more reserved Unitarians, evangelical Arminians such as the Freewill Baptists and Methodists clung to what Stephen Marini has termed "an experiential imperative in religious epistemology."[101] One knows one is saved because one experiences it. That is, the experience of accepting Christ as

---

[97] On the growth of the Freewill Baptists in Rhode Island see ibid., 147–154.

[98] See David Richard Kasserman, *Fall River Outrage: Life, Murder, and Justice in Early Industrial New England* (Philadelphia, 1986).

[99] See Avery Trial Papers, RIHS.

[100] Stephen A. Marini, *Radical Sects of Revolutionary New England* (Cambridge, Mass., 1982), 136.

[101] Marini, *Radical Sects*, 137–138. On the approach taken by the Unitarians see Sydney E. Ahlstrom, *A Religious History of the American People* (New Haven, 1972), 388–402.

your savior provides the basis for knowledge about the state of your soul. The "experiential imperative" thus laid the foundation for a religious culture that venerated intense displays of emotion rather than dispassionate intellectual debate. It proved to be the cornerstone of plebeian Arminianism.[102]

Descriptions of Methodist and Freewill Baptist worship underscore its exuberant quality. After hearing a Methodist minister at Wickford, Daniel Waldo reported glumly that "there was more sound than substance in his discourse."[103] He also related an account of a Methodist revival in Hopkinton that lasted four days. "They would frequently jump, clap their hands & halloo untill exhausted; then fall on the floor & roll over & over like a dog—Thus some were jumping, others rolling, & some running backward till they almost fell on those who were rolling—Some stomping about the house like one in a high fit of passion."[104] Catherine Williams, too, included a scene from a camp meeting near Smithfield, Rhode Island, at the conclusion of her 1833 work, *Fall River:* "Many were struck down, they said, with conviction of their sins, throwing themselves in the dirt and calling loudly for mercy."[105] Williams depicted a scene of complete chaos and social disorder, stocked with unsavory rum sellers, young women and men of lustful proclivities with parents nowhere in sight, and female and "African" preachers. "Who can contend," she wrote, "that this free intermingling of society is not dangerous, this tumbling and falling about not indecent."[106] What she described was nothing less than a world in which normal authority was turned upside down. While Williams presented this account in part to condemn Rhode Island Methodism and the controversial Ephraim Avery, her rendering does resemble other more impartial accounts. The Freewill Baptists, too, favored services that gave free reign to the spirit. When John Colby, an early Freewill Baptist missionary, visited the state, he evidently encouraged the direct participation of laypeople in the service itself. "Mr. Colby encourages his hearers to speak in his meetings," reported a

---

[102] In attributing an Arminian perspective to plebeian piety, this study parts company with Charles Sellers's *The Market Revolution,* a work that casts the central religious struggle of the age as a contest between bourgeois Arminianism and plebeian antinomianism. Sellers's rather problematic use of the terms "Arminian" and "antinomian" is explored in detail in essays by Daniel Walker Howe and Richard Carwardine in Melvyn Stokes and Stephen Conway, eds., *The Market Revolution in America: Social, Political, and Religious Expressions, 1800–1880* (Charlottesville, 1996).
[103] Waldo diary, March 31, 1818, RIHS.
[104] Waldo diary, July 21, 1817, JCB.
[105] Catharine Williams, *Fall River: An Authentic Narrative* (1833), ed. Patricia Caldwell (New York, 1993), 154. All quotations are from the 1993 edition.
[106] Williams, *Fall River,* 145.

dismayed Ephraim Abbott, "& tells them they can do more good than he can."[107] Hosea Smith, a Rhode Island mill worker who became a Freewill Baptist preacher, recorded numerous scenes of emotional conversion in his spiritual autobiography. During one revival, Smith sought to bring two lost souls to Christ. "They wept and cried bitterly for mercy," he recalled. "My heart felt so much for them I thought I could not sleep any that night and that I would pray for them all night."[108] Emotional release and the language of the heart thus constituted the core of worship among the early Methodists and Freewill Baptists.

More practical matters of polity and organization galvanized the popularity of the Methodists and Freewill Baptists among Rhode Island's working people. The Methodist camp meeting, held in groves and fields throughout the state, was the ideal forum in which to attract the "floating population" of rural operatives.[109] As workers moved from mill to mill in search of employment, they could follow camp meetings as they went. Moreover, the natural settings of camp meetings nurtured the life of the spirit. "In the stillness of the forest and in the retirement of nature," *Zion's Herald* reported in 1824, "it is well known, from experience, that religious discourses often make the most lasting impression on the human heart."[110] Rather than seeing religious culture as a way of overcoming the crudeness of nature, as Samuel and John Slater did, the Methodists rooted their piety in the wilderness. And while the Methodists certainly paid attention to building churches, the camp meeting itself denied the distinctions of wealth and prestige based upon the practice of pew ownership. In such ways did the camp meeting function as "a ritual recovery of unities, openness, inclusiveness, and flexibility that had characterized early American Methodism."[111]

Freewill Baptists, too, took strides toward inclusivity and flexibility. From the outset, they held to a policy of "open communion," the practice of inviting all Christians to join with them in the Lord's Supper. This policy distanced the Freewill Baptists from the Six-Principle Baptists and positioned them to increase their numbers. In 1822, for instance, when Daniel Mathhewson petitioned the Rhode Island state legislature for permission to hold a lottery for the purpose of constructing a Freewill Baptist church in Smithfield, he announced his determination to "build a house for the pub-

---

[107] Ephraim Abbott to Edward Pearson, November 30, 1812, Abbot Papers.
[108] Hosea Smith, *The Life of Hosea Smith, A Travelling Minister, who was left without father or mother, or any connexion. Also an account of his sufferings and cruel treatment, and his conviction and conversion. Also his calls into the ministry* (Providence, 1833), 34.
[109] Domestic missionaries often used this phrase to describe the transiency of workers. See "Religion in Rhode Island, 1828–1829," 7.
[110] Quoted in Kasserman, *Fall River Outrage*, 41.
[111] Russell E. Richey, *Early American Methodism* (Bloomington, 1991), 23.

lic worship of God which shall be free & open to all denominations." More-over, the pews in the church would "be free to all persons."[112] Over time, the Freewill Baptists joined the Methodists in constructing a finely organized and hierarchical structure of church governance, complete with quarterly meetings, annual conferences, and plans for a Freewill Baptist seminary. "The genius of the Freewill Baptists," Daniel Jones has written, "lay in their ability to mix a strong and simple faith of piety and good works with an in-stitutional network of growing sophistication."[113] Although they moved de-cisively toward respectability in the 1850s, the Freewill Baptists retained a radical edge that prevented them from fully embracing refined religion. In 1851 the Rhode Island Quarterly Meeting openly denounced the Fugitive Slave Law as "anti-Christian" and encouraged its members to engage in civil disobedience.[114] The premium the Freewill Baptists placed on the liberty of the human soul never quite left the movement.

Itinerant ministers and lay exhorters embodied the freedom prized by the Methodists and Freewill Baptists. Both denominations made extensive use of these preachers in carrying their respective messages to the country-side. While the Methodist circuit riders are better known to historians, the Freewill Baptists also employed a traveling ministry. "The Free-will revival-ists," according to Joseph Brennan, "were uneducated but colorful charac-ters, were paid no stated salary and preached where they might."[115] In the late eighteenth and early nineteenth centuries, the Freewill Baptists had still not reconciled themselves to a paid, professional clergy, and upon occasion they criticized the Congregationalists and other entrenched ministers for their interest in salaries. Ephraim Abbott recalled one such insult: "the only call Congregational & C. ministers have is money. The more money is offered he said the louder is their call."[116] Even when the Freewill Baptists began to pay their clergy, they remained dedicated to funding missionary preaching throughout the small towns and factory villages of Rhode Island. In May 1826, the inaugural issue of the *Free-will Baptist Magazine,* published in Providence, dedicated "a part of the profits" from the journal "to the sup-port of an itinerant ministry."[117] The mobility of the Methodist and Freewill

---

[112] *Petitions to the Rhode Island General Assembly,* vol. 50, June 15, 1822, Rhode Island State Archives, Providence.

[113] Jones, *Economic and Social Transformation,* 154.

[114] *Minutes of the Ministers' Conference, and also of the Quarterly Conference, of the Rhode Island Quarterly Meeting of Freewill Baptists; Together with a Circular in relation to a plan for aiding Feeble Churches* (Pawtucket, 1851), 7–8.

[115] Joseph Brennan, F.S.C., *Social Conditions in Industrial Rhode Island: 1820–1860* (Washington, D.C., 1940), 69.

[116] Ephraim Abbott to Edward Pearson, November 30, 1812, Abbot Papers.

[117] *Free-will Baptist Magazine* 1 (May 1826): 3.

Baptist clergy thus mirrored the transiency of the rural workers to whom they ministered.

Women also played a central role in bringing the gospel to the back-country. While Methodist women did not enjoy the authority conferred by ordination, they nevertheless found their voices in love feasts and camp meetings. In 1818, Daniel Waldo heard Methodist women pray and exhort near Slatersville although he did not experience the event as edifying. Catherine Williams, as we have seen, also identified female preachers at a Methodist camp meeting in Smithfield, Rhode Island. Prominent "female preachers," such as Nancy Towle and the celebrated Salome Lincoln, also made frequent appearances among the Methodists at groves and glades throughout New England. The Freewill Baptists exceeded the Methodists in their commitment to female preaching and exhortation. At least ten women preached among the Freewill Baptists of Rhode Island in the early nineteenth century.[118] The heroic and charismatic Susan Humes sparked a spectacular revival "in the little village called Swansecut Factory in Scituate" before her untimely death at the age of twenty-four.[119] Clarrisa Danforth, sometimes preached with Charles Bowles, the black Freewill Baptist who had converted her, and drew massive crowds throughout New England. John Colby, a leader among the early Freewill Baptists wrote of Danforth "that there has never been a preacher through these parts, that called out such multitudes."[120] And Nancy Towle, whose autobiography provides an extraordinary glimpse into this network of female evangelists, crisscrossed the mill villages and hamlets of Rhode Island speaking among both Methodists and Freewill Baptists. Female itinerants who claimed the authority to raise their voices "were unconstrained and outspoken, and

---

[118] Nancy Towle's autobiography of her ministry cites Martha Spalding, Mrs. Thompson, Susan Humes, Clarissa Danforth, Almira Bullock, Hannah Fogg, Judith Prescott, and Mrs. Quimby as having preached among the Freewill Baptists. As we shall observe, Susan Humes and Clarissa Danforth received significant recognition within the Freewill Baptist movement, as did Salome Lincoln. On female preachers in Rhode Island see Towle, *Vicissitudes Illustrated, in the Experience of Nancy Towle, in Europe and America, Written by Herself* (Charleston, 1832), esp. 21, 23–26, 33–34. See also Louis Billington, "'Female Laborers in the Church': Women Preachers in the Northeastern United States, 1790–1840," *Journal of American Studies* 19 (December 1985): 369–394; and Catherine A. Brekus, *Strangers and Pilgrims: Female Preaching in America, 1740–1845* (Chapel Hill, 1998).

[119] On the factory revival see *Free-will Baptist Magazine* 1 (November 1826): 94–95; *Free-will Baptist Magazine* 1 (February 1827): 112–113. Susan Humes's obituary appears in the *Free-will Baptist Magazine* 1 (August 1827): 191. She also delivered an "exhortation" before the Rhode-Island Quarterly Meeting in Rehoboth, Massachusetts, in 1826. See *Free-will Baptist Magazine* 1 (November 1826): 88–89. Zalmon Tobey, of the Fourth Baptist Church in Providence, spoke at the same meeting.

[120] Quoted in Billington, "Female Laborers," 384.

as the nineteenth century unfolded, they moved farther from the evolving ideal of femininity we know as Victorian, which effaced the existence of women so deeply autonomous and independent of mortal men."[121]

It should not be surprising that the rural Methodists and Freewill Baptists listened to women preachers. For the experience and rhetoric of emotional conversion that proved so central in both denominations—one that emphasized tears, tender sentiment, and a change of the heart—was clearly gendered female in the early nineteenth century. Methodism, according to Diane H. Lobody, "was a women's church because it spoke a women's language."[122] A similar argument could be made for the early Freewill Baptists, with whom the Methodists shared so much. We should also remember that the majority of Rhode Island's factory operatives in this era were women and children, an audience with whom this language might have resonated. In taking on a strongly feminine dimension, the religion of the Freewill Baptists and Methodists stood in sharp contrast to the masculine world embraced by the Congregationalists and Calvinistic Baptists. The distinction between the plebeian religious culture of small farmers and factory operatives and the refined religion of the elite was defined by gender as well as by indices of social prestige and wealth.

As preachers and exhorters, Freewill Baptist and Methodist women also made claims to public power that projected them onto masculine terrain. Indeed, the very act of female preaching confounded traditional gender roles and represented a substantial threat to the established lineaments of authority throughout society. "I sometimes felt," Nancy Towle remembered, "in delivering my message to the people, like one, possessed of great authority, and its effects appeared visible on all that heard."[123] The genteel Catherine Williams reviled female preaching precisely because it made women seem like men. She wrote of one female preacher that "the great effort of retaining such a masculine attitude destroyed entirely the effect" of her sermon.[124] In marking a reversal of gender roles, female preaching may well have been one of the most authentically revolutionary features of plebeian religious culture.[125]

Almond Davis, in his account of the life of the female preacher Salome

---

[121] Nell Painter, *Sojourner Truth: A Life, A Symbol* (New York, 1996), 72.

[122] Diane H. Lobody, "'That Language Might Be Given Me': Women's Experience in Early Methodism," in Russell E. Richey, Kenneth E. Rowe, Jean Miller Schmidt, eds., *Perspectives on American Methodism: Interpretative Essays* (Nashville, 1993), 141.

[123] Towle, *Vicissitudes Illustrated*, 24.

[124] Williams, *Fall River*, 158.

[125] Teresa Anne Murphy argues that the feminine cast of plebeian religion generally sparked a crisis in family authority among working-class families. See her excellent chapter "Popular Religion and Working People," in *Ten Hours' Labor: Religion, Reform, and Gender in Early New England* (Ithaca, 1992), esp. 89–100.

Lincoln, confirmed Williams's fears regarding the subversion of gender roles.[126] Throughout his biography of her, Davis described Lincoln in both masculine and feminine language. Salome Lincoln emerged as one of the most prominent members among the cadre of female preachers who worked in the Rhode Island countryside. She attained fame in her day not only for her oratory but for leading a textile strike at a mill in Taunton, Massachusetts, where she had worked as an operative. She entered the religious life in 1823 when Elder Reuben Allen baptized her as a Freewill Baptist. After a brief period of backsliding, she heard the call to preach the gospel. Once she began to speak in public, she proved enormously popular throughout the New England countryside. "In her discourse," Davis wrote, "there was no artificial arrangement; yet clearness of reasoning—the sound argument—and the motives warm and from the heart."[127] Lincoln's preaching thus blended manly virtues (her solid reason and ability to form an argument) with womanly attributes (her sincerity and empathy). It proved to be a compelling mixture.

The ability to combine the masculine and feminine seems to have been at the center of Salome Lincoln's appeal. Davis acknowledged Lincoln's "striking manner" by making reference to both her "strong mind" and "a character signalized for its deep toned piety."[128] He produced a sermon outline Lincoln had written to demonstrate that "the arrangement of her discourses, was usually very clear, and her divisions were distinctly marked," but simultaneously insisted that she delivered discourses in which "many who heard her, *were melted to tears.*"[129] In such ways did Lincoln combine calculation with passion, cool reason with appeals to the heart. She retained this balance even while in the clutches of consumption. From her deathbed in Warwick, Rhode Island, she struggled to keep both a clear head and a heart willing to accept the fate that God had planned for her. In the end, Salome struck the perfectly balanced chord. "She was calm and resigned," Davis wrote, "and appeared more rational, and seemed more like herself."[130] In death, she evidenced female resignation to God's will tinged with masculine reason and courage in the face of fear. From start to finish, Davis's rendering of Salome Lincoln provides us with a picture of an "androgynous saint," a powerful woman who blurred the conventions of gender.[131]

---

[126] Almond H. Davis, *The Female Preacher, or Memoir of Salome Lincoln* (1843; reprint, New York, 1972).
[127] Davis, *Female Preacher,* 45.
[128] Ibid., 75.
[129] Ibid., 85, 81.
[130] Ibid., 150.
[131] See Susan Juster, *Disorderly Women: Sexual Politics and Evangelicalism in Revolutionary New England* (Ithaca, 1994), 51–53; 106–107 especially.

In addition to embracing female preaching, the plebeian religious culture of the countryside contained another strongly feminine element in its
adherence to visionary experience.[132] Residents of the backcountry understood that dreams should be taken seriously. In the mill village of Pawtucket,
Daniel Waldo recorded a striking account in which a prophecy made
public created an uproar. "A young girl called together a number of
witnesses to hear her deliver a revelation from God," he recalled. She
announced that a young man responsible for burning down a barn "would
die shortly if he did not confess his guilt." Although she did not predict
exactly the hour of his death, this divine message split the community. "This
has excited great division among the baptists," Waldo reported, "& very
much disturbed the whole village."[133] This prophecy clearly held enough
credibility to be hotly debated by the villagers. The dream of a young man
from Burrillville provoked consternation of a different kind. According to
Daniel Waldo, the "thursday night preceeding his death" the young man
had dreamed "that he was assaulted by an inormous serpent & a terrible dog
& in the barn where he put an end to his life." Mr. Brown, the young man's
father, offered him an interpretation of this frightening spectacle. "You
have enemies against whom you must guard by good conduct," he tried to
explain. The young fellow, twenty years old and "the most steady of five
sons," found the exegesis unconvincing. The next night, he had the same
dream, "with the addition that he cut off one of the dog's paws & viewing it
he found in it a ladies' hand with a glove on it." He found it intolerable. The
next day the family found his body, dead and hanging from a rope in the
barn. On the wall inside the barn, the younger Brown had scrawled this last
message, "The Lord be blest to save my soul."[134] What could have driven this
"steady" young man to pursue such drastic measures? Waldo tried unsuc-
cessfully to console the distraught father, who heaped responsibility for the
tragedy upon himself.

Dreams brought messages of hope and reassurance as well as leaving lega-
cies of conflict and confusion. Ministers, especially, traced their conversions
and calls to preach to divine intervention. Shortly after her baptism in the
Christian Church, Nancy Towle recalled that "I had at that time, an impression from a dream, that I should one day, become religious, and bear testimony to the word of God's grace over the earth."[135] Hosea Smith, the mill
hand turned preacher, based his ministerial authority on divine interven-

[132] See Smith-Rosenberg, *Disorderly Conduct*, 135; Phyllis Mack, *Visionary Women: Ecstatic
Prophecy in Seventeenth-Century England* (Berkeley, 1992).
[133] Waldo diary, September 17, 1818, JCB, for all quotations.
[134] Waldo diary, April 17, 1817, JCB, for all quotations.
[135] Towle, *Vicissitudes Illustrated*, 9.

tion. After praying for God's grace, Smith remembered, "That night I dreamed of discharging a gun and it set the whole world on fire. I thought the fire blazed up under my feet and all around me, but it did not burn me." He considered briefly whether the flames were a foretaste of the Last Judgment but decided against this view since they had not harmed him. Rather, he "felt the dream was a call from God."[136] Thus fortified, Hosea Smith proceeded to join the Freewill Baptist Church. Abel Thornton, another Freewill Baptist, laced his conversion account with numerous references to dreams and supernatural interventions. After hearing Clarissa Danforth preach during a revival, Thornton listened to a young man who "told a number of visions of the night which he had passed through. He also related a dream which a man in the neighborhood had dreamed."[137] Considering eternal topics, Thornton retired to his bedchamber, and "when I lay down on my bed and shut my eyes, it appeared as though the judgment day was fast approaching."[138] He took this as a sign that he should seek the forgiveness of God and prayed for grace. Although he heard "a still small voice" assure him that his sins had indeed been forgiven, Thornton yearned for decisive proof.[139] He worried that the voice in his head might not be authentic. "Therefore I prayed to the Lord to give me a further evidence the following night in a dream," he wrote, "which I accordingly received, and it set my soul to rejoicing, and I began to tell all around what a Saviour I had found."[140] For Abel Thornton, this dream delivered assurance of salvation and provided the "text" for his first sermon.

Even as these visionaries united to form congregations, they manifested a spirit of feisty independence. Like other common folk in New England, Rhode Islanders often linked their religious loyalties to charismatic figures rather than to specific church buildings or denominations.[141] Preachers such as Salome Lincoln, Hosea Smith, and Nancy Towle shuttled between gatherings of Methodists, Christians, and Freewill Baptists with such ease that it is occasionally difficult to nail down their precise religious affiliation at any given moment in time. Given the common anti-Calvinist perspective articulated by these groups as well as their dedication to an experiential epistemology, however, such doctrinal precision might have seemed superfluous to their hearers. Some backcountry Christians jettisoned

---

[136] Smith, *Life of Hosea Smith*, 29–30.
[137] Abel Thornton, *The Life of Elder Abel Thornton, Late of Johnston, R.I., A Preacher in the Free-will Baptist Connexion and a Member of the R.I.Q. Meeting. Written by Himself* (Providence, 1828), 16.
[138] Ibid.
[139] Ibid., 21.
[140] Ibid.
[141] See Karen V. Hansen, *A Very Social Time: Crafting Community in Antebellum New England* (Berkeley, 1994), 151–152.

denominational language altogether and took the name of their minister as their own. Henry Tatem's followers, according to one Congregational missionary, simply referred to themselves as "Tatemites."[142] The "Tatemites" proved popular in the Phenix factory village in Cranston and eventually joined with a splinter group of Freewill Baptists known as the Rhode Island Union Conference. The Union Conference included the cantankerous elder Ray Potter, who had been expelled from the regular Quarterly Meeting of Freewill Baptists owing to his dispute with Daniel Greene, one of the founders of the Freewill Baptist Church in Pawtucket and a mill owner. Potter rendered his battle with Greene as an apocalyptic struggle between the forces of gospel liberty and the tyrannical designs of a cabal of the rich.[143]

During precisely the same historical moment in which Ray Potter was battling Daniel Greene for authority in the Pawtucket church, the plebeian residents of Providence worked to stake out their own religious terrain. During the great revival of 1820 and in its wake, the common citizens of the city joined the residents of rural Rhode Island in forming a distinctive religious culture. They, too, embraced the Freewill Baptists, the Methodists, and, as we shall see, the Universalists as well. They, too, embodied a challenge to Calvinist orthodoxy and sought to create churches over which they exercised control. Although the rural and urban versions of this plebeian religious culture were not absolutely identical, they shared a fundamental commitment to the kind of religious autonomy evidenced by Ray Potter and his followers in Pawtucket. In giving articulation to the spiritual concerns of common citizens, the revival of 1820 proved to be a turning point in the religious and social history of Providence and of Rhode Island as a whole.

---

[142] "Religion in Rhode Island, 1828–1829," 12.

[143] Elder Ray Potter, *The Poor Man's Defence, Exhibiting a Brief Account of the Circumstances Connected with the Difficulty Which of Late Has Transpired in the Village of Pawtucket* (Providence, 1823). Potter's battle with Greene took place the year before Pawtucket women launched a major strike against local manufacturers. See Gary Kulik, "Pawtucket Village and the Strike of 1824: The Origins of Class Conflict in Rhode Island," *Radical History Review* 17 (1978): 5–37

3

"From Nature's Darkness into God's Marvellous Light"

The Revival of 1820

Throughout the spring of 1820, a revival of extraordinary power engulfed Providence. Sparked by Second Baptist Church, the blaze of religious enthusiasm "soon spread and the glorious work of the Lord was extended throughout the town at large."[1] In a town of not quite 12,000 persons, nearly 500 converts stood before their respective congregations to pronounce declarations of faith. (See Table 8 for a breakdown of converts by church.) They not only joined established churches, such as First Baptist Church and Beneficent Congregational Church, but connected themselves with new congregations launched by the Freewill Baptists, Methodists, and the Universalists. The revival also provided the flame that led to the creation of the African Union Meeting House, the city's first independent black church. Neither Charles Finney's well-orchestrated visit to the city in 1831 nor the ripple of genteel enthusiasm of 1857–58 surpassed it for sheer scale and transformative power. As an event that reconfigured the religious landscape of antebellum Providence, the revival of 1820 proved to be unmatched.

Although revivals had touched Providence before, the town's religious leaders acknowledged readily the singular character of this most recent evidence of God's grace. Willard Preston, a Congregationalist pastor, firmly declared to Brown University students that "Never did the inhabitants of this town experience such a season of refreshing from the presence of God,

---

[1] Stephen S. Wardwell diary, September 1820, Beneficent Congregational Church, Providence, Rhode Island.

Table 8. Revival converts of the 1820 era

Church	Members joining in 1820
Beneficent Congregational	163
First Baptist	161[a]
Second Baptist	61
Chestnut Street Methodist	39[b]
Pacific Congregational	20
First Congregational	20
TOTAL	464

Sources: Record Book, Beneficent Congregational Church, Vestry, Beneficent Congregational Church; Record Book, First Baptist Church, RIHS; Record Book, Chestnut Street Methodist Church, Vestry, Trinity United Methodist Church; Record Book, First Universalist Society, RIHS; accounts in Providence *Religious Intelligencer and Christian Monitor*, May 13 and 20, 1820.
Note: The above figures do not include those who joined the African Union Meeting House or those who founded Fourth Baptist Church. Membership data for the African Union Meeting House do not exist for this period, and the members of Fourth Baptist Church cannot be considered converts because they already belonged to Henry Tatem's Six-Principle Baptist Church in Cranston. The ninety-four Universalists who purchased pews in 1821–22 are also not included because they cannot be considered converts in a strict sense. Therefore, the total number of revival converts, substantial though it was, does not fully represent the sweeping power of the revival years.
[a] First Baptist Church records show that 147 members were baptized during the revival. I have included the total of 161 new members who joined by letter or other methods that year.
[b] The *Religious Intelligencer and Christian Monitor* gives the figure for Methodist converts as 61. I have obtained the total of 39 professors of faith directly from the church minutes.

it is believed, as they now experience."[2] In nearby Seekonk, Massachusetts, the Baptist minister John Pitman felt the reverberations of the Providence revival. As he made his way to the city to watch his colleague Stephen Gano conduct mass baptisms, Pitman, too, proved an instrument of God. As he moved from house to house, he recorded striking instances of conversion, including that of a sea captain who related his experience in the home of "an ancient black sister." Retiring from his pastoral calls, Pitman wrote of the revival, "I think it exceeds anything I have seen & may be said that God has visited every home."[3] Stephen Wardwell, himself a convert at Beneficent

[2] Willard Preston, *Motives to Early Piety, A Sermon Preached March 5, 1820* (Providence, 1820), 11.
[3] John Pitman diaries, April 24 and April 27, 1820, Manuscript Collection, Rhode Island Historical Society, hereafter cited as RIHS.

Congregational Church, agreed with Preston and Pitman. "This town has been visited by many times of refreshing from the presence of the Lord," he observed in his diary, "but this time is thought to be the greatest of them all."[4]

Even those citizens who cast a dubious eye toward the revivalists conceded without question that the hand of God was visible everywhere. Attorney Philip Crapo, possessed of a disposition toward free-thinking, outlined with dismay the frenzied pace of church activity for his friend Samuel Eddy. He discovered that the Baptists, Congregationalists, and Methodists had gathered "every night for a long time & have had crowded assemblies." If this were not enough, Crapo noticed that private meetings "are almost without number at all times of day from morning till late in the evening." Indeed, he lamented, "Everything which goes forward seems to be preaching, praying, exhorting & singing without any time or disposition for reflection."[5] Moses Brown, the aging Quaker merchant and manufacturer, noted an especially stunning example of spiritual transformation. "Anson Potter," he recalled, "a Professed Deist or Thomas Pain's Man has become a Seriously Concerned Man; from Rejecting the Bible from his house, has bo't one and Read Abundance now says it is the Best and most Consistent Book he ever read."[6] As Anson Potter's case indicates, the heat of the revival penetrated even the stone-cold hearts of the rational.

It might be tempting to explain the burst of religious enthusiasm that transfigured Providence as a reaction to the economic panic of 1819. Throughout the country, the panic and the depression that followed threw thousands out of work and sent numerous banks into ruin.[7] But in New England, and in Rhode Island especially, a tradition of conservative banking practices sheltered Providence residents from the harshest features of the panic.[8] While the panic and depression crippled commercial centers such as New York and Philadelphia, it skipped over Providence rather lightly. Moreover, the tone of this revival embedded in the discourses of the clergy and in the accounts of converts does not reveal a somber mood but rather one of exuberant expectation. Unlike the depressions of 1837 or 1857, when Providence clergy announced that economic downturns had led to a renewed interest in the life of the spirit, the panic of 1819 does not

---

[4] Wardwell diary, September 1820.

[5] Philip Crapo to Samuel Eddy, April 17, 1820, Samuel Eddy Papers, RIHS.

[6] Moses Brown to Samuel Eddy, April 21, 1820, Samuel Eddy Papers.

[7] See Charles Sellers, *The Market Revolution: Jacksonian America, 1815–1846* (New York, 1991), 137–171.

[8] Peter J. Coleman, *The Transformation of Rhode Island, 1790–1860* (Providence, 1963), esp. 191–195.

seem to have prompted this kind of thinking.[9] In searching for the impulse that inspired converts, we must look beyond an explanation that sees revivalism as a salve for the wounds inflicted by a hurtful economy.[10]

The argument in this chapter is that the revival of 1820 was the crucible in which laborers, artisans, and small shopkeepers forged a plebeian religious culture of their own making. It examines the creation of five new congregations—First Universalist Chapel, Chestnut Street Methodist Church, Third Baptist Church, Fourth Baptist Church, and the African Union Meeting House—as institutional manifestations of this plebeian religious life. It sheds light on these congregations by examining their geographic locations, their leaders and members, and the theological stances they embraced. As we have seen, despite the inclusive character of religious life in early national Providence, the town's "best men" and affluent pewholders ruled within each congregation. The revival provided the spiritual momentum that empowered common citizens to establish their own churches, beyond the direct control of the merchant and manufacturing elite. In giving working people a central voice in institutions of their own making, the revival may be interpreted as an integral part of the process of class formation in antebellum Providence. "Many of the classic struggles at the entry to the industrial revolution," wrote E. P. Thompson, "turned as much on customs as upon wages or conditions of work."[11] If we think of religious culture as a set of customs, then the struggles of Providence working people to create their own religious terrain can be viewed as a key element in the making of class relationships in Rhode Island.

The geographic location of the new churches provides the first clue to their humble character. All of them claimed territory on the perimeter of the town's central development. They spread out beyond the increasingly refined houses and shops along Benefit Street on the East Side and along Westminster Street on the West Side.[12] The Methodists and Universalists found congenial settings in the rapidly expanding commercial district of the West Side. The Baptist congregations bracketed the heart of the city on

---

[9] See Chapters 4 and 7 below.

[10] For a powerful formulation of the relationship between despair and religious enthusiasm among working people, see E. P. Thompson, *The Making of the English Working Class* (New York, 1966 edition), 375–400. American historians have applied Thompson's insights to the revivalism following the panic and depression of 1837. See Bruce Laurie, *Working People of Philadelphia, 1800–1850* (Philadelphia, 1980), 118; Sean Wilentz, *Chants Democratic: New York City and the Rise of the American Working Class, 1788–1850* (New York, 1984), 300.

[11] E. P. Thompson, *Customs in Common: Studies in Traditional Popular Culture* (New York, 1993), 4–5.

[12] See Richard L. Bushman, *The Refinement of America: Persons, Houses, Cities* (New York, 1992), 370–371, on the refinement of East Side Providence.

the East Side, with the Fourth Church set along North Main Street and the Third Church tucked between India Point and Fox Point at the extreme south end of town. Only the African Union Meeting House, set back a block from Benefit Street, was built within sight of the merchant mansions of East Side Providence. To some degree, the peripheral location of the churches may simply reflect the institutional needs of residents in the more recently developed regions of the town. Nonetheless, the creation of congregations around the edge of city also suggests the economic marginality of their members.

In selecting West Side Providence for their churches, the Methodists and Universalists placed themselves in town's new commercial district. Home to dozens of small shops and groceries, the West Side enjoyed a wave of development symbolized by the construction of the Arcade in 1828. A three-story building in the Greek Revival style, the Arcade comprised a business and commercial center now recognized as America's first enclosed shopping mall. Brisk economic development proceeded with a rapid increase in the number of West Side residents. By 1825 the West Side pulled almost even to East Side Providence in population, containing 7,212 occupants compared to 8,729 residents in the oldest area of settlement.[13] The Universalists, dedicating their chapel in 1822, occupied the most ample and impressive building. With the total value of pews amounting to nearly $23,000, this congregation evidenced a concern for detail in construction.[14] On September 29, 1823, for instance, the trustees instructed S. W. Wheeler to "cause a sufficient number of Cushions to be put on the seats of the female singers."[15] In May, 1825, a mysterious blaze destroyed the Universalist church, wasting such careful attention to congregational comfort. Undaunted, the Universalists revalued their smoldering pews and six months later commenced the process of construction.[16] The Methodists put together two less elaborate churches. In 1816, under the direction of the untiring pastor Van Rensselaer Osborn, the community's Methodists launched their first housed congregation. This meetinghouse on Aborn Street suited the Methodists for only a few years, since the revival of 1820 produced enough coverts to render the first chapel "overflowing."[17] By all accounts, the new Methodist church, near the intersection of Chestnut,

[13] Edwin M. Snow, *Census of the City of Providence, Taken in July 1855; with a brief account of the manufactures, trade, commerce, and other statistics of the city; and an Appendix, giving an account of previous enumerations of the population of Providence* (Providence, 1856), 8.
[14] Record Book, First Universalist Society, November 9, 1822, RIHS.
[15] Record Book, First Universalist Society, Trustees Meeting, September 29, 1823.
[16] Record Book, First Universalist Society, re-valuation of pews on December 26, 1825.
[17] *Seventieth Anniversary of the Chestnut Street Methodist Episcopal Church and Sunday School in Providence, R.I., December 13 and 14, 1885* (Providence, 1886), 60.

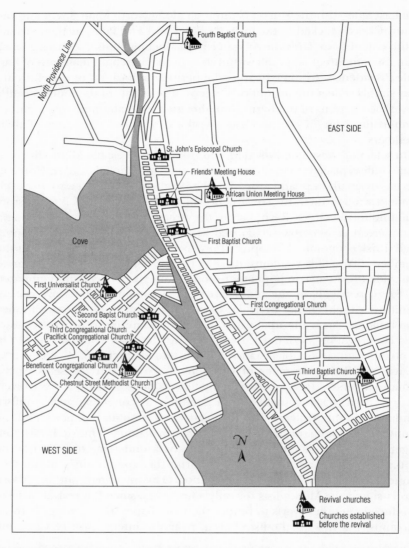

Providence churches in the era of the 1820 revival, based on Daniel Anthony's map of the Town of Providence, 1823. Courtesy of The Rhode Island Historical Society, RHi (×3) 1264.

Clifford, and Ship Streets, while large enough to contain new members, was a modest affair. Stephen Wardwell considered the new church "very convenient" but also noted that the total value of auctioned pews amounted to only $8,000.[18] The Chestnut Street Church included few architectural embellishments. As another account maintained, "Neither spire, nor fresco, nor arches adorned it, and yet the fathers thought it perfect."[19] Simplicity of style characterized the Methodist approach to church construction.

On the East Side of Providence, the communicants of Fourth Baptist Church and Third Baptist Church built churches that served as bookends on that side of town. Fourth Baptist Church stood on North Main Street, along the road that stretched out to meet the mill village of Pawtucket. A warehouse of the United Manufacturing Company, owned primarily by cotton entrepreneur Dexter Thurber, stood virtually next door to the church. Although actual spinning was not performed in the warehouse, Daniel Anthony's 1823 map places a mill pond along the Moshasuck River, within walking distance of the church. Whether some Fourth Baptist Church members worked as operatives cannot be conclusively determined from existing church or business records. More certain, however, is that this new church took hold in a neighborhood with a strong working-class flavor. Dedicated in 1822, Fourth Baptist Church cost slightly more than $6,000. A wooden church containing space for some sixty-eight pews, it made only one concession to East Side fashion—a ninety-foot steeple equipped "with a good bell."[20] Despite the imposing bell tower, the interior of the church left room for refinement. As late as 1830, minutes of the Fourth Baptist Society record that lack of heating in the upper part of the meetinghouse continued to chill worshippers.[21] On the opposite end of the East Side, the members of Third Baptist Church settled near the docks between Fox Point and India Point, a region one historian of the church claimed to be "beyond the settled portion of the city."[22] Although they were not draymen or dock workers, the first male communicants worked as carpenters, masons, and laborers and lived along Transit and Wickenden Streets. George Dods, a cooper and a guiding spirit of the church, roamed for three years—one excursion took him as far as New Hampshire—to raise subscriptions for a church of "the plainest description" measuring some 45 by 50 feet in size.[23]

[18] Wardwell diary, December 29, 1821.
[19] *Seventieth Anniversary*, 61.
[20] Rev. Francis Smith, *A Discourse Delivered in the Fourth Baptist Meeting-House, Providence, on the re-opening of the house, after its enlargement, October 20, 1850* (Providence, 1851), 7.
[21] Record Book, Fourth Baptist Society, July 15, 1830, RIHS.
[22] E. H. Johnson, *History of the Third and Brown Street Baptist Churches of Providence, R.I.* (Providence, 1880), 9.
[23] Ibid., 4.

By June 27, 1822, Dods's persistence finally paid off in the official dedication of the Third Baptist Church.

While the new Baptist congregations straddled the East Side, the members of the African Union Meeting House established themselves near the center of town. Moses Brown's donation of a piece of land to the black community determined, in large part, the precise site for the church. A small building that required only $2,200 to complete, the meetinghouse would have been dwarfed by the First Baptist and First Congregational churches, which stood a few blocks away.[24] In its location and design, the African Union Meeting House could function to remind blacks of their subservient position within the community. Members of the Providence elite may also have taken comfort in the knowledge that they could carefully oversee the religious activities of their employees. The area near the intersection of Meeting and Congdon Streets served as one of the town's first black neighborhoods. At a time when many of Providence's black residents lived or worked as servants in white homes, the selection of a church location near the heart of town made sense for both employers and employees. Thus, only the African Union Meeting House remained in the neighborhood of the stately homes and churches that distinguished the East Side of Providence.

The small shopkeepers, artisans, and laboring people of Providence led the drive to establish the revival era congregations. But it must be recognized that the converts did not hail exclusively from the same niche in the town's social structure. Hezekiah Anthony, a prosperous Methodist grocer, and George Dods, a cantankerous Baptist cooper, did not travel in precisely the same circles of Providence society. But they did have more in common with each other than they did with the men of the merchant and manufacturing elite. That Pardon Hawkins, a common laborer, could be named deacon of Fourth Baptist Church lends support to the assertion that "the great democratic revivals of the early nineteenth century emerged primarily not from the new middle class but from Americans whom the market revolution had either bypassed or hurt."[25] While the elite contributed in some measure to the formation of the revival churches, they did not dominate them by purchasing ranks of expensive pews. Although the members of Providence's plebeian congregations accepted support from some of their refined brethren, they proved vigilant in the defense of their own independence.

[24] *A Short History of the African Union Meeting and School-House, erected in Providence (R.I.) in the years 1819, '20, '21; with rules for its future government* (Providence, 1821), 12–13.
[25] Paul E. Johnson and Sean Wilentz, *The Kingdom of Matthias: A Story of Sex and Salvation in Nineteenth-Century America* (New York, 1994), 9.

The movement that culminated in the creation of the Universalist Chapel in 1822 began in the 1790s as a series of individual protests. In the early national period, as we have observed, the members of First Baptist Church and Beneficent Congregational Church worked assiduously to rid themselves of the Universalist menace and disciplined members who professed those sentiments. Even into the 1820s, the Universalists in Providence carried the aura of being a dangerous group. On November 24, 1822, the day following the dedication of their chapel, James Wilson, the pastor of Beneficent Congregational Church, weighed into the Universalists from his pulpit. For his sermon text that day he selected Matthew 25:46: "And these shall go away into everlasting punishment but the righteous into life eternal."[26] In 1825, when fire consumed the Universalist church, James Wilson may have felt vindicated by God's fierce judgment.

Despite their unsavory image, the Universalists represented the most affluent of the revival era congregations. With the average cost of pews running about $175 per seat, the Universalist Chapel contained seats that rivaled those in established congregations in sheer cost. (See Table 9.) Merchants and manufacturers such as Edward Carrington, Amasa Mason, and Rufus Waterman all contributed to the congregation by purchasing pews. Master craftsmen, too, bought seats, accounting for about 15 percent of the total, when measured against membership in the Providence Association of Mechanics and Manufacturers. (See Table 10.) Artisans clearly continued to support Universalism even as it faced the ongoing disapprobation of the community. In April 1826, PAMM voted to hold its annual anniversary meeting at the Universalist Chapel, where they heard a prayer by David Pickering. Voicing sentiments in accordance with Universalist doctrine, the artisans sang, "Religion, that most darling theme, Thro' which eternal life is seen; To ev'ry name or sect is free, Who stands in gospel liberty."[27] In housing a handful of elite pewholders and in serving the needs of Providence's aspiring master craftsmen, the Universalists comprised members of comfortable means.

But the Providence economic elite did not dominate the pews of the Universalist Chapel. Grocers and petty merchants constituted the largest single occupational group of pewholders. (See Table 11.) Following close behind these shopkeepers, house carpenters, masons, and a variety of other craftsmen found places in the chapel. Rounding out the pewholders, were an ensemble of "white-collar" workers, including publishers, agents, and one

---

[26] Wardwell diary, November 24, 1822.
[27] *Celebration at the Universalist Chapel, Order of Exercises at the Anniversary Meeting of the Providence Association of Mechanicks and Manufacturers, April 10, 1826*, Harris Collection, Large Broadsides, Brown University Library.

Table 9. Pew valuations in new revival churches

Church	Average pew value	Most expensive pew	Least expensive pew
First Universalist, 1824	$174.71	$350.00	$36.00
Fourth Baptist, 1822	85.22	135.00	40.00
African Union Meeting House	20.00	20.00	20.00

Sources: Record Book, First Universalist Society, RIHS; Record Book, Fourth Baptist Society, RIHS; *A Short History of the African Union Meeting and School-House, erected in Providence (R.I.) in the years 1819, '20, '21; with rules for its future government* (Providence, 1821).

Table 10. PAMM members among revival era pewholders

		PAMM members	
Church	Pewholders	Number	% of pewholders
First Universalist, 1824	94	14	14.89
Fourth Baptist, 1822	37	10	27.02
TOTAL	131	24	18.32

Sources: See Table 9; Gary Kornblith, PAMM master list.

Francis C. Shaffer, "professor of dancing." Despite their relative wealth in comparison to other revival era pewholders and communicants, the Universalists made provisions for the less affluent within their Society. (See Table 12.) In 1836 the Universalist Society empowered the trustees to remit even the minimal two-dollar pew tax for impoverished pewholders.[28] David Pickering, the first minister of the Universalist Chapel, expressed sympathy for the propertyless citizens of Providence and had no patience with nabobs. In his 1828 oration on American Independence, Pickering assailed what he called "some remains of aristocracy among us." Adumbrating by almost two decades the role William S. Balch would play in the Dorr Rebellion, Pickering articulated a democratic social vision that took aim at Rhode Island's restrictive suffrage. He identified some wealthy men "who have yet to learn that the right of suffrage properly belongs to men, and not to the soil, which they enjoy the privilege of cultivating." Recalling his audience to an ethic of social responsibility, Pickering maintained that "it requires neither the powers of a Locke nor of a Newton, to discover that the rich are

[28] Record Book, First Universalist Society, Article 4 of By-Laws, August 15, 1836.

Table 11. Occupations of revival era pewholders

Occupation	Number of pewholders
First Universalist Church, 1824	
Grocers	10
House carpenters	6
Masons	5
Merchants	4
Blacksmiths	3
Publishers	3
Agents	2
Butchers	2
Jewelers	2
Paperhangers	2
Shoemakers	2
Tallow chandlers	2
Other[a]	27
Occupation unknown	24
TOTAL	94
Fourth Baptist Church, 1822	
Grocers	4
House carpenters	3
Jewelers	3
Manufacturers	3
Masons	2
Other[b]	11
Occupation unknown	11
TOTAL	37

Sources: Record Books, Fourth Baptist Society, First Universalist Society, RIHS; 1824 *Providence Directory*.

[a] One each of the following: accountant, architect, auctioneer, baker, book store owner, Boston wagoner, brush maker, cabinetmaker, coach and chaise maker, collector of customs, colorer, coroner, customs house officer, deputy sheriff, dry goods merchant, fancy goods dealer, glazier, guager, livery stablehand, painter, paper and oil store owner, professor of dancing, shoe store owner, tin plate worker, truckman, variety store owner, wheelwright.

[b] Baker, chaise and wagon maker, colorer, constable, iron founder, painter, physician, road maker, shoemaker, tanner, yeoman.

dependent upon the poor for the most of their luxuries and enjoyments."
Yet, these people were precisely the citizens who did not own the $134
worth of property required in order to vote. Pickering hoped to see "this
disgusting limb of tyranny amputated from the fair colassal statue of our

Table 12. Wealth distribution among revival era pewholders

Tax value in dollars[a]	First Universalist Church, 1824		Fourth Baptist Church, 1822	
	Pewholders	%	Pewholders	%
500+	1	1.0	1	2.7
101–500	5	5.3	—	—
51–100	4	4.3	—	—
41–50	3	3.2	2	5.4
31–40	5	5.3	2	5.4
21–30	9	9.5	2	5.4
11–20	13	13.8	7	18.9
0–10	27	28.7	9	24.3
Total listed	67	71.1	23	62.1
Pewholders not listed	27	28.7	14	37.8

Sources: Pewholders identified in Record Book, First Universalist Society, RIHS; Record Book, Fourth Baptist Society, RIHS. Data on pewholders from other new revival era church are not available.
[a] Total tax valuation, both real and personal, as listed in the Providence Town Tax List for 1824, RIHS.

country's venerated institutions, buried in the grave of eternal oblivion."[29] In no uncertain terms, Pickering condemned the political arrangements that allowed Rhode Island's men of property to govern the state.

For the emerging network of Methodists, both pewholders and communicants, poverty represented a more pressing concern than it did for the Universalists. According to one chronicler of the congregation, some neighbors mocked them, saying "they have no house, and they are so poor they cannot build one."[30] Another denominational record pointed out that "Methodism was cradled in a hovel. It worshipped in some ally, or by-place, quite unobserved by the more wealthy and honorable."[31] A glance at the occupations of the thirty-one men who made up the Methodist Episcopal Society in 1817 validates observations of the denomination's slender means. Formed after the construction of the Aborn Street Church but before the Chestnut Street Church was built, the society included members who may be taken as key lay leaders in the emergence of Providence Methodism. While occupational data are available on only thirteen of the original members, they suggest the plebeian character of the Methodist leadership: two

[29] David Pickering, *Address Delivered Before the Citizens of Providence, in the Universalist Chapel, on the Fifty-Second Anniversary of American Independence* (Providence, 1828), 12, for all quotations from this address.
[30] *Seventieth Anniversary*, 57.
[31] W. McDonald, *History of Methodism in Providence, Rhode Island, from its introduction in 1767 to 1867* (Boston, 1868), 46.

laborers, two cabinetmakers, a machine maker, a carpenter, a mason, a shoemaker, a rope maker, a tailor, a silversmith, and an oysterman.[32] Unlike their Universalist neighbors, the fresh Methodist congregation included few grocers or shopkeepers, with the notable exception of Hezekiah Anthony. Instead, house carpenters, masons, and shoemakers constituted the leading occupational groups in the church. (See Table 13.) The large number of Methodist men who do not appear in either the town tax lists or in the city directory further suggests the marginal resources and transiency that characterized the communicants. (See Table 14.)

The leaders of Providence Methodism took to heart the relative poverty of their members. In their original design for the 1816 Aborn Street Church, they experimented with a "Free Church" plan.[33] Implicitly recognizing that many of their prospective members might not be able to purchase seats, the church leaders considered doing away with pew auctioning altogether. Such considerations proved critical to the success of Methodism not only in Providence but in America as a whole. In 1866, Reverend C. C. Goss outlined the features that contributed to the Methodist "miracle," the transformation that moved the Methodists from being a small sect to the largest Protestant church in America in less than a century. Among the factors Goss considered crucial was "the system of free churches." Aware that Methodist communicants were typically not "blessed with an abundance of this world's goods," Goss knew that the practice of selling pews could limit church membership. "The system of renting pews in the house of God," he wrote, "or of selling them, is very deleterious to the spread of the gospel."[34] Providence Methodists, too, balked at commodifying the religious space within their new church. Unlike the efforts of reformers in the 1850s, who also praised a system of free churches for the poor, the Methodist initiative sprang not from well-meaning philanthropists but from the ranks of the members themselves. Their eventual decision to auction the pews in the Chestnut Street Church emerged out of monetary necessity rather than from the initial wishes of the congregation.

The early Methodists conceded that financial muscle as well as devotion was essential to their success. In 1815, while collecting subscriptions for the Aborn Street Church, they received contributions from the members of the merchant elite, including Edward Carrington, Nicholas Brown, and Sullivan

---

[32] Methodist leaders identified from the July 14, 1817, Articles of Agreement forming the Methodist Episcopal Society, in *Seventieth Anniversary*, 78–79. Occupational data are from *The Providence Directory* (Providence, 1824), the earliest record of its kind for the city.
[33] McDonald, *History of Methodism*, 52–53.
[34] Goss quoted in Roger Finke and Rodney Stark, *The Churching of America, 1776–1990: Winners and Losers in Our Religious Economy* (New Brunswick, N.J., 1992), 105.

Table 13. Occupations of revival era communicants (male)

Occupation	Number of members
First Baptist Church: New members, 1820	
House carpenters	7
Grocers	3
Masons	3
Shoemakers	3
Editors/publishers	2
Laborers	2
Other[a]	11
Occupation unknown	40
TOTAL	70
Third Baptist Church: New members 1820–22	
House carpenters	5
Other[b]	11
Occupation unknown	4
TOTAL	20
Fourth Baptist Church: New members, July 5, 1823, to December 1824	
Laborers	2
Ministers	2
House carpenter	1
Rope maker	1
Shoemaker	1
Tanner	1
Turner	1
Occupation unknown	6
TOTAL	15
Beneficent Congregational Church: New members, 1820	
Accountants	4
Grocers	4
Clerks	2
Hat store owners	2
House carpenters	2
Mariners	2
Shoe store owners	2
Other[c]	18
Occupation unknown	33
TOTAL	69

Table 13. *Continued*

Occupation	Number of members
Chestnut Street Methodist Church: New members, 1818–24	
House carpenters	5
Masons	5
Shoemakers	4
Mariners	3
Blacksmiths	2
Other*d*	13
Occupation unknown	60
TOTAL	92

Sources: Record Books, First Baptist Church; Third Baptist Church; Fourth Baptist Church; Beneficent Congregational Church, Vestry, Beneficent Congregational Church; Chestnut Street Methodist Church, Vestry, Trinity United Methodist Church; 1824 *Providence Directory.*
a One each of the following: baker, cooper, dry goods merchant, jeweler, mariner, merchant, millwright, ship carpenter, shoe store owner, tailor, weaver.
b Clerk, cooper, grocer, laborer, mason, minister, ship carpenter, shoe store owner, tailor, teamster, yeoman.
c Assistant postmaster, baker, blacksmith, bleacher, boardinghouse owner, druggist, editor, laborer, merchant, morocco dresser, paperhanger, saddler, sexton, shoemaker, tailor, teamster, tin plate worker, turner.
d Baker, barber, cabinetmaker, cooper, druggist, grocer, jeweler, machine maker, saddler, ship carpenter, tobacconist, toolmaker, yeoman.

Dorr, as well as a $20 gift from Samuel Slater.[35] When they sold pews for the Chestnut Street Church, they encouraged "several liberal minded gentlemen" who did not profess membership to purchase seats. Purity of doctrine did have its limits.[36] The Methodists, like members of other established churches, tapped the resources of wealthy patrons in constructing their meetinghouses. Two of Methodism's most steadfast sponsors aligned themselves closely with the congregation. Daniel Field, Esq., could not bring himself to a public profession of faith but did donate the land for the new Chestnut Street Church and paved the way for other Field family members to join the congregation. The grocer Hezekiah Anthony proved an even more energetic advocate for Providence Methodism. A resident of Weybosset Street and an owner of two stores there, Anthony represented the growing number of entrepreneurs located on the West Side. Equally

[35] *Seventieth Anniversary,* 77.
[36] Ibid., 61.

Table 14. Wealth distribution among revival era church members

Tax value in dollars[a]	First Baptist Church		Third Baptist Church		Fourth Baptist Church		Beneficent Congregational Church		Chestnut Street Methodist Church	
	N	%	N	%	N	%	N	%	N	%
501+	—		—		—		—		—	
101–500	1	1.4	—		—		—		1	1.0
51–100	—		—		—		1	1.4	—	
41–50	—		1	5.0	—		—		1	1.0
31–40	—		—		—		1	1.4	—	
21–30	—		—		—		2	2.9	1	1.0
11–20	1	1.4	—		1	6.6	2	2.9	5	5.4
0–10	12	17.1	5	25.0	2	13.3	11	15.9	10	10.8
TOTAL LISTED	14	19.9	6	30.0	3	19.9	17	24.5	18	19.2
Church members not listed	56	80.0	14	70.0	12	80.0	52	75.3	74	80.4

Note: These are male church members, from the sources described in Table 8 with the addition of Record Book, Third Baptist Church, RIHS. To obtain a larger number of Methodist men, beyond the total actually joining in 1820, I have included all Methodist men who joined the Chestnut Street Church between 1818 and 1824. When white men aged sixteen and over in the town are considered as a group, about 43 percent were assessed in the tax lists. Those not assessed comprised 57 percent of the population of white men over 16 years old. Of the revival members, about 70–80 percent cannot be located in the town tax lists, suggesting that the converts were, on balance, among the less prosperous citizens of the community.
[a] Total Tax Valuation, both real and personal, as listed in the Providence Town Tax List for 1820, RIHS.

ambitious in advancing worldly and spiritual affairs, he served as a trustee of the church for forty-one years and also helped settle the Power Street Methodist Church on the East Side in the early 1830s. Unlike some hefty contributors, Anthony claimed Methodism as his faith by joining the congregation. In such ways did the humble Methodists seek and capture affluent supporters for their cause.[37]

But Providence Methodism also nurtured at least two of the city's earliest labor activists. During November 1818, James Lewis and Samuel Lewis, both masons, confessed their faith in the Chestnut Street community. Both men, residents of Point Street near the West Side waterfront, paid modest real estate taxes in 1820. By 1822 James Lewis expanded his property holdings

[37] On Hezekiah Anthony's role in promoting early Providence Methodism, see *Seventieth Anniversary*, 60, 85; McDonald, *History of Methodism*, 58–59; on Anthony's property holdings see *Providence Directory*, 1824.

to include pew no. 23 in the newly constructed Fourth Baptist Church. Even though he purchased this pew, Lewis continued his allegiance to Methodism. In 1833 he purchased a pew in the new Power Street Methodist Church, on the East Side. As a capstone for their rise to prominence, both Lewises joined PAMM. The respectability of church membership, pewholding, and membership in PAMM did not dull the Lewises interest in labor activism and reform. In the summer of 1832, James Lewis assumed the presidency of the Providence Association of Practical Carpenters and Masons, perhaps the first labor union in the city's history. Samuel Lewis served as secretary for the same group. Beyond issues of hours and wages, Samuel Lewis also embraced the growing movement to extend voting rights in Rhode Island. In March 1834 he won a place as one of twenty-four Providence delegates to a statewide convention to debate suffrage reform. The cases of James and Samuel Lewis illuminate how the enthusiasm generated among the revival era communicants could carry over into labor activism and the broader currents of political reform.[38]

The new Baptist congregations shared with the Methodists deep roots in the Providence artisan community. George Dods, a cooper, proved to be the guiding spirit as well as the most controversial figure in the formation of Third Baptist Church. Even before the advent of the revival, Dods displayed a penchant for engaging in theological speculations. As a member of First Baptist Church, he had debated attorney Samuel Eddy on the fine points of Trinitarian doctrine. Eddy did not appreciate it. "The principal talkers are old father Dods and two or three apprentice boys," Eddy complained to his daughter, "who of course must know all about the subject."[39] Whatever the intellectual merits of his arguments, it is clear that Dods craved authority over his own body of believers. On November 2, 1820, he officially founded Third Baptist Church by leading fourteen members away from First Baptist Church. The Dods faction insisted that their request to form a new congre-

---

[38] Information for the profiles of James and Samuel Lewis is collected from the following sources: Records of Chestnut Street Methodist Episcopal Church at Trinity United Methodist Church, Providence, Rhode Island; 1820 Providence Town Tax List, RIHS; *Providence Directory*, 1824; Record Book, Fourth Baptist Society, August 26, 1822; Power Street Methodist Church Records, 1833 Pew Records, RIHS; and Gary Kornblith's unpublished masterlist of the memberships in PAMM. On the political activities of the Lewises see *The New England Artisan and Laboring Man's Repository*, preamble and constitution of the Providence Association of Practical Carpenters and Masons, July 26, 1832; and on the suffrage convention see the *Rhode-Island Constitutionalist*, March 12, 1834, list of Providence delegates. For a treatment of the connection between an artisan "producerist ethic" and Methodism, see William R. Sutton, *Journeymen for Jesus: Evangelical Artisans Confront Capitalism in Jacksonian Baltimore* (University Park, Pa., 1998), esp. 122–128.

[39] Samuel Eddy to Martha Mauran, May 30, 1818, Samuel Eddy Papers, Brown University Library.

gation "does not originate from any dissatisfaction with the church or the preaching we hear from time to time."[40] This was probably a genuine statement. The residences of the communicants reveal that they lived along Transit and Wickenden Streets and thus may have desired a congregation in their own neighborhood. House carpenters formed the largest single group of male communicants at the new church, followed by a smattering of other craftsmen and a lone grocer (see Table 13).

The members of Fourth Baptist Church, too, claimed plebeian origins. The original membership of the congregation had belonged to Henry Tatem's Six-Principle Baptist Church in Cranston, Rhode Island. Weary of making this substantial journey for worship, they wanted to establish a church in their own vicinity. Pardon Hawkins, a laborer and the first deacon of the church, brought the members together at his residence for that purpose. On July 5, 1823, a date capturing the independent spirit of the congregation, the church declared itself a separate body of worshippers.[41] The original band of fifteen male members included a handful of artisans, of whom only one, Nicholas S. Dawley, joined PAMM. When the Fourth Baptist Society auctioned its pews on August 26, 1822, the church included some of the most reasonably priced seats in town. The pews ranged from $135 to $40, with the average going for about $85. Among the original thirty-seven pewholders of the Fourth Baptist Society could be found ten who affiliated themselves with PAMM at about the same time they purchased their seats. When measured against the total number of pewholders, the Fourth Baptist Society contained an even larger proportion of artisans than did the Universalists. (See Tables 9 and 10.)

At the same time, the Fourth Baptist Society did have strong links to the merchant and manufacturing community. From the outset, members of the Providence elite had assisted the struggling church members in their efforts to construct a meetinghouse. For all their zeal, the members possessed scant resources. Elder Ray Potter, the fiery Freewill Baptist from Pawtucket whom we have already met, crisscrossed the region to collect money for the congregation. He apparently did not enjoy the gift of George Dods for fundraising. Although Potter held a certificate from Moses Brown confirming his character and verifying the poverty of the Fourth Baptist members, he collected only $171 of the $611 needed to purchase the lot for the church.[42]

---

[40] Record Book, Third Baptist Church, November 2, 1820, RIHS.

[41] Record Book, Fourth Baptist Church, July 5 and August 6, 1823, RIHS.

[42] See Moses Brown Papers, box 4, certificate of August 10, 1820, endorsing Elder Ray Potter as an agent for the Fourth Baptist Church, RIHS. Brown thought the new members "not being very wealthy nor fully United with other Societies." On the funds collected see Fourth Baptist Society Minutes, August 26, 1822, RIHS.

With such a substantial shortfall, the members looked to the merchants and manufacturers for help. The Browns, Thomas P. Ives, Edward Carrington, Seth Wheaton, Samuel Eddy, Earl D. Pearce, and William Almy provided the remainder of the funding necessary to acquire the land. Dexter Thurber, the owner of a cotton manufactory, a warehouse, and a tannery, also owned six pews in the new church, making him the most important property owner in the society. He also served as the first president of the Fourth Baptist Society and exercised considerable influence in launching the drive to establish a church and society at the north end of town.[43]

By 1828 a controversy erupted between the members of the Fourth Baptist Church and members of the society for control of the space within the meetinghouse. The issue at stake concerned the time at which each group could use the church building for its evening meetings. Since the communicants and the pewholders constituted two entirely distinct groups—the original lists of members and pewholders contained *no* members in common—disagreement over the use of church space was a serious problem. After a series of meetings, a committee of both church members and pewholders arranged a settlement that divided the use of the church rather equally between both groups. The congregation won control of the building on Wednesday, Thursday, Friday, and Sunday evenings while the pewholders could occupy the church on the other three nights. Both groups solemnly accepted this accord, agreeing that "this arrangement is not to be interrupted by either party unless by mutual consent by both." The settlement worked. Records of both bodies testify that controversy over the use of church space did not erupt again. More than simply a wrangle over meeting arrangements, the communicant-pewholder conflict at Fourth Baptist Church reveals that the plebeian members of the congregation did not shy away from contesting the more affluent members of the society for a measure of control over the church.[44]

The formation of the Rhode Island Union Conference, including the Fourth and Third Baptist churches, reveals another dimension of the plebeian quest for religious independence. Established in 1824, the Union Conference was a subgroup within the Freewill Baptist movement.[45] United largely by their belief in "free Communion," the churches of the Union

---

[43] Ibid. See also Smith, *Discourse Delivered in the Fourth Baptist Meeting-House,* 5–7.

[44] On the settlement of the contest over the use of church space see Record Book, Fourth Baptist Church, December 3, 1828; Fourth Baptist Society Minutes, October 6, 1828.

[45] On the formation of the Rhode Island Union Conference see Isaac Dalton Stewart, *The History of the Freewill Baptists for Half a Century, Volume 1, From the Year 1780 to 1830* (Dover, N.H., 1862), 397–398; A. D. Williams, *The Rhode Island Freewill Baptist Pulpit* (Boston, 1852), 139; and George T. Day, *The Life of Rev. Martin Cheney* (Providence, 1853), 35–54.

Conference allowed themselves great latitude in local congregational polity. Although some of its members eventually joined the Rhode Island Quarterly Meeting of Freewill Baptists, during the 1820s they sought freedom from the dictates of the larger denomination. The ministers who gathered in the Rhode Island Union Conference gave particularly clear expression to Stephen Marini's judgment that the Freewill Baptists in general "envisioned a direct democracy of the saints founded on mass consensus and mutual discipline."[46] Two of them we have already met in the Rhode Island countryside. One was Ray Potter, who joined the Union Conference after contending with a Pawtucket mill owner for control of the Freewill Baptist church there. Potter lost the struggle but called attention to his plight by publishing a populist discourse concluding with the text "Do not rich men oppress you? Go to, ye rich men, weep and howl for the miseries that shall come upon you."[47] The other was Henry Tatem, whose parishioners formed the nucleus of the Fourth Church. Tatem also joined the Union Conference. A leader of considerable charisma, he attracted a dedicated following, some of whom preferred the name "Tatemites" to any denominational label.[48] Pastor Martin Cheney, who made his commitment to democracy clear in 1845 when he delivered a plea for the release of Thomas Dorr from prison, also attached himself to the group.[49] The peripatetic Cheney had deep personal connections among Providence Freewill Baptists. On February 5, 1824, the members of Fourth Baptist Church granted him a license "to preach the gospel wherever God in his providence may cast his lot."[50] Zalmon Tobey and Allen Brown, pastors of Fourth and Third Baptist Churches in Providence, rounded out the Union Conference membership. On September 3, 1824, when the members of Fourth Baptist Church voted to join the Union Conference, they simultaneously embraced an especially democratic and populist sect within the larger Freewill Baptist movement.

Of all the congregations established during the early 1820s, the members of the African Union Meeting House may have evidenced the strongest desire for religious independence. The black residents of Providence confronted not only relative poverty, which they shared with some members of the other predominantly white churches, but also a rising tide of racial hostility.[51] The creation of the African Union Meeting House thus

---

46 Stephen A. Marini, *Radical Sects of Revolutionary New England* (Cambridge, Mass., 1982), 174.
47 On Potter's controversy in Pawtucket, see Chapter 2.
48 "Religion in Rhode Island, 1828–1829," 12, Brown University Library.
49 Day, *Life of Martin Cheney*, 300–311.
50 Record Book, Fourth Baptist Church, February 5, 1824.
51 On the escalation of white hostility toward blacks in the antebellum urban North, see especially Gary B. Nash, *Forging Freedom: The Formation of Philadelphia's Black Community, 1720–1840* (Cambridge, Mass., 1988).

expressed a sense of racial identity and solidarity, but it also connected Providence blacks to the broader plebeian quest for religious autonomy. "The church, almost entirely responsible to the community," James Oliver Horton has written, "was generally the black institution most independent of white society."[52] The efforts of black residents to control their own meetinghouse thus paralleled the project undertaken by predominantly white residents in launching the Universalist, Methodist, and Freewill Baptist congregations.

The revival of 1820 coincided almost exactly with an intensified wave of racism sweeping not only Rhode Island but the nation as a whole. As postrevolutionary possibilities for gradual emancipation dimmed after the War of 1812, Americans took measures to insure the perpetuation of the peculiar institution. When Providence residents flocked to church meetings, the United States Congress passed the Missouri Compromise, promising the virtually unhindered expansion of slavery into the Southwest. Closer to home, Rhode Island's blacks confronted constricting opportunities for political expression. In 1822 the General Assembly restricted voting rights to white men only, rolling back earlier provisions that had allowed free black men of property to go to the polls.[53] Even marginal economic success among a handful of blacks threatened the white community. And increasingly, Providence whites eyed black efforts at self-improvement with apprehension. In 1815 Sarah Latham, who also taught a school for the Providence Female Tract Society, opened a school for blacks. The ubiquitous Daniel Waldo recounted a conversation with the governor of Rhode Island, in which the magistrate questioned whether the school was a good idea. According to Waldo, the governor reported that "some complain that it made their servants proud and less faithful."[54] In an effort to allay white fears of well-educated and saucy servants, the Providence *Religious Intelligencer* averred that "every effort to correct the morals and benefit the souls of this class is an essential service to the community."[55] Leaders in the black church understood accurately the coercive purposes behind the white-run school. They countered by suggesting that some Rhode Island whites "have wished, like the Southern slave-holders, to keep them in ignorance."[56] William J.

[52] James Oliver Horton, *Free People of Color: Inside the African American Community* (Washington, D.C., 1993), 34–35.
[53] See J. Stanley Lemons and Michael A. McKenna, "Reinfranchisment of Rhode Island Negroes," *Rhode Island History* 30 (February 1971): 3–4; Robert J. Cottrol, *The Afro-Yankees: Providence's Black Community in the Antebellum Era* (Westport, Conn., 1982), 67–112.
[54] Daniel Waldo diary, October 5, 1818, John Carter Brown Library, Brown University.
[55] *Religious Intelligencer* 1 (May 27, 1820): 11.
[56] *Short History of the African Union Meeting and School-House*, 10–11.

Brown summed up the hostility that Providence blacks experienced daily when he wrote, "the feeling against the colored people was very bitter."[57] Amid accounts of religious conversions and the glorious work of the Lord, the city's blacks perceived a different reality.

In the early national era, Providence's churches had been the central civic institutions bridging the races. And to some degree, even as racial animosity increased, the churches continued to function as cultural brokers. The revival era plebeian churches, especially, welcomed some black members. Given what we know about the pervasiveness of racism among white, working-class people in the antebellum North, these clues pointing toward harmony are worth noting. Black communicants, for instance, made up twelve of the original 111 members of the Aborn Street Methodist Church.[58] Fourth Baptist Church minutes relate the appointment of a special minister to tend to the spiritual needs of "the people of color in this town."[59] The Universalist pastor David Pickering made himself available to black residents. Between 1827 and 1832 he presided at the marriage ceremonies of five black couples.[60] While the participation of blacks in the city's pre–revival era churches appears to have dropped off after 1820, full-scale racial segregation did not evolve overnight. As late as 1832, for example, some thirty black members continued to worship with whites at First Baptist Church.[61] In early nineteenth-century Providence, churches still provided a context for cordial encounters among whites and blacks in a civic environment bent on cutting social ties between them.

Although free blacks could sit in predominantly white churches, and even vote in church affairs—a fundamental right they were *denied* in the larger civic polity—they understood all too well that whites conferred upon them an inferior status. Recall William J. Brown: Although he identified a lively free black contingent at First Baptist Church, he also noted that "many attended no church at all, because they said they were opposed to going to churches and sitting in pigeon holes, as all the churches at that time had some obscure place for the colored people to sit in."[62] Cato Pearce, another black Rhode Islander and lay preacher, knew of a Presbyterian church in Killingly, Connecticut, that contained "nigger

[57] William J. Brown, *The Life of William J. Brown, of Providence, R.I. with personal recollections of incidents in Rhode Island* (Freeport, N.Y., 1971), 88.
[58] McDonald, *History of Methodism*, 51.
[59] Record Book, Fourth Baptist Church, March 2, 1831; see also August 3, 1831.
[60] "Marriages of Colored People, celebrated by David Pickering, Pastor of the First Universalist Society and Church in Providence, State of Rhode Island," David Pickering Papers, RIHS.
[61] See *A List of Members of the First Baptist Church in Providence, with Biographical Sketches of the Pastors* (Providence, 1832), 46.
[62] Brown, *Life of William J. Brown*, 46.

pews."[63] Like Brown and Pearce, Frederick Douglass experienced the pains of outright discrimination when he sought to worship at a church in New Bedford, Massachusetts.[64] Although white members might pronounce religious sentiments assuring blacks that all were equal in the sight of God, the pew plats of their churches reminded blacks of their marginal position.

In creating the African Union Meeting House, black residents insured that they would exercise control over the seating of the church. Led by George McCarty, a trader, the original church committee composed pew deeds which restricted the ownership of seats to blacks. Black owners could dispose of their pews with complete freedom, with the single exception of sale to nonblacks. If such a transaction were attempted, the deed specified that "said Pew shall be forfeited by——and be considered as the property of said African Union Meeting and School-House, subject to be retained or sold by the Committee of said building."[65] The members of the African Union Meeting House claimed the most reasonably priced pews in the city. All of the pews in the Meeting House carried a twenty-dollar valuation (see Table 9). In giving the seats in the church a uniform price, the Committee of the Meeting House departed from the prevailing pattern of seating arrangements followed by white churches. In their more egalitarian seating procedures, the black church leaders may have found an additional way to distinguish their polity and thereby assert their independence. Inexpensive seats recognized the limits of economic black power. While leaders such as George McCarty did possess property, the vast majority of Providence blacks simply could not have afforded pews of higher price. Unfortunately, membership lists for the African Union Meeting House are not available. And before 1832, Providence blacks were invisible to those who made the city's directories. Still, we can make reasonable projections about the kinds of citizens who populated the African Union Meeting House. The first official accounting of the city's blacks in 1832 listed three out of five male occupations as laborers.[66] Moreover, as William J. Brown's record attests, black men could rotate through seafaring work back to land-based jobs, attempting to pick up knowledge of a craft in the process. In 1820, according to one scholar, domestic work provided the daily routine for more than half of the town's free blacks.[67] Seafaring, barbering, craft work, casual labor, domestic

---

[63] *A Brief Memoir of the Life and Religious Experience of Cato Pearce, A Man of Color. Taken Verbatim From His Lips and Published For His Benefit* (Pawtucket, R.I., 1842), 27.

[64] Frederick Douglass, *My Bondage and My Freedom* (1855; reprint, New York, 1969), 350–353.

[65] *Short History of the African Union Meeting and School-House*, 8.

[66] *The Providence Directory* (Providence, 1832), 130–133.

[67] Julian Rammelkamp, "The Providence Negro Community, 1820–1842," *Rhode Island History* 3 (1948): 21–22.

service, needlework—these were the tasks that occupied the hands of Providence's black community.[68] Since much of this work was done for whites and even required residence in white homes, the prospect of a separate arena for worship may have proved particularly compelling to the church's first members.

The procession to celebrate the dedication of the church in 1821 highlights an extraordinary act of spiritual autonomy on the part of the communicants. These early nineteenth-century black processions differed markedly from the black festivals of the colonial era. Unlike eighteenth-century festivals, which were designed largely for consumption within the black community, nineteenth-century parades took on an "overtly public and political cast" aimed at dramatizing a vibrant black identity within the town at large.[69] Although Moses Brown had mobilized Quaker support for the African Union Meeting House and had personally donated the land for the building, black leaders used the dedication festivities to embody their own declaration of independence. Given the prevailing climate of race relations in antebellum Providence, the procession they planned was nothing short of audacious. They carefully orchestrated a march to their new meetinghouse in which the African Greys, a militia group, would take a leading role. Various "African societies," complete with a commander decked out in "a red pointed cap" and equipped with "an elephant's tusk in his hand," also planned to participate in the festivities. This brilliant assembly intended to swing by the Quaker meetinghouse on Meeting Street to gather Moses Brown and other Friends en route to the new church. When the blacks arrived, the Quakers were aghast. And while some Friends evidently made their way to the African Union Meeting House, even the tolerant Moses Brown demanded that the African Greys deposit their weapons outside before worship services began. Such a display could not have been better crafted to challenge Quaker sensibilities. Drilling in the militia constituted a serious breach of Quaker ethics, and the blacks met them with a battalion. Simplicity of dress governed the Friends' code, and the African societies confronted them in tribal regalia. The free-singing and spirited quality of black worship must have scandalized the Quakers, whose services were based on silence. The leaders of the black church most certainly recognized that such a procession would have offended some of their most powerful

[68] See W. Jeffrey Bolster, "'To Feel Like a Man': Black Seamen in the Northern States, 1800–1860," *Journal of American History* 76 (1990): 1173–1199. See also Bolster, *Black Jacks: African American Seamen in the Age of Sail* (Cambridge, Mass., 1997), 158–160.
[69] Shane White, "'It Was a Proud Day': African Americans, Festivals, and Parades in the North, 1741–1834," *Journal of American History* 81 (1994): 15.

allies, including Moses Brown. But they took the risk. In constructing this festival, the members of the black church demonstrated in powerful fashion their desire for spiritual independence.[70]

Following its dedication, the African Union Meeting House continued to nurture black political aspirations. Shortly after they were disfranchised from the electoral process, the few blacks who did own real estate were hit with a real estate tax. The new tax sparked controversy, and "several colored gentlemen," including George McCarty, gathered at the church to decide whether or not to comply with the request of the town officers for payment. Those who debated the matter concluded that "taxation and representation went together; and they were unwilling to be taxed and not allowed to be represented."[71] Thus did members of the African Union Meeting House make supple use of the Anglo-American political language of republican-ism while simultaneously affirming their distinctive African-American identity. "Even as their institutional names identified black Americans as an African people," James Oliver Horton has observed, "they utilized many of the tools of American politics to organize themselves in their struggle for self-improvement and mutual support."[72] After taking the sense of the meeting, a delegation was dispatched to Newport to request voting rights rather than an abrogation of the tax. Confronted with this conundrum, the General Assembly backed off on the taxation question rather than to return the vote to black men of property. The small amount of revenue at stake did not seem to justify the risks involved in cutting black men a small slice of political power. Although they had lost their right to vote in civic affairs, the African Union Meeting House sustained and gave expression to black civic life.

Providence women, too, gained a substantial measure of political empowerment from the revival. In the postrevolutionary era, as we have seen, churchgoing women suffered a precipitous decline in their abilities to participate in matters of congregational governance. With their voices effectively silenced or severely circumscribed, women found themselves subject to a flurry of church disciplinary cases that targeted them for the crimes ascribed to their gender. With the coming of the revival, women's voices began to be heard, literally, once again. At the most basic level,

---

[70] Brown, *Life of William J. Brown*, 83–84. For a wider consideration of the political ramifications of black celebrations and parades in the early national era see David Waldstreicher, *In the Midst of Perpetual Fetes: The Making of American Nationalism, 1776–1820* (Chapel Hill, 1997), 328–348.

[71] Brown, *Life of William J. Brown*, 86.

[72] Horton, *Free People of Color*, 154.

women far outdistanced men in making professions of faith before their respective congregations. In 1820, women outnumbered men at Beneficent Congregational Church by a margin of 94 to 69. During the same year, at First Baptist Church, female additions to the congregation ran ahead of male participation by a ratio of 91 to 70.[73] At Fourth Baptist Church, 26 women and 15 men made up the first membership list.[74] Among Methodists, the dominance of women among professors reached the ratio of two to one, the most lopsided margin in town.[75] If judged simply by sheer numbers, then the revival of 1820 pointed toward a feminine millennium.

In addition to crowding tallies of the converted, revival era women projected themselves into positions of real political power. At Third Baptist Church, for instance, they took a central role in sorting out a struggle for control of the church between the cooper George Dods and the new minister, Allen Brown. Since Dods had supplied most of the energy for collecting the funds for the new congregation, it is hardly surprising that he came to see the church as his own property. Unfortunately for him, the rest of the congregation did not see it that way. Between 1822 and 1824, Dods and a small faction of dedicated followers battled Allen for leadership of the congregation. Only a congregational vote solved the crisis and sent Dods packing back to First Baptist Church. On April 5, 1824, the communicants, with "the Sisters voting," passed a unanimous resolution to "withdraw their watch care and Fellowship" from seventeen members, with George Dods's name heading the list.[76] In addition to bolstering Allen Brown's authority, female members also saved Willard Preston's ministry at Pacific Congregational Church. As early as 1817, Preston had been gearing up for a season of spiritual renewal. In a sermon delivered that year, he insisted that "without an experiential acquaintance with the truths of the gospel, there is no salvation for any of us." For Preston, true religion was a matter of the heart. "What is that repentance which is not felt?" he wondered. "Can we conceive of repentance, as distinct from feeling of the heart?"[77] Preston's emotional tones did not win universal plaudits, especially among the men of the Congregational Society to whom he had conveyed them. By November 1820, a

---

[73] See Table 8 for sources on Beneficent Congregational Church and First Baptist Church.

[74] Record Book, Fourth Baptist Church, July 5, 1823.

[75] Women outdistanced men 184 to 92 among the 276 members who joined the Chestnut Street Church between 1818 and 1824. Records of the Chestnut Street Methodist Episcopal Church, Vestry.

[76] Record Book, Third Baptist Church, April 5, 1824.

[77] Willard Preston, *A Sermon Preached Before the Pacific Congregational Society in Providence, R.I. March 9, 1817* (Providence, 1817), 17, 13.

crisis brewed that put Preston's job at risk. The men seemed equally divided on the subject of Preston's tenure, but the women of the church forced the issue by lending overwhelming support to the beleaguered minister. "The sisters of the church had feelings also," one account reported, "which were not to be disregarded, and they were almost all in favor of Mr. Preston."[78] Once again, women intervened decisively in rescuing the minister of their church.

Even when they failed to sway their congregations, women took center stage in proclaiming the necessity of a religion of the heart. Such was the witness of Mrs. Lydia Metcalf, a member of First Congregational Church. In October 1821 the First Congregational Church firmly declared itself to be within the Unitarian fold. This doctrinal shift signaled an effort by the Providence elite—which counted some of the wealthiest merchants and manufacturers among its members and pewholders—to distance themselves from the plebeian revivalists. The revision of the covenant "had long been desired by many of the Members." Under the guidance of the Harvard-trained divines Enos Hitchcock and Henry Edes, some members may have harbored Unitarian views well before the official doctrinal change. But in the midst of change Mrs. Lydia Metcalf clung to a religion of the heart. She voiced the only sustained dissent from the move to Unitarianism. In a gesture that required significant courage and intelligence, Mrs. Metcalf addressed the congregation about one year after the new covenant had been approved. According to the clerk's transcription of her remarks, she considered first the issue of the nature of Christ. She claimed Jesus "to be the Supreme and Self-existent God, and that in that Character he suffered and died on the Cross." Mrs. Metcalf, like the revivalists and Willard Preston, held to the centrality of repentance. She insisted "that it is necessary to the Character of a Christian to be able to tell the day, hour, or moment of conversion. That in consequence of such views she could not be satisfied in sitting under Preaching not in accordance with them."[79] Even in dissent, Lydia Metcalf articulated a powerful statement of the meaning of the revival.

For all of this, the expansion of female roles within revival era churches and institutions took place within a broader context of church building that continued to be gendered male. The process by which American Protestantism became "feminized" during the first half of the nineteenth century

---

[78] *A Candid Statement of Facts, Relative to the Difficulties between Pacific Congregational Church in Providence, R.I. and Those Brethren Who Withdrew and were formed into a Separate Church, with the documents which passed between the Two Parties on the Subject of a Mutual Council* (Providence, 1823), 5–6.

[79] Record Book, First Congregational Church, October 29, 1821, and March 5, 1822, RIHS.

has, in at least one crucial respect, been overstated.[80] The formation of new plebeian congregations, inasmuch as this process involved the acquisition of property, the collection of money for church buildings, and the auctioning of pews, remained a masculine exercise in public institution building. The plebeian enthusiasts, in this respect, did not depart from the understandings of gender evinced by their refined and affluent social betters. In the city, especially, church building remained the preserve of men. In examining the revival era congregations, the evidence does not point us toward charismatic leaders of the caliber of Nancy Towle, Susan Humes, or Salome Lincoln—women who shaped profoundly the plebeian religious institutions of the countryside. While women in Providence did exercise political power within congregations, the leadership roles within those churches were claimed by petty proprietors and artisan men such as George Dods, Pardon Hawkins, and George McCarty.

Moreover, the language of spiritual independence that undergirded the plebeian congregations was deeply indebted to the masculine language of republicanism. When the members of Fourth Baptist Church gathered at Pardon Hawkins's home on July 5, 1823, they connected themselves to a political tradition that equated femininity with notions of moral corruption. When the members of the African Union Meeting House formed their parade, they did so in a way that put women on the sidelines. The militia display projected an image of vigorous African-American manhood but simultaneously marginalized African-American womanhood.[81] And David Pickering, who blasted the prerogatives of a tainted and corrupt aristocracy, took a dim view of women's activism in Sunday schools and tract societies. He called for "an Instructress" to tutor them in "the theory and practice of looking well to the affairs of the *household*; of confining themselves more uniformly to the use of the *needle* and the affairs of the *kitchen*. This instruction would qualify them to become *good Wives* and *prudent Mothers*."[82] For Pickering, the spiritual independence for men was predicated on notions that assumed the dependence of women within a patriarchal household.

Even if the revival did not place women at the forefront of the new churches, it gave them authority over a vast array of reform efforts. As we have observed, groups such as the Female Charitable Society and the Providence Female Tract Society were institutions over which women exercised administrative and financial control. Many of the women who joined the Providence Female Tract Society had professed their newly found faith

---

[80] Ann Douglass, *The Feminization of American Culture* (New York, 1977).
[81] See White, "'It Was a Proud Day,'" 47–48.
[82] "Domestic Missionary," *Christian Telescope and Universalist Miscellany* 4 (March 28, 1828): 243.

during the revivals of 1805, 1815, and 1820.[83] As the work of Sarah Latham in the school for blacks suggests, participation in reform groups also provided the medium through which women shaped the civic life of the town in an era in which the vote was still beyond their grasp. During the 1830s and 1840s, as we shall observe in the next chapter, women in tract societies and temperance groups would expand the circle of female social and political activism. Despite the misgivings of men such as David Pickering, the revival did enable women to create institutions over which they held control. The religion of the heart articulated by Lydia Metcalf pointed women on a mission to reform society at large.

The churches created during the revival energized the common residents of Providence, laying a foundation for labor reform and demands for an expanded suffrage during the 1830s and 1840s. Among the Universalists, David Pickering aimed at the residue of "aristocracy" and voiced demands for a more democratic state government. The Methodists challenged the prevailing custom of pew auctioning and also provided a home for some of Providence's early labor activists. The creation of the Rhode Island Union Conference within the Freewill Baptist movement, too, reveals another dimension of plebeian grassroots organizing. There can be no doubt that the communicants of the African Union Meeting House understood well how an independent church fostered political action. Seth Luther himself, perhaps the most important plebeian labor and suffrage leader in antebellum Rhode Island, had been a revival convert at First Baptist Church in 1815. And when the Dorr Rebellion broke out in 1842, the suffrage insurgents would gather strength from the Freewill Baptists, Methodists, and Universalists, the very denominations fostered by the revival. Rather than pacifying the small proprietors, artisans, and laboring folk of Providence with hopes of justice meted out in heaven, the revival fired the imaginations of common people to improve their lot on earth.

As the new communicants bound themselves together in solemn covenant, they simultaneously proclaimed a broadly anti-Calvinist theology that gave ample room for the flexing of the human will. Like the rural operatives and farmers of the countryside who joined the Freewill Baptists and the Methodists, the urban revivalists took an Arminian stance that placed a premium on the emotional experience of religion. They insisted on an understanding of salvation that accentuated the freedom of both the mind and the spirit. They retained a belief in the profound significance of dreams and visions in the process of conversion.

[83] Joining the Tract Society from First Baptist Church alone were seven female converts from 1805, nine from 1815, and four from 1820. See *The First Annual Report of the Providence Female Tract Society* (Providence, 1816), 14–18; and membership records, First Baptist Church, RIHS.

In identifying a central key for plebeian religion, this analysis does not intend to collapse into a single melodic line the polyphony of voices singing in the revival. Universalists, for instance, distrusted and condemned the exercise of the emotions when they threatened to dethrone human reason. Methodists and Freewill Baptists would have quarreled over the proper relationship of local congregations to the denomination as a whole. Because the African Union Meeting House served an interdenominational constituency, it is difficult to assign a uniform theological perspective to its communicants. But precisely because the revival triggered the expression of such a diversity of views, it worked to undermine the established religious order of the town. To be sure, Calvinism in Rhode Island never had the hold that it did in Massachusetts. But if Calvinism represented the theology of community order, discipline, and authority in early-nineteenth-century New England, then the revival era congregations challenged the reigning spiritual order.

Although revival era churches did not speak in unison on what they affirmed, they were quite certain about what they opposed: Calvinism. David Pickering attacked the establishment of Sunday schools, not because he doubted the importance of the Bible in the life of spirit, but because he saw in them an effort to indoctrinate students "in the gloomy and soul chilling absurdities of Calvinism."[84] The Universalists considered it an affront to God-given human reason that the almighty would consign some to damnation and others to eternal bliss even before the dawn of creation. In the dedicated efforts of domestic missionaries—a zeal that he thought "rages like a malignant disease"—Pickering perceived an evangelical plan to promote a modern orthodoxy that would crush the freedom of the mind.[85] When the first members of Fourth Baptist Church met at Pardon Hawkins's home to articulate their beliefs, the church clerk recorded "a brief statement of the religious sentiments of the Church which were decidedly Anticalvinistick."[86] At Third Baptist Church, pastor Allen Brown swelled the chorus of Providence anti-Calvinism. In a June 22, 1822, letter to the communicants, who had originally come from the First Baptist Church, he wrote "that I did not believe in the doctrine of personal unconditional election, and that I did not dare to preach the perseverance of the saints, according to the creed of John Calvin." Brown's personal statement of belief drew approval from "a large majority of the members" of the church.[87] In taking the Arminian position of their denomination, the members of the Chestnut Street Methodist

---

[84] *Christian Telescope and Universalist Miscellany* 3 (April 28, 1827): 69.
[85] *Christian Telescope and Universalist Miscellany* 1 (January 8, 1825): 89.
[86] Record Book, Fourth Baptist Church, July 5, 1823.
[87] Record Book, Third Baptist Church, July 22, 1822.

Church simultaneously distanced themselves from notions of predestination and unconditional election.

While taking jabs at the Calvinists, the new churches proved reluctant to enforce strict doctrinal conformity over their members. Even Allen Brown, who registered his dissatisfaction with the tenets of predestination and the perseverance of the saints, admitted that he had no "objection that calvinists should belong to a church over which the Lord may place me."[88] He rejected only that these ideas be the litmus test for membership at Third Baptist Church. Since it served the full gamut of Episcopalians, Methodists, and Baptists, the African Union Meeting House announced that it "is to be open and free for all Christian professors, and not confined to any one profession of the Christian religion." The founders believed that "there are pious people or Christians, in and among the various denominations, as well as some who make no outward profession."[89] The Freewill Baptists, too, eschewed creeds. A "Brief Statement of the Faith and Practice of the Freewill Baptists," published in Zalmon Tobey's *Free-will Baptist Magazine,* asserted that they "universally adopted his [Christ's] perfect laws of liberty [the holy Scriptures] as their only true rule of faith and practice, and the book of church discipline, to the exclusion of all creeds, articles of faith, church platforms, etc., made by men."[90] The members of Fourth Baptist Church took this position quite seriously, managing to avoid even writing a church covenant until 1827. Moreover, as we have seen, the Freewill Baptists adopted an open communion policy, allowing any professing Christians to join them in the Lord's Supper. The Universalists applauded such sentiments, holding their communion table open to "all the members of other Churches who may be present, without regard to denomination."[91] In its brief "Compact," the members of the church echoed the Freewill Baptists by simply taking the example of Jesus "as the rule of our conduct, and his commands as our directory in the duties of religion."[92] Moreover, the members of the society of pewholders insisted that "no subscription to any Creed, articles of Faith, or Covenant shall ever be required of others, by those who meet for Public Worship."[93] They affirmed, too, that members had "free and perfect liberty to give that meaning to the writings of the New and Old Testaments, which shall best accord with his or her own understanding of

---

[88] Ibid.

[89] *Short History of the African Union Meeting and School-House,* 25.

[90] *Free-will Baptist Magazine* 1 (May 1826): 21.

[91] Constitution, Article 13, Record Book, First Universalist Church, RIHS.

[92] Compact and Rules of the First Universalist Church, Providence, R.I., Record Book, First Universalist Church, RIHS.

[93] Copy of the charter of the First Universalist Society, section 2, Record Book, First Universalist Society.

the same."[94] Only the Methodists, among revival era congregations, exercised a vigorous denominational discipline over their members.

Although the revival era churches did not police carefully the intellectual life of their members, it would not be accurate to depict them as "antinomians."[95] To the contrary, converts and new members pledged themselves to look after the moral conduct and behavior of each other. Even the Universalists adopted the principles expressed in Matthew 18:15–17, common among other evangelical congregations, in order to discipline "disorderly or immoral members."[96] The members of Third Baptist Church promised to "watch over each other in the love of God; to abstain from all foolish talking, viz., jesting, vain disputing, backbiting, and all unnecessary worldly conversation on Lord's day."[97] The covenant at Fourth Baptist Church agreed with these principles and added that the members should avoid "things which gender strife, disregarding promises and not fulfilling engagements, tatling, and backbiting, spending our time idly at taverns or elsewhere and vain and unnecessary worldly conversation on Lord's day and whatever else is contrary to sound doctrine according to the glorious gospel of Christ."[98] Both Universalists and Baptists could agree that Christian conduct and right behavior weighed more heavily in the scales of salvation than did assent to the finer points of doctrine.[99]

For new members making professions of faith, the behavior that mattered most was conversion. And here we find the point of sharpest disagreement between the Universalists and their Baptist, Methodist, and African-American colleagues. By and large, Universalists deplored revivalists and the excessive displays of emotion they sanctioned. David Pickering's journal, *The Christian Telescope and Universalist Miscellany*, blasted religious enthusiasm in a column titled "Revivals," written by one "Candour." "What have groans and sighs, and hollow whispers, forged *experiences*, and grimaces, distorted countenances, and frightful and unnatural sounds, which are practiced by religious deceivers," inquired the columnist, "to do with the solid, rational and mild religion of Jesus!"[100] From nearby Pawtucket, the Universalist minister Jacob Frieze took an equally firm stand against "reli-

---

[94] Ibid.
[95] See Sellers, *Market Revolution*, for a work that casts the Methodists in this role.
[96] Compact, Article 6, Record Book, First Universalist Church.
[97] Covenant, Record Book, Third Baptist Church.
[98] Covenant, Record Book, Fourth Baptist Church.
[99] On the growing importance of character and outward behavior in the Christian life during this period see James Turner, *Without God, Without Creed: The Origins of Unbelief in America* (Baltimore, 1986), 126–130; Richard Rabinowitz, *The Spiritual Self in Everyday Life: The Transformation of Personal Religious Experience in Nineteenth-Century New England* (Boston, 1989), 79–151.
[100] *Christian Telescope and Universalist Miscellany* 3 (June 9, 1827): 116.

gious excitements" by delivering two sermons on the subject. He walked his communicants through a comprehensive litany of condemnation, exposing revivals as irrational, uncharitable, and disruptive of family order since they encouraged young women to attend the "midnight haunts" where such meetings were held. In the end, Frieze thought that revivals created more "gloomy bigots" than they did authentic and clear-eyed Christians.[101]

The shrill rhetoric of the Universalists should not obscure the highly Christo-centric character of the movement's church in Providence. Recall that the communicants dedicated themselves to the example of Jesus Christ as the guide for all of their behavior. And they received instruction from the pulpit to coach them along the way. According to David Pickering's own catalogue, he delivered slightly more than thirteen hundred sermons to his congregation between 1822 and 1835. More striking than his boundless energy are the Biblical texts that consumed his attention. A glance over the texts of Pickering's sermons shows that he returned with regularity to the books of Matthew, Romans, Psalms, Proverbs, and Isaiah. His love of the New Testament revealed itself particularly in two monumental sets of orations—a fourteen-sermon series exploring the Sermon on the Mount and a twenty-seven-sermon series explicating the entire book of Romans.[102] Pickering's communicants shared his love of the Bible. Not even the most indefatigable of evangelical congregations could have surpassed the zealous scholars of the Universalist Sunday School. In 1833, a banner year for the group, a class of 126 young students committed to memory a staggering total of fifty-two thousand verses of the Scriptures.[103] The Universalists might have been closer to their enthusiastic cousins than they cared to admit.

Zalmon Tobey and David Pickering edited magazines that carried the banner for their respective denominations in Providence and, perhaps, in Rhode Island as a whole. Tobey launched the *Free-will Baptist Magazine* in 1826 and kept it afloat until 1830. Pickering began working on the *Christian Telescope and Universalist Miscellany* in 1824 and edited it through 1828. On an institutional level, these journals served to accentuate the presence and independence of the Freewill Baptists and the Universalists in the constellation of Providence churches. But they did more than trumpet the formation of new denominations. Both journals employed the rhetoric of

---

[101] Jacob Frieze, *Two Discourses, Delivered in the Universalist Church, in Pawtucket, On Sunday, August 30, 1829* (Pawtucket, R.I., 1829), 20, for both quotations. See Teresa Anne Murphy, *Ten Hours' Labor: Religion, Reform, and Gender in Early New England* (Ithaca, 1992), 94–100.

[102] Book of Sermon Texts Preached, David Pickering Papers.

[103] See chart of scholars and verses memorized, 1829–1834, Record Book, First Universalist Sunday School, RIHS.

freedom and emancipation to promote their respective denominations. But each took this language of liberty in a different direction. Pickering and the *Christian Telescope* emphasized consistently the role of the Universalists in liberating the human intellect. In contrast, Tobey and the *Free-will Baptist Magazine* underscored regularly an understanding of the gospel as both "free and precious" to new converts. If Pickering sought to unshackle the mind from the biases of unreasonable doctrine, Tobey wanted to free the soul from the wages of sin.

The first issue of the *Christian Telescope* made clear Pickering's mission. Taking its text from the gospel of John, the paper's masthead proclaimed, "Ye Shall Know the Truth and the Truth Shall Make You Free." Pickering drove home the message of intellectual freedom in a statement accompanying the laying of the cornerstone for the Universalist Chapel. "The class of religionists to which we belong," he announced, "has contributed in an eminent degree to the emancipation of the human mind, by calling in question the unreasonable dogmas of the church."[104] In starting their own Sunday school, the Universalists planned "to leave the mind unbiased by any sectarian prejudices."[105] While he had nothing against memorizing Biblical texts, Pickering sought to avoid the indoctrination he thought inevitably accompanied instruction in the schools operated by the Rhode Island Sunday School Union. "The great object of these schools was *not* to instruct the child of *poor parents* in the First Rudiments of Useful Science," the *Christian Telescope* maintained, "but to impress the infant mind with the *peculiar tenets of orthodoxy.*"[106] The Universalist assessment of the aims of the Rhode Island Sunday School Union, of course, missed the mark in important ways. As we have seen, the students did receive training in basic reading and writing in a context that was decidedly nonsectarian. Still, Pickering and his fellow Universalists remained dedicated to a faith that allowed individual believers a maximum degree of free inquiry.

The Freewill Baptists also accorded freedom a place of prime importance in their theological lexicon. But unlike the Universalists, who stressed the liberation of the intellect, the Freewill Baptists insisted on a "free and precious gospel" given to all humanity who would freely accept this wonderful gift.[107] In elucidating the meaning of gospel liberty, Zalmon Tobey verged on sentiments that would have been acceptable in David Pickering's church. In an 1828 sermon delivered before the Rhode Island Quarterly Meeting,

---

[104] *Christian Telescope and Universalist Miscellany* 1 (July 18, 1825): 203.
[105] *Christian Telescope and Universalist Miscellany* 4 (June 28, 1828): 322.
[106] *Christian Telescope and Universalist Miscellany* 3 (March 31, 1827): 39.
[107] Freewill Baptists employed this phrase so pervasively in the *Free-will Baptist Magazine* that a catalogue citing its uses would fill many pages.

Tobey declared flatly that "God is not willing that any should perish, but that all should come to repentance."[108] No humans on the planet stood beyond the offer of free salvation. He urged his listeners to spread the word of God "to the American, the European, the Asiatic, the Islander, the Indian; nor even is the poor African, though groaning beneath the heavy burden of slavery, and smarting under the rod of a cruel master, forgotten."[109] The Freewill Baptists thus coupled a firm belief in free human agency with a deep trust in the generosity of God to produce a capacious vision of global salvation.

In offering the prospect of "free" salvation, the Freewill Baptists selected a language that was strikingly at odds with the rhetoric of an emerging market society. In their view, the gospel had no price, it was not something to be purchased, it did not represent a commercial exchange or even a contract. To the contrary, the Freewill Baptists explicitly rejected the idea of salvation as a kind of market transaction in which the convert surrendered to the will of God in exchange for the reward of eternal life. Quoting the prophet Isaiah, the Freewill Baptists insisted instead that the gift of salvation was "without money and without price."[110] Indeed, the phrase "salvation is free" was repeated like a mantra in the pages of the *Free-will Baptist Magazine* and was even featured on a list of "a few Reasons for joining the Free Will Baptists."[111] But the fact that salvation was unearned did not cheapen its value. Rather, as Martin Cheney explained, the free offer of salvation made it even more valuable. "Believing, as I sincerely do, in a free and precious gospel, and that whosoever will may take the water of life freely," he wrote, "I can sincerely ascribe all the blessings we have received to the unmerited, unbounded goodness of God."[112] In emphasizing the degree to which salvation was not a matter of human striving, effort, or work, the Freewill Baptists divorced the workings of grace from the transactional language of the marketplace.

The plebeian enthusiasts sometimes spoke in ways that not only removed them from the market economy but distanced them from the temporal world as well. Like their counterparts in the countryside, the urban enthusiasts embraced the deep mysteries of faith. Even church covenants invoked celestial beings. At Third and Fourth Baptist churches, the members pledged their faith before God and his "angels." They prayed "that the head of the church will lead us into the mysteries of his kingdom," where they

---

[108] *Free-will Baptist Magazine* 2 (December 1828): 157.
[109] Ibid., 158.
[110] *Free-will Baptist Magazine* 1 (August 1826): 56; 2 (August 1828): 49.
[111] *Free-will Baptist Magazine* 3 (April 1830): 250–255.
[112] *Free-will Baptist Magazine* 3 (October 1829): 114.

would find "the pardon for our many sins."[113] If the Freewill Baptists pinned their hopes for forgiveness on a heavenly existence, the Methodists sought perfection on earth. Pastor Van Rensselaer Osborn, "the man by whom, God established the Methodists church in Providence," possessed "superhuman energy" as well as a tenacious belief in the doctrine of sanctification. Nearing death in 1846, Osborn announced earnestly, "I am sinless, now."[114] Daniel Waldo, too, thought the doctrine of sanctification part of the source of Methodist appeal. Although Waldo disdained this position, he discovered a Methodist preacher who argued that "sanctification was an instantanious work & after it we are perfectly sinless, & every real Christian knows when he is in this state. The prayers of such will be litterally answered & he can heal all manner of diseases, if the patient has faith."[115] The Methodists thus melted the distinction between heaven and earth, preserving a belief in the unmediated intervention of the holy in the midst of profane life.

William J. Brown and Cato Pearce, both black Rhode Islanders, preserved in the accounts of their respective conversion experiences profound testimony verifying the direct intervention of the sacred in their lives. Brown, a shoemaker and sailor who became a key civic leader in the Providence black community, experienced salvation at an 1835 revival sparked by the Freewill Baptist minister John W. Lewis. Pearce, who had been born to slave parents in Kingston, Rhode Island, worked as a seaman and an agricultural laborer before he set out on his career as a traveling preacher. Unlike Brown, who had learned to read and write and set down his story in his autobiography, Pearce spoke to an amanuensis in Pawtucket, Rhode Island, who published his remarks in 1842. While neither man grasped religion at the African Union Meeting House in 1820, their accounts do provide us with rare glimpses of the conversion experiences of communicants from the first generation of blacks who formed independent churches in Rhode Island. They testify, as well, to the prominence of intense and unmediated experiences of the sacred in the lives of plebeian residents.

Like other Providence men, William J. Brown owned a pew before he felt the stirrings of saving faith. Because he had been active in the temperance cause, had displayed talents as a fund-raiser, and could read and write, Brown had been asked to serve on a committee at the African Union Meeting House. Because he did not own a pew (his mother owned a quarter of one pew), he was not eligible to sit on the committee. The leaders of the church, who evidently considered Brown to be a talented man, presented him with a pew of his own—no. 47, which had previously "belonged

---

[113] Covenants, Record Books, Third and Fourth Baptist Churches.
[114] *Seventieth Anniversary*, 59 for both quotations.
[115] Waldo diary, October 7, 1818.

to a man named William Brown, who went to Hayti"—in order that he might serve.[116] Still, even as a pewholder and secretary of the temperance society, the experience of religion had eluded him. A profession of faith could have exposed Brown to dangers that pew ownership did not. He knew well that Providence blacks faced more than the temptations of the flesh when trying to practice lives of Christian duty. He had observed that whites sought to provoke churchgoing blacks to violence, rough words, and uncharitable behavior in an effort to expose the alleged weakness of their faith. "It was a common thing for colored people to be disturbed on the street," Brown wrote, "especially on the Sabbath."[117] Prospective black communicants had to conquer the normal doubts confronting struggling sinners and then bear with equanimity the threats and jeers of their fellow citizens.

By 1835, when the revivalist John Lewis came to Providence, William J. Brown made these twin burdens his own. He attended revival meetings over a period of four days, but prospects for his conversion looked grim. Overcome with emotion at one gathering, Brown had "reeled to and fro like a man intoxicated." This behavior earned him only the rebuke of a minister, who scolded, "If you have come here to get these brethren to pray for you in order to make fun, it will be the means of sinking you into perdition."[118] But Brown's distress over the state of his soul was authentic. He lost his taste for food. He sought solitude. He couldn't concentrate on his work. He examined his behavior, prayed devoutly for deliverance from sin, and still found no relief. Then, at the moment of his most profound despair, came a gentle voice. "Just then a thought ran across my mind," Brown recalled, "like some one whispering in my ear, saying, do you want religion enough to go down on Market square and pray, if by so doing you could get it."[119] Humbling himself, Brown agreed that he could. Then, "a light as large as the full moon shone in my face, and a voice spoke within me, saying, thy sins, which are many are forgiven." Liberated from his past, Brown's conversion sent him into a liminal state of religious ecstasy: "for a while I could not tell whether I was dreaming or awake; my heaviness was gone, and my soul was filled with joy; everything seemed lovely and beautiful; I had never enjoyed or had any conception of such a feeling before; it was indescribable."[120] Powerful visionary experiences such as Brown's proved central in the lives of plebeian enthusiasts in both the countryside and the city.

[116] Brown, *Life of William J. Brown*, 123.
[117] Ibid., 126.
[118] Ibid., 137.
[119] Ibid., 141–142.
[120] Ibid., 142.

Unlike William J. Brown, Cato Pearce did not grow up with firm religious moorings. As a young man, Pearce had run away from his master in Wickford, Rhode Island, and sailed to the West Indies, where he had indulged the wicked habits of a seafaring life—drinking, swearing, and a propensity to overlook prayer. Back in Providence for a time, Pearce had hired himself out to James Rhodes and attended the Methodist meetings of "one Elder Osborne" (the Van Rensselaer Osborn we have met above). Whereas William J. Brown only gave the impression of being intoxicated at church, Cato Pearce confessed that he "used to go hear him [Osborn] sometimes half drunk."[121] Pearce eventually found religion and began a career as an itinerant preacher, ministering to Methodists, Baptists, and to anyone else who might listen. It proved a profitable venture, enabling Pearce to purchase "a very fine nice shirt" with ruffles, a breast pin, and white gloves in which to preach.[122] Although he possessed the external accouterments of a fancy preacher, Pearce was illiterate and could only crib his sermon texts from other, more learned ministers—memorizing their verses and his variations on them before appearing before his congregations. Eventually, it was the issue of literacy that blocked Pearce's advancement as a respectable clergyman. "I told 'em I couldn't preach," he related to one audience, "for I had no larning." His inability to read and write made him feel "cold and dark."[123]

The transformative moment in Cato Pearce's life took place in a vision. According to his anonymous amanuensis, it was this extraordinary religious experience that prompted Pearce to tell his story in the first place. In that place between sleep and full consciousness, Pearce heard the Lord call to him by name. "He handed me the bible and told me to read," he recalled, "Well, I looked into the bible and I know'd every letter, but couldn't pronounce the words." Even though the Lord had commanded Pearce to read from the Scriptures, he could not do it. Seeing his dilemma, the Lord asked Pearce to follow him to his house where He would teach him how to read. On the way to the Lord's house, Pearce nearly took the wrong turn, barely avoiding the devil's efforts to take him to hell. But Pearce soon regained the right tack, along "a narrow path—a beautiful, straight, level path that led right back by the side of the gates where I came up." He kept to the right, stepping carefully around the devil, who by this time "had turned into a dog and lay there." Finally, Pearce came to a "large new house" in the middle of rich, green fields where fruit "looked beautiful and temptin'" along the roadside. He heard a voice command him not to eat it. He knew he had arrived at the house of God.

---

[121] *Brief Memoir of the Life of Cato Pearce*, 8.
[122] Ibid., 17–18.
[123] Ibid., 20.

Pearce described the scene in the Lord's home with astonishing detail and enormous theological license. Into the kitchen he went, where angels with "wings as white as the drippin' snow" sang hymns of praise overhead. The Lord was seated, in his robe, at the kitchen table with his daughter and wife close at hand. Then Pearce related the strange story of how he came to have the ability to read. The Lord commanded his daughter to go to another room and to return with the New Testament, in which Pearce's name now appeared. The Lord's wife, too, took part in Pearce's transformation. She brought forward a communion cup with a potion that "will make him pray, preach, or sing." The Lord himself then began to preach and told Pearce that he must then follow Him to the pulpit. "Then I began to preach—and could read and preach—I could read in any part of the bible, and I could 'splain upon it; and I *never* was so happy in all my life—I can't 'spress my feelin's." In his vision, Pearce had found what his earthly life had denied him, the ability to read the Scriptures.[124]

Pearce's baroque vision, which has been presented here only sparely, is significant from a number of angles. It reveals, obviously, the persistence of magical thinking and visionary religion in the plebeian religious culture of Rhode Island. It shows, too, how these experiences empowered even illiterate citizens to hold religious authority. Although Pearce enjoyed the gift of literacy only in a liminal state, it is plain that this experience bolstered his sense of clerical legitimacy, allowing him to continue preaching and to stake a claim in the world of print culture. Finally, Pearce's vision is striking in its portrayal of a profoundly patriarchal god. Arguably the most fantastic invention of this multifaceted vision is its placement of the Lord at the head of a family unit, ordering his daughter and wife to serve his needs in the kitchen. In crafting an image of a strongly masculine god, in adorning himself in fancy clothes, and in his endorsement of an ornate and syncretistic religious experience, Pearce shares much with the figure of the New York street preacher Matthias.[125] Pearce's vision exposes the strongly patriarchal dimension of male street preaching, which would characterize other self-anointed ranters in the streets of Providence during the 1830s and 1840s.[126]

In his judgment of the overall impact of the 1820 revival, Stephen S. Wardwell, the revival's most devoted convert, wrote with confidence that "many were brought from nature's darkness into God's marvellous light."[127] Given the number of freshly awakened souls who tendered professions of

---

[124] The text for Pearce's dream is from *A Brief Memoir of the Life of Cato Pearce*, 21–26.
[125] Johnson and Wilentz, *Kingdom of Matthias*, esp. 10–11, 94–95, 172–173. See 98 for a description of Matthias's dress.
[126] See Chapter 5 below.
[127] Wardwell diary, September 1820.

faith and built new churches, Wardwell's observation appears amply justified. But the revival did more than harvest new converts. It reconfigured decisively the religious landscape of the town. The revival provided the energy used by the shopkeepers, artisans, and laborers of Providence to form their own congregations. Its power verifies the observation made long ago by Ernst Troeltsch, that "the really creative, church-forming, religious movements are the work of the lower strata."[128] Unlike the churches of the pre-revival era, which embraced the full range of Providence residents from the most humble to the most exalted, the revival era congregations claimed more modest constituents. In the crucible of the religious enthusiasm, plebeian revivalists established their own churches. In the process, they fractured the organic sense of religious community that had characterized the city's congregations before the revival.

The revival of 1820 launched the process of "cultural bifurcation" in the Providence religious community.[129] In the years following it, we can begin to detect the emergence of two religious cultures, each with its own denominational basis, notion of authentic religious experience and ethical perspective. While communicants did not queue up neatly on one side of this cultural fault line or the other, by the 1830s and 1840s the outlines of these two religious cultures—plebeian and bourgeois—can be fairly well traced. On the one hand, the revival fomented a plebeian religious culture in the Universalist, Methodist, and Freewill Baptist congregations, a culture dedicated to a flexible anti-Calvinism, to intense religious experiences and street preaching, and, as we shall observe, to its own political and economic agenda. But the revival also produced a response on the part of the more genteel and refined members of Providence society. In the decades after the revival, these prosperous Christians forged a bourgeois religious culture centered especially in Calvinist Baptist congregations, among Congregationalists, Episcopalians, and polished Unitarians. These were churchgoers who valued high-toned and well-appointed meetinghouses, trusted in the social order and sobriety, and embraced values that complemented an emerging capitalist society. It is to the creation of bourgeois religious culture that we now turn our attention.

[128] Troeltsch quoted in H. R. Niebuhr, *The Social Sources of Denominationalism* (1929; reprint, Gloucester, Mass., 1987), 29.
[129] The phrase is from Lawrence W. Levine, *Highbrow/Lowbrow: The Emergence of Cultural Hierarchy in America* (Cambridge, Mass., 1988), 81.

4

"The True Use of Riches"

The Emergence of Bourgeois Religious Culture

On November 3, 1841, Francis Wayland, president of Brown University and a prominent Baptist clergyman, delivered a funeral oration for Nicholas Brown. The occasion marked the passing of one of Providence's leading citizens and wealthy benefactors. Born in 1769, Nicholas Brown was the son of the Nicholas Brown, one of four brothers who, along with his brothers John, Moses, and Obadiah, had made up the town's most important eighteenth-century family. The younger Nicholas carried the family's fortunes with success into the early nineteenth century. His business partnership with Thomas P. Ives in "one of the largest commercial houses in New England" had established Brown's position in the front rank of the Providence elite.[1] Wayland acknowledged Brown's financial triumphs, pointing out that "the success of his diversified operations testified that boldness of enterprise may be harmoniously united with vigorous and deliberate judgment." He praised Brown's "largeness of mind," and his uncanny ability to "look at results, and frequently at results long distant."[2] In Wayland's eulogy, Nicholas Brown emerged as a visionary capitalist, one gifted with the insight to bestow wisely the fruits of his benevolence upon the community.

Francis Wayland knew firsthand the benefits of Nicholas Brown's prescience and care. In 1826, as Wayland applied for the presidency of Brown University, Nicholas Brown, then a trustee of the school, had written

---

[1] Francis Wayland, *A Discourse in Commemoration of the Life and Character of the Hon. Nicholas Brown, Delivered in the Chapel of Brown University, November 3, 1841* (Boston, 1841), 14.
[2] Ibid., 15.

119

to assure him that his candidacy was unassailable.[3] After Wayland had accepted the job, Brown made a series of prodigious gifts to support his program for reforming the university. Although Wayland's students sometimes considered him a prodding and pedantic intellect, as neatly ordered and arid as his treatises on moral science and political economy, he felt great loss on the occasion of Brown's death. "His manly and venerable form," Wayland lamented, "will no more meet us at his hospitable fire-side, in the mart of business, or in the house of God."[4] The funeral oration thus developed not only as an acknowledgment of a life gracefully lived, but also as the testament of one friend to another.

Francis Wayland built his account of Nicholas Brown's life on the topic of benevolence. He began with comments on the place of benevolence in human life, in the sphere of what he called "our sublunary existence." Sounding a conservative note, he announced that "from the very constitution of our being, we mutually influence and are influenced by the character of others. To isolate ourselves from society is impossible." Given this organic conception of the social order, Wayland stressed the obligations and duties that members of society owed one another. From this theoretical scaffolding he then constructed a compelling case for the necessity of benevolence. Aside from benefiting society, good deeds also conferred a kind of immortality upon those who undertook them. "It is by what we ourselves have done," concluded Wayland, "and not by what others have done for us, that we shall be remembered by after ages." Finally, he maintained that the practice of benevolence was "in harmony with the interests, the affections and the conscience of man; and thus the strongest and the noblest principles of our nature co-operate in rendering it ultimately successful."[5] For him, a life lived in the spirit of benevolence was nothing less than the working out of a divine impulse, planted by the Creator in every human heart.

The life of Nicholas Brown described a pattern that Francis Wayland held up for all to imitate. Although he harbored a deep skepticism with respect to institutional or governmental efforts to ameliorate the conditions of the poor, he cheered acts of charity undertaken by individuals, and here Brown's record was peerless. Wayland pointed to Brown's patronage of the American Tract Society, to his key role in sponsoring the Providence Atheneum, and to his generous support of the town's churches. "Although he was conscientiously a Baptist," Wayland remarked, "yet his charities

---

[3] See William G. Roelker, "Francis Wayland, A Neglected Pioneer of Higher Education," *Proceedings of the American Antiquarian Society* 53 (1943): 32.
[4] Wayland, *Discourse in Commemoration of Nicholas Brown*, 3.
[5] Ibid., 5, 6, 9, 12.

were rarely solicited in vain by Christians of every other denomination."[6] Wayland also took pains to observe Brown's remarkable contributions to the school itself. He noted Brown's gifts of a "law library of considerable value," funds for an endowed professorship of Oratory and Belles Lettres, the purchase of scientific instruments, the donation of three lots of property for a presidential mansion, and a building for the study of natural philosophy, chemistry, mineralogy, and natural history. Crowning these impressive achievements, Wayland explained, Brown "erected, at his own expense, the beautiful edifice in which we are now assembled, for a library room and a chapel."[7] Even in death, the reach of Brown's charity literally encircled audience and speaker alike, reminding them of Wayland's assertion that the work of benevolence could transcend the passage of time.

Francis Wayland's reflection on the life of Nicholas Brown reveals something more than the tribute of one friend to another or the traces of a philosophy of benevolence. It exposes, as well, one dimension of a bourgeois religious culture that emerged in Providence during the middle decades of the antebellum era. The personal friendship between Wayland and Brown symbolizes in some measure the coalescence of a wider cultural collaboration between the city's respectable Protestants and its rising business and manufacturing classes. While it was rooted largely among the more affluent residents of the city, bourgeois Protestantism cannot be neatly categorized as "middle class" because it found adherents among both the city's most wealthy residents, such as Nicholas Brown, and those of much more humble means. Bourgeois religious culture claimed a substantial following well beyond the circle of the merchant and manufacturing elite, especially among shopkeepers, clerks, and master craftsmen.

Although I emphasize the bifurcation of religious culture in Providence, I do not intend to present antebellum American society through the lens of a Manichaean dualism. I take seriously the insightful critiques made of the concept of "bourgeois" culture offered by scholars such as Peter Stearns, who argues that "with no effort at social-structural definition or precision, the notion of bourgeois culture becomes an absurdity."[8] Nor do I employ the term "bourgeois" in a pejorative or trivial sense. To the contrary, I hope to portray something of the quandaries and the heart-wrenching dilemmas experienced by these people of faith. These caveats notwithstanding, I do employ a two-tiered model of American social and cultural development in

---

[6] Ibid., 18.

[7] Ibid., 25; for an inventory of Brown's donations, see 22–25.

[8] Peter N. Stearns, "The Middle Class: Toward a Precise Definition," *Comparative Studies in Society and History* 21 (1979): 389.

contrast to one that discovers clear markers between the triad of upper, middle, and lower classes.[9]

In this chapter I explore bourgeois religious culture as it manifested itself in individual congregations, in evangelical reform movements, and in the thought of Francis Wayland. Adherents to the bourgeois religious perspective could be found not only among refined Congregational, Episcopal, and Unitarian churches but also among Baptists and Methodists who yearned for a sense of respectability in the years following the revival of 1820. The prevalence of pew auctioning and, especially, the widening practice of multiple pewholding among the Providence faithful testified to the profound linkages between the culture of the marketplace and that of the meetinghouse. Outside their churches, bourgeois Protestants sought to sacralize their cityscape through a wide array of reform efforts, especially through championing the cause of temperance and by distributing religious tracts to all of its residents. These reform movements revealed the twin passions of bourgeois Protestants for both individual self-control and social order. And in a series of textbooks and addresses, Wayland gave voice to the concerns of bourgeois Protestants on a national level. To a degree greater than that evinced by his ministerial predecessors of the early national period, he worked to reconcile the spirit of capitalism with the ethics of Christianity.

The religious culture of bourgeois Protestants differed from that of the plebeian enthusiasts we considered previously. Rather than worshipping in humble churches or in fields or in factories, bourgeois Protestants appointed their meetinghouses with rich pew cushions and expensive organs. Whereas plebeian revivalists prized emotional expression and the liberty of the soul, bourgeois Protestants valued coolheaded deliberation and social

---

[9] For classic works that probe the emergence of the middle class in America see Mary P. Ryan, *The Cradle of the Middle Class: The Family in Oneida County, New York, 1790–1865* (Cambridge, 1981); Karen Halttunen, *Confidence Men and Painted Women: A Study of Middle Class Culture in America, 1830–1870* (New Haven, 1982); Stuart M. Blumin, *The Emergence of the Middle Class: Social Experience in the American City, 1760–1900* (Cambridge, 1989).

The major work exploring the rise of the middle class in Providence is John S. Gilkeson Jr., *Middle-Class Providence, 1820–1940* (Princeton, 1986). Probing a vast array of civic and reform groups, especially those promoting the temperance movement and abolitionism, Gilkeson charts the emergence of a "middle-class consciousness" during the antebellum period, defined, for the most part, as a producer ideology that venerated self-discipline and hard work. While intricately researched, Gilkeson's argument tends to link the emergence of this producer ideology too closely to the rise of the middle class as an economic group, thus ignoring how elite residents and even working-class Americans could lay claim to that very same language. One could make the case, for instance, that a producer ideology was at the heart of the Providence workingmen's movement of the 1830s. In my reading of the evidence, this producer ideology claimed a much wider following than Gilkeson allows and cannot be identified as the sole possession of the middling ranks of American society.

cohesion. Connecting the resurgent Calvinism and the Unitarian influence in Providence during these years (groups that could not have been more at variance theologically) was an emphasis on the "emotional control" that proved to be a central component in the configuration of bourgeois culture.[10] This restrained style of piety surfaced in the faith of Nicholas Brown himself, who, according to Wayland "was never connected with any Christian church" yet proved himself a patron of Baptist ministerial students and a host of other religious causes.[11] In emphasizing emotional control, decorum, and rationality, bourgeois religious culture was also profoundly masculine in contrast to its plebeian counterpart. Wayland's selection of Nicholas Brown as an example worthy of imitation suggests that he had in mind the particular form of a "manly" and Christian saint.

The resurgence of masculine religion placed bourgeois women in a precarious position. The undeniable reality that women constituted the majority of church members in antebellum America has sometimes masked the limitations of power they faced within their own congregations. As the diaries of Stephen S. Wardwell and Emeline Barstow reveal, the bourgeois passion for the creation of a public social order privileged an especially male domain of activity. While it has become a commonplace to emphasize the importance of bourgeois women in the reform activities of the Second Great Awakening, the work conducted by women was often guided by and financed by men. This proved to be true, especially, of the movements to promote temperance and to spread tracts. Simultaneously, bourgeois women offered stinging critiques of the worst abuses wrought by the market economy. During the 1830s, they championed the case of Elleanor Eldridge, a black domestic worker who had been cheated out of her home by the machinations of devious men of property and their lawyers. They voiced concerns about the conditions faced by needlewomen, much as the women of the Providence Female Tract Society had done in earlier decades with respect to textile operatives. The "iconoclastic" and oppositional quality of aspects of female reform made it difficult for bourgeois Protestants to speak with unanimity on important issues of religious and civic reform.[12] It was not until the 1850s that bourgeois women and men closed ranks to present a more united front toward their social and economic inferiors.

Bourgeois Protestants also wrestled with a troubling paradox. For even as

[10] John F. Kasson, *Rudeness and Civility: Manners in Nineteenth-Century Urban America* (New York, 1990), 147–181.
[11] Wayland, *Discourse in Commemoration of Nicholas Brown*, 16.
[12] Carroll Smith-Rosenberg, "The Cross and the Pedestal: Women, Anti-ritualism, and the Emergence of the American Bourgeoisie," in *Disorderly Conduct: Visions of Gender in Victorian America* (New York, 1985), esp. 134.

they applauded the divinely sanctioned fruits of individual acquisitiveness, they feared that unbridled greed would tear apart the social order. As Francis Wayland himself recognized, the quest for material goods could sap the desire to love God and to serve one's fellow creatures. Although Wayland more typically raised such concerns in times of economic panic, such as in 1837 and 1857 when he targeted speculation as one of the most baneful features of the market economy, he also expressed them in Nicholas Brown's funeral oration. "Why should a man postpone the period of his benevolence," asked Wayland in his peroration, "until the time when the love of wealth, eating like a canker into his soul, has paralyzed every generous sentiment; or until death, loosening by force his grasp upon his possessions, has rendered the *virtue* of charity impossible." The full measure of Brown's life, Wayland concluded, could be found in his "true use of riches" for the public good.[13] That Wayland felt compelled to articulate the evils of the love of wealth while eulogizing one of Providence's richest citizens speaks to the depth with which even refined Protestants struggled to reconcile the love of profit with the love of God.

Nicholas Brown's good fortune was only one manifestation of the city's prosperity. Indeed, Providence revealed signs of God's generous hand. In the two decades between the revival of the early 1820s and the Dorr Rebellion of 1842, its population grew steadily from about 12,000 to just over 23,000 persons.[14] While Irish immigration had begun to increase during the late 1830s, its full impact would not be felt by the city until the 1840s and 1850s. More spectacular than Providence's modest population growth was its economic dynamism. Providence entrepreneurs, bankers, and manufacturers pioneered the expansion of turnpikes, canals, railroads, banks, and insurance companies, thereby solidifying their preeminence over Newport's elite. Manufacturing, too, spread from the mill villages surrounding Providence into the city itself. By 1840 the development of steam power contributed to the rise of textile works and machine shops that employed some twenty-five hundred men, women, and children.[15] Artisans, especially those in the building trades, stayed busy constructing these workplaces as well as accommodations for the city's expanding population. The city also boasted institutions of intellectual cultivation and commercial innovation. The dedication of the Providence Atheneum in 1838 and the presence of Brown University gave Providence residents sustenance for the life of the

---

[13] Wayland, *Discourse in Commemoration of Nicholas Brown*, 28.

[14] Peter J. Coleman, *The Transformation of Rhode Island, 1790–1860* (Providence, 1963), 220.

[15] *Statistics of the United States of America, as collected and returned by the marshals of the several Judicial Districts, under the Thirteenth Section of the Act of Taking the Sixth Census; Corrected at the Department of State, June 1, 1840* (Washington, D.C., 1841), 59.

mind. In 1828 the construction of the Arcade on the west side of town allowed citizens to celebrate the creation of the first enclosed shopping mall in America. While Providence would have been dwarfed by Philadelphia, New York, and even Boston, it had emerged as the "metropolis" of southeastern New England.[16]

Respectable residents of the city nonetheless perceived danger in the midst of progress. The expansion of urban manufacturing sharpened fears that a population of degraded factory operatives would blight the moral and religious health of the city.[17] In 1833 Providence master craftsmen and journeymen squared off in bitter confrontations involving the ten-hour workday and proposed reforms to Rhode Island's restrictive suffrage requirements.[18] Providence citizens also wrestled with the wider problem of poverty. In 1824 the *Christian Monitor and Weekly Register* claimed with alarm that "Support of the Poor" had cost the city $8,390.47 during the previous year—by far the single largest town expense.[19] In 1828 the creation of the Dexter Asylum gave concrete form to civic concerns regarding the governance and control of the poor.[20] The explosion of racial violence divided Providence society along another axis. Major riots in 1824 and 1831 set working-class whites and blacks at each other's throats.[21] The violence of 1831 proved especially convulsive. It took the governor, sheriff, and four companies of state militia, complete with field artillery, to drive the rioters from the field. The scale of the violence, the destruction of entire neighborhoods, and the helplessness of the town meeting to handle the crisis convinced men of property that new measures to ensure social stability were needed. On October 5, 1831, scarcely one month after the rioting, they decided "that it is expedient to adopt a city form of government."[22] They resoundingly affirmed a city charter and so launched the town of Providence as a new administrative entity.

This quest for order revealed itself not only in the creation of a city government but in the churches of refined Protestants as well. The formation of new churches and the maturation of the congregations nurtured by the

---

[16] "Metropolis" is Peter J. Coleman's term; see *Transformation of Rhode Island*, 161–217.

[17] *Literary Subaltern*, November 19, 1830.

[18] See *New England Artisan and Laboring Man's Repository*, April 19, May 24, June 14, 1832; more generally, Marvin E. Gettleman and Noel P. Conlon, eds., "Responses to the Rhode Island Workingmen's Reform Agitation of 1833," *Rhode Island History* 28 (1969): 75–94.

[19] *Christian Monitor and Weekly Register*, June 12, 1824.

[20] *Rules and Regulations for the Government of the Dexter Asylum, established at a town meeting of the Freemen of Providence, on the 26th day of July, 1828* (Providence, 1828).

[21] See Howard P. Chudacoff and Theodore C. Hirt, "Social Turmoil and Governmental Reform in Providence, 1820–1832," *Rhode Island History* 31 (1972): 21–33.

[22] Quoted in Chudacoff and Hirt, "Social Turmoil," 28.

revival of 1820 may have been more important in promoting social order than even the creation of the new city charter, since the number of Providence faithful (pewholders and members) exceeded by far the approximately 650 voting freemen of the town meeting. And the churches they created promoted reform movements that touched ordinary lives at least as intimately as did city ordinances.

If the revival era provided a boost to Baptist membership, the decades following 1820 allowed the Congregationalists, Episcopalians, and Unitarians time to catch up. In 1827 the feuding factions at Pacific Congregational and the "Calvinistic" Congregational Church reunited to establish the Richmond Street Congregational Church. By 1834, High Street Congregational Church joined this denomination's West Side renaissance. The Episcopalians gathered two new communities as well: Grace Church in 1829 and St. Stephen's in 1839. By 1828 the Unitarians gained a hold in West Side Providence with the creation of Westminster Congregational Church. In the wake of the revival, the more high-toned Protestant denominations collected significant strength.

The simultaneous resurgence of Calvinism among the communicants of the Richmond Street and High Street churches and the expansion of Unitarianism would seem to present a stark theological contradiction within the ranks of bourgeois Protestants. Indeed, the two denominations held opposing views with respect to the dispensation of God's grace. High Street communicants agreed in their "Confession of Faith" that God had selected "a certain number of mankind who were from eternity predestined to be holy and to inherit everlasting life." The final article of the document preserved the assertion that God would "sentence the wicked to endless punishment."[23] Frederick A. Farley, pastor of the Unitarians at Westminster Congregational Church, dismissed this as nonsense. What kind of theology "demands conformity on peril of future damnation," he asked?[24] The theological disputes between Calvinists and Unitarians must be taken seriously, especially in an age that took such matters with an earnestness that modern folk can scarcely summon. But battles over the doctrine of election should not blind us to what Calvinists and Unitarians shared. Both denominations valued a religion of the intellect over one of the heart, both proved themselves attractive to Providence's rising business classes, both auctioned their pews, and both committed themselves to programs of religious reform in the community. Thus Farley, the Unitarian pastor, clasped hands with Josiah

---

[23] Record Book, High Street Congregational Church, "Confession of Faith of the High Street Congregational Church," Manuscript Collection, Rhode Island Historical Society, hereafter cited as RIHS.

[24] Frederick A. Farley, *A Discourse Delivered at the Dedication of Westminster Church in Providence, Rhode Island, March 5, 1829* (Boston, 1829), 16.

Chapin, a Calvinist deacon and cotton merchant, in support of the Rhode-Island State Temperance Society.

Those churches that had prospered during the turbulence of the revival era tried to keep pace with the newer congregations of refined Congregationalists and Unitarians. Three of these congregations undertook plans to renovate, improve, or expand their facilities. On September 21, 1832, the men of the Charitable Baptist Society announced the revaluation of all the pews in the church building and publicized a full-scale auction to pay for the recently completed work. On the floor of the church, the society ripped out the old pews to make space for "more comfortable and more fashionable seats."[25] The society tempted prospective pew purchasers by advertising the acquisition of "a new Organ (of the first class)" worth some three thousand dollars.[26] Moreover, in the course of the rebuilding project, the upper balcony of the church had been removed. The elimination of these seats, traditionally reserved for black worshippers, suggests a hardening of racial attitudes on the part of the pewholders. In constructing a more comfortable site for devotion, the Charitable Baptist Society planned for a more fashionable, wealthy, and white congregation. The members of the African Union Meeting House countered this move with their own bid for refinement. Between 1840 and 1841, the pastor Jeremiah Asher presided over efforts that rendered it "one of the best, the neatest, and most commodious places of worship in the city, so much so, that many of the colored people regarded it as quite aristocratic."[27] Like their white neighbors at First Baptist Church, the members of this black congregation moved to define themselves in a more exclusive fashion. The Methodists, too, sought a more respectable profile in the city. Under the leadership of Hezekiah Anthony, a grocer, they overcame their qualms about pew auctioning and constructed a fine meetinghouse in East Side Providence, containing pews prized as highly as those of the Richmond Street Congregational Church. (See Table 15.) The trajectory of some of the revival era churches in the 1830s and 1840s is suggestive of the process, once described by H. R. Niebuhr, by which "a church of the poor sloughs off its original endowment and accepts a type of religious life more in conformity with its new economic interests and status."[28]

---

[25] Norman M. Isham, *The Meeting House of the First Baptist Church in Providence: A History of the Fabric* (Providence, 1925), 20.

[26] See Pew Plat for September 21, 1832, in Charitable Baptist Society Records, box 2, folder marked "Pews 1805–1859," RIHS.

[27] Jeremiah Asher, *An Autobiography, with Details of a Visit to England, and some account of the history of the Meeting Street Baptist Church, Providence, R.I., and of the Shiloh Baptist Church, Philadelphia, Pa.* (Philadelphia, 1862), 75.

[28] H. Richard Niebuhr, *The Social Sources of Denominationalism* (1929; reprint, Gloucester, Mass., 1987), 89.

Table 15. Providence pew valuations, circa 1832

Church	Average pew value	Most expensive pew	Least expensive pew	Number of pews valued
Westminster Congregational Church, 1832	$355.33	$550.00	$90.00	105
St. John's Episcopal Church, 1832	348.45	430.00	200.00	71
First Congregational Church, 1832	342.00	700.00	75.00	119
First Universalist Church, 1832	216.00	380.00	50.00	99
High Street Congregational Church, 1832	207.42	350.00	85.00	64
Power Street Methodist Church, 1833	189.76	402.50	42.40	70
Richmond Street Congregational Church, 1828	183.00	350.00	30.00	110
First Baptist Church, 1832	181.94	400.00	30.00	144
Fourth Baptist Church, 1832	99.61	135.00	40.00	39[a]

Sources: Westminster Congregational Society, Pew Records, RIHS; St. John's Episcopal Church Records, box 14, folder 119, University of Rhode Island Archives; Benevolent Congregational Society Records, box 12, see "Assessment From Nov. 1, 1831 to Nov. 1, 1832," RIHS; First Universalist Society Records, volume for Pew Taxes, 1832–1838, RIHS; High Street Congregational Church Records, RIHS; Richmond Street Congregational Church Records, RIHS; Power Street Methodist Church Pew Records, 1833–1866, RIHS; Charitable Baptist Society Records, box 2, folder "Pews 1805–1859," see also pew plat for September 21, 1832; Fourth Baptist Church Records, Treasurer's Book, RIHS.
[a] Includes only purchasers of pews, not renters.

As they remodeled their churches, refined Protestants also sought to bring more exclusivity to the ranks of those who owned their pews. A survey of these congregations, with special attention to the pewholders of First Baptist, Power Street Methodist, High Street Congregational, and Westminster Congregational (Unitarian) churches, reveals that pew costs crept higher from their relatively low levels during the revival era. Among the new congregations, the pews at Westminster Congregational Church carried the highest valuation. Reaching an average cost of over $350 per seat, the new Unitarians held even more expensive pews than those owned by the established East Side Unitarians and Episcopalians. The new seats offered by the First Baptist Society, the Methodists, and the Calvinist Congregational churches fell between $180 and $210 per pew. Although not excessively expensive, these seats still commanded greater valuations than those offered by the Fourth Baptist Church, for example, during the revival years. The trend toward more standardized pew assessments suggests, as well, that society members attempted to define more exactly their economic criteria for membership.[29]

The new pewholders demonstrated an extraordinary spirit of individual acquisitiveness. Especially among merchants, manufacturers, and master craftsmen, multiple pew ownership became a passion. In the early national period it was not uncommon for members of the merchant elite to own more than one pew. A privileged coterie of such men owned clusters of pews in the town's most prestigious meetinghouses. These purchases solidified business partnerships and sealed family relationships. By the early 1830s, men such as Nicholas Brown and Josiah Chapin raised the art of multiple pew ownership to new heights. They owned ranks of pews and were poised to exert extensive personal control within the denominations they funded. Unlike the prevailing pattern evident before the revival, single entrepreneurs emerged as the benefactors of individual congregations and denominations.

By standing as patrons of their respective churches—Nicholas Brown among the Baptists, Josiah Chapin among the Congregationalists, Hezekiah Anthony among the Methodists—those who had amassed large numbers of pews could also display their commitment to benevolence. These men and their extended families could not possibly have filled all of the seats in the pews they purchased. Although it is difficult to determine with precision, it is quite likely that holders of multiple pews allowed others to sit in the spaces they did not occupy. Moreover, as the 1832 pew plat of First Baptist Church makes clear, Nicholas Brown purchased a large number of pews that did not sit in prime locations, suggesting that he bid on these pews since they were less likely to be attractive to prospective buyers. His willingness to buy these relatively undesirable seats, and to pay taxes on them, represented another kind of contribution to the welfare of the church. By purchasing multiple pews, bourgeois Protestants could thus join displays of financial acumen with great generosity, personal self-interest with public spirit, individual ambition with Christian charity. It was a combination that many refined pewholders found irresistible, for it reconciled some of the deepest contradictions within their religious culture.

Elite merchants and manufacturers such as Nicholas Brown and Josiah Chapin held the most exalted places among the ranks of Providence pewholders. During the 1832 auction of seats at First Baptist Church, Nicholas Brown collected nineteen pews worth more than two thousand dollars, making him the most powerful member of the First Baptist Society. Because he never joined the church, however, Brown appears not to have meddled

---

[29] Evidence on pewholding patterns is derived from Table 15 and its sources.

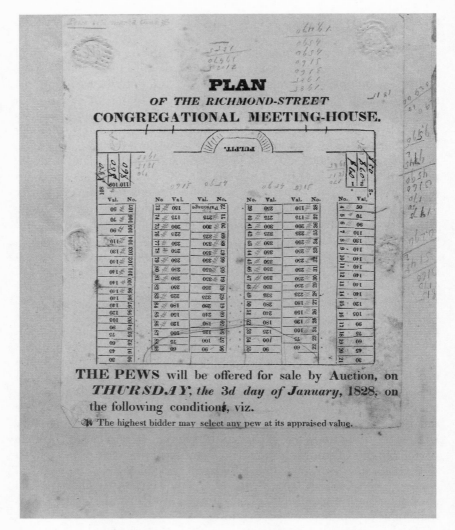

This pew plan emphasizes the degree to which pewholding might be considered an essentially financial transaction. Note that the highest bidder was eligible to purchase any pew. Church membership was not a requirement for prospective bidders. Courtesy of The Rhode Island Historical Society, RHi (×3) 8973.

directly in the affairs of the communicants. Josiah Chapin, like Brown, dominated the list of pewholders in his meetinghouse. At the 1835 auction of High Street Congregational seats, the cotton broker purchased eighteen pews assessed at nearly $3,900. Virtually unchallenged as the society's leading figure, Chapin owned three times as many pews as James Eames, whose collection of six pews placed him second among the owners. Perhaps even more impressive, Chapin's total of eighteen seats represented 38 percent of all the pews sold outright in the meetinghouse. Elected the first deacon of the congregation, Chapin did not think it an inappropriate display of pride to have his name entered at the head of the ledger of original members.

The ambition to seize religious property extended beyond the merchant and manufacturing elite. Aside from Nicholas Brown, eleven other Baptists owned more than one seat. At High Street Congregational, four men jointly held more than half of all the seats purchased. Among the Unitarians at Westminster Congregational, thirteen men owned at least two places. Even among the Methodists, the Power Street Society recorded eleven members taxed on two or more pews. The ownership of multiple pews, once restricted to only the wealthiest of citizens, came increasingly to distinguish respectable members of Providence society. Master craftsmen, particularly, could be counted among those not satisfied with a single seat. Rather than owning a single pew, or even sharing the costs of a place, as had been prevalent during the early national period, these artisans wanted greater individual recognition.

If piety were measured as a function of pew property, then the tin-plate worker James Eames could claim title as the most devout of Providence artisans. In 1835 he owned six pews valued at $1,455 at High Street Congregational Church. Moreover, in joining this particular church, Eames strategically located himself among some of Providence's rising businessmen. An association with Josiah Chapin could certainly have given Eames more business contacts. Amos C. Barstow, a future mayor of Providence and a successful stove dealer, also committed himself to the church the same day Eames did. The relationship between their two families deepened when Eames's daughter Emeline married Barstow in the same year both joined the church. By purchasing seats in the High Street Church, Eames showed a keen sensitivity to shifts of power in the Providence business community as well as a dedication to Congregationalism. Unitarian and Methodist artisans joined Eames in their quest for religious property. At Westminster Congregational Church, Nathaniel F. Potter, a mason, acquired two pews which carried a total valuation of $670. In the same meetinghouse, tallow-chandler Henry L. Kendall picked two places totaling a hefty $750 assess-

Table 16. Wealth distribution among bourgeois pewholders in select congregations

Tax value in dollars[a]	First Baptist Church		Power Street Methodist Church		High Street Congregational Church		Westminster Congregational Church	
	N	%	N	%	N	%	N	%
501+	3	3.7	4	7.7	—		—	
101–500	21	25.9	13	25.0	4	10.8	9	9.9
51–100	10	12.3	4	7.7	4	10.8	8	8.3
41–50	5	6.1	2	3.8	2	5.4	1	1.0
31–40	4	4.9	2	3.8	2	5.4	10	10.4
21–30	3	3.7	3	5.7	2	5.4	4	4.1
11–20	7	8.6	5	9.6	2	5.4	13	13.5
0–10	5	6.1	8	15.3	5	13.5	20	21.0
TOTAL LISTED	58	71.3	41	78.8	21	56.7	64	67.7
Pewholders not listed	23	28.4	11	21.1	16	43.2	31	32.2

Sources: Providence Town Tax List for 1832; also sources noted in Table 15.
[a] Total tax valuation, both real and personal, as listed in the Providence Town Tax List for 1832, RIHS.

ment. Among the multiple pew owners at Power Street Methodist Church, master craftsmen also held their own. Robert G. Corey, a baker, and Phillip H. Durfee, a house carpenter, each purchased two seats with a combined valuation of better than $300. The desire of some craftsmen to accumulate religious property spanned theological distinctions.

The prevalence of multiple pewholding in the bourgeois churches suggests the affluence of the members. Whether Baptist or Congregationalist, Methodist or Unitarian, the new pew owners claimed an impressive level of prosperity. Indeed, an exploration of pewholders in the 1832 city tax list exposes hefty numbers of them who were assessed for more than fifty-one dollars of real and personal property (see Table 16). Merchants and grocers headed the lists of those who bought pews in these churches (see Table 17). Compared to those who purchased pews in the revival era, or even in the early national period, pewholders in the bourgeois churches were, on the whole, a more consistently wealthy group. By 1832, even the communicants of First Baptist Church and Beneficent Congregational Church, the churches that gathered the most revival converts in 1820, attained a significant degree of affluence (see Tables 18 and 19). Henry Trumbull, a member of Beneficent Congregational Church, noticed that the poor seemed to have been culled from the ranks of respectable churchgoers. In his 1829 address to the Brothers Charitable Society, he called for greater attentiveness to the needs of the lowly. He chided his fellow communicants,

Table 17. Occupations of bourgeois pewholders

Occupation	Number of pewholders
First Baptist Church, 1832	
Merchants	10
Grocers	8
House carpenters	3
Jewelers	3
Mariners	3
Masons	3
Attorneys	2
Cashiers	2
Glaziers	2
Manufacturers	2
Widows	2
Other[a]	18
Occupations unknown	23
TOTAL	81
Power Street Methodist Church, 1833	
Merchants	8
Mariners	8
Grocers	7
House carpenters	5
Masons	2
Bakers	2
Other[b]	13
Occupation unknown	7
TOTAL	52
High Street Congregational Church, 1835	
Merchants	5
Butchers	3
Dry goods	2
Other[c]	11
Occupation unknown	13
TOTAL	37
Westminster Congregational Church, 1832	
Merchants	12
Dry goods/grocers	6
Accountants	3
Attorneys	3
Hat stores	3
Manufacturers	3

Table 17. *Continued*

Occupation	Number of pewholders
Westminster Congregational Church, 1832	
Brokers	2
Cashiers	2
Clerks	2
Druggists	2
Hardwares	2
Innkeepers	2
Jewelers	2
Mariners	2
Physicians	2
Preceptors	2
Other[d]	14
Occupation unknown	30
TOTAL	95

Sources: Data on pewholders taken from materials listed for Table 15; Occupational data from the *Providence Directory*, 1832.

[a] One each of the following: agent, baker, blacksmith, calenderer, cooper and founder, hat store owner, judge, lumber and coal, machine shop, publisher, sail maker, ship joiner, surveyor, tailor, tailoress, tanner, watchmaker, yeoman.

[b] Agent, blacksmith, boardinghouse owner, clerk, druggist, manufacturer, painter, plumber, sail maker, shoemaker, steamboat captain, tailor, yeoman.

[c] House carpenter, laborer, mariner, painter, stove dealer, tailor, temperance store owner, tin plate worker, tobacconist, wheelwright, woodenware maker.

[d] Shoe store owner, agent, bookbinder, chaise harness maker, house carpenter, marshall, mason, pewterer, salt store owner, sign painter, tallow chandler, treasurer, watchmaker, yeoman.

some of whom had "no conception that whilst they are feasting for joy, there are others afflicted in penury."[30] That Trumbull felt it necessary to remind his fellow church members about the reality of poverty suggests that respectable communicants no longer brushed up against the poor as they had in the late eighteenth century.

The trade in pews also accentuated the profoundly gendered features of bourgeois religious culture. As space in meetinghouses became calibrated

---

[30] Henry Trumbull, *Address on the Importance of Charity* (Providence, 1829), 16. Stuart M. Blumin, in *The Emergence of the Middle Class,* also observes that church records in Philadelphia point toward a trend in which Presbyterian congregations sorted themselves out along class lines. Church membership, Blumin concludes, not only was determined by factors such as neighborhood, doctrinal disputes, or the popularity of individual ministers but "was also (and increasingly) shaped by class" (221).

Table 18. Wealth distribution among bourgeois church members in select congregations

Tax value in dollars[a]	First Baptist Church, 1832		Beneficent Congregational Church, 1832	
	N	%	N	%
501+	0		1	1
101–500	5	5.6	8	8
51–100	3	3.3	8	8
41–50	5	5.6	5	5
31–40	1	1.1	2	2
21–30	8	8.9	5	5
11–20	7	7.8	15	15
0–10	7	7.8	15	15
TOTAL LISTED	36	40.4	59	59
Church members not listed	53	59.5	41	41

Sources: Providence Town Tax List for 1832; *A List of Members of the First Baptist Church in Providence, with biographical sketches of the Pastors* (Providence, 1832), 33–43; *The Annual Report of the Beneficent Congregational Church, Providence, R.I., Presented, November, 1832, to which is added, the Articles of Faith, and Covenant, and a list of the Officers and Members* (Providence, 1832), 54–60.
[a] Total tax valuation, both real and personal, as listed in the Providence Town Tax List for 1832, RIHS.

increasingly in terms of the market values, women became ever more marginalized in the churches where they worshipped. Simultaneously, the world of bourgeois religion offered men advantages tied to their prowess in the market economy. Some idea of the gendered quality of this religious experience can be seen through an analysis of two ordinary Providence communicants who have left us extraordinary records of their spiritual lives. We have already met Stephen S. Wardwell, the young Sunday school teacher who ventured to Killingly, Connecticut, in the early 1820s. A cashier and later a director of Providence's Eagle Bank, Wardwell served as organist for Beneficent Congregational Church and appears to have been ubiquitous in the arena of religious reform. We have also met Emeline Eames, who became Emeline Barstow when she married Amos Barstow of High Street Congregational Church in 1834. As the wife of the mayor of Providence, she traveled within the ranks of the town's political leaders and even met Andrew Jackson on a trip to Washington, D.C. Although both Wardwell and Emeline Barstow moved in the circles of West Side Congregationalism, the

Table 19. Occupations of church members at First Baptist Church and Beneficent Congregational Church, 1832

Occupation	Number of church members
First Baptist church members	
Grocers/dry goods	8
Tailors	6
Jewelers	3
Meal dealers	3
Accountants	2
Bakers	2
Masons	2
Shoemakers	2
Other[a]	30
Occupations unknown	23
TOTAL	81
Beneficent Congregational church members	
Grocers/dry goods	13
Cashiers	5
Bakers	4
House carpenters	4
Merchants	3
Printers	3
Accountants	2
Cabinetmakers	2
Jewelers	2
Painters	2
Physicians	2
Shoe store owner	2
Shoemakers	2
Tailors	2
Other[b]	29
Occupations unknown	23
TOTAL	100

Sources: See Table 18 and the *Providence Directory*, 1832.

[a] One each of the following: accountant, and com. store owner, blacksmith, boardinghouse owner, cashier, city sergeant, confectionery store owner, cooper, cooper and founder, glazier, hairdresser, hat colorer, hatter, house carpenter, laborer, lumber and coal dealer, machinist, mariner, merchant, president of Brown University, printer, professor, pump and block maker, sail maker, shoe store owner, steamboat captain, surveyor, tanner, tax collector, umbrella maker, watchmaker.

[b] Barber, block maker, bookstore owner, butcher, caulker, chair maker, clerk, dyer, glazier, hardware store owner, hat store owner, insurance secretary, justice of the peace, manufacturer, mason, merchant tailor, messenger, saddler, sexton, silversmith, stonecutter, tanner and currier, teamster, temperance grocer, tin plate worker, turner, upholsterer, watchman, wool and leather goods dealer.

documents they left speak to the profound differences that separated the religious experiences of women and men.

In terms of sheer volume and scope, Stephen Wardwell's massive diary overshadows the slim journal and commonplace books of Emeline Barstow. Wardwell began his diary shortly after his conversion experience in 1820 and kept it for nearly twenty years, leaving fully seventeen volumes of work.[31] Each volume, painstakingly organized and lined with a cashier's steady hand, is a carefully crafted production. In them he recorded events both large and small, public and private. Thus the death of a family cat in 1824 shares space with an elaborate description of Charles Finney's revival in Providence in the summer of 1831. But what is most striking about these volumes, aside from their immaculate script and impressive size, is how compulsively they were organized and kept. In nearly twenty years of writing, there is hardly a day skipped, hardly a sermon text ignored, hardly a community event overlooked. The act of keeping a diary of such size must have been, in itself, an act of ambition, iron will, and enormous self-discipline. Emeline Barstow, on the other hand, has left us two slender volumes, filled largely with poetry. Some of these efforts she composed herself and others were evidently copied after the manner of a commonplace book. In one of the volumes she included a brief journal, spanning the years from 1836 to 1839. Unlike Wardwell's compulsive creation, Barstow's journal is not as carefully linked to chronology. She wrote some extensive entries and also skipped weeks and even months at a stretch before she wrote again, sometimes punctuating these lapses in regularity with doses of self-deprecation and laments about poor health. Also included in her papers are some notes and letters written by her husband, Amos C. Barstow. Indeed, Emeline's papers are included as part of her husband's collection and do not have an archival existence distinct from his.[32] If Stephen Wardwell's entries are prodigious, precise, and self-possessed, Emeline Barstow's writings are fragmentary, ethereal, and self-effacing.

Both journals are self-consciously chronicles of spiritual journey and struggle. In 1836, at the age of twenty-three, Barstow determined it her duty to God to record her feelings as a way to chart her growth in grace. "My feelings are ever open to the inspection of the Omniscient God," she wrote on August 28, "If recorded they may though past be open to my own inspection." On May 14, 1837, after failing to write for three months, she reaffirmed her mission. "I cannot describe the feelings of my heart this

---

[31] Stephen S. Wardwell diaries, Beneficent Congregational Church, Providence. All citations that appear in the text can be found here.

[32] Emeline Barstow's papers and documents are included in the collection of Amos C. Barstow, RIHS. All citations that appear in the text can be found here.

morning in viewing the blank pages of this book," she wrote, "in which I have from a deep sense of duty solemnly promised to keep a faithful record of the feelings of my heart." Although she had joined the High Street Congregational Church in 1834, Emeline continued to struggle for a sense of certainty that she numbered among the elect. She set May 24, 1838, aside as a day of private fasting and prayer because she "felt I must do something to obtain a more lively assurance of my adoption into the family of Christ." For Emeline Barstow faith was a matter of feeling. Faithfully recording and examining those feelings was the key to understanding her own spiritual state.

Stephen Wardwell also sought to comprehend the state of his soul, but he took a different approach. "I have procured this book," he wrote near the opening of his first volume, "to keep a memorandum or journal of whatsoever I may think of importance to note down, such as the texts of sermons that I may hear preached, etc. and may I be directed in the right way of truth, and be enabled with the assistance and in the strength of Almighty God, to do what I may do, and write what I may write in his fear and in his service."[33] Whereas the texts that interested Emeline Barstow were the "feelings" of her own soul, the texts that absorbed Stephen Wardwell's attentions were the Biblical passages that he heard expounded upon in church. Whereas Emeline Barstow searched for assurance of salvation within herself, Stephen Wardwell charted his spiritual progress in deeds of service performed in the community at large. Whereas Emeline Barstow sought "adoption into the family of Christ," Stephen Wardwell rooted his Christian identity in the public world of civic reform and religious activism. But the very act of charting his public deeds could also imperil the humility that Wardwell claimed was essential to the Christian life. On January 1, 1822, he prayed, "Grant O Lord that in writing this volume I may feel humble before thee and be kept from pride." Over the years, Stephen Wardwell struggled to balance the satisfaction he took in his religious work with the appropriate measure of humility. As he glanced over his pages, he could take solace in the number of sermons he had heard, the number of tracts he had distributed, and the causes of religious reform he had championed. At the same time, the very prosperity of his efforts could give rise to feelings of pride—sentiments that throughout his life he sought to hold at bay.

Given his concern for a life informed by benevolent action, the character of Stephen Wardwell's diary is relentlessly public. While he does mention important personal events, such as his marriage in 1823, he typically reports church services, hymns, and sermon texts. The account of his marriage, for

---

[33] Wardwell diaries, September 1820.

instance, takes only a few sentences, while an 1825 "Skeleton of a Sermon" on II Corinthians 8:9 spans several pages. On January 1, 1833, he found space to provide an inventory of all the religious activities in which he had participated during the previous year: 162 sermons, 90 preparatory conferences, 25 prayer meetings, 40 teachers' meetings, 26 meetings of religious and benevolent societies, and 54 "other" religious meetings, yielding a grand total of 397 meetings for a single year, or more than one per day—a pace that proved fairly typical for his active career. And, of course, there was always his music. As church organist, Wardwell noted with only slightly restrained glee the purchase of a new piano forte in 1824 and, in 1825, the arrival of a fine new organ from Boston. "It is an excellent instrument," he wrote, "and has a fine tone."[34] He played it for the first time in public worship on July 10, 1825. Through his diary, Stephen Wardwell could observe himself as an authentically pious man, tallying his religious deeds and performances with the sharp eye of a banker.

The compass of Stephen Wardwell's public activities extended well beyond the pew he owned in Beneficent Congregational Church. On January 17, 1825, he recorded the founding meeting of the Providence Religious Tract Society and could not resist mentioning that he "drew up a Constitution" that the group voted to adopt. In August, 1831, he took careful note of Charles G. Finney's activities in Providence. Three years later he marked his growing interest in the emerging abolitionist movement. On August 1, 1834, he wrote that "this day all the slaves in the British West India Islands have become free. When shall it be said that American Slavery is at an end. Hasten the time O Lord."[35] Not surprisingly, Stephen Wardwell was a lifelong proponent of public observance of the Sabbath. The Sabbath was a means of providing a kind of divine order over the life of the city in which he lived, and it was clear to him that God meant to enforce it. On May 1, 1825, he recorded what he considered to be "a very solemn dispensation of divine Providence." Five young "lads" had been out in a boat, relaxing and enjoying themselves on Sunday instead of attending religious services. Four of the young boys had drowned, among them two sons of another Providence banker. "This is a solemn warning," Wardwell concluded, "to parents to restrain their children; & to children to abstain from indulging themselves in breaking the Lords Day." From Stephen Wardwell's point of view, God clearly stood in awful judgment over the acts of men.

In some respects, the journal and poetry of Emeline Barstow resonate

---

[34] Ibid., June 30, 1825.
[35] The Providence abolitionist movement is treated by Gilkeson, *Middle-Class Providence*, esp. 35–54.

with the religious sensibility described by Stephen Wardwell. To be sure, her writings provide glimpses of her connection to aspects of religious reform and public life. Before her marriage she had written a short selection titled "The Christian Religion" that might have served as her own personal creed. "How unlike all others is the religion of Christ," it began. "It is a religion which requires us to do unto others as we would have them do unto us." For her, the Christian faith served to "prompt us to all benevolent acts, that render us happy and useful in life." These were words with which Stephen Wardwell could have agreed. Although she did not write about it (and the omission is revealing), we also know that she served, at least briefly, as a tract distributor for the Providence Religious Tract Society, the group for which Wardwell had written a constitution. There is also, preserved with her papers, a list of contributors to the High Street Female Charitable Society "kept by Mrs. A. C. Barstow for February to October, 1835." During the 1830s Emeline Barstow also became increasingly interested in the abolitionist movement. On July 4, 1836, she took time in her journal to enter, in one of its longest entries, a condemnation of slavery. "This is nominally a free and happy land; but o! the thraldom not only of sin, and satan, but a portion of this free and happy people hold in bondage, servile bondage more than two millions of their fellow men. O! I blush for my country." Emeline Barstow's writings percolate with knowledge of the public world in which men like Stephen Wardwell and her husband, Amos, circulated.

But it is not the world of public benevolence that organizes Emeline Barstow's religious experience. In contrast to Stephen Wardwell's diary, Emeline Barstow's journal and poetry possess a striking measure of interiority. Rather than recording her attendance at worship, Barstow's journal more frequently notes those occasions when she was not able to attend church. It is her confinement, not her involvement in public affairs, that runs like a thread through her journal. On September 7, 1837, she wrote, "It is now more than three years since I enjoyed health and have been a stranger to it and the comfort it bears on its wing." Her ill health often prevented her from joining in public worship, but she does not reveal the specific source of her complaints. Since her first child, Sarah Sophie, did not arrive until 1839, it is unlikely that her trials sprang from the rigors of raising a young family.[36] It might be more revealing that she dates her illness to the year of her marriage. As Barbara Epstein has observed, nineteenth-century Victorian wives often suffered from a range of mysterious maladies that were linked to "the loss of self that domestic dependence

---

[36] Evidence from the 1850 federal census shows that Emeline and Amos Barstow presided over a household of seven children and two Irish servant girls. The oldest child, Sarah Sophie, was eleven years old in 1850.

brought with it."[37] While Emeline's marriage to Amos seems, from the fragments of evidence that have survived, to have been warm and affectionate, we cannot know with certainty how difficult those first years with him may have been. What is visible here, however, is a young woman in profound need of spiritual assurance. While Stephen Wardwell's outward conduct provided him with some measure of knowledge about God's grace, Emeline Barstow struggled with deeper demons. On January 8, 1837, she confided that "I sometimes feel I have a nearness of access to God, and that I do love him supremely," yet she acknowledged that "when I recollect the deceitfulness of the human heart, every evidence that I may have had of living in favor with God vanishes like the morning cloud and early dew." Try as she might, she could not be certain of God's favor.

Emeline Barstow's doubts followed her into the night. Perhaps the most arresting bit of writing in her papers is an episode titled simply "A dream." In this elaborate account, she reported that she walked through the streets of a city. "The heavens were shrouded with blackness and the streets through which I passed were literally filled with men," she said, "some of whom were dead, wounded or dying, while others were set in hostile array every man against his brother each seeming intent on the destruction of the other." The men wielded strange, and oddly domestic, weaponry. "Some were making use of broken glass and china to hurl at each other," she recalled, "altogether producing a scene of horror and confusion as in my wakeful hours I could have formed no just conception of." In her dream, she hurried to reach her home, "fearing lest I might become a victim in this contest of carnage and blood." Her arrival home brought not relief but even greater consternation. The "Thing of Terrors," she wrote, "had taken captive one beloved object of my heart's affections and that no less a one than her who gave me birth and had cradled and nourished me in infancy, restrained my waywardness in childhood and youth and been friend, guide, and counsellor of riper years." Gripped by terror, she awoke.

The interpretation Emeline Barstow gave of her dream was as unique as the dream itself. Taking an allegorical approach to her Dante-like fantasy, she reasoned that "if men do not literally 'bite and devour each other,' they do that which is in many respects worse. They bite with the tongue of slander, and take away that good name which we are told by the wise man is

---

[37] Barbara Leslie Epstein, *The Politics of Domesticity: Women, Evangelism, and Temperance in Nineteenth-Century America* (Middletown, Conn., 1986), 85–86. Like other young New England women, Emeline Barstow may have suffered from tuberculosis. Her writings bear some resemblance to the "narratives of illness" produced by these women. On these points see Sheila M. Rothman, *Living in the Shadow of Death: Tuberculosis and the Social Experience of Illness in American History* (Baltimore, 1995), 77–127.

rather to be chosen than great riches." The message of the dream, for her, was a warning to avoid gossip and the evils of the tongue, for these evils tear apart the social fabric just as surely as does rioting in the streets. "And how very little," she concluded, "is thought upon those things which are pure, lovely, and of good report among men." Viewed from one perspective, the lesson Emeline Barstow drew from her nightmare touched on the wider bourgeois concern with the consolidation of social order. Perhaps in her dreams she had fought her own version of the real battle that had been fought in the streets of Providence in 1831. But her lesson was also an ad-monition to herself, for she had already chastised herself for partaking in "vain and frivolous conversation. The Lord has frequently checked me in my mad career by laying his hand on me in sickness." The illnesses that had confined her, then, she interpreted as divine judgment for her sins. Even in her dreams Emeline Barstow could not find peace.

The introspective Emeline Barstow and the energetic Stephen Wardwell shared much that this brief analysis has glossed over. Both of them were Congregationalists. Both proved themselves intensely devoted to their fam-ilies and children. Both of them dabbled in sentimental poetry. Both of them knew that this earthly realm was "transitory" and looked for salvation to a world beyond. Both of them wrote about death and heaven, both lived in comfortable circumstances, and both saw the threat that material pros-perity posed to the life of the spirit. Emeline Barstow lamented that she dis-covered in herself "so much that savours of a worldly spirit, so much pride, and selfishness, and so much in every form that opposeth itself to God."[38] Stephen Wardwell, too, struggled with the blessings of his own prosperity. After hearing Charles Finney preach, he began thinking "whether it is my duty to sell my Real Estate & give it to promote the cause of Christ or not." During the same revival, he cried, "O may the Lord cut down the hearts of rich men that they may be humbled in the dust and cry out for mercy."[39] Both Barstow and Wardwell recognized that the attractions of this world distracted Christians from the true goal of salvation.

For all that they agreed upon, the journals and religious outlooks of Stephen Wardwell and Emeline Barstow are suggestive of the ways in which gender shaped bourgeois religious culture. In emphasizing the world of public order and social reform, bourgeois religious culture afforded men like Stephen Wardwell ample opportunity to exercise their spiritual gifts. Wardwell's diary bears rich testimony to the variety of his roles in the community—organist, Sunday school leader, Sabbath advocate, tract

[38] Emeline Barstow diaries, June 18, 1837, RIHS.
[39] Wardwell diaries, August 22 and 28, 1831.

distributor, budding abolitionist. The experience of Emeline Barstow suggests that while this public world was increasingly open to men, women could be folded inward upon themselves. While Wardwell's religious experiences launched him into roles of public power and prestige, Barstow's primed her doubts and plagued her dreams. This does not mean that bourgeois women retreated from the world of religious reform. But Emeline Barstow's and Stephen Wardwell's experiences reveal that bourgeois religious culture, in its emphasis on pews and property, in its zeal for public reform and civic order, and with its connections to the world of the market, contained a profoundly masculine component.

The distance that separated evangelical women and men also appeared in the arena of reform. While turbulent debate over the nature of Christ, the conditions for salvation, and the mystery of the Trinity had punctuated the revival era, these concerns faded during the 1830s. As students of antebellum religion have observed, respectable Protestants had begun to move toward the cultivation of "moral character" rather than strict doctrinal conformity as the true measure of the life of faith. These same Protestants edged, too in the direction of a more "rational" religion, shorn of its earlier adherence to a transcendent and mysterious God.[40] These shifts in Protestant culture toward a religion of character and rationality fit remarkably well with notions of masculine identity prevalent in the era. As Karen Halttunen has written, "character formation was the nineteenth-century version of the Protestant work ethic." Advice books taught young men that through their own efforts and the cultivation of character, they could rise in the new world of "self-made" men.[41] And to the degree that bourgeois Protestants cast themselves as defenders of the civic order, they simultaneously cast their religious culture in manly terms. Recall that even Francis Wayland had identified Nicholas Brown's "manly and venerable" form as one especially suited to the performance of benevolent acts. If Nicholas Brown stood as the apotheosis of bourgeois Protestantism, it was because he evinced the particular kind of Christian manhood that Francis Wayland so lavishly praised.

Even within the home—a domain that genteel Protestants in antebellum America generally conceded to the authority of females—men seemed determined to shore up their influence. The formation in 1831 of the

---

[40] See here especially James Turner, *Without God, Without Creed: The Origins of Unbelief in America* (Baltimore, 1985), 73–113; Richard Rabinowitz, *The Spiritual Self in Everyday Life: The Transformation of Personal Religious Experience in Nineteenth-Century New England* (Boston, 1989), 79–151.
[41] Halttunen, *Confidence Men and Painted Women*, 28, 29; see also Kasson, *Rudeness and Civility*, 92–111.

Providence Society for the Encouragement of Faithful Domestic Servants embodied a surprisingly bold reassertion of manly influence at the domestic hearth. Led by Samuel W. Bridgham, the first mayor of Providence, and Nathan Crocker, the Episcopal minister of St. John's Cathedral, the group set itself the task of regulating more closely the character and governance of household servants by creating a registration service to monitor them. Revealing the bourgeois passion for order, the society began its first annual report with the claim that "the comfort of house-keeping depends upon the orderly arrangement of the household."[42] For civic leaders such as Bridgham, the correspondence between a comfortable and orderly home and a comfortable and orderly city must have been self-evident.

According to members of the society (all of them men), housekeepers had failed utterly as employers of domestic servants. Their first annual report amounted to an assault on what they considered to be the shortcomings of housekeepers as managers of workers. Housekeepers had not investigated sufficiently the character of those they employed, they were too indulgent, they were fickle and unpredictable, and they allowed "service by the day" rather than hiring servants for lengthy contracts. Given the wholesale condemnation of housekeepers outlined in this document, it is little wonder that not a single woman appeared on the society's roster of members. According to the society, women were the problem. Yet, the men, in tones that strain credulity, professed astonishment that women refused to cooperate with their efforts to "reform" the home. "The Managers also regret," the annual report chided, "that the ladies, who are generally so active in all benevolent institutions, should not have taken a more active part in this."[43] The men concluded their remarks by appealing to housekeepers for support of their society, but they did so in language that could hardly have rallied members. "It is therefore for the housekeepers to determine," they warned, "whether they will continue to submit to evils which throw into confusion and disorder the whole household concerns, or by exertion end them."[44] That the society produced only one annual report may suggest the extent of support that it received from Providence women.

When Providence women did enter directly the debate about the treatment of servants, they did so on their own terms. In 1838, a group of women, Frances McDougall and Catherine Williams among them, brought to the public *The Memoirs of Elleanor Eldridge*, a story detailing the case of a black woman who had been swindled out of her home by unscrupulous

---

[42] *First Annual Report of the Providence Society for the Encouragement of Faithful Domestic Servants* (Providence, 1832), 3.
[43] Ibid., 9.
[44] Ibid., 10.

white men.[45] Although Elleanor Eldridge was a free woman, the narrative
shared much with the literary genre of the slave narrative, including a har-
rowing account of how her paternal grandfather had been captured in
Africa, enslaved, and brought to America. Anonymously written, the document nonetheless included testimonials from a number of women who had
employed Elleanor, all testifying to the veracity of the story. In weaving her
tale, the author (or perhaps authors, since several women contributed
testimonials) cast Elleanor as a woman of industry, integrity, thrift, and
childlike innocence. She was also a woman of deep faith, who "subscribes
for papers which she cannot read, in order to promote the circulation of
truth, whether moral or religious."[46] In condescending tones, the authors
claimed that the facts of Elleanor's life would provide an example of "industry and untiring perseverance" for the "colored population" of the city.[47]

The *Memoirs*, in over one hundred pages of text, presented the following
dilemma. After some thirty years of labor, working variously as a dairymaid,
paperhanger, whitewasher, and domestic, Elleanor Eldridge had been able
to purchase a sizable amount of property, including a lot in Providence with
a house. Having no husband or children, Elleanor Eldridge's accomplishment derived from her own prodigious efforts. In the cause of loyal service,
however, she was called away, during which time she became ill and rumors
of her death began to circulate in town, taking on increasing credibility with
each passing week. Believing that she had died, her creditors attached her
property, put it up for auction, and sold it. Elleanor thus returned to Providence to find herself deprived of her home. She was "by a single stroke of
the hammer, deprived of the fruits of all her honest and severe labors."[48]
The white women who rallied to help her determined to raise the funds
necessary for her to reclaim her property.

Corrupt men were to blame for this brazen injustice—the *Memoirs* left no
doubt about that. Elleanor's status as a colored woman put her doubly at
risk. "No man," the narrative maintained, "ever would have been treated so;
and if a white woman had been the subject of such wrongs, the whole
town—nay, the whole country, would have been indignant." It also implicated sleazy lawyers as responsible for her plight and for the legal technicalities she struggled against to reclaim her property. "This poor woman,"
the *Memoirs* cried, "ignorant of the technicalities and sinuosities of the law,
reposed in the vain confidence, that others would be guided by the sense of

[45] *Memoirs of Elleanor Eldridge* (Providence, 1838). On McDougall's key role in publishing this
work, see Sidney Rider, *Rhode Island Tracts, No. 11* (Providence, 1880), 35.
[46] *Memoirs of Elleanor Eldridge*, 92.
[47] Ibid., preface.
[48] Ibid., 85.

justice, that she had imbibed herself; nor dreamed but that law and justice would go hand in hand." Although the narrative had conceded, early in its pages, that domestic servants needed more attention to their "moral health," it is clear that it cast men, rather than women, as the abusers of domestics. At the conclusion of the story, an anonymous "Lady of Providence" contributed a poem, "Hard Fate of Poor Ellen," that asked, "Where is the man, could be so base— / Against the helpless and forlorn? / Let him, forever, hide his face! / If he would shun *deserved scorn*."[49] The female supporters of Elleanor Eldridge clearly held Providence men, and especially their legal system, accountable for her hard times.

In describing Elleanor Eldridge as "our heroine," the ladies of Providence selected a woman who stood at odds with the picture of orderly family life. Although the author (or authors) of the *Memoirs* spiced it with an early tale of girlish romance, it is clear that Elleanor Eldridge was celebrated as an independent entrepreneur. She also chose not to marry. "When questioned on the subject," the narrative reported, "she says that she has determined to profit by the advice of her aunt, who told her never to marry, because it involved such *a waste of time*, for said she, 'while my mistress was courting and marrying, I knit five pairs of stockings.' "[50] Throughout the narrative there is, aside from its occasional condescension, also a tinge of admiration for the property and independence that Elleanor Eldridge had been able to attain. In taking on her cause as their own, some white women in Providence celebrated a woman whose life called into question the very domesticity they were pledged to uphold.

Providence women did not confine their critiques of the economic order to the treatment of black domestics. In 1837 the elite women of First Congregational Church led a movement that accused Providence entrepreneurs of immoral behavior in managing their seamstresses and garment workers. In surveying conditions in the sweating trades they argued that "there is no difficulty in finding employment for any class of workers, if they will work for nothing, or work for the interest of their employers, and starve themselves." They deplored, too, the nefarious "system of underbidding," particularly damaging to women struggling for decent employment. Under this arrangement merchant tailors attempted to squeeze out a few more pennies of profit by giving work to those who would accept the least amount of pay. The church women considered such profits to be excessive—providing the employers six times what they paid their seamstresses for each

[49] Ibid., 91, 110, 27, 108.
[50] Ibid., 100.

garment produced.[51] During the depression of 1837, the plight of these seamstresses prompted their more affluent sisters to create the Providence Employment Society. The women who created this group ventured into the male world of the marketplace by establishing themselves as a "model employer" for seamstresses. "The business that the Society established," according to Susan Porter Benson, "sought to upgrade rather than to degrade the seamstresses' skills, paid higher wages than the commercial labor market, raised the rates in times of inflation and refused to cut them in depression, and avoided competitive practices that the board considered illegitimate—all the while keeping the operation in the black through clever management."[52] Like the women of the Providence Female Tract Society in earlier years, the women of the Providence Employment Society challenged the notion that entrepreneurs conducted their pursuits in a moral and Christian manner.

But civic and religious leaders worried more about the pernicious effects of intemperance than they did about the plight of needleworkers. In 1831, Francis Wayland explained the heartache that alcohol could bring home and community. Before members of the Providence Association for the Promotion of Temperance, he evoked images that would become archetypal in the cause. There could be no doubt, he proclaimed, that the "common tippling shop" overturned the "cup of domestic happiness." Wayland then placed scenes of horror from the streets beside "all the delights of an innocent and lovely fireside."[53] The parade of destitute men, struggling widows, and crying orphans that crowded other temperance literature suggests that respectable citizens earnestly fretted over the crumbling of family life. Wayland also drew attention to the wider civic polity by offering an interpretation of the race riot of 1831. He presented a frightening catalogue of the upheaval that would have been still fresh in his listeners' minds. He recalled for them the work of "a lawless and infuriate mob," of "the crash of falling habitations," of "the sharp peal of musquetry," and finally, "the long drawn sigh and gurgling death groan" of the victims. According to the Wayland, the root cause of all of this suffering was clear: "It was all the deed of RUM."[54] Here was a revealing reduction of a complex event. By portraying drink

---

[51] *Report and Proposal to the Public on the Subject of Female Wages, by a Committee of the Female Benevolent Society, Providence, March 6, 1837*, 4, 5–6.

[52] Susan Porter Benson, "Business Heads and Sympathizing Hearts: The Women of the Providence Employment Society, 1837–1858," *Journal of Social History* 12 (1978): 303.

[53] Francis Wayland, *An Address Delivered Before the Providence Association for the Promotion of Temperance, October 20, 1831* (Providence, 1831), 7.

[54] Ibid., 10–11.

as the sole basis of the disturbance, he obscured the reality of racism and allowed sober citizens to wash their hands of any responsibility for civic disorder.

As they cast themselves as defenders of hearth and home, temperance advocates sometimes described the temptations of drink in unmistakably feminine terms. In 1844 the Congregationalist minister Thomas T. Waterman presented a shocking portrait that cast the evils of intemperance in the service of a wider diatribe against overconsumption. Speaking before the Rhode-Island State Temperance Society, he reminded his listeners that the "tendency of the age to self-indulgence and consequent effeminacy is proverbial." In the course of his republican tirade he blasted those who feasted upon sumptuous meals, crying out that "the great ruling passion seems to be what shall we eat, and what shall we drink!" The result of giving in to these desires, warned Waterman, would be disastrous. As was the case with "luxurious France," he argued, some Americans would make "the cook their priest, the table their altar, and meat and wine their God!"[55] If individuals failed to curb their appetites, then society would be doomed to chaos and effeminacy. The members of the Rhode-Island State Total Abstinence Society agreed. At their 1854 annual meeting, they resolved that "the chief obstacles to the final triumph of this cause are Perverted Appetite, Sordid Interest, and Heartless Fashion."[56] By pitting "Heartless Fashion" against virtuous restraint, temperance advocates cloaked their cause in the powerful language of republicanism.

Manly fortitude provided the antidote for feminine indulgence.[57] Temperance advocates styled themselves a "brotherhood of interest" and deployed military imagery to gather support.[58] In 1832 the board of managers for the Providence Association for the Promotion of Temperance conjured the spectacle of a pious temperance army marching against a dangerous enemy: "Our young men, the hope and joy of friends and our community, especially those who are *enrolled* as members of our *military companies*, marching under the banner of Temperance, what a phalanx would they present to resist the advance of a foe, more dangerous to our happiness and freedom than the approach of hostile armies." If such support were

[55] *Address to the Rhode-Island State Temperance Society for 1844* (Providence, 1844), 21–23.
[56] *Proceedings of the Rhode-Island State Total Abstinence Society at Their Annual Meeting in Providence, January 25, 1854, with the Report of the Corresponding Secretary, and the Speech of J. P. Knowles, Esq.* (Providence, 1854), 4.
[57] For an exploration of the masculine tone of the Washingtonian temperance movement and its implications for working people in New England, see Teresa Anne Murphy, *Ten Hours' Labor: Religion, Reform, and Gender in Early New England* (Ithaca, 1992), 101–130.
[58] *Total Abstinence: A Report of the Board of Managers of the Providence Association for the Promotion of Temperance* (Providence, 1832), 8.

mustered, the managers announced, "the battle of temperance would be fought, the victory won, and our city saved."[59] A mass temperance rally held in Providence in February, 1842, also pulsed with martial spirit. As supporters marched into Beneficent Congregational Church, they sang a "national ode" that cast the temperance struggle in explicitly republican terms. "The tyrant is—Destroying Drink— / Who chains his slaves in the links of fire; / The slave is he whose manhood sinks / Beneath his withering sceptre dire." Could such a deplorable situation be allowed to stand? The song supplied the answer. "It cannot be!" the participants sang, "Man's nobler part / Yearns for his fellow-suffering man— / Haste, then, each patriot, Christian heart, / The revolution is begun!"[60] In such ways did the contest over temperance emerge as America's next struggle for independence.

But freedom from drink could not be won until the sellers of alcohol suffered a crippling defeat. In the rhetoric of sober Rhode Islanders, no one was more responsible for perpetuating the evils of intemperance than the morally corrupt grocers, merchants, and vendors who engaged in this "immoral traffic." In an 1834 temperance address, the Congregationalist minister Jotham Horton argued that "every merchant should be made to feel, that when he sells a cask of liquor, he performs an action the immorality of which must be estimated by the number of glasses it contains." Horton compared alcohol dealers with the most evil of characters. "Like the kidnapper and the slave-dealer," he proclaimed, "they will meet in the brow of every virtuous man an open rebuke."[61] In 1844 the Rhode-Island State Temperance Society took aim at grocers who stood behind the mask of "respectability" in order to sell their deadly drink. "The Rumseller who robs and murders his victims, who fills our poor houses with paupers and our jails with criminals," scoffed Thomas T. Waterman, "is suffered to go at large, and is called respectable!"[62] In 1854 advocates of total abstinence cried out that "the liquor sellers are another class altogether, and by far the most guilty. Indeed, the wickedness is mostly chargeable to them."[63] The grocers and merchants who populated the pews of Providence churches faced a moral challenge that pitted their drive for profits against the need for sobriety and civic order.

Temperance advocates recognized the offensive against alcohol needed

---

[59] Ibid., 11.

[60] "Simultaneous Temperance Meetings, February 22, 1842," Harris Collection, Large Broadsides, Brown University Library.

[61] *Report of the Board of Managers of the Providence Association for the Promotion of Temperance* (Providence, 1834), 5, 12.

[62] *Address of the Rhode-Island State Temperance Society for 1844* (Providence, 1845), 9.

[63] *Proceedings of the Rhode-Island State Total Abstinence Society*, 10.

to be waged along a wide front, stretching from individual congregations to the Rhode Island General Assembly. Through the instrument of the temperance pledge, individual communicants throughout the city dedicated themselves to the cause.[64] Outside their churches, temperance leaders created city- and statewide organizations to publicize the evils of drink and to propose measures to check them. Under the aegis of The Rhode-Island State Temperance Society members of different denominations buried doctrinal distinctions to attack alcohol. In 1833 the Calvinist deacon and merchant Josiah Chapin and the Unitarian pastor Frederick A. Farley attended the same Providence meeting of the organization. To cement solidarity, the Rhode-Island State Temperance Society gathered smaller societies in rural counties, particularly in mill villages. By 1838 it explicitly advocated the establishment of local groups which would "bring the working classes together. And if there were no other object to be gained in organization of County Societies but this, it would be worthy of attention."[65] Like other reform groups of the early nineteenth century, the society took on features of a complex governmental entity, complete with slates of elected officers, local auxiliaries, and annual conventions.

In wearing the appearance and function of a quasi-governmental agency, the temperance movement remained firmly in the grip of men. Not a single woman appears to have been accorded a leadership role in the Providence City Temperance Society or in the Rhode-Island State Temperance Society. The annual reports of the State Temperance Society printed odes—contributed by men—heralding the importance of sobriety in promoting happy and orderly family relationships. Moreover, temperance advocates held an ultimate goal that, perforce, excluded direct female participation: the passage of state legislation banning the sale and "alcoholic liquors." In 1846 the Rhode-Island State Total Abstinence Society included in its annual report a "memorial" directed to the General Assembly. It claimed that "patriotism, humanity, benevolence, philanthropy, and religion" all called for the enactment of stiffer laws, overturning the local licensing system. "We believe that the use of alcoholic liquors as a beverage," they explained, "is attended with evil, and only evil, to any community: that it promotes disease

---

[64] For examples of temperance pledges see Record Book, First Baptist Church, February 2, 1832; Record Book, Richmond Street Congregational Church, May 8, 1827; Record Book, Fourth Baptist Church, March 25, 1835; Record Book, Third Baptist Church, April 19, 1832; and High Street Congregational Church Covenant, all at RIHS.

[65] *The Seventh Annual Report of the Rhode-Island State Temperance Society, Read at the Adjourned Meeting Held in Providence, January 11, 1838, Together with the Correspondence of Local Societies* (Providence, 1838), 7.

in individuals, discord and poverty in families and communities, and hastens multitudes to a premature grave."[66] Because alcohol played such a large role in "sapping the very foundations of order, peace and happiness," the state should "entirely" prohibit its sale. In 1852 they achieved their end: the General Assembly "enacted a version of the Maine Law, which mandated statewide prohibition."[67] By coupling the cause of temperance with the exercise of the ballot, reformers insured that the public contest over the issue would be decided by men.

Tract distributors differed from temperance reformers in three important ways. First, their main goal was to convert individual souls rather than to pass legislation. While temperance advocates strode confidently into the political arena, tract distributors understood their activities in exclusively spiritual terms. Although the tracts they carried were designed to promote Christian sobriety, tract distributors considered abstinence from alcohol to be the fruit of the saved soul rather than something to be sought in its own right. Second, while temperance reformers tried to include virtually all religious groups within their embrace, thus papering over denominational bickering, tract distributors stuck to their evangelical guns. By 1832 Providence Unitarians, disgusted with the orthodoxy of the intrepid Providence Religious Tract Society, split away and formed their own group.[68] Third, whereas the temperance movement assumed a political agenda, thus marginalizing the role of women, the tract reformers' insistence that their movement was essentially a spiritual one opened the door for a larger female role. Women took to the streets, handing out literature and visiting families in their homes. They were listed, too, as officers in "auxilliary societies" based largely in individual congregations and in smaller communities around the city.[69] While women did not occupy the leadership positions in the Providence Religious Tract Society, they nevertheless found a significant institutional role at the local level.

Tract reformers shared with temperance advocates an abiding concern with social order. In 1825 the Providence Religious Tract Society orchestrated the first systematic distribution of religious literature within the city. They carefully divided the town by ward, neighborhood, street, and family.

[66] *Extracts From the Proceedings and Reports of the Rhode-Island State Total Abstinence Society, From its Organization, Jan. 1841 to Jan. 1846. With the Constitution of the Society and the License Law of 1846* (Providence, 1846), 10, 23.
[67] Gilkeson, *Middle-Class Providence*, 35.
[68] See *First Semi-Annual Report of the Providence Auxiliary Unitarian Association* (Providence, 1832).
[69] *The Fourth Annual Report of the Providence Religious Tract Society* (Providence, 1829), 17.

Individual missionaries then held responsibility for visiting persons within their specified zones. The very orderliness of their method bespoke what they hoped to accomplish. As they moved from street to street and from house to house, the distributors sought to bring souls to Christ and, simultaneously, to create harmony among the social classes. These two goals, they thought, were interconnected. The tract they carried for the month of April 1832, *A Persuasive to Public Worship*, made this point explicitly. It argued that in the fellowship of worship "a friendly intercourse is maintained between the different ranks of society. These are too apt to dislike each other; and their different situations keep them at a distance; but in the house of God, 'the rich and poor meet together, the Lord is the maker of them all.' "[70] Tract distributors believed that converted souls would build a harmonious social order.

By the 1830s, tract society missionaries in Providence presided over an operation of extraordinary scope and complexity. Their sturdy belief in the nearly magical power of religious print strikes the modern observer as evidence of both tremendous faith and enormous innocence. In 1829 the Providence Religious Tract Society trumpeted the power of tracts: "the mass of men at present, as in the days of our Saviour, must be instructed in an easy and familiar manner."[71] As we have glimpsed already in the mill villages, missionaries imbued their literature with mysterious power. Faith in these little documents inspired a virtual army of volunteers. In a single year, 1832, they distributed more than twenty-three thousand religious tracts, or more than one document for every man, woman, and child in town.[72] Although the missionaries believed that the tracts could conquer sinners through the unaided influence of the Holy Spirit, they did make room for human agency. They visited, prayed, preached, and sometimes even argued with the persons they encountered in their districts. In 1837 the society reported that its volunteers had "visited from month to month nearly four thousand families; they have reported twenty-five hopeful conversions, four *at least* of which were through the instrumentality of the Tracts."[73] Spreading through the city street by street and family by family, the society sought to leave no one untouched by their prodigious efforts.

The Providence distributors selected tracts that emphasized simple tales of spiritual regeneration, the staple literature of the American Tract

---

[70] *A Persuasive to Public Worship*, no. 41, 2. All tracts are cited here according to the tract number assigned by the American Tract Society.

[71] *Fourth Annual Report*, 16.

[72] John Bours Papers, Distribution throughout the City, 1832, RIHS.

[73] *The Twelfth Annual Report of the Providence Religious Tract Society* (Providence, 1837), 5.

Society.[74] The traditional, even conservative, message was that the attractions of worldly wealth posed the greatest threat to the salvation of the soul. *The Barren Fig Tree* described a hustling farmer who repents before his minister: "I have been striving to get a few dollars together, and to lay up the things of this world. O what a wonder that the Lord has not long before this cut me down."[75] The selection for August 1833, *I am an Infidel*, chronicling the plight of a Universalist, announced that "it is easy for men, immersed in the bustle of business, or running in the giddy round of fashionable amusements, or listening to the pleasant song to forget God."[76] In *The World's Conversion*, distributed in June 1834, Providence readers could find described the most substantial obstacle standing between them and the salvation of their nation. "Look into the churches," the tract observed, "their members are so much like the world, that their spiritual influence is almost extinguished. They lay up wealth for their families, when they ought to expend it for Christ and souls."[77] Money, according to these tracts, led men astray from God. According to *The Harvest Past*, a popular tract written by Timothy Dwight of Yale College, "in the language of most men, worldly success is the only meaning of prosperity."[78] And yet this form of prosperity could lead to eternal damnation. The tract *On Repentance* laid out a truly terrifying prospect before those refined Protestants who staked the disposition of their eternal souls on decorous behavior and the outward signs of character. "It matters not," it averred, "that you be sober, industrious, moral, amiable, and respected: if you have ever for one moment loved the Lord your God with less than your whole heart, and soul, and mind, and strength, then you are a sinner in the sight of the great God."[79] In such ways did the tracts place in tension the things of this world with the goal of attaining salvation.

Throughout the course of his extensive career, Francis Wayland strove to reconcile the pursuit of piety and the drive for wealth. Although not as charismatic as his contemporaries Lyman Beecher and Charles G. Finney, Wayland may well have been the most influential Protestant clergymen in the antebellum North. His twin textbooks, *The Elements of Moral Science* (1835) and *The Elements of Political Economy* (1837), provided guidance to

[74] Detailed lists of the titles of tracts distributed in Providence during the 1830s may be found in the John Bours Papers. For an assessment of the American Tract Society's literature see Mark S. Schantz, "Religious Tracts, Evangelical Reform, the Market Revolution in Antebellum America," *Journal of the Early Republic* 17 (1997): 425–466.
[75] *The Barren Fig Tree*, no. 148, 7.
[76] *I Am an Infidel*, no. 267, 4.
[77] *The World's Conversion*, no. 297, 13.
[78] *The Harvest Past*, by President Dwight, no. 302, 4.
[79] *On Repentance*, no. 183, 2.

college students for decades. The first text proved especially popular, selling over a hundred thousand copies throughout the nineteenth century. In the space of twenty years, the treatise on political economy reached fifty thousand readers.[80] Hardly a college senior could be found who had not imbibed the texts of "the Ricardo of evangelists."[81] Abraham Lincoln counted himself among Francis Wayland's disciples. According to Herndon, Lincoln "ate up, digested, and assimilated" Wayland's work in moral philosophy.[82] From the university hall to the White House, Francis Wayland's thinking engaged the generation that came to maturity on the eve of the Civil War.

Wayland had more modest concerns when he arrived in Providence in December 1826. Not yet thirty-one years of age, he tackled the thorny problem of restoring discipline to Brown University undergraduates. To achieve this goal, he removed the traditional "barrel of ale always kept on tap in the cellar to which all students had free access."[83] Faculty and instructors were to keep a close eye on student behavior through a system of dormitory room inspections. Wayland also initiated a new grading system, the results of which were to be communicated to parents at the end of each term. Student dissent simmered under the new regime. Wayland admitted to President Everett of Harvard that "a pony had been carried up two flights of stairs and put in his recitation room."[84] But, on the whole, he proved himself deft in scuttling more organized acts of rebellion. He imported the "spy system" he had learned from Eliphalet Nott while he taught at Union College, thus averting the confrontations that plagued other campuses of the era. In

[80] On the popularity of Wayland's textbooks see Joseph Blau's introduction in Blau, ed., Francis Wayland, *The Elements of Moral Science* (Cambridge, 1963), xlii; Michael J. L. O'Connor, *Origins of Academic Economics in the United States* (New York, 1944), 172–190; Charles C. Cole Jr., *The Social Ideas of the Northern Evangelists* (New York, 1954), esp. 178–183; William G. McLoughlin *New England Dissent 1630–1833*, vol. 2 (Cambridge, 1971), 1274. More recent works that set Wayland's work in the context of antebellum intellectual life include Mark Y. Hanley, *Beyond a Christian Commonwealth: The Protestant Quarrel with the American Republic, 1830–1860* (Chapel Hill, 1994), 35–39; Martin J. Burke, *The Conundrum of Class: Public Discourse on the Social Order in America* (Chicago, 1995), 108–113.

[81] Cole, *Social Ideas of the Northern Evangelists*, 178.

[82] Quoted in Daniel Walker Howe, *The Political Culture of the American Whigs* (Chicago, 1979), 270.

[83] See Roelker, "Francis Wayland," 36.

[84] Ibid. On Wayland's career at Brown University see the series of four articles by Theodore R. Crane: "Francis Wayland and the Residential College," *Rhode Island History* 19 (1960): 65–78; idem, "Francis Wayland and the Residential College," *Rhode Island History* 19 (1960): 118–129; idem, "Francis Wayland: Political Economist as Educator," *Rhode Island History* 21 (1962): 65–90; and idem, "Francis Wayland: Political Economist as Educator," *Rhode Island History* 21 (1962): 105–124.

establishing himself as an apostle of discipline, Wayland departed from the more relaxed attitudes held by Asa Messer, his immediate predecessor.

If one word claimed pride of place in Francis Wayland's intellectual lexicon, then that word was "law." From his vantage point, laws governed virtually all aspects of the human experience, laying out patterns for understanding the universe, God, and one's relationships with other human beings. In *The Elements of Moral Science*, Wayland defined what he meant by "Moral Law." He did not invoke the Decalogue or the Sermon on the Mount but turned instead to Sir Isaac Newton as his principal authority. Moral laws shared much with the physical laws that Newton himself had discovered. Thus, a moral law is "a form of expression denoting an order of sequence established between the moral quality of actions and their results."[85] In the course of his treatise, Wayland made seemingly innumerable references to laws of various sorts: "the law by which conscience is governed," "the law of marriage," "the law of benevolence."[86] In 1837 he explored in some detail "the moral law of accumulation."[87] At every intellectual turn, Wayland concerned himself with understanding, categorizing, and then applying moral law to each discrete aspect of human experience. So did the leading Protestant moralist of antebellum America verge on articulating a Thomistic vision of the moral life.

Although the Scriptures figured heavily in defining the content and scope of these moral laws, they did not provide Wayland's starting point. Indeed, he explained that "the truths of revealed religion *harmonize* perfectly with those of natural religion. The difference between them consists in this—that the one teaches plainly what the other teaches by inference; the one takes up the lesson where the other leaves it, and adds to it other and vitally important precepts."[88] Aside from deploying evidence from physics and natural religion to advance his arguments, Wayland also turned to poets and essayists. His text is laced with quotations from Shakespeare as well as Cowper and Dr. Johnson. It brims with observations lifted from the classical economists. Wayland's work on moral science may be treated as an eclectic amalgam of the major intellectual interests of his era. It provides evidence, too, for historians who see in antebellum moral philosophers and theologians the seeds of "unbelief" in America.[89] The Bible, while still

---

[85] Wayland, *Elements of Moral Science*, 17, 18.

[86] See ibid., 63, 279, 339.

[87] Francis Wayland, *The Moral Law of Accumulation: The Substance of Two Discourses, Delivered in the First Baptist Meeting House, Providence, May 14, 1837* (Providence, 1837).

[88] Wayland, *Elements of Moral Science*, 123.

[89] See, especially, Turner, *Without God, Without Creed.*

essential, is ranked alongside a host of other authorities to be consulted in the discovery of moral law.

The orderly ethical system advanced by Wayland was simultaneously a masculine one. From the start, he had set out to create at Brown University "the paternalistic atmosphere he had known at Schenectady" while at Union College.[90] In pointing to Issac Newton and in adopting his mechanistic language and its metaphors, he also enlisted a particularly masculine way of understanding the world. As Carolyn Merchant has argued, the "founding fathers" of the seventeenth-century scientific revolution, Newton among them, sought to systematize the "disorder" that had, for millennia, characterized "feminine" nature.[91] Wayland's passion for order was rooted, in part, in an intellectual tradition that saw it as the preserve of men. His text on *Moral Science*, too, left no ambiguity about the authority of men over women in day-to-day life. Its discussion of "the law of marriage" assigned dominion over the household to husbands. He did give lip service to the notion of "separate spheres," explaining that "it is the duty, in the first instance, of the husband to provide for the wants of the family; and of the wife to assume the charge of the affairs of household. His sphere of duty is *without*, her sphere of duty is *within*." But duty and authority did not amount to the same thing, and Wayland could not resist extending his judgment into the domestic realm. He excoriated the woman who was "a useless and prodigal appendage to a household, ignorant of her duties and her manner of discharging them." Such "useless" women had acquired bad habits "from a life of childish caprice, luxurious self-indulgence, and sensitive, feminine, yet thoroughly finished selfishness." Wayland blamed "the system of female education at present in vogue" for these woes, yet his own educational reforms, as we shall observe, were directed almost exclusively toward men. Women could fend for themselves. That he felt it necessary to lecture wives on their proper duties, while assuming that men already understood theirs, suggests that in some respects the notion of separate spheres was pure fiction. As Wayland finally settled the matter, "the duty of the wife is submission and obedience."[92]

As Francis Wayland said, men fulfilled their primary duties in the marketplace. In considering this arena of life, he distanced himself from the college's previous leadership. Both Jonathan Maxcy and Asa Messer, in their addresses and sermons, had juggled the interlocking concerns of individual gain and community welfare. They had, along with other Providence clergy,

[90] Crane, "Francis Wayland and the Residential College," 69.
[91] Carolyn Merchant, *The Death of Nature: Women, Ecology, and the Scientific Revolution* (New York, 1983), esp. 164–191.
[92] Wayland, *Elements of Moral Science*, 284–285.

attempted to balance the competing claims of personal profit and corporate fairness without conceding victory to either side. By the 1830s the writing of Francis Wayland evinced a decided emphasis on personal profit. The conservative tone of earlier nineteenth-century Providence churchmen was slowly giving ground to a more liberal economic ethic. This is not to suggest that Wayland's ethic could be used to rationalize all of the moral dilemmas inherent in market society. During the panic of 1837, for instance, he pulled up short of embracing outright speculation. But Wayland did envision a social and economic order animated by individual pursuit of wealth. This trend was revealed in his two major books and in his controversial 1850 plan for curricular change at Brown University.

The first traces of Wayland's acquisitive individualism appear in *The Elements of Moral Science*. In his consideration of "Practical Ethics," Wayland included a resounding defense of property rights. "The right of property is founded on the will of God," he intoned, "as made known to us by natural conscience, by general consequences, and by revelation." Moreover, individuals could exercise the right to accumulate property without limit—provided that they "not so use it as to interfere with the rights of my neighbor." The pursuit of private property, for Wayland, made progress possible. For without the right of individual gain, "there would be no accumulation; of course no capital, no tools, no provision for the future, no houses, no agriculture."[93] Thus, Wayland attempted to blend the rights of individuals with the good of society. At the same time, he stressed the need for accumulation of capital as a condition for social progress.

The importance Wayland attached to property rights is evident in his views on slavery. *The Elements of Moral Science* clearly connects these two topics; the consideration of property immediately follows a discussion of domestic slavery. It is likely Wayland's rigid adherence to notions of private property conditioned his perceptions of Southern slavery, especially his reluctance to condemn its practice outright. To be sure, Wayland advanced arguments against the institution of slavery, which, he believed, stood in opposition to the moral teaching of the Bible. Slavery, too, retarded the accumulation of national wealth. Sounding very much the "free labor" advocate, Wayland insisted that slavery "takes from the laborers the *natural stimulus* to labor." He observed that "the slaveholding States had every advantage, both in soil and climate, over their neighbors. And yet the accumulation of capital has been greatly in favor of the latter."[94] Slavery, he thought, was responsible for this differential. The coercive nature of the

[93] Wayland, *Elements of Moral Science*, 210, 211.
[94] Ibid., 190, 191.

master-slave relation, he said, also inhibited the enslaved person from the full exercise of conscience, without which eternal happiness was impossible. Given the centrality of the conscience in Wayland's ethic, these were serious incriminations. But he stopped short of charging slaveholders with holding property rights in another human being. Although in his consideration it was unlawful to obtain property "by consent *violently obtained*," he used highway robbery, not slavery, as an example of that sin.[95] Because he considered it plausible that the slaves "are not competent to self-government," he conceded that "immediate abolition" might not be a prudent course of action.[96] This being the case, Wayland offered sets of obligations and duties, for both masters and bondsmen, under the current system of slavery. Although some Southerners railed against Wayland's treatment of the slavery issue, *The Elements of Moral Science* could hardly be construed as a document of radical abolitionism.[97]

Considerations of economy and society did not fully surface in Wayland's thought until he brought out *The Elements of Political Economy*. Like his contemporaries Horace Bushnell, Lyman Beecher, and Charles Finney, Wayland understood these topics as being within the purview of his ministerial calling. He told his Brown students, in unmistakable terms, to get rich. In considering how human productivity could be increased, Wayland declared, "it is a benefit to a whole neighborhood, for a single member of it to become rich."[98] This was so because capital was essential to the employment of all. At points, Wayland carried his praise of material consolidation to extremes. He argued, for instance, that "the accumulation of capital is more to the advantage of the laborer than the capitalist."[99] This was so because capitalists created jobs. There were, in his view, hardly any limits to what a man might earn. Since God had designed man to labor, he must "be allowed to gain all that he can; and 2nd. That having gained all that he can, he be allowed to use it as he will."[100] One could scarcely imagine a more unequivocal endorsement of individual acquisitiveness.

Throughout the work, Wayland argued that harmony should prevail between employers and laborers. In fact, he saw no fundamental distinction between labor and capital in the first place, since he considered the financing of a factory to be every bit as much work as laboring in one. According

---

[95] Ibid., 217–218.

[96] Ibid., 196.

[97] See Blau's introduction to *Moral Science*, xliv–xlvi; Kenneth Moore Startup, *The Root of All Evil: The Protestant Clergy and the Economic Mind of the Old South* (Athens, Ga., 1997), 127–128.

[98] Francis Wayland, *The Elements of Political Economy* (New York, 1837), 93.

[99] Ibid., 93; see also 354–355.

[100] Ibid., 111.

to Martin J. Burke, "for Francis Wayland every individual engaged in 'human industry' was a laborer. Philosophers, lawyers, clergymen, and physicians were as much laboring men as those who worked on farms, in mines, or in factories." Indeed, in Burke's view, Wayland was "one of the most prominent antebellum proponents of class harmony."[101] He viewed the wage relationship itself to be one of complete parity, the "result of a partnership," in which the two parties "are equally necessary to each other."[102] At the same time, however, Wayland recognized accurately the power of employers to regulate wages and introduce labor-saving machinery. Like many antebellum Rhode Islanders, Wayland loved the gadgets and mechanical equipment that increased the efficiency of industrial production. "He who, by an ingenious contrivance, is able to save the hire of one laborer," he remarked with admiration, "will find himself, at the end of the year, richer by precisely this amount saved."[103] Despite insisting upon accord between entrepreneurs and workers, he realized that the businessmen held the upper hand. Perhaps Francis Wayland was thinking of his friend Nicholas Brown when he argued that every man "be allowed to gain all that he can."

Francis Wayland's vision for the future of Brown University connected the purposes of education with the continuing expansion of the market economy. He had long been dissatisfied with a curriculum that seemed suited to producing cultivated gentlemen rather than useful and industrious workers. He wanted to revamp college curricula to make them more beneficial for the wide run of "farmers, mechanics, manufacturers, merchants." As he explained to a Boston audience, "we in the Baptist denomination are all on the level and we ought to endeavor to educate the masses. All of our academies ought to be so arranged to meet the wants of the people at large."[104] Wayland believed a curriculum heavy with practical courses of a vocational bent would best serve the interests of most citizens. In 1850 he had put these proposals into concrete form in a report to the University Corporation. He called for a "new system" to be implemented that would increase Brown's enrollment, allow students greater choices in the classes they took, and institute practical courses in engineering, applied science, and applied chemistry. Despite considerable resistance from those who clung to the classics, Wayland prevailed, and the new program was launched in the fall of 1850.[105]

[101] Burke, *Conundrum of Class,* 109.
[102] Francis Wayland, *Elements of Political Economy,* 336.
[103] Ibid., 424.
[104] Quoted in Crane, "Francis Wayland: Political Economist as Educator," 123.
[105] On the "new system" and the challenges it faced in the late 1850s, see ibid., 117–122; Roelker, "Francis Wayland," 66–78.

While Wayland's proposal has been heralded under the rubric of democratic reform in American higher education, its author clearly harbored doubts about the political sense of most people. In the crucible of the Dorr Rebellion of 1842, he had already proven himself an indefatigable supporter of the "Law and Order" party against the popular, revolutionary movement championed by Thomas Wilson Dorr. While Wayland, no doubt, did want to open wide the doors of higher education, it is also clear that he wanted students trained for particular and practical ends. As Theodore Crane has argued, Wayland justified his position "with a blunt vocationalism and revealed his increasing distrust of the 'aristocratic' College of his former associates."[106] The "new system" thus blended Wayland's incipient democratic leanings with a curriculum designed for a capitalist future. In championing education of a vocational and practical nature, he sought to enable students to accrue the gains he had described so glowingly in *The Elements of Political Economy.*

The panic of 1837 pushed Wayland to reconsider the almost headlong rush for wealth he advocated in his textbook. In two emotional sermons preached in First Baptist Church, he offered a moral interpretation of the recent collapse of business. In tones appropriate for a Puritan jeremiad, Wayland considered the economic disaster as the judgment of God. Whereas colonial New Englanders perceived divine intervention in fires, floods, and earthquakes, bourgeois Rhode-Islanders sensed God's presence in the business cycle. Financial ruin had struck, according to Wayland, because of "an excessive avidity for the rapid accumulation of property. In the words of the Scriptures, men have hasted to be rich." Although he continued to maintain, in agreement with *The Elements of Political Economy*, that the Bible allowed for the increase of wealth, what disturbed him was the frenzy of speculation. He had not grappled with such blatant displays of greed in his masterpiece. Echoing the earlier text, Wayland repeated that "God intends that man should grow rich by adding something to the means of human happiness."[107] Speculation simply involved the rapid buying and selling of property without adding any real value to it. Speculators thus fell outside even Wayland's elastic definition of an authentic laborer.

Francis Wayland surveyed with horror the actions of those who sought wealth but were not willing to labor for it. Speculation, he wrote, "has a direct tendency to foster a spirit of avaricious worldliness." Taking chances,

---

[106] Crane, "Francis Wayland: Political Economist as Educator," 122. On the trend toward creating a "usable" education for students see Burton J. Bledstein, *The Culture of Professionalism: The Middle Class and the Development of Higher Education in America* (New York, 1978), 318–331.
[107] Wayland, *Moral Law of Accumulation*, 9, 10.

anticipating prices, playing the market, all contributed to a spirit of "practical atheism." For in these endeavors, "The fact that God governs the world becomes less and less an element in our calculations." Adumbrating Thomas T. Waterman's temperance address, Wayland expressed concern about "lavish expenditure and self-indulgence." At the close of his second sermon, he summed up his anxiety over the panic. "I do greatly fear," he admitted, "that this intense love of wealth is, more than almost any other cause, destroying men's souls."[108] As fervently as Wayland had advocated enrichment in *The Elements of Political Economy*, so he recoiled from the reality of avarice in *The Moral Law of Accumulation*. While Wayland did not repudiate the mission of capitalists as such, it is clear that his writings in time of economic panic "blended with a larger Protestant yearning for traditional faith to offset the materialism of the age."[109]

Bourgeois Protestants reconciled the tension between the pursuit of worldly wealth and the practice of piety through the exercise of religious benevolence. As Charles Cole noted in his landmark study, Northern evangelicals were of three minds when it came to money, simultaneously "despising it, embracing it, and putting it to use."[110] Benevolence, or putting one's fortune to work, allowed one to avoid the pitfalls of either of the first two alternatives. Wayland made this point clear not only in his Nicholas Brown funeral oration, but in his text on moral science as well. Among the four virtues that he cherished most highly—justice, veracity, chastity, and benevolence—he saved benevolence as the capstone for his ethical system. Unlike Plato, who cemented the virtues of wisdom, courage, and moderation with the ultimate virtue of justice, Wayland placed benevolence at the apex of his work. In the final pages of his text, his rhetoric soared in describing the glories of benevolence, suggesting that in it lay hopes for world peace and harmony. Because he believed that the primary causes of war "are most commonly the love of plunder and the love of glory," he posited that the practice of benevolence was a nation's best protection from its ravages. True benevolence, authentic regard for others, Wayland thought, quelled the motives that caused nations to take up arms in the first place. With an innocence startling to twentieth-century sensibilities, he announced "that there is not a nation in Europe that could be led on to war against a harmless, just, forgiving, and defenseless people."[111]

---

[108] Ibid., 15, 16, 21, 33.
[109] Hanley, *Beyond a Christian Commonwealth*, 103.
[110] Cole, *Social Ideas of the Northern Evangelists*, 168.
[111] *Moral Science*, 362.

The years immediately following Nicholas Brown's death proved Wayland's postulates of universal harmony to be illusory. In 1842 the Dorr Rebellion revealed deep conflicts within Providence society between those who had power in the state government and those who did not. The conflict was shaped, as we shall see, not only by bourgeois Protestants but by a plebeian religious culture that flourished during the 1820s and 1830s.

5

"The Voice of the People Is the Voice of God"

The Emergence of Plebeian Religious Culture

In 1836, perhaps while Francis Wayland was preparing his lessons on moral science for Brown University undergraduates, Seth Luther rallied a crowd of workingmen in Brooklyn, New York. On July 4 of that year Luther, a prominent Rhode Island labor radical and suffrage advocate, had traveled to New York, to commemorate the sixtieth anniversary of American independence. Already a seasoned speaker and fiery agitator, he treated his audience to a display of verbal pyrotechnics that befit the occasion. In his view, a new American aristocracy of wealth had betrayed the principles of equality and liberty for which the revolutionary generation had suffered and died. "The pretended Representatives of the people of ALL PARTIES have been for years pursuing a course of self-aggrandisement, and ruinous corruption," he explained, "while the Workingmen have been deceived and juggled out of their rights by the cry of whigism or democracy triumphant, as the case might be."[1] Luther had taken a careful measure of his audience and made certain to observe the recent trial and conviction of twenty New York journeymen tailors for their role in creating a trade union. The decision of Judge Ogden Edwards, that the journeymen had created an "illegal combination" by organizing a union, seemed to Luther to be irrefutable proof that the American political and legal system was arrayed in battle against the interests of workingmen.[2] The betrayal of the revolutionary heritage by men

---

[1] Seth Luther, *An Address Delivered Before the Mechanics and Working-Men, of the City of Brooklyn, on the Celebration of the Sixtieth Anniversary of American Independence, July 4, 1836* (Brooklyn, 1836), 7.
[2] See Sean Wilentz, *Chants Democratic: New York City and the Rise of the American Working Class, 1788–1850* (New York, 1984), 290–292.

of large property cut Seth Luther to the core. "I am ashamed of my country, ashamed of its unjust and unequal laws, ashamed to acknowledge," he cried, "myself a son of a revolutionary soldier."[3] Luther experienced the withering of the Revolution's promise as a matter both personal and political.

At virtually every turn, Seth Luther took issue with the orderly ethic articulated by Francis Wayland. While Wayland clung to a vision of social harmony in which capitalist and laborer were equal partners in the process of production, Luther blasted the "aristocracy" and claimed that workingmen were "the real and only producers of wealth." While Wayland organized his worldview around the concept of law, Luther condemned American courts, observing that "the Great Lawgiver of the universe requires none of his creatures to respect injustice."[4] Luther then rattled off an entire litany of laws that deserved nothing but contempt, including the stamp tax and the tea tax that had sparked the revolution in the first place. But even deeper than their differences on the social order and the role of law were the contrasting visions of true Christianity held by the two men. For Wayland, Nicholas Brown emerged as the ideal saint, embodying the spirit of business acumen and ingenuity braided with an abiding sense of benevolence. For Luther, true Christianity belonged to the poor.

At key points in his Independence Day address, Seth Luther hammered away on the theme that Jesus, himself a mechanic, would most certainly have favored the cause of the workingmen. The Bible, Luther said, lent its authority to laborers. "Hundreds of passages in that book," he argued, "may be found containing denunciations against the rich for their oppression of the poor." And if any in his audience suspected that God had taken the part of employers, Luther knew that they had fallen victim to yet another instance of deception. A favorite trick of tyrants, he proclaimed, "is to pervert the benevolent religion of him who was despised by the aristocracy of Jerusalem because he was poor; because he was born in a stable and cradled in a manger." During his life on earth, Luther observed, Jesus had spent most of his time among the poor and the dispossessed: "He while on earth went about doing good; healing the sick, opening the eyes of the blind, and restoring the dead to life. A great, *very* great share of his attention and mercy was given to the poor, and for this he was hated by the rich." Luther conjured a God of miracles rather than immutable laws, whose chosen people were the infirm and the lowly. Perhaps speaking autobiographically, he noted a parallel between the world of the New Testament and the world of antebellum America. "Thus it is in our days," he observed, "if a Mechanic, a

---

[3] Luther, *Address Delivered Before the Mechanics*, 15.
[4] Ibid., 3, 9.

poor man, endeavor to speak in public, he is despised by the learned, so called, and what he says is considered of little or no consequence."[5]

But what Seth Luther had to say on July 4, 1836, was of importance both for his contemporaries and for students of antebellum America. His address leads us into a consideration of the plebeian religious culture that formed a counterpoint to the bourgeois religious culture we have already considered. If bourgeois Protestants sought to forge a united front to keep social chaos at bay, plebeian religion displayed a greater degree of diversity and syncretism, manifesting itself in Catholic and Protestant congregations and in a full range of self-anointed street preachers as well. Where bourgeois religious culture wedded itself to decorum and rationality, plebeian religious culture mixed well with emotional outbursts and evidenced an enduring belief in the supernatural and the miraculous.[6] As bourgeois Protestants sought a religion of refinement and taste, plebeian enthusiasts participated in a "rough religion" that embraced the polarities of boisterous laughter and righteous wrath.[7] And plebeian spokesmen such as William Apess and Seth Luther articulated political visions that stood at odds with acquisitive individualism prized by Nicholas Brown and Francis Wayland.

To help us grasp the distance separating the plebeian and bourgeois religious perspectives, it is worth recalling the distinction Max Weber drew between charismatic leaders and movements, on the one hand, and the routines of bureaucracy and rationality, on the other. While he recognized the processes by which charismatic religion could be "routinized" in institutional form, Weber's analysis highlighted essential differences that separated the charismatic from the bureaucratic. One of these differences turned on the issue of gender. Weber maintained that "'pure charisma,' is contrary to all patriarchal domination (in the sense that the term is used here). It is the opposite of all ordered economy. It is the very force that disregards economy."[8] His assertion that charisma and patriarchy are fundamentally incompatible is revealing and important for this analysis because it suggests that plebeian religious culture manifested a distinctively "feminine" quality. (In Weber's notion of the term in this context,

---

[5] Ibid., 13, 24, 25.

[6] On the persistence of magical thinking in the early republic, see especially Alan Taylor, "The Early Republic's Supernatural Economy: Treasure Seeking in the American Northeast, 1780–1830," *American Quarterly* 38 (1986): 6–34; Jon Butler, *Awash in a Sea of Faith: Christianizing the American People* (Cambridge, Mass., 1990), 225–256.

[7] See E. P. Thompson's essay "Rough Music," in *Customs in Common: Studies in Traditional Popular Culture* (New York, 1993), 467–531.

[8] See S. N. Eisenstadt, ed., *Max Weber on Charisma and Institution Building, Selected Papers* (Chicago, 1968), 21. Eisenstadt's collection gathers important pieces of Weber's work on these topics.

patriarchy refers to a particular type of household organization that creates an "ordered base" for rational economic activity.) This is not to suggest that early American Catholicism or antebellum street preachers accorded women any more political power or social regard than did their bourgeois counterparts. But in holding to certain forms of magical and visionary thinking (evident especially among Mormons and Millerites), in venerating emotion over rationality, and in distancing itself from the values of the market, plebeian religious culture took on features that could be construed as feminine in the context of nineteenth-century America.

The feminine quality of plebeian religion was revealed in the variety and "disorderly" quality of its adherents. As we have already observed in the Rhode Island countryside, one of the hallmarks of popular religious culture was its tremendous diversity. Six-Principle Baptists, Freewill Baptists, Methodists, Universalists, and a host of other independent preachers and visionaries competed for the spiritual allegiance of rural Rhode Islanders. This diversity manifested itself in the urban expression of plebeian religious culture as well. In Providence, humble residents joined Roman Catholic parishes (the Cathedral of SS. Peter and Paul dedicated in 1838 and St. Patrick's Church dedicated in 1842) and two new Baptist communities (the Roger Williams Baptist Church formed in 1830 and the Abyssinian Freewill Baptist Church gathered in 1835). Aside from its ethnic and cultural variants, plebeian religious culture also dissolved denominational boundaries, unleashing street preachers of various stripes. In a Protestant religious culture in which ideas of "disorder" were increasingly gendered as female, plebeian religious culture necessarily partook of the feminine.[9]

Weber's analysis of charisma also helps us to make sense of other aspects of plebeian religious culture. For him, charismatic leaders drew their strength from internal sources, from their abilities to conjure and perform magical acts, and from being recognized as charismatic by their followers. Like some of the street preachers we will consider, charismatic leaders moved—in Weber's words—"outside the ties of this world, outside of routine occupations, as well as outside the routine obligations of family life." Bourgeois Protestants, by contrast, immersed themselves in worldly cares, applied themselves to steady jobs, and gloried in the pleasures of the domestic hearth. Moreover, in Weber's analysis authentic charisma stood in sharp contrast to the preoccupation with rational economic calculation. "In general," he wrote, "charisma rejects all rational economic conduct."[10]

---

[9] See Susan Juster, *Disorderly Women: Sexual Politics and Evangelicalism in Revolutionary New England* (Ithaca, 1994).

[10] Eisenstadt, *Max Weber on Charisma*, 21.

While Providence's plebeians did take some regard for rational economic behavior, their bourgeois counterparts embraced more fully the values of the market, evident especially in the carefully calibrated ranks of pews that subdivided their meetinghouses. Indeed, plebeians did not even require church buildings in which to practice their faith. When plebeian churches did auction their pews and collect pew rents, they offered their seats at much more modest prices.[11] In practicing a religion that retained roots in modest churches, in private homes, and in the streets, plebeians implicitly limited the penetration of the market into their religious culture.

Rhode Island's Catholics first gathered for worship wherever they could find space. Some of the earliest Catholic services were conducted in an old schoolhouse on Benefit Street that fell victim to the great gale of 1815. In September 1828, Bishop Benedict Fenwick of Boston came to Providence to celebrate Mass in Mechanics' Hall. Other services were held in the Providence Town House, a location that would become a favorite forum for street preachers when visiting the city.[12] "In industrial regions," Joseph Brennan reports, "Mass was said in private homes, sometimes in those of persons who were not Catholics, or in public houses."[13] In mill villages, fear that Protestant mill bosses might not approve of their devotions forced devout Catholics underground. As late as 1858, some factory workers in Rhode Island asked for Mass to be said in their homes near dawn because "the presence of a priest in the village would have given offence to the mill-owners."[14] Some evidence suggests that textile entrepreneurs were, indeed, hostile to the Catholic devotions of their workers. At Cranston, for instance, the Catholic workers in the Sprague family's mill complex had to walk to Providence to attend Mass because the Spragues had provided a Protestant chapel.[15] In gathering in public places and in the privacy of their own residences, Rhode Island's early Catholics resembled the Protestant itinerants of the countryside.

[11] Evidence on pew costs in Providence's Catholic congregations was not available to me. In his study of Catholic parishes in antebellum New York, Jay P. Dolan noted that Irish churches did sell and rent pews but notes that perhaps as few as 10 to 25 percent of parishioners actually paid for their places, with the most expensive seats renting for $100 to $150 per year. He observes, as well, that "the renting of pews was not a custom familiar to Irish immigrants." See Dolan, *The Immigrant Church: New York's Irish and German Catholics, 1815–1865* (Baltimore, 1975), 51–52.
[12] See Patrick T. Conley and Matthew J. Smith, *Catholicism in Rhode Island: The Formative Era* (Providence, 1976), 18–20; Joseph Brennan, *Social Conditions in Industrial Rhode Island, 1820–1860* (Washington, D.C., 1940), 63–67.
[13] Brennan, *Social Conditions*, 65.
[14] William Byrne, *History of the Catholic Church in the New England States* (Boston, 1899), 1:421.
[15] See Conley and Smith, *Catholicism*, 52–55; Charles Hoffman and Tess Hoffman, *Brotherly Love: Murder and the Politics of Prejudice in Nineteenth-Century Rhode Island* (Amherst, Mass., 1993), 21–22.

Poverty and internal dissent plagued Providence's Catholics as they sought a more permanent foothold in the city. By all accounts, they were working-class people, who worked for the Boston & Providence Railroad, in textile mills, and as domestic servants or other "common laborers" in the neighborhoods along the West Side. In 1838, under the direction of Father John Corry, the Cathedral of SS. Peter and Paul opened for worship. The cathedral's congregation included some fifteen hundred members, drawn principally from the ranks of "laboring people." Hence, financing the construction was a struggle.[16] When the building was dedicated, it carried a debt of about five thousand dollars. To offset the costs of constructing the narrow 80' × 40' structure, Corry canvassed Providence for donations and even sold one-dollar tickets for the opening ceremonies. Even as he scoured the city for funding, a protest movement within the church doubled Corry's worries. In 1841 a coterie of disaffected communicants led by John McCarthy, a worker at Philip Allen's Calico Print Works, approached Bishop Fenwick with a proposal for a new church, St. Patrick's. The reasons for Corry's difficulties with the dissidents remain obscure, but the experience soured him on his mission. In the first baptismal register for the new church he complained, "It is not to be found in history that ever was a Catholic Church built with so much opposition on the part of Catholics as this."[17]

A Protestant entrepreneur stepped forward as the most important patron of early Rhode Island Catholicism. Philip Allen, the enterprising brother of Zachariah Allen, employed some three hundred Irish Catholic workers at his print works in Providence and had intimate connections with that community. Displaying the sense of benevolence that animated Nicholas Brown's charitable ventures, Allen made the cause of Rhode Island Catholics his own. It may have been his own high-toned Episcopalian background that led him to bestow upon them a "splendid Spanish bell" weighing some one thousand pounds. Two years later, when St. Patrick's Church was established, Allen contributed another three hundred dollars for the purchase of a second bell. On January 26, 1842, Bishop Fenwick traveled from Boston to bless Philip Allen's bells.[18] Allen treated the bishop to a tour of the print works, which left the churchman impressed. Allen's donations to his Catholic workers contained multiple messages. On one level, of course, the bell was a symbol of early factory discipline. It is doubtful that Allen's workers, many of whom worshipped at the two Catholic churches, missed the industrial implications behind the gift. In symbolic form, the fine Spanish bell brought Allen's authority even into the realm of worship.

[16] Byrne, *History of the Catholic Church*, 1:394.
[17] Quoted in Brennan, *Social Conditions*, 66.
[18] On the bells see Byrne, *Catholic Church*, 1:394, 397–398.

Simultaneously, the bell functioned in a mystical fashion during the celebration of the Mass, communicating the transformation of the host into the body and blood of Christ. Since the Cathedral church initially possessed no organ, the clanging of the bell would have been the only sound the parishioners heard, above the soft background of the priest's Latin.[19] The ritual of the Mass, then, transformed the meaning that the communicants attached to the bells, which simultaneously represented coercion and freedom, temporal discipline and spiritual autonomy.

Although Catholic parishioners warmly accepted Philip Allen's bells, they were less certain about the tract distributors and temperance reformers who entered their neighborhoods. Some Catholic residents cordially entertained their Protestant visitors. One "Brother Fuller" appears to have had some success in convincing factory operatives—Catholics among them—to receive religious literature and pious newsletters. Throughout 1834 he recorded numerous instances in which Catholic families accepted the materials he carried. In February he reported that he distributed sixty religious newspapers "on Eddy's point many of which were given to Catholics." In July he ventured to the countryside, calling on two factory villages in Johnston where "20 papers were dist. to Catholic families in a factory village." Back in Providence in September, Fuller ventured into the city's rougher neighborhoods to hand out literature at India Point and near the North Burial Ground, where, again, Catholics took hold of his papers. By November, he had visited Carpenter's Point and delivered twenty religious papers "chiefly to Catholics." Since Fuller was not ashamed to record instances in which his efforts were rejected, it is likely that virtually hundreds of Catholic families took literature from his hands.[20]

Other tract distributors did not have Brother Fuller's touch. They found Irish Catholics to be highly resistant to spiritual transformation of any kind. One Irish woman explained to her distributor that "the priest would not allow her to read such books & she thought they could do her no good."[21] Another Catholic family stiffly informed their visitor that "We are no tract receivers."[22] Part of the problem for the missionaries stemmed from the fact that the Irish could not read the literature they were handed.[23] Given the

---

[19] On the Mass see Dolan, *Immigrant Church*, 59–60. On the use of bells see *The Catholic Manual, Containing a Selection of Prayers and Devotional Exercises, for the use of Christians in Every State of Life* (Baltimore, n.d.), 35.

[20] See John Bours Papers, distributions for February 1834, 26; July 1834, 9; September 1834, 18; November 1834, 22, Manuscript Collection, Rhode Island Historical Society, hereafter cited as RIHS.

[21] John Bours Papers, distribution for August 1832, 2.

[22] John Bours Papers, distribution for September 1832, 15.

[23] Ibid., 14–15.

deep roots of Irish Catholic culture in traditions of the verbal arts, song, and storytelling, the primacy that Protestant reformers placed on written tracts must have seemed baffling.[24] Others immigrants took issue with Protestant dogma. One "Roman Catholic" turned the tables on an unsuspecting distributor by arguing "with me that *that* [Catholicism] was the only true religion."[25] Some Catholic families regarded the tract distributors as troublesome and contentious guests, complicating their already complex adjustment to a new society and culture.

The temperance issue also divided Irish Catholics and bourgeois Protestants. In the midst of growing Protestant concerns that strong drink caused most of society's problems, "the Irish in their open and undisguised drinking were more noticeable than their neighbors and more subject to blame and abuse."[26] The issue of alcohol also figured prominently in the spectacular murder trial of the Gordon brothers in 1844 and 1845. The brothers stood accused of the murder of Amasa Sprague, one of Rhode Island's most prominent industrialists. In 1843 Sprague had pressured the Cranston Town Council to repeal the liquor license of an Irish immigrant, Nicholas Gordon, who operated an ale house in his grocery store. In the case brought by the prosecution against the Gordons, the revocation of the liquor license became "the core" issue.[27] Protestants implicated the Irish thirst for liquor in Sprague's death.

Irish Catholics embraced the temperance cause on their own terms. From his earliest days in Providence, Father Corry had championed a Catholic Temperance Society. In February 1841, he had boasted to a Providence newspaper that "twelve hundred of the Irish laborers" had already dedicated themselves to sobriety, maintaining that "there is no longer any need of giving employment to a drinking Irishman."[28] While some dissenters refused to join the temperance cause, enough Irish Catholics embraced it to prompt a massive temperance rally on July 4, 1844. The meeting, which drew fifteen hundred members from both the Cathedral Church and from St. Patrick's, convened at a picnic on Smith Hill. But this "Arcadian festivity" had a flavor quite distinct from the huge 1842 Protestant rally we have previously considered. Recall that this rally had featured a martial theme, revealed in calls for republican virtue and the recruitment of a "Cold Water

---

[24] On the orality of Irish culture see Kerby A. Miller, *Emigrants and Exiles: Ireland and Irish Exodus to North America* (New York, 1985), 71–72.

[25] John Bours Papers, distribution for February 1833, 10.

[26] Brennan, *Social Conditions*, 80.

[27] See Hoffman and Hoffman, *Brotherly Love*, 28–29 and passim.

[28] *Manufacturer's and Farmer's Journal, Providence and Pawtucket Advertiser*, February 11, 1841. See also March 22, 1841.

Army." The Catholic rally avoided military pomp, employing instead imagery of a pastoral and spiritual nature. "The women wore white. The men had green ribbon scarfs, and all wore medals of the Blessed Virgin suspended from the neck."[29] The tone of this event and the attire of its participants would have made it clear that the Catholic and Protestant movements sprang from divergent understandings of what the drive for temperance was about. The political objectives of the Protestant movement would have held little promise for Irish Catholic immigrants, who, given Rhode Island's substantial property and residency requirements for suffrage rights, walked near the edges of formal party politics.

Differences over religious tracts and temperance among bourgeois Protestants and Irish Catholics point to an even deeper divide in religious sensibility. As their medals commemorating the "Blessed Virgin" make clear, Rhode Island Catholics prized both the feminine and the miraculous in their religious devotions. As students of Irish Catholic culture have long understood, the religious beliefs that the immigrants carried with them in the antebellum period contained strong doses of folk customs and beliefs that only lightly touched orthodox Christianity. A minority of them attended church. "The figures on church attendance in pre-famine Ireland," Emmet Larkin has pointed out, "indicate that only thirty-three percent of the Catholic population went to mass."[30] Sacraments such as baptism and marriage "were also frequently celebrated in private houses rather than in churches," a practice that seems to have endured in the early days in Rhode Island as well.[31] The point here is not to impeach the faithfulness of Rhode Island's first Catholics. "In fact, pre-Famine Catholics *were* devout," Kerby A. Miller has written, "but their piety was expressed primarily in archaic, communal traditions, which had originated in pre-Christian times and had since acquired only a thin veneer of medieval Catholicism."[32] Moreover, even where Catholics held more orthodox views, their belief in the primacy of the sacraments, in the mystery of the Eucharist, and in their veneration of the "Blessed Virgin" could not have been more alien from the ethic of rational order embraced by bourgeois Protestants. In practicing a religion that continued to make room for miracles, Rhode

[29] See Byrne, *Catholic Church*, 1:399, on the Catholic temperance rally; for the Protestant rally see Chapter 4 above and "Simultaneous Temperance Meetings, Feb. 22, 1842," broadside in Harris Collection, Large Broadsides, Brown University Library. Dissent from the temperance movement is explored in Robert W. Hayman, *Catholicism in Rhode Island and the Diocese of Providence 1780–1886* (Providence, 1982), 40.

[30] Emmet Larkin, "The Devotional Revolution in Ireland, 1850–1875," *American Historical Review* 77 (1972): 636.

[31] Ibid.

[32] Miller, *Emigrants and Exiles*, 73.

Island's Catholics shared much the street preachers and the prophets we will take up shortly.

Like the city's first Catholics, new Protestant groups also met in private homes. In 1830 thirteen residents gathered at the residence of Peleg Boss, a carpenter. While all who attended the meeting considered themselves to be Baptists, they did not wish to connect themselves with any of the city's standing churches. Instead, they sought to form their own congregation, based on the doctrinal positions of the Six-Principle Baptists. A rustic sect whose primary areas of strength could be found in Rhode Island's farming villages, the Six-Principle Baptists remained something of an oddity among the increasingly respectable Providence Baptist communities. They felt cool about evangelical reform, doubted the wisdom of an educated clergy, and looked with disdain on hymn singing and the fine musical instruments prized by bourgeois communicants. By 1833 this small group of believers managed to erect their own house of worship on Burgess Street. Pew prices in their church may have been among the lowest in the city. Even in 1870, the price range of pews auctioned by the church fell between seven and sixty dollars per year.[33] Known as the Roger Williams Baptist Church, the first communicants prided themselves on fostering a "progressive and independent spirit."[34]

The lure of respectability made it difficult for the communicants to maintain their spiritual independence. In 1835 a convention of Six-Principle delegates assembled in Cranston to consider whether instrumental music should be allowed during worship. By a narrow margin, the delegates affirmed the traditional sectarian stand against the use of such music. The members of the Roger Williams Church, who evidently had warmed to singing with accompaniment, removed themselves from these restrictions. Floating without a denominational connection for nearly two years, the communicants finally voted to affiliate with the Freewill Baptists. In May 1837 the Roger Williams Church joined the Rhode Island Quarterly Meeting of the Freewill Baptists, which welcomed the use of musical instruments. By selecting to affiliate with the Freewill Baptists, the communicants of the Roger Williams Church took significant strides toward respectability. The use of fine organs and elaborate arrangements for hymns characterized the best Providence churches. Like the communicants of revival era churches before them, the members of the Roger Williams Church moved into the mainstream of Providence's Protestant culture.

For the Providence black community, the emergence of a new Freewill

---

[33] *Manual of the Roger Williams Church. Providence, R.I., with a Sketch of its Early History* (Providence, 1873), 18–19.
[34] Ibid., 20.

Baptist church spurred a renewed dedication to practice of enthusiastic religion. In September 1835 Reverend John W. Lewis, a fiery Freewill Baptist preacher, began a lengthy revival at the African Union Meeting House. By 1838 Lewis had left Providence, but he had also stirred the congregation to the point of schism. Chafing under the guidance of the Calvinist Jeremiah Asher, the Lewis converts broke away to form their own congregation, the Abyssinian Freewill Baptist Church. They held fast to the traditional Freewill Baptist drama of redemption that stressed the "Freeness of Salvation" to all sinners.[35] In taking up the central idea of the "Freeness of Salvation," the members of the Abyssinian Church spoke not only an anticommercial language but one that emphasized the fundamental concept of freedom as well. They also voted that "all evangelical Christians shall have full liberty to commune with us."[36] In 1835, the same year in which Fourth Baptist Church moved to restrict their communion practices, the Abyssinian Freewill Baptist Church retained an open communion policy. This exuberant and flexible doctrinal style recalled the theological tone of the 1820 revival era.

Like Providence Catholics, the members of the Abyssinian Church entered religious reform activities on their own terms. Their church covenant demanded that members "wholly abstain from the use of ardent spirits, except when they are recommended for medical purposes by a temperate physician."[37] Upon leaving Providence, the pastor John Lewis took command of the New England Temperance Convention of People of Color in Boston. Moreover, during the 1840s black Freewill Baptists contributed support to the growing antislavery network within their denomination.[38] Still, the communicants of the Abyssinian Church did not join forces with white Protestants in distributing tracts or in promoting citywide temperance rallies. Despite their initiatives in religious reform, the black Freewill Baptists found that respectability in Providence was defined largely in terms set by white Protestants of substantial property.

The street preachers who typified plebeian religious culture struck an ambivalent posture with respect to the bourgeois concept of respectability. On the one hand, this collection of dissidents, ranters, and self-styled theologians cared little for conventional notions of decorum and restraint. They gloried in the very chaos that bourgeois reformers sought to contain.

---

[35] *A Short Summary and Declaration of Faith of the Abyssinian Free-will Baptist Church in Providence, R.I., to which is added The Church Covenant* (Providence, 1836), 4.
[36] Ibid., 8.
[37] Ibid., 7.
[38] See Jay Coughtry, *Creative Survival: The Providence Black Community in the Nineteenth Century* (Providence, n.d.), 66.

In contrast to the systematic rotation of visits planned by the tract distributors, these ministers of the streets held forth whenever an audience could
be found. At the same time, they sought a measure of authority and respect.
William Apess and Seth Luther, especially, claimed that *they*, rather than
the formally educated, ordained clergy, were the true prophets of the
gospel. The poles of rebelliousness and respectability described a con-
tinuum along which the street preachers shuttled as circumstance dictated.
They occupied a middle ground between these two extremes that made
them difficult for respectable residents to define, but impossible for them
to ignore.

In September 1826, the Providence *Beacon* featured the letter of a
Pawtucket resident who complained of a certain "Dr. Preachloud."[39] The
correspondent characterized him as "a religious quack, who has cracked
eardrums, and turned the heads of half the females in this place, by his loud
exhortations and pourings out of the spirit." Although the newspaper account did not furnish a precise identity for the infamous Preachloud, the
piece claimed that he was "by trade a Cobler." Because he was "of that class
of mechanics, who are termed 'religious,' he left the trade of St. Crispian,
for the purpose of separating sinners, and bringing them, 'out of darkness
into marvelous light.'" A man with a shadowy past and without definite occupation, Dr. Preachloud is an excellent example of the Weberian charismatic figure—a man standing outside the normal routines and attachments
of social life. An artisan possessed of substantial magnetism and a strong
pair of lungs, Dr. Preachloud and his antics created a stir in the Pawtucket
community.

The account of Dr. Preachloud's revival underscored its deeply seductive
and provocative character. Providence's ordained clergy had long worried
about the impact that roving itinerants might have on their congregations
and sometimes articulated their fears in ways that recognized the sexual
component of revival preaching. For example, James Wilson, the pastor of
Beneficent Congregational Church, warned his flock to be wary of the dangers of visiting Methodists. In his diary he recalled publishing a work which
"opened the eyes of many to discover the danger of itinerant preachers aiming at seduction of members from settled churches."[40] Wilson's recognition
that revival preachers played out "seduction" scenes with their hearers is
precisely what bothered some of Preachloud's critics in Pawtucket. One
critic lamented that "so very pious have a great many of his female converts
become that they refuse to do any kind of work on the Sabbath." As a result,

[39] All citations for "Dr. Preachloud" come from the Providence *Beacon*, September 9, 1826,
American Antiquarian Society Library, Worcester, Mass.
[40] James Wilson Memoirs, 274, Manuscript Division, Library of Congress.

"their parents and guardians have been obliged to have recourse to the birch in order to make them return to their duty." In short, Dr. Preachloud inspired insubordination against the proper ties of family authority.

But even as Dr. Preachloud generated religious controversy, he based his dissent on an entirely orthodox and Biblically sound issue. Stephen S. Wardwell himself could have applauded Preachloud's strict Sabbatarian views as well as his implication that God's laws reigned supreme over all earthly authorities, including parents. Preachloud's sweeping Sabbatarianism would have accorded well with the positions held by refined Providence churches during the 1840s. In April 1843, for instance, the Richmond Street Congregational Church voted to restrict "travel, on the Sabbath, in Steam Boats, Stages, or other conveyances for purposes of business or pleasure, or to visit the Post-Office for the same purposes on the Lord's Day."[41] By holding to a rigid position on the issue of Sabbath observance, Preachloud clung to a thoroughly respectable idea to make trouble for the Pawtucket community. He blended in strange combination the competing ideas of dissent and obedience, rebellion and respectability.

The liminality of the street preachers within the town's religious culture sometimes obscured their real identities. In October 1829, the Providence *Literary Subaltern* complained bitterly about a "wandering vagabond" who held forth in the old Town House.[42] Courting the favor of the "mischevous boys" among his listeners, the street preacher called "Phileo" held forth on a Monday evening. "He would have the whole of our clergy," lamented the report, "as ignorant as himself, and as he insists on opposing education, our respectable clergymen, have wisely and prudently closed their doors against him." Resigned to collecting a congregation at the Town House, Phileo continued his work. The "boys" in the streets, at least, found his freewheeling style of preaching entertaining and applauded "the Reverend gentleman" with "vehemence" and "frequency." The newspaper's account, with understandable sarcasm, repeatedly referred to Phileo as a "reverend gentleman," thereby mocking his crude, untutored rhetoric and the mob to which it appealed. But could it also be possible that Phileo really was a minister of some sort?

Evidence suggests that Phileo may not have been the opponent of the established clergy that he first appeared to be. Records of First Baptist Church in nearby Pawtucket document that in July 1829 David Benedict, the settled minister of the congregation, stepped down in the midst of controversy. During the fall and winter of 1829, church minutes reveal that one "Elder

[41] Record Book, Richmond Street Congregational Church, April 1843, RIHS.
[42] All citations for Phileo's visit come from *Literary Subaltern* (Providence), October 2, 1829, American Antiquarian Society Library.

Philleo" achieved remarkable success in adding new members to the congregation, baptizing over seventy members between September 19 and December 12. On March 6, 1830, the church voted to "give Rev. Calvin Philleo call to settle as our pastor for one year."[43] Was Calvin Philleo the "Phileo" who had been ridiculed in the Providence newspaper? Chronology makes a case for this point. The *Literary Subaltern's* article appeared on October 2, 1829, at precisely the moment that the Pawtucket church records show "Elder Philleo's" revival in full swing. The very slight difference between "Phileo" and "Philleo," especially slight when we remember the elastic conventions of spelling in the early nineteenth century, also suggests that these two men were actually the same person. The *Literary Subaltern's* characterization of Phileo as a "reverend gentleman" may have contained a double meaning, simultaneously lampooning Phileo's style while also identifying him correctly as a minister, albeit one who did not receive the approbation of established Providence churchmen. However plausible the case may be, we cannot be certain in the end that Philleo and Phileo were one and the same. His appearance at the fringes of respectable Providence society reveals, however, an important dimension of plebeian religious culture.

The case of Calvin Philleo (or Phileo) is evocative of wider problems of authenticity and character in antebellum America. In their fluid and mobile market economy, where one did business with strangers as a matter of course, Americans struggled to detect the fraudulent among the honest, to sort out the unscrupulous from the sincere, and to guard themselves against the growing numbers of "confidence men" who walked the streets looking to prey upon the innocent.[44] Etiquette books and advice manuals on manners and proper demeanor only complicated the matter, since devious characters could easily act as well-behaved gentlemen. Providence communicants knew that the outward appearance of piety did not always betoken authentic faith. Temperance advocates, for example, understood that men who appeared as devout pewholders on Sunday might well operate groceries that sold alcohol during the week. Even the most sincere of converts, such as Emeline Barstow and Stephen Wardwell, constantly searched their hearts and deeds for signs that would either buoy or sink their hopes for salvation. When we recall that the master of "humbug," P. T. Barnum himself,

[43] Record Book, First Baptist Church, Pawtucket; see meeting of July 18, 1829, on the Benedict situation; meetings of September 19, 26, October 22, November 6, 21, 28, December 12 for baptisms; and meeting of March 6, 1830, on the vote to call Calvin Philleo as pastor, RIHS.
[44] See Karen Halttunen, *Confidence Men and Painted Women: A Study of Middle-Class Culture in America, 1830–1870* (New Haven, 1982); John F. Kasson, *Rudeness and Civility: Manners in Nineteenth-Century Urban America* (New York, 1990), 92–111.

once tried his hand as a Bible salesman, we can gain some understanding of the depth of the problem that people of faith were up against.[45]

Edward Quarles, a Providence paperhanger and amateur actor, exploited the problem of religious deception in his stunning performance in the comic play *The Hypocrite*.[46] In 1828 he made his stage debut by taking the part of Mawworm, an evangelical minister identified with the tag line "I wants to go a preaching." That this phrase enjoyed some currency in Providence at the time is illustrated by the fact that it appeared in the *Literary Subaltern*'s piece on Phileo. In poking fun at popular preachers in general, Quarles simultaneously assaulted the wandering theologians who frequented the Providence Town House. He planned his performance as a "caricature of the productions of an itinerant sensationalist, who was then preaching in this town." Simultaneously, however, by taking the stage and "acting" the part of a minister, Quarles perpetrated a sleight of hand that rivaled the hypocrisy of those he sought to mimic.

The theater that hosted Quarles's thespian efforts had become the focus for a kind of artistic class struggle by the time he mounted the stage. In the early national era, theater productions tended to attract prosperous "federalist" audiences. Sometimes pampered by servants in livery, prominent citizens feasted upon patriotic sketches, adventure stories, and numerous Shakespearean dramas. By the late 1820s, however, the Providence Theater drew a less decorous class of patrons. Journeymen and apprentices interrupted performances and created mayhem for actors who could not contend with their participation. Like other theater audiences of the antebellum period, Providence artisans expected to take an active role in the productions they witnessed. Their shared "similarity of tastes" led them to establish their own club, the "Shoemakers' Literary and Dramatic Society."[47] In 1828 they succeeded in creating their own productions for the stage. Quarles's appearance in *The Hypocrite* constituted one of the first efforts by Providence working people to project an organized presence in the community at large.

The play brought Edward Quarles instant popularity. Thirty-three years old, he had obtained little formal education but was "endowed with unusual sarcastic powers." Quarles employed these gifts to full effect in his performance. In the play's famous pulpit scene, he nearly lost his composure. He discovered that the sermon he had intended to deliver had been removed

---

[45] See Neil Harris, *Humbug: The Art of P. T. Barnum* (Chicago, 1973), 29.
[46] The material on Edward Quarles is from Charles Blake, *An Historical Account of the Providence Stage, being a paper read before the Rhode Island Historical Society, October 25, 1860* (Providence, 1868), 211–213.
[47] See Blake, *Historical Account of the Providence Stage*, 75–76 and 199.

and another text had been placed there instead. Flexible enough to roll with adversity and with the participation of the audience, Ned Quarles worked his way into an extraordinary performance. He delivered the satire with such force that "the audience were in ecstasies." At the conclusion of the play, the patrons clamored for Quarles to step forward to deliver a speech. To their dismay, he explained that "his first appearance on the stage should also be his last." He was right. A few years later, authorities discovered his body floating in the Providence Cove.

Even as Edward Quarles jabbed at the figure of the "itinerant sensationalist," his own dramatic performance took on features of a popular religious revival. The interior of the Providence Theater itself, with its boxed seats and balcony, resembled a church complete with pews. In executing his part in the play, Quarles made use of the same earthy and common language that revival preachers employed. He also employed the same extemporaneous methods of his enemies by daring to use a sermon script that he had not seen before. Moreover, both Quarles and the evangelical ministers schemed to put their respective audiences "in ecstasies." While Quarles certainly did not intend to produce conversions among theatergoers, he did succeed in inducing emotional release. In presenting his parody of a revival preacher, Quarles edged toward creating a religious atmosphere of his own design.

The "worship service" crafted by Edward Quarles, however, bore little resemblance to the services conducted in refined Protestant churches. In accepting the suggestions of his audience, Quarles diffused his own version of ministerial authority.[48] Control of his performance rested equally with audience and performer. The satire itself, with its rough humor, came perilously close to an open expression of anger—which, as John F. Kasson has argued, respectable citizens suppressed at all costs. "Of all emotions," he writes, "anger most violently betrayed a loss of self-possession and irreparably shattered the spirit of civility."[49] Moreover, in throwing himself on the mercy of his audience, in exhibiting dangerous behavior such as laughter, and in acknowledging anger, Quarles created a scene of disorder and chaos that could never have been tolerated in a bourgeois worship service. The values that Quarles and his colleagues exhibited in this performance could not have cut more fully against the grain of respectable piety.[50] This production by the "Shoemaker's Literary and Dramatic Society" may have

[48] On the participatory quality of theatergoing in the nineteenth century and the controversies it spawned, see Kasson, *Rudeness and Civility*, 217–228.

[49] Ibid., 157.

[50] The intricate interplay between the stage and the rise of capitalist culture is explored in Jean-Christophe Agnew, *Worlds Apart: The Market and the Theater in Anglo-American Thought, 1550–1750* (New York, 1986).

prompted orderly Providence citizens to hasten their campaign to shut down the theater. Like Edward Quarles, the Providence theater died a few years later.

Unlike Edward Quarles, whose oration traded on parody, the shoemaker Melvin Wilbour fought earnestly for the opportunity to express his own beliefs. A resident of North Main Street, he had been one of the original members who joined the Fourth Baptist Church in 1823.[51] He also possessed a deep desire to preach. Perhaps trusting in the flexible doctrinal stance of the original congregation, Wilbour approached the communicants about his call to speak. In July 1830 they granted him a trial run. They decided to select "a suitable time and place in which he will preach before the church in order that they may decide definitely as regards his call to Preach the Gospel." He passed the test. By March 1831 the congregation acknowledged that the shoemaker had "for a long time been seriously impressed that it is his duty to improve his gifts in public." They endorsed him as a member in good standing and recommended him "to all who are disposed to encourage him in his efforts."

The members of Fourth Baptist Church quickly came to regret their vote of confidence. By August 1832 they learned that Wilbour had been "rebaptized and ordained to preach by certain Ministers called Mormonites now Preaching in this City." The issue of rebaptism, especially, caused trouble for the Mormons as they sought converts. "No single teaching," Richard Bushman has written, "caused the early missionaries more trouble than the requirement of rebaptism, with its implication of universal Christian apostasy."[52] Alarmed, the congregation sent Allen Brown and Zalmon Tobey to confront Wilbour about the report. At first, he apologized for his conduct. He acknowledged the grief he had brought the church and "desired their forgiveness." Persuaded by Wilbour's apparent repentance, the communicants did not suspend his membership, but they did revoke his right to preach in public "until the excitement was alayed and he again aprobated by the Church." Given the substantial nature of Wilbour's theological deviance, the members of his church displayed remarkable patience in dealing with him.

Melvin Wilbour soon demonstrated that he did not merit such forbearance. Within a month, he appeared at a church meeting to express his determination "to resist the injunction placed upon him by the Church." In

---

[51] This account of the Melvin Wilbour case is drawn from Record Book, Fourth Baptist Church, meetings of July 28, 1830; March 2, 1831; August 1, 8, September 26, October 8, 1832; February 27, 1833, RIHS. On March 25, 1835, the church also cut off from their membership one Unis Wilbour, probably Melvin's wife.

[52] Richard L. Bushman, *Joseph Smith and the Beginnings of Mormonism* (Urbana, 1984), 153.

response to his open defiance of their authority, the members again moved cautiously. On October 8, 1832, they gathered in a special meeting to give the case their full attention. Despite Wilbour's challenge, the congregation once again "earnestly entreated" him to "desist from his intention to preach in public." By the winter of 1833, the members proved less tolerant. Already weary of the case, they heard reports that "Brother Wilbour continued to preach as often as an opening presented and was determined thus to do." Even more disturbing to them was word that Wilbour now "considered himself a regular ordained Minister." Deeply concerned that he would represent his brand of Mormon-Baptist theology as that of the congregation, they withdrew their fellowship from him. As if to punctuate their intentions, the communicants stressed that they would leave Wilbour "to act on his own responsibility." This may have been exactly what Melvin Wilbour had wanted all along.

If Melvin Wilbour absorbed the spirit and doctrine of Mormonism in the early 1830s, then his views would have clashed with those held by bourgeois Protestants. The first Mormons were people of the miracle. The story of Joseph Smith's visions and his discovery of the golden plates (upon which the Book of Mormon was inscribed) speaks to the profound grip that supernatural thinking continued to have on antebellum Americans. "Despite the disdain of the educated," Richard Bushman has argued, "ordinary people apparently had no difficulty reconciling Christianity with magic."[53] John L. Brooke has traced the origins of Mormon cosmology to a hermeticism that had deep roots in early modern Europe, especially in seventeenth-century England. "The restoration of a miraculous connection between heaven and earth, between spirit and matter," Brooke writes, "was the most powerful attraction drawing adherents to Smith's new church." Joseph Smith and those he anointed as his leaders had a special role to fill in manifesting those connections between the sacred and the profane. "Smith's God was a God of miracles," Brooke continues, "but so too were his agents, his priests, men of miracles."[54] From what we know of Melvin Wilbour's case at Fourth Baptist Church, it is unlikely that he performed any miracles. Yet, it is equally clear that Wilbour felt empowered by some force, some higher call or authority, to repeatedly and openly defy the members of a church he had helped to establish. If not an outright miracle, then the strength and tenacity of Melvin Wilbour's call to preach may have had its origins in an experience of the sacred.

The economic ethic of the *Book of Mormon* also did not square with the

[53] Ibid., 72.
[54] John L. Brooke, *The Refiner's Fire: The Making of Mormon Cosmology, 1644–1844* (New York, 1994), 184, 186.

acquisitiveness that characterized refined Protestants. According to Nathan O. Hatch's reading, the *Book of Mormon* "is a document of profound social protest, an impassioned manifesto by a hostile outsider against the smug complacency of those in power and the reality of social distinctions based on wealth, class, and education." He goes on to maintain that "the single most striking theme in the *Book of Mormon* is that it is the rich, the proud, the learned who find themselves in the hands of an angry God. Throughout the book, evil is most often depicted as the result of pride and worldliness that comes from economic success and results in the oppression of the poor."[55] To be sure, it is tempting to overstate the "counter-cultural" stance of the first Mormons. Indeed, Joseph Smith himself had to live down accusations of using his prophetic gifts to hunt treasure. And, as Grant Underwood has observed, "most Latter-day Saints seem to have imbibed the prevailing ethos of economic liberalism a little too fully to fit the description of being antibourgeois or radically communitarian."[56] Even if we concede that the Mormons were not "radically communitarian," that admission still leaves a considerable gap between the *Book of Mormon* and Francis Wayland's *Elements of Political Economy*.

Despite their hold on Melvin Wilbour, the Mormons were not the only religious group agitating for converts within the city. In 1841 William Miller, the celebrated Adventist, visited Providence preaching his own peculiar version of Christ's return to earth. He preached to "crowded audiences, and is said to have had some converts to his opinions upon the interpretation of the prophecies."[57] Unlike Joseph Smith, William Miller did not insist that his followers rebaptize themselves and follow him into a new church. For this reason, Providence Millerites are difficult to track; they floated within the ranks of established congregations. Yet, some evidence hints that Providence Millerites may have gathered informally and discussed the prophetic chronology that the founder had outlined. Ruth Doan points out, for instance, that Providence's Millerites "were said to have chosen the fifteenth of February 1843 as a likely time for the end."[58] That this consensus seems to have been reached and publicized by Miller's adherents in Providence suggests that subterranean meetings took place. Since Miller insisted that simple folk armed or'y with a Bible could follow his prophecies, it is little wonder he attracted a following.

While some spectators may have regarded Miller's preaching as street

---

[55] Nathan O. Hatch, *The Democratization of American Christianity* (New Haven, 1989), 116, 117.

[56] Grant Underwood, *The Millenarian World of Early Mormonism* (Urbana, 1993), 103.

[57] *Manufacturer's and Farmer's Journal, Providence and Pawtucket Advertiser*, April 8, 1841.

[58] Ruth Alden Doan, *The Miller Heresy, Millennialism, and American Culture* (Philadelphia, 1987), 48.

theater, it changed Timothy J. Aldrich's life. A molder who worked in the factory of the New England Butt Company, Aldrich became profoundly impressed with Miller's doctrines. On September 12, 1843, he admitted to the members of Richmond Street Congregational Church that he "is deeply interested in the 2nd advent and deems it his duty to attend meetings where his peculiar views are advocated."[59] What is remarkable here is the matter of timing. Aldrich seems to have deepened his commitment to the Adventists even as the specific dates outlined by Miller and his followers for the coming of the millennium melted away without the blessed event. The Providence date of February 15 had passed as did days in April, May, and July 1843. Aldrich may have been following the lead of other Millerites, who, after a series of disappointments, tried to avoid naming specific dates for Christ's second coming even as they cleaved to the broad outlines of Miller's teachings.

In the ensuing months, Timothy Aldrich weighed the nature of his connection with the Richmond Street Church. In January 1844 he appeared before them again to defend his opinions. He claimed openly to have "conscientiously embraced views touching on the second advent of Christ which this Church reject." Indeed, Aldrich admitted that he had originally entered into the Congregational covenant while "in the dark." Now enlightened by Miller's teachings, he claimed theological expertise as his own. Following the flow of Aldrich's testimony, the church clerk recorded that he "called no man master—and regarded human covenants as the work of men and of no binding nature." Moreover, Aldrich laid out the only condition under which he would accept continuing membership in the congregation: "the privilege of advocating his own views in the social meetings of the Church." If such a requirement could not be met, as Aldrich of course understood it could not, then he asked that his membership be "dissolved in any manner the Church might deem proper."[60] Hence, Aldrich simultaneously gained an audience for his views and preempted the impact of a vote for exclusion of membership by suggesting it himself. His bold move provides evidence for the claim that "the demands of God, as perceived by individual Millerites, took precedence over subjection to the community of the church."[61]

Although antebellum churches treaded carefully in confronting the Millerite heretics in their midst, they found that they could not tolerate the "radical supernaturalism" that pervaded Adventist thought.[62] In looking for the personal return of Christ to earth, and in dating its timing with

---

[59] Record Book, Richmond Street Congregational Church, September 12, 1843.
[60] Record Book, Richmond Street Congregational Church, January 8, 1844.
[61] Doan, *Miller Heresy*, 140.
[62] The term "radical supernaturalism" is from ibid., 54–82.

precision, William Miller and his followers insisted that the distance between earthly and heavenly realms would soon collapse. As they preached
Christ's physical return to earth, Millerites made room for the intervention
of the miraculous in their daily lives, thus rejecting pretensions to a rational
religion. The audacity with which Miller announced the specific timing of
this blessed event seemed to his critics to verge on sheer insanity. At the very
least, as Timothy Aldrich's case made clear, the dedication of individual
Millerites to their particular vision of millennial prophecy challenged the
sober and careful Biblical hermeneutics practiced by their contemporaries.
Aldrich's insistence that human covenants were not binding was, in turn,
based on the belief that the teachings of the Bible as understood by individuals outweighed the judgment of the community of faith.

Some skeptics accused the Millerites of adopting a posture of passivity
and outright laziness as they counted down the days before Christ's return.
With dreams of the dawning millennium racing in their heads, putting in a
regular day's work seemed somehow less important for some Adventists. Exaggerated as they may have been, charges of Millerite passivity are important for two reasons. First, they suggest, as Ruth Doan has argued, that even
when Millerites exhibited all the evidence of hard work and personal discipline, they did so for reasons that separated them from their bourgeois
brethren.[63] Millerites worked only because God had told them to, not to
bound ahead in the world of the market economy. If the millennium were
truly on its way, then the cultivation of character and the goal of laying up
earthly riches represented endeavors of paltry significance. Second, to the
degree that their opponents charged them with passivity, they simultaneously marked the Millerites as a particularly "feminine" form of religious
dissent. Nineteenth-century Americans understood the qualities of passivity
and even "passionlessness" as belonging especially to women.[64] In this respect, too, Timothy Aldrich's dispute with the Richmond Street Church
demonstrated a break with the manly and market-oriented outlook manifested in bourgeois religious culture.

Still, Timothy Aldrich launched his rebellion from what he understood
be the high ground of Biblical authority. Aldrich, and Millerites in general,
based their beliefs on their own understanding of the Scriptures. In a world

---

[63] Ibid., 151–158.

[64] See especially Nancy F. Cott, "Passionlessness: An Interpretation of Victorian Sexual Ideology, 1790–1850," *Signs: A Journal of Women in Culture and Society* 4 (1978): 219–236. On women
among Millerites see Jonathan M. Butler, "The Making of a New Order: Millerism and the
Origins of Seventh-Day Adventism," in Ronald L. Numbers and Jonathan M. Butler, eds., *The
Disappointed: Miller and Millenarianism in the Nineteenth Century* (Bloomington, Ind., 1987),
196–197.

that still settled disputes by means of appeal to Biblical teachings, Timothy Aldrich rested his case on the most solid of all sources. Inspired not by visions, angels, or dreams but by Biblical calculation, Millerites seemed far more conventional than Joseph Smith and his Mormon followers. At points, Miller and his disciples appeared to be even more conventional than their opponents. "At a time when the seminary trained, at least, were aware of challenges to the integrity of the Bible on a variety of fronts," Ruth Doan writes, "the Millerites seemed most content to assert simply that they believed in an inspired Bible, including the whole Bible, and consistent within itself."[65] Like Dr. Preachloud's relentless Sabbatarianism, Timothy Aldrich's dissent drew strength from the major source that legitimated evangelical culture in antebellum America.

William Apess, too, mobilized traditional religious and political themes in the cause of social protest.[66] A Pequot Indian from Massachusetts, Apess became one of the leading Native American voices of the 1830s. He composed an autobiography, *A Son of the Forest* (1831), and other works critical of the Puritans' "providential" interpretation of how God had disposed of his people. While Apess may be better known for his public role in the Mashpee Revolt of 1833–34 in Massachusetts, he lived and worked for a time in Providence, Rhode Island. In *A Son of the Forest*, Apess claimed that he had a sister in Providence and that he lived in the city from 1825 to 1827. These proved to be especially critical years in Apess's development, coming as they did on the heels of a profound experience that confirmed his call to preach the gospel. During his years in the city, Apess took a leading role among the Methodists, serving as a class leader and obtaining a certificate to preach.[67] His life and work are significant, not only for what they illuminate about the study of Pequot culture and Native American history, but also for what they reveal about "the lower strata of the laboring classes in this period of New England history."[68] His religious experience, especially, exposes important dimensions of plebeian piety that blend with those of the street preachers considered here.

[65] Ruth Alden Doan, "Millerism and Evangelical Culture," in Ronald L. Numbers and Jonathan M. Butler, eds., *The Disappointed: Miller and Millenarianism in the Nineteenth Century* (Bloomington, Ind., 1987), 127.
[66] The classic modern volume assembling Apess's work is Barry O'Connell, ed., *On Our Own Ground: The Complete Writings of William Apess, a Pequot* (Amherst, Mass., 1992). All citations to Apess's work are from O'Connell's collection.
[67] Apess, *A Son of the Forest*, in O'Connell, *On Our Own Ground*, 47–48.
[68] O'Connell, *On Our Own Ground*, xxvii. Much of what O'Connell writes in his excellent introduction with respect to Apess's subversive use of Methodism and republicanism could be applied more widely to the study of working-class Americans of the antebellum period. Thus, Apess emerges as a key figure in the study of labor history as well as Native American history.

Born in 1798 in Colrain, Massachusetts, William Apess could not have come from a more marginal background. He was a member of the Pequots, a people who had fallen victim to the genocidal war waged upon them by the Puritans in 1637 (it was widely believed by whites that the Pequots had been completely exterminated). As a child, he was sent to live with his grandparents to avoid the quarrelsome relationship of his parents. Then followed a series of stints as an indentured servant. He converted to Methodism in 1813 and was condemned for his faith by one of his masters. "Now the Methodists and all who attended their meetings were greatly persecuted," he recalled. "All denominations were up in arms against them, because the Lord was blessing their labors and making them (a poor, despised people) his instruments in the conversion of sinners."[69] William then joined the army during the War of 1812, a move that only made worse his growing fondness, and quite possibly his addiction, to rum. A Pequot among white New Englanders, a transient laborer among settled farmers and townspeople, a drinker among sober churchgoers, and a Methodist among the state-supported Congregationalists of Massachusetts, William Apess laid claim to the social and economic marginality that Max Weber argued characterized charismatic religious figures.

William Apess made room for the supernatural in his religious world view. This is evident, especially, in the passages in *A Son of the Forest* where Apess describes how he received the confidence to begin his career has a preacher. In particular, he sought a sign from God that would single him out as a man especially anointed to preach, since, he wrote, "we read in the Bible that in former days holy men spoke as they were moved by the Holy Ghost."[70] Apess, too, wanted a sign. He struggled with his soul on the matter, and wrestled especially with a strange dream that troubled his sleep. He dreamed that he had taken a journey "through a miry place in a dark and dreary way" when he saw a bright plain, bathed in sunlight. Upon reaching the plain, he discovered "an angel of the blessed Lord stood in my way. After having addressed me, he read some extracts from St. John's Gospel, respecting the preaching of the word of life." Disturbed by the encounter (did the angel mean to block his desire to preach?), Apess called on God to give him a sign to confirm his ministerial authority. Soon after the dream, he preached a series of powerful messages in which "the Lord laid too his helping hand." The success of his preaching, and his conviction that the Lord had made it so, thus assured Apess "that my call was of God."[71] At this point, Apess's Methodism and traditions of Native American religion merged. As

[69] Apess, *Son of the Forest*, 19.
[70] Ibid., 43.
[71] Ibid., 44–45.

Karim Tiro has argued, through Methodism's validation of "the individual's direct relationship with the supernatural through visions and other forms of sensible revelation, praying outdoors, and emphasizing oral communication and the personal charisma of the preacher, enthusiastic evangelicals achieved a closer approximation of Native American traditions, however superficially, than their more liturgical peers."[72]

William Apess turned his Methodism into a powerful weapon of social protest. From the beginning, his embrace of the Methodism "was a real act of defiance towards his masters."[73] By the 1830s, he turned that defiance toward the white community at large. His people, he argued, had conducted themselves in greater accordance with Christian values than had the whites, who had taken their land and sold them alcohol. Relying heavily on the work of Elias Boudinot, Apess took the position that Native Americans "are none other than the descendants of Jacob and the long lost tribes of Israel."[74] Touching on a point that resonated with the beliefs of Joseph Smith and the Mormons, Apess posited the history of a devout population of Native Americans that inhabited North America well before contact with modern Europeans.[75] In 1836 Apess also brought his Methodist perspective to bear in an address he delivered in Boston, *Eulogy on King Philip, as Pronounced at the Odeon, in Federal Street, Boston*. Blending republican rhetoric with Methodist egalitarianism, Apess resurrected King Philip as the Pequot version of George Washington, a chief fighting for the freedom and independence of his people in 1676, just as Washington had led his people a century later. Blasting the hypocrisy of the Puritans and their historians, Apess argued that "it appears that King Philip treated his prisoners with a great deal more Christian-like spirit that the Pilgrims did."[76] Apess's Methodist identity afforded him the advantage of taking on the dominant culture of his day in a language that they had to take seriously.

Seth Luther, too, brought the full force of Christianity to bear on the injustices of his day. A Providence carpenter, he played a key role in the labor and suffrage reform agitation of 1832–33. He served as secretary for the Providence Association of Practical Carpenters and Masons and delivered a powerful oration in 1833 titled *An Address on the Right of Free Suffrage*. He worked closely with the New England Association of Farmers, Mechanics, and Other Workingmen and promoted the workingmen's cause from

---

[72] Karim M. Tiro, "Denominated 'SAVAGE': Methodism, Writing, and Identity in the Works of William Apess, A Pequot," *American Quarterly* 48 (1996): 659–660.
[73] Tiro, "Denominated 'SAVAGE,'" 658.
[74] Apess, *Son of the Forest*, 53.
[75] See Bushman, *Joseph Smith*, 134–136.
[76] Apess, *Eulogy on King Philip, as Pronounced at the Odeon, in Federal Street, Boston* (1836), in O'Connell, *On Our Own Ground*, 300.

Boston to New York. In addition to his writings on voting rights in Rhode Island, Luther published three other major orations, which propelled him into the front ranks of antebellum labor agitators. Blending natural rights philosophy with his Baptist heritage, Luther demonstrated an impressive understanding of European political developments and their relevance to American life. Virtually every one of his published addresses compared the situation of American workers with that of laborers in other nations. "No American thinker in the whole early labor movement," Louis Hartz wrote in a pathbreaking essay, "was so acutely conscious as Seth Luther of the world-wide implications of the egalitarian drive."[77] Back in Rhode Island during the early 1840s, Luther threw himself behind Thomas Wilson Dorr's political insurgency to demolish the property requirement for Rhode Island's voters. A stalwart in Dorr's battalions, Luther paid for his role in the rebellion with imprisonment. Despite his "somewhat erratic" reputation, even his opponents came to respect his integrity and dedication. Reporting on his death in 1863, the Providence *Evening Post* acknowledged that "he did not embrace Dorrism as many of its followers did, because it promised promotion; it had been his political creed all his life."[78] Assessed by any relevant standard, Seth Luther measures up to be one of the most significant figures in the antebellum labor movement.

Despite Luther's manifest importance, his life was marked by a marginality that, perhaps, has played a part in rendering him invisible to all but a handful of historians. The story of Luther's relationship with the communicants of First Baptist Church suggests the volatility and liminality that characterized his career. During the revival of 1815–16, he joined the congregation along with dozens of other town residents, including the pastor Stephen Gano's daughter Maria, and some fifteen black residents.[79] After recording his baptism, church minutes do not mention him again for nearly a decade. On July 29, 1824, the congregation pressed charges against Seth Luther for the crime of "disorderly walking," a form of deviance that attached itself with increasing frequency to female communicants.[80] In Seth

---

[77] Louis Hartz, "Seth Luther, the Story of a Working-Class Rebel," *New England Quarterly* 13 (1940): 415. For works that explicate Luther's work in broader context see especially Jama Lazerow, *Religion and the Working Class in Antebellum America* (Washington, D.C., 1995), 208–213 and passim; Edward Pesson, *Most Uncommon Jacksonians: The Radical Leaders of the Early Labor Movement* (Albany, 1967), 87–90. See also the articles by Carl Gersuny, "A Biographical Note on Seth Luther," *Labor History* 18 (1977): 239–248, and "Seth Luther—The Road from Chapachet," *Rhode Island History* 33 (1974): 47–55.

[78] Quoted in Gersuny, "Biographical Note," 248.

[79] On the Baptist converts see Henry Melville King, ed., *Historical Catalogue of the Members of the First Baptist Church in Providence, Rhode Island* (Providence, 1908), 46–50.

[80] Record Book, First Baptist Church, July 29, 1824, RIHS. On the identification of "disorderly walking" with femininity see Juster, *Disorderly Women*.

Luther's case, the church did not spell out exactly how he had challenged their authority. Perhaps he had simply missed too many worship services. Indeed, Luther claimed to have traveled at least forty-five thousand of miles as a young man, ranging along the frontier as far west as Cincinnati, Ohio, through Indian and slave territory, and as far south as Florida. Even if he exaggerated the mileage of his journeys, as he probably did, the chances that he attended Stephen Gano's preaching are slim. Still, church members typically reserved the charge of "disorderly walking" for something more than neglect of Sabbath duties. Criminals tagged with this breach of conduct openly flaunted the authority of the church or bucked the legitimacy of the disciplinary process itself. It stands to reason that the members of First Baptist Church pursued Luther for reasons other than failing to take his place at worship.

Seth Luther's desperate financial condition may provide important clues as to his difficulties at First Baptist Church. In October, 1823, a few months before his excommunication, Luther petitioned the Rhode Island General Assembly for debt relief.[81] Composing his request from jail, Luther inventoried nearly two thousand dollars in debts and losses which he had sustained over the past three years. Chief among those with claims on Luther was his own brother, Thomas Luther Jr., to whom Seth owed $377.97. Ironically, Luther counted among his only possessions at this time a volume titled *Advice to a Younger Brother*.[82] During a decade in which debt law in Rhode Island hardened and respectable communicants looked askance at the impoverished, a business failure, especially one that burdened family members, may have generated friction between Luther and the members of First Baptist Church. But there may have been even more to this dispute. Among his financial losses, Luther listed a hundred dollars he had spent "on getting a Portrait of Rev. S. Gano Engraved and in attempting to sell the same." Stephen Gano, of course, was the immensely popular minister at First Baptist Church. It may be that the congregation frowned on Luther's efforts to profit by hawking portraits of the pastor. What is more certain, however, is that by 1824 Seth Luther had failed utterly in business and had been cut loose from the community of faith to which he had belonged for nine years.

Given Luther's increasingly marginal position in relation to churchgoing and prosperous Providence citizens, it is not surprising that his religious and social criticism carried such a sharp edge. In 1834, for instance, when

[81] Luther's petition for debt relief may be found in *Petitions to the Rhode Island General Assembly*, 52:88, Rhode Island State Archives, Providence.
[82] I am indebted to a conversation with Carl Gersuny for this insight. See his article "Young Luther in Debt," *Rhode Island History* 56 (1998): 53–60.

he lectured on the evils of avarice, Luther spoke with no small authority when describing how a debtor froze to death in the Providence jail.[83] He, too, had been imprisoned for debt. For his part in the Dorr Rebellion, Luther was sent to jail again. Following his release in 1843, Luther took to the open road, agitating for the release of Thomas Wilson Dorr from prison. The fragments of correspondence that survive from this period show a man desperate for recognition, driven by his convictions yet fearful that he would be forgotten. From Springfield, Illinois, he wrote to his colleague Walter S. Burgess that if Dorr were not "*unconditionally Liberated* and that too in short order Rhode Island will be desolated even as was Moscow when the Head Quarters of Napoleon were in the Kremlin." Conjuring legions of imaginary supporters, Luther pictured himself returning triumphantly to Providence as the leader of an army of liberation. Luther's final lines to Burgess, however, betrayed such grandiose schemes: "Yours a Survivor from the Chains and dungeons of Rhode Island in Exile."[84] His grip on reality began to loosen. At the outbreak of the Mexican War, he fired off a letter to President Polk pledging his enlistment for this patriotic crusade. He never went. By 1846 he had been committed to an asylum near Boston before being returned to the Butler Hospital for the Insane in Providence. Appropriately, Francis Wayland had been one of the guiding spirits behind the establishment of the Butler Hospital. Luther's behavior and opinions, which paralleled some of the Old Testament prophets whom he deeply admired, alienated him from those he fought so hard to free.

Seth Luther thus skirted the edges of the society that he sought to redeem. He stood without family (evidence reveals he did not marry), without formal church affiliation, and without steady employment against his bourgeois counterparts. He lived the life of a free-ranging agitator, traveling thousands of miles in his career and never settling in a single community. He was poor. Jailed twice, Seth Luther well understood that he lived under the power of a state in which he had no voice. Even his association with labor's cause and trade union activism placed him in quasi-legal terrain, for he lived in an age in which unions had only begun the struggle for official recognition. We might well conclude that the only "homes" Seth Luther really had were the reform organizations and unions that he had nurtured and who had given him voice. Yet, Seth Luther, like the other street preachers we have considered, sought a legitimacy of his own grounded in the principles of the American Revolution and,

[83] Seth Luther, *An Address on the Origins and Progress of Avarice, and its Deleterious Effects on Human Happiness* (Boston, 1834), 27.
[84] Seth Luther to Walter S. Burgess, September 7, 1844, Dorr Correspondence, Brown University Library.

especially, in the fundamental tenets of Christianity as he comprehended them.

Religious principles drove Seth Luther's critique of American capitalism. From his perspective, God had not sanctioned the acquisitive spirit that propelled entrepreneurs in the market place. To the contrary, Luther essayed "that Avarice is not implanted in the human breast by the Great God of heaven and earth."[85] He held that it was absurd to believe "that the great Author of our existence designed that *many* should be poor and miserable, in order that the *few* may roll and riot in splendid luxury."[86] "Avarice," he told New England workers in 1833, "manufactures drunkards, chains and lashes the slave, and crowds down and oppresses the poor, the friendless, and the destitute: it is the father of *all crime* from the days of Adam until the present time."[87] He did not concur with Francis Wayland, who believed that whole communities would benefit from the exertions of a few ambitious and wealthy members. Instead of perceiving a fundamental harmony between individual gain and divine purpose, Luther knew that the precepts of Christianity clashed with the values of commerce. He assailed those "who profess to have their treasure in heaven, grasping with intense desire the world, the world, the world."[88] Those Christians who rested in finely appointed pews sheltered in comfortable meetinghouses he ranked first among hypocrites. "How can I sit easy, and look on splendid pulpits, and crimson damask curtains, pews lined with costly stuffs, luxuriously carpeted and cushioned, for the seat of the opulent," he cried, "when I know that the inmates of that republican bastille, in Leverett Street, Ward 5, have nothing but the floor, on which to sit or lie down, night or day?" Speaking from personal experience, he questioned how charitable Christians could imprison a man "for the crime of being poor." Seth Luther thus argued that the current arrangements of the market economy in antebellum America could not be reconciled with the spirit of true Christianity. In the end, he affirmed bluntly, "Ye cannot serve GOD and mammon."[89]

In light of this perspective, Seth Luther offered a harsh condemnation of master mechanics and manufacturers. Unlike Francis Wayland, who sought to promote harmony among the social classes, Luther denounced in shrill language textile entrepreneurs who exploited their operatives, especially those who abused women and children. Chiding employers who cited church attendance as proof of manufacturing's wholesome effects, Luther

---

[85] Luther, *Address on the Origins and Progress of Avarice,* 19.

[86] Luther, *An Address Delivered Before the Mechanics,* 12.

[87] Seth Luther, *An Address to the Working Men of New England, on the State of Education, and on the Condition of the Producing Classes in Europe and America* (New York, 1833), 7.

[88] Luther, *Address on the Origins and Progress of Avarice,* 34.

[89] Ibid., 30, 34.

doubted that "after working like slaves for 13 or 14 hours every day" anyone "ever *thanked* God for *permission* to work in a *cotton mill.*"[90] More broadly, he found any form of labor exploitation to clash with Biblical teaching. Recalling the Old Testament prophet Isaiah, Luther blasted the rich: "Why do ye grind the faces of the poor?"[91] In establishing the rigorous routine of factory labor, entrepreneurs also robbed their operatives of education. In the cotton manufactories, maintained Luther, "it is *impossible* to attend to education among children, or to improvement among adults."[92] He accused manufacturers of "extinguishing the flame of knowledge" throughout New England.[93] Unlike Francis Wayland, Luther held out little hope that a disciplined college system could meet the requirements of an informed citizenry. "We boast of our colleges, our academies, our primary and other public schools," he argued; "some wise ones assert that every child in the nation has an opportunity to obtain a good common school education. *But this is not so.*"[94] Kept in ignorance, factory operatives would be deprived of their mental independence and would "become mere machinery of a monied aristocracy."[95] In denying workers education, employers quashed intellectual freedom and excluded "the producing classes from a participation in the fountains of knowledge, and the benefits equally designed for all."[96] God, said Luther, had constructed all human beings for education and moral improvement.

Seth Luther blended Biblical language with the rhetoric of republicanism to confront Rhode Island's $134 property requirement for suffrage rights. Property ownership, he said, should not determine the shape of popular political participation. Luther based this claim of political equality on the notion of human equality before God. "Has the great Author of our existence," he asked, "scattered blessings with a partial hand?" No. All persons were "made of the same materials, and subject to the same laws of our common nature."[97] God had designed a just universe in which all men could

[90] Luther, *Address to the Working Men of New England*, 18.
[91] Luther, *Address on the Origins and Progress of Avarice*, 42. This passage from Isaiah regarding the "grinding" of the poor resonated with the rhetoric of other labor activists of the antebellum period. See, for example, William R. Sutton, *Journeymen for Jesus: Evangelical Artisans Confront Capitalism in Jacksonian Baltimore* (University Park, Pa., 1998), esp. 24–25, 64–65. Jama Lazerow rightly emphasizes the theme of "Christian vengeance" that sprang from Luther's prophetic roots. See *Religion and the Working Class*, 208–211.
[92] Luther, *Address to the Working Men of New England*, 21.
[93] Luther, *Address on the Origins and Progress of Avarice*, 32.
[94] Luther, *An Address Delivered Before the Mechanics*, 16.
[95] Ibid., 17.
[96] Luther, *Address to the Working Men of New England*, 6–7.
[97] Seth Luther, *An Address on the Right of Free Suffrage, Delivered by the Request of Freeholders and others of the City of Providence, in the Old Town House, April 19, and Repeated April 26, at the Same Place* (Providence, 1833), 6.

participate. Aware that such opinions placed him at odds with Rhode Island property holders, he invoked the heritage of the Protestant Reformation. "Martin Luther," he reminded his critics, "was cautioned by the Pope of Rome, not to make an excitement," yet he held to his principles. Seth Luther concluded his address insisting that *"the voice of the People, is the voice of God."*[98] This plain phrase captured the essence of the religious culture of the streets.

Unlike Francis Wayland, who held tightly to the sanctity of law in all human affairs, Seth Luther looked critically upon Rhode Island's Constitution and its statutes. Because these had been framed by only a tiny minority of the state's residents, he thought they carried little authority. "The government of this state," he announced, "is not even republican in its form; it was formed under a king, and it is an aristocratical form government." Luther probably had in mind here Rhode Island's ancient constitution, which had remained virtually intact since 1663, and its sharp contrast with the guarantees of Article 4, Section 4 of the United States Constitution that insures that all states operate under a "republican" form of government. Luther maintained that since the majority of Rhode Islanders could not vote, they were in even worse shape than the vassals of feudal times, who at least "paid taxes and fought in consideration of holding the lands they defended." In Rhode Island, he observed, men are "actually compelled to watch over the lives and property of men, who do not think them worthy or fit for any other use." He went on to deny the validity of the State's requirement that citizens who did not vote for taxes must still pay them. Drawing a parallel between the colonists' plight in 1776 and Rhode Island's suffering citizens, Luther held that "no law made by either Legislative body assessing a tax on non-voters, can with justice be collected; for they have never given their assent to the tax, directly or indirectly, by themselves or their representatives."[99] By 1833 Seth Luther had already articulated the rationale that Thomas W. Dorr and his associates would use in their uprising almost a decade later. For men like Seth Luther, the legitimacy of the state to rule was based upon its adherence to the Biblical and revolutionary principles of equality. If the state failed to rest its authority on such grounds, Luther reasoned, it could not expect citizens to obey its laws.

Seth Luther's conviction that true Christianity was the possession of the poor bolstered his economic, social, and political claims. As did other labor leaders of the antebellum era, he drew a distinction between the "practical Christianity" practiced by Jesus and the first disciples and the "churchianity"

[98] Ibid., 25.
[99] Ibid., 15, 20, 21.

practiced by many churchgoing Christians who had forsaken the principles of their Founder.[100] As we have seen, he charged the established clergy with an attempt "to pervert the benevolent religion of him who was despised by the aristocracy of Jerusalem because he was poor."[101] He condemned as hypocrisy the "splendid pulpits, and crimson damask curtains, pews lined with costly stuffs, luxuriously carpeted and cushioned for the seat of the opulent."[102] He excoriated church members who refused "2000 Mechanics" in Brooklyn the opportunity to gather in city meetinghouses for the Fourth of July. "They refused us liberty to enter the house of God," he cried, "and then scoffed at us for being infidels, unbelievers."[103] Luther's language here cannot be interpreted through the lens of a generic anticlericalism or as evidence of the blanket hostility of the antebellum labor movement to Christianity. Far from it. "Believing, as I do, in the precepts of the Christian faith," he explained, "I am compelled to say, that I do not consider any community can deserve the name of Christian, if that community permit such things to exist, as I have described; for every principle, every precept, and all the practice of Jesus Christ, is entirely set at nought, and trampled under foot."[104] In Luther's estimation, the authentic believers had gathered outside the walls erected by high-toned communicants.

Still, for all his railings against bourgeois religion, Seth Luther advanced an agenda for economic, educational, and political reform that was, in fact, rather conventional. In the final pages of his *Address on the Origins and Progress of Avarice*, he inventoried a list of proposals familiar to all students of labor reform in Jacksonian America: he wanted to abolish private monopolies, end capital punishment and imprisonment for debt, revise the militia system, revamp lien laws, and reform other aspects of the legal establishment.[105] He brushed aside as nonsense charges that workingmen wished to do away with private property. Instead, steps must be taken to "make labor respectable."[106] Manual labor schools should be made available to all. And Luther sang the praises of sobriety: meetings of workingmen "should be conducted free from the excitement induced by the free use of stimulating liquors."[107] Moreover, in agitating for suffrage reform, he

---

[100] See Lazerow, *Religion and the Working Class*, 47–68 and passim.

[101] Luther, *Address Delivered Before the Mechanics*, 24.

[102] Luther, *Address on the Origins and Progress of Avarice*, 30.

[103] Luther, *Address Delivered Before the Mechanics*, 25–26.

[104] Luther, *Address on the Origins and Progress of Avarice*, 29.

[105] Ibid., 43. For good summaries of the workingmen's programs for reform see Bruce Laurie, *Artisans into Workers: Labor in Nineteenth-Century America* (New York, 1989), 63–64; Walter Licht, *Industrializing America: The Nineteenth Century* (Baltimore, 1995), 52.

[106] Luther, *Address on the Origins and Progress of Avarice*, 35.

[107] Luther, *Address Delivered Before the Mechanics*, 20.

appealed directly to the spirit of the American revolution and heroes such as Benjamin Franklin.[108] Despite the steely edge on his rhetoric, Luther sometimes softened the character of his concrete reform proposals. Why?

Like other street preachers, Seth Luther displayed a highly ambivalent attitude toward religious and secular authority. Of course, he launched assaults on Christian hypocrisy, labor exploitation, and political oppression. Simultaneously, Luther wished to capture a measure of religious authority and respectability for himself and for the causes he championed. He was keenly aware of his precarious position within the Providence community. In 1833, speaking before a suffrage rally, Luther recognized "that a prophet is not without honor save in his own country and among his own kindred."[109] By clothing his social criticism in the languages of Christianity and revolutionary republicanism, Luther legitimated his ideas in terms of the most powerful rhetoric available to him.[110] While it is unlikely that he consciously diluted his convictions to gain a larger audience, Seth Luther did want to be recognized, applauded, and even followed. Ironically, it was the profound desire to be taken seriously, to be acknowledged as respectable, to be counted as a full citizen, that drove him into outright rebellion.

If plebeian religious culture straddled the fence on issues of respectability and rebellion, it also assumed an ambiguous posture with regard to gender. At first glance, the masculine character of much of plebeian religious culture appears self-evident. Most obviously, the street preachers whom we have considered were all men. They hailed from the "mechanic preacher" tradition so evident during the revolutionary era of seventeenth-century England and (as they would have been quick to remind us) from the world of the Scriptures as well.[111] Jesus, they said, had been a carpenter. Urban artisans turned preachers should not be confused with the other classic form of plebeian religious leadership, the pious "factory girls" and "female preachers" who led services in the Rhode Island countryside.[112] Unlike women such as Salome Lincoln, Nancy Towle, and Susan Humes, who gained legitimacy from their connection with denominations such as the Freewill Baptists and the Methodists, the mechanic preachers lashed out at established congregations. If the female preachers spoke the language of love, of the heart, and of a transcendent and mysterious God, the mechanic preachers engaged in verbal combat with their social betters, employed a

---

[108] Luther, *An Address on the Right of Free Suffrage*, 17.
[109] Ibid., 3.
[110] On the legitimating function of religion see especially Peter L. Berger, *The Sacred Canopy: Elements of a Sociological Theory of Religion* (New York, 1967), esp. 29–51.
[111] On "mechanic preachers" see Christopher Hill, *A Tinker and a Poor Man: John Bunyan and His Church, 1628–1688* (New York, 1990), 135–140 and passim.
[112] On female preaching see Chapter 2 above.

rugged and bombastic rhetoric, and, more often than not, drew attention to themselves as well as to God. While female labor leaders, such as Sarah Bagley and Huldah Stone, did ground their agendas in religious precepts, the "mechanic preachers" were more likely than the female preachers to hoist the banner of social criticism. As we have seen with William Apess and Seth Luther, street preachers often carried with them a clear political program for which they sought support. In all these ways, the mechanic preachers of Providence distinguished themselves as a particularly masculine expression of plebeian religious life.

For all of these clear differences with the tradition of the female preacher, the mechanic preachers of the city embodied features that might be considered feminine. In the first place, the crimes of which they were accused—disorderly walking especially—were gendered female in the early-nineteenth-century evangelical community. In this sense First Baptist Church accused Seth Luther, manly though he was, of the most feminine of churchly crimes. Moreover, in venerating a religion that made room for miracles, for emotional verve, and for the millennial expectation of primitive Christianity, the mechanic preachers articulated a religious vision that had more in common with that of the female preachers than with that of bourgeois Protestants such as Francis Wayland. The mechanic preachers also drew female audiences. Here we can recall Dr. Preachloud's ability to capture the attention of Pawtucket's women. We can also point to a little-discussed but vitally important poem written by Seth Luther during his second imprisonment.

In 1842, languishing in prison for his role in the Dorr Rebellion, Seth Luther composed a thirty-six-stanza poem titled "The Garland of Gratitude: Respectfully Dedicated to the Constitutional Suffrage Ladies of Rhode Island."[113] Those historians who do examine Seth Luther's works typically focus on his major political addresses, casting aside the "Garland of Gratitude" as a piece of poetic fluff written by a man of unstable mind. Yet, for what it says about plebeian religion and politics, Luther's poem claims a place of equal importance alongside his more lengthy and scholarly orations. For it reveals a connection between the mechanic preachers, political activism, and the women of Providence. That he wrote the poem (and published it) in the first place suggests that women may have been acquainted with his life and work.

In the "Garland of Gratitude," Seth Luther sang of the virtues of the "Suffrage Ladies" who had supported his cause. A suffrage woman was a

---

[113] Seth Luther, *The Garland of Gratitude: Respectfully Dedicated to the Constitutional Suffrage Ladies of Rhode-Island* (Providence, 1842). All citations that follow are to this brief edition, which has no pagination.

"ministering angel," who brought relief to the weary and oppressed prisoners. "Let me but gaze on woman's eye," he intoned, "and see Heaven's sunlight from its beaming." Fearlessly the suffrage women had taken up the cause of the prisoners, an act for which "trumpets silvertoned are sounding, / spreading for your spotless fame." Luther then heaped scorn and sin on another class of women: the "'Law and Order' daughters," who had supported the established government. "Hide your heads and weep in vain," he told them, "All Niagara's vast waters, / Cannot purge your dawning stain." But Luther's protagonists were something more than angelic, heavenly visitors; they were women possessed of authentic political zeal. "Sisters!" he lauded them, "ye have done your duty, / In the days of dread distress, / Adding lustre to your beauty / When ye ran, The Crushed to bless." Nor did suffrage women shrink in the face of criticism from their opponents. Rather, they held firm in their convictions, "the tyrants *sneer* ye *boldly* braved / And hurled defiance at their spite." Defiant and dutiful, beautiful and angelic, the suffrage women in Seth Luther's poem combined the attributes of manly citizenship with those of female piety. This tribute to his "Sisters" in the cause of suffrage reform speaks to the high regard Seth Luther held for them. The public did not share Luther's zest for his own poem. From prison, two months after its publication, he wrote to Walter S. Burges that he was "much surprised that to my knowledge not a single request respecting the Garland of Gratitude has been replied to, in any many whatever."[114] The poor public response to Luther's poem is understandable: it was, after all, a marginal artistic effort composed by a man now being held for treason against the state. But Luther's disappointment may also have sprung from the deep appreciation he felt for the subjects of his poem.

The "Garland of Gratitude" tells us much about plebeian religious culture and the political activism that it sustained. It evokes the female audiences to which street preachers such as Seth Luther appealed. It suggests, too, the feminine dimension of a religious culture that, on the surface, would appear to be almost entirely masculine. In carrying with it a strong feminine component, plebeian religious culture distinguished itself from its more manly bourgeois counterpart. Moreover, the "Garland" leads us to think about the delicate interplay of politics, religion, and gender in the Dorr Rebellion. For in the context of this struggle, Rhode Islanders discovered that such issues were inseparable. They all influenced the course of this most stormy chapter in antebellum Rhode Island's history.

[114] Seth Luther to Walter S. Burgess, September 5, 1842, Dorr Correspondence.

6

"A Taste of Civil War"
The Dorr Rebellion of 1842

In the early morning hours of May 18, 1842, the citizens of Providence experienced "a taste of civil war."[1] Thomas Wilson Dorr, the recently elected "People's Governor" of Rhode Island, marched on the city arsenal with a rebel force of slightly more than two hundred men and two pieces of field artillery. Desperate to achieve recognition as Rhode Island's legitimate executive, Dorr risked all in this reckless encounter. Inside the arsenal a militia force of nearly equal size armed with five six-pound cannons prepared for his assault. The defenders of the Whig governor Samuel Ward King's government included Dorr's father and his younger brother. When the militia force refused to surrender, Dorr ordered his men to fire their cannons at the arsenal's eighteen-inch walls. Owing to the damp, foggy night and the incompetence of Dorr's gunners, the weapons stood silent. With little stomach for a pitched battle, the rebel force melted away as dawn broke. Dorr fled. In the wake of the arsenal fiasco, Dorr's mission to bring political reform to the state seemed doomed. Only his poor grasp of military tactics had kept a single Rhode Islander from being killed or wounded in the bungled attack.[2]

[1] D. Macdill, "Free Institutions, Regulated Liberty, and Pure Religion. Three National Blessings," *Biblical Repertory and Princeton Review for the Year 1843* 15 (1843): 111.
[2] The account of the attack on the arsenal and other aspects of the political history of the Dorr Rebellion have been drawn from: Arthur May Mowry, *The Dorr War; Or the Constitutional Struggle in Rhode Island* (Providence, 1901); Marvin Gettleman, *The Dorr Rebellion: A Study in American Radicalism: 1833–1849* (New York, 1973); George M. Dennison, *The Dorr War: Republicanism on Trial, 1831–1861* (Lexington, 1976); Patrick T. Conley, *Democracy in Decline: Rhode Island's Constitutional Development 1776–1841* (Providence, 1977).

Francis Wayland attributed the peaceful resolution of the crisis to God's merciful intervention. On May 22, he confessed to the members of First Baptist Church that "never in the whole course of my life have I seen so clearly, as in this instance, the indubitable evidence of Divine interposition." In his view, God had delivered Providence from the threat of social anarchy and had restored due respect for lawful government. He considered Dorr's effort to storm the city arsenal as nothing less that the resurgence of "the horrors of revolutionary France." Even worse, he had heard that church members could be found in the Dorrite ranks. "I have been informed," Wayland lamented, "that a considerable number of professing Christians in this city have been deluded into a participation in these transactions." He called on Baptists, and residents throughout the city, to reflect upon their conduct during the recent confrontation. Had they taken the side of godly obedience or had they allied themselves with the forces of godless anarchy and rebellion?[3]

Francis Wayland's response to the arsenal incident points to the key role that religion played in the Dorr Rebellion of 1842. He observed, quite rightly, that Christians had aligned themselves on both sides of the political divide, some supporting Governor King and others backing Thomas Dorr and his suffrage reformers. For this reason the political conflict of the Dorr Rebellion marked a contest between the bourgeois and plebeian religious cultures. Bourgeois Protestants, with their dedication to property and the standing social order, lined up behind Governor King's administration. As good evangelicals and Whigs of a conservative bent, bourgeois Protestants could at once embrace the forces of economic modernization while holding to the traditional political order of the state and to deferential social relationships.[4] Adherents of the plebeian religious culture, on the other hand, gave strength to the Dorrite insurgents. Their dedication to spiritual freedom, their belief in self-expression, their ambivalence toward established authority, and their fondness for prophetic language made them natural allies in a political movement that championed equal rights. It was more than coincidence that many regular Baptists, Congregationalists, and Episcopalians threw their weight behind the Law and Order Party, while Universalists, Methodists, and independent Baptists often bolstered the Dorrites. The political loyalties of members, however, did not follow exactly denominational affiliation. Within individual congregations, the political

[3] Francis Wayland, *The Affairs of Rhode Island. A Discourse Delivered in the Meeting-House of the First Baptist Church, Providence, May 22, 1842* (Providence, 1842), 20–21, 7, 30.
[4] On this point see Daniel Walker Howe, *The Political Culture of the American Whigs* (Chicago, 1979), 219; Richard J. Carwardine, *Evangelicals and Politics in Antebellum America* (New Haven, 1993), 110–111.

passions unleashed by the rebellion turned brothers and sisters in Christ against one another. Only after considerable struggle were bourgeois Protestants able to vanquish their plebeian adversaries.

The political question that carried Thomas Wilson Dorr to the gates of the Providence arsenal hinged on the expansion of Rhode Island's restrictive qualifications for voting rights. Early in the nineteenth century, the General Assembly, with an eye toward the original colonial charter of 1663, set the minimum property requirement for suffrage at $134 of real estate. In the Age of Jacksonian Democracy, as other states sank their property requirements, Rhode Island's suffrage rules pushed against the national political tide. By the 1830s the property requirement disfranchised most of the state's adult white men. It fell particularly hard on urban laborers, petty clerks, industrial employees in Providence, and inhabitants of mill villages in the hinterland. In 1840 a survey of the entire state reported that nearly 58 percent of all adult white males in the state could only watch the hotly contested presidential campaign between William Henry Harrison and Martin Van Buren. During an era in which "the common man" found political voice, most common men in Rhode Island remained mute.[5]

Thomas Wilson Dorr, the scion of a prominent merchant family, capitalized on the political marginality of the propertyless. In the spring of 1840, he joined with other reformers to create the Rhode Island Suffrage Association, an organization dedicated to extending the vote to all white men. By 1841 the reformers had concocted a "People's Constitution" that won the support of an overwhelming number of citizens and led to Dorr's claim to have been elected "People's Governor" in early 1842. Law-abiding Rhode Islanders cast their votes for the Whig governor Samuel Ward King under the franchise requirements of the state's current constitution. The state thus possessed two governors—one enormously popular and illegally elected, the other perfectly legitimate but representing only a tiny minority of the citizens. The electoral standoff, the moves of the General Assembly to jail Dorrite officeholders under the provisions of the "Algerine Law," and dwindling support prompted Dorr to gamble his future on the arsenal attack. In the wake of this failure, Dorr scampered to the mill villages of Woonsocket, Smithfield, Cumberland, and Chepachet, the bastions of his greatest support. But facing the threat of nearly three thousand militia troops ready to march on the rebels from Providence, most of Dorr's demoralized followers fled. In 1843, after hiding out in New Hampshire and Massachusetts, Dorr surrendered and was eventually sent to prison.

[5] See Conley, *Democracy in Decline*, 236–237, 296–297. On the extension of suffrage rights generally, see Harry L. Watson, *Liberty and Power: The Politics of Jacksonian America* (New York, 1990), 232.

This serpentine story of political rebellion is inseparable from the religious themes that informed it.[6] As it grew into the Rhode Island Suffrage Association, the cause of suffrage reform had always carried the force of Christian rhetoric. Almost a decade before Dorr, Seth Luther had framed the issue of expanding the franchise in theological language. God, he had said, did not intend for democratic rights to be parceled out according to the amount of property one owned. The barber William I. Tillinghast, one of Luther's associates in the agitation of 1833, also employed a religious justification for the democratic state. "My creed," he explained, "is that the principles contained in the holy Bible & the true principles of Republicanism (or liberty & equality) both came from God." He maintained that "no tyrant can be a true Christian, for how can he 'do as he would be done by'?"[7] The members of the Rhode Island Suffrage Association, too, believed in the Biblical basis of democracy. Their newspaper, the *New Age and Constitutional Advocate*, frequently joined the mission of suffrage reform with divine sanction. "Say not," announced one editorialist, "that religion has nothing to do with government. A true democracy has its root in Christianity."[8] In January 1841, one anonymous "Roger Williams" put the case even more militantly. He pointed to the example of "Christ, the bold and efficient Reformer; the democrat and radical, laying the axe at the root of the vile abuses of His age."[9] In the minds of suffrage reformers, God Himself had endorsed their cause.

On April 17, 1841, a rally organized on the Jefferson Plain introduced the Universalist minister William S. Balch as a major advocate for the Suffrage Association. Called to be pastor of First Universalist Church in 1838, he served as chaplain for the Suffrage Association at this rally and then delivered the keynote address at the mass meeting held on the Dexter Training Grounds two months later. Even after he left Providence in the wake of Dorr's defeat, he maintained warm relations with the imprisoned "People's Governor." In 1844, from his New York pulpit, Balch proclaimed that "good men, like a good cause, deserve no less of our favor because unfortunate."[10]

---

[6] More broadly see Daniel Walker Howe, "The Evangelical Movement and Political Culture in the North during the Second Party System," *Journal of American History* 77 (March 1991): 1216–1239.

[7] See notes for a suffrage address by W. I. Tillinghast in Dorr Manuscripts, vol. 7, Brown University Library. Marvin E. Gettleman and Noel P. Conlon, eds., "Responses to the Rhode Island Workingmen's Reform Agitation of 1833," *Rhode Island History* 28 (1969): 75–94.

[8] "A Short Sermon," *New Age and Constitutional Advocate*, December 11, 1840, American Antiquarian Society Library, Worcester, Mass.

[9] "Christianity—Democracy," *New Age and Constitutional Advocate*, January 8, 1841.

[10] William S. Balch, *A Sermon Preached on Thanksgiving-Day, December 14, 1844 in the Bleeker Street Church* (New York, 1845), 21.

A year later speculation surfaced that he might return to Providence to re-
new Dorr's struggle. One Whiggish commentator admitted that Balch "is
better qualified than anyone here to reorganize the Dorrite party and to
join together its divided forces."[11] By this time Balch had publicly embraced
the "Associationist" doctrines of Charles Fourier and seemed primed for yet
another round of radical activism.[12] From start to finish, supporters and
critics alike recognized him as a leading light among the Dorrites.

William S. Balch had never hid his political lamp under a bushel. In 1839,
during July Fourth festivities in Pawtucket, he intoned a jeremiad against
the abuses of American government since the Revolution. "We have departed," he lamented, "from that simple and beautiful mode of government
adopted by the early sages of our land." Now, he said, Americans allowed
"other considerations than a pure regard for personal rights, the public
weal, the good of all, to prejudice our minds and lead us astray." He called
on Rhode Islanders to restore their true principles of the Revolutionary
founders. Like other Americans of the Jacksonian era, Balch drew rhetori-
cal strength from what Marvin Meyers has called the "restoration theme" in
American politics, a device that harkened listeners to the moral and political purity of the revolutionary generation.[13] "I can conceive no form of government so perfectly compatible with the sublime principles of christianity,"
he announced, "or so directly calculated to promote the happiness of all
mankind, as a democracy." Given such political sentiments, he moved
easily into the suffrage reform camp.[14]

The April 17 rally cemented William S. Balch's position as a major figure
in the Suffrage Association. The rally itself took on the flavor of a religious
festival. The suffragists had decided to launch the rally with a procession
from Edward Hall's First Congregational Church on Benefit Street. This
church, where men of property dominated, refused to acknowledge the
marchers by not joining with other churches in ringing its bells. Upon ar-
riving at the Plain, the demonstrators joined Balch in singing a psalm. He
then offered a prayer, "perfectly appropriate to the occasion," before a great
feast commenced. Even as the crowd of three thousand persons devoured
an ox, a calf, and a pig, they behaved with a certain measure of decorum.
The coachmen and draymen participating in the event voted to consume

[11] "Balch's Political Sermon," *Manufacturer's and Farmer's Journal, Providence and Pawtucket
Advertiser*, February 27, 1845.
[12] Balch's flirtation with Fourierism is indicated in Russell E. Miller, *The Larger Hope: The First
Century of the Universalist Church in America 1770–1870* (Boston, 1979), 212.
[13] Marvin Meyers, *The Jacksonian Persuasion: Politics and Belief* (Stanford, 1960), 16–32.
[14] William S. Balch, *Individual Freedom the Foundation of Democratic Government. An Oration,
Delivered in Pawtucket, Rhode Island, July 4, 1839* (Pawtucket, 1839), 23, 19–20.

no spirituous liquors for the day. While other marchers may have imbibed during the meal, this gesture toward temperance reform imparted a quality of respectability to the gathering. The Suffrage Association aimed to give their rally exactly that image. "We have often been told that we are but a discontented rabble," observed the *New Age and Constitutional Advocate*. "The 17th showed to our State that this rabble produced the largest and most orderly procession ever seen in Rhode Island." With Balch presiding over its festivities, the Suffrage Association staked a claim to political and religious legitimacy.[15]

William S. Balch took center stage again when the Suffrage Association met on the Dexter Training Ground on July 5, 1841.[16] Here he delivered an oration titled "Popular Liberty and Equal Rights" that the *New Age and Constitutional Advocate* deemed "one of the most talented pieces of composition that we have heard for many days."[17] Like Seth Luther, Balch took as his starting point the idea that "man was originally created to be free." Rhode Island's current constitution, with its property requirement, had robbed men of their basic and divinely inspired political freedoms. In Balch's view, the property requirement marked a betrayal of Rhode Island's heritage as a haven for religious and political liberty. "Ask the hovering spirit of Roger Williams," he suggested, "if liberty is to be measured by dollars and cents, and parcelled out by feet and inches to his descendants?" In the final passages of his speech, Balch turned to the potentially dangerous question of whether or not the views articulated by the Suffrage Association were "revolutionary." Because the Suffrage Association planned to call for a "People's Convention" to meet in October, this question assumed great importance. Balch tried to have it both ways on this issue. Of course, he argued, all those who fought for liberty were committed to a revolutionary task—as were Adams, Jefferson, Patrick Henry, and most especially, Jesus. Simultaneously, Balch echoed the position that the goals of the reformers meshed perfectly with the traditions of the Revolutionary founders. "Call it a Revolution," he questioned, "that we say, intelligence, virtue, honor, and patriotism, makes the man and not dirt and primogeniture?" Balch pleaded guilty to being a revolutionary, but only insofar as Jesus and the heroes of '76 had been rebels as well.[18]

---

[15] This account is drawn from "Suffrage Meeting on Jefferson Plain," *New Age and Constitutional Advocate*, April 23, 1841.

[16] According to the *New Age and Constitutional Advocate*, July 9, 1841, over three thousand persons heard Balch's July 5 oration.

[17] Ibid.

[18] William S. Balch, *Popular Liberty and Equal Rights. An Oration Delivered Before the Mass Convention of the R.I. Suffrage Association, Held on Dexter Training Ground, in Providence, July Fifth, 1841* (Providence, 1841), 4, 18, 21.

Thomas Dorr's decision to attack the city arsenal placed his religious supporters in a precarious position. Some were willing to support Dorr, even to the point of quasi-legal political maneuvering, but they balked at the prospect of shooting it out in the streets. Jacob Frieze, a Universalist minister, suffrage advocate, and labor leader, broke openly with Dorr on the point. As a former member of the Suffrage Association, Frieze recognized the legitimacy of the principle of popular sovereignty, but he had no interest in fighting a war. He argued with Dorr "that force is never to be exercised for redress of grievances, till in the last extremity, all peaceable remedies shall have been applied, and proved ineffectual."[19] Among the Freewill Baptists, a denomination that lent considerable sympathy to Dorr, the attack on the arsenal and subsequent militia crackdown sparked a lengthy debate as to whether Christians might take up arms under any condition.[20] In edging toward open warfare, Dorr risked losing an important basis of his political support.

Some ministers remained loyal to Dorr's cause even in the days following the arsenal debacle. Leonard Wakefield, a Methodist pastor from Cumberland, proved his mettle as a staunch supporter of the "People's Governor." Like other suffrage reformers in the northern and western manufacturing towns, he continued to pray for Dorr's ultimate victory. In Woonsocket, Smithfield, and Chepachet, suffragists continued to hold rallies and local elections even after Dorr's military failure. Wakefield participated in the town elections in the mill village of Cumberland and secured himself a position as the postmaster.[21] On June 30, state militiamen arrested him as he sat down to dinner. With a batch of twenty other prisoners, he was loaded into a wagon headed for the Providence jail. As they neared the prison, Wakefield endured the taunts and jeering of a large crowd that had assembled to observe the spectacle of a suffrage minister being held at the point of a musket. One spectator declared, "d——m him, the next time he preaches it will be in the State prison!" Under formal questioning, Wakefield admitted that he had delivered a sermon that endorsed "the suffrage side." And although he had been at Chepachet to visit the Cumberland men there, he insisted that his role was peaceful. He had not run bullets. He had not encouraged fighting. He had done nothing "except

[19] Jacob Frieze, *A Concise History of the Efforts to Obtain an Extension of the Suffrage in Rhode Island: From the Year 1811 to 1842*, 3d ed. (Providence, 1912), 108.

[20] Record Book, Elder's Conference of the R.I. Quarterly Meeting of Freewill Baptists, May 17, 1843, and subsequent meetings through August 1842, Manuscript Collection, Rhode Island Historical Society, hereafter cited as RIHS.

[21] On Wakefield's election see *Manufacturer's and Farmer's Journal, Providence and Pawtucket Advertiser*, June 9, 1842. On the general strength of Dorr's following in the mill villages see Gettleman, *Dorr Rebellion*, 85, 120, 130–134; Conley, *Democracy in Decline*, 242, 295, 326, 339, 344.

to express my opinions freely and fearlessly, with a temperate zeal."[22] With little to hold him on, the authorities released him. But by September 1842 he was back at it, lending his voice to a clambake in Millville conducted on Dorr's behalf. According to the *Providence Express*, Wakefield offered "a fervent and appropriate prayer," after which other speakers praised the suffrage cause.[23] An indefatigable political activist, Leonard Wakefield sustained his dedication in the weeks after Dorr's arrest for treason.

As the Law and Order Party rejoiced in its victories of the summer of 1842, other Providence ministers worried about the flexing of military and political muscle they had recently witnessed. On August 14, Archibald Kenyon, pastor of West Baptist Church, considered the proper relationship Christians should cultivate with their government. Moving away from the claims made by William S. Balch and the Suffrage Association, he postulated that no specific form of civil government could claim the status of a divine institution. Because the Bible mandated no particular frame of civil authority, governments could function as "a blessing and a curse to the world." If they were rooted in mutual consent and protected God-given rights, then governments should be obeyed. But no Christian could be required to bend to an authority that contradicted Scripture or that denied basic rights granted by God. For example, Christians could refuse to obey a magistrate who required them to break one of the Ten Commandments. "Universal obedience to civil laws" he reminded his congregation, "is not required either by the law or example of Jesus Christ." Since Rhode Islanders had recently been pushed to the brink of civil war and militiamen now patrolled the streets, Kenyon's affirmation of the limited role of governmental authority and the right of Christians to dissent was radical stuff.[24]

James A. McKenzie, pastor of Roger Williams Baptist Church in Providence, took an even more direct and active role in championing Dorr and his cause in the dark days following the summer of 1842.[25] In his journal and papers, McKenzie lamented that the rebellion had caused such great turmoil among Providence communicants by "creating such divisions and enmities in families, neighborhoods, and chhs [churches] —presenting such spectacles of christian armed against christian— threatening life mutually—binding—imprisoning—proscribing—

[22] Wakefield's account is taken from Edmund Burke, *Interference of the Executive in the Affairs of Rhode Island, 28th Congress, 1st Session, House Report No. 546, serial 447* (Washington, D.C., 1844), 313–315. On the biases of Burke's Report see Gettleman, *Dorr Rebellion*, 156–157.

[23] "Millville Clam Bake," *Providence Express*, September 13, 1842.

[24] Archibald Kenyon, *The Object and Principles of Civil Government, and the Duty of Christians Thereto. Being a Discourse Preached Before the West Baptist Church and Society, August 14, 1842* (Providence, 1842), 5, 7.

[25] Materials on McKenzie are in the James A. McKenzie Papers, RIHS.

oppressing—reviling—defrauding." Such torments did not plague his own members, among whom "were some Algerines and the rest Dorrites." With the backing of his Dorrite congregation, McKenzie preached a sermon before a quarterly meeting of Freewill Baptists in August 1842, in which, like Archibald Kenyon, he confronted the obligations of Christians to the state. In what sounded, at times, like an unqualified endorsement of pacifism, McKenzie fashioned an argument in which he denied that Christians could, for any reason, take up arms.[26] His pronouncements against war and the taking of human life, however, were not abstract theological arguments. Rather, they were aimed at those Christians, notably members of the established order, who held the guns in August 1842.

The sermon rankled local authorities. "I found my duty to be to preach against all carnal war on a great or little scale," he wrote, "and the inconsistency of christians taking or using swords, guns, cannon or any instrument of death against mankind or of overcoming evil with evil." In May 1842, McKenzie's comments might have been interpreted as a homily against Dorr and his followers. In August 1842, the members of the Law and Order faction knew that McKenzie was talking about them. Indeed, McKenzie recalled that in giving the sermon he risked being arrested. "I was told the Sabbath following as I was preaching in the Roger Williams chh there were some that came to take me away to prison—but they did not come in [and] I did not see them." But McKenzie, an advocate of peace now spoiling for a fight, was somewhat disappointed that he had not been carted off to jail. He knew "there were several ministers beside myself that were upon the list to be apprehended as I was told—but they did not take us—and I am rather sorry they did not for I was ready to go."[27]

Perhaps because James McKenzie had nearly become a political prisoner himself, he led the charge to have Thomas Dorr released after his conviction for treason in June 1844. On July 4, 1844, he agreed to participate in a rally on the Dexter Training Ground, a meeting that drew some five thousand people in his count, to advocate Dorr's release. He observed that whereas the "nation as a nation rejoices this day we as a portion of it feel a gloom overspreading us." The state founded by Roger Williams had turned its back on his example, for it held in its clutches Thomas Wilson Dorr. "Here alone in all this wide spread country is found the victim of political oppression—incarcerated in this State by arbitrary power—here is found the confessor and virtually the Martyr to honesty, integrity, liberty and equality," he cried. That McKenzie claimed that Dorr had been imprisoned

---

[26] See James A. McKenzie, *A Discourse Delivered by Request, and Before the Rhode-Island Quarterly Meeting, in Tiverton, August 24, 1842* (Providence, 1842).

[27] James A. McKenzie Papers.

with "arbitrary power" when he had been convicted in a court of law measures the depth of his political radicalism. Noting other instances in Biblical history in which God had released prisoners, McKenzie hoped Rhode Island's authorities would do the same. "Give us as a State and as a nation," he prayed, "just men and true men that will not fawn upon the rich and frown upon the poor—men of liberal views, holding to equal rights— men fearing God and working righteousness to rule us in thy fear and in thy Providence remove from power men whose principles are subversive of pure religion, true liberty and equal rights." In his prayer McKenzie offered a heartfelt endorsement of Dorr and an equally acerbic condemnation of his opponents.

William S. Balch, Leonard Wakefield, and James McKenzie were not alone in crying for Dorr's support. Alongside them, the "suffrage ladies" of Rhode Island organized, agitated, and worked for the Dorrite agenda and for the release of Dorr from prison. In the weeks and months following the military and political defeat of Dorr, these women became a powerful and visible presence in Rhode Island. In ways that previous scholars not acknowledged, the Dorr Rebellion afforded Rhode Island women a direct entrance into the world of partisan politics. While we have begun to recognize the powerful role played by Whig women in America's second party system, women on the Democratic and even more radical wing of the political spectrum have not received their due.[28] Like their Whiggish sisters, the Dorrite ladies, too, entered the world of political debate, wrote broadsides and songs, organized rallies, offered advice, and raised money. They approached their political work with a religious zeal and insisted that true Christianity bolstered the suffrage cause.

Since neither Thomas Wilson Dorr nor the Rhode Island Suffrage Association ever dreamed of extending voting rights to women, we need to think carefully about why the "suffrage ladies" rushed to their aid. Writing to the *New Age and Constitutional Advocate*, one "Ann Page" wrote that "the rights of women remain to be better understood than at the present time, even by some of the most genuine advocates of liberty; yet, let us not be hindered from doing all we can."[29] While Page acknowledged, quite rightly, that female suffrage had no place on the Dorrite list of reforms, she did recognize

---

[28] The political participation of Whig women is noted in Watson, *Liberty and Power*, 221–223; Carwardine, *Evangelicals and Politics*, 32–35; and explored in more detail by Elizabeth R. Varon, *We Mean to Be Counted: White Women and Politics in Antebellum Virginia* (Chapel Hill, 1998), and Ronald J. Zboray and Mary Saracino Zboray, "Whig Women, Politics, and Culture in the Campaign of 1840: Three Perspectives from Massachusetts," *Journal of the Early Republic* 17 (1997): 277–315.
[29] *New Age and Constitutional Advocate*, August 13, 1841.

that the language of rights and liberties offered women new domains for action. Perhaps, too, the suffrage ladies believed that the enfranchisement of propertyless men might be a first step down the road toward full female citizenship. The political upheaval created by the constitutional crisis in Rhode Island also afforded women an opportunity to step into new political roles. As did women in the Revolutionary era, women in Jacksonian Rhode Island took advantage of a crisis. Finally, the religious flavor of the Dorr insurgency meshed well with a traditional domain of female activism. If women understood Dorr's movement as a religious crusade, they could enter its ranks just as they had joined charitable groups, tract societies, and temperance organizations. Indeed, Catherine Williams wrote in one of her many letters to Thomas Dorr that the suffrage women in Providence met weekly, asking their members to contribute a penny each time.[30] In effect, the Dorrite ladies modeled their political gatherings on the precedent of the female "mite society," one of the oldest and most pervasive forms of organization used by women within their congregations.

The political activities in which the suffrage ladies engaged hardly seemed separable from the work of religious reform. Throughout the fall and winter of 1842, they hosted clambakes and raised money for the "suffrage poor" and for the prisoners being held in Newport.[31] Such efforts to relieve the needy had deep roots in the Providence religious community. Even the names that women selected for their organizations, such as the "Benevolent Suffrage Association," pointed toward the traditional work of female charity.[32] Like tract distributors, some women sent Dorr religious reading material. On September 5, 1842, Caroline Ashley wrote to him on behalf of "the young ladies of Providence who sympathize with you in your efforts in behalf of the people of Rhode Island." She asked his "acceptance of a pocket Bible as a slight testimony of the deep interest we feel in the cause in which you are engaged." She added that "they sincerely regret that the principles contained in this Holy Book should in this community be so little regarded; and that one of its abilist advocates remains of necessity in exile from his home state."[33] Sometimes women rooted their political activism in local congregations. On October 14, 1842, the *Woonsocket Weekly Patriot* reported that the "Ladies Benevolent Suffrage Association" had

[30] Catherine R. Williams to Dorr, October 9, 1842, Dorr Correspondence, vol. 5, Brown University Library.

[31] For some flavor of these events see "Suffrage Ladies of Providence" to Dorr, August 20, 1842, Dorr Correspondence, vol. 4; Mary Anthony and Sarah E. Anthony to Dorr, October 31, 1842, Dorr Correspondence, vol. 5; Catherine R. Williams to Dorr, December 28, 1842, Dorr Correspondence, vol. 5.

[32] Catherine R. Williams to Dorr, July 1, 1845, Dorr Correspondence, vol. 9.

[33] Caroline Ashley to Dorr, September 5, 1842, Dorr Correspondence, vol. 5.

launched a procession from the "Methodist Chapel" there that included over one thousand persons, "a majority of whom were ladies."[34] In some ways, the political insurgency of Dorrite women meshed with the traditional patterns and methods of religious reform.

The "Woonsocket Suffrage Song," composed by an anonymous "suffrage lady," captures how religious language carried the message of political reform.[35] The text called on the friends of suffrage reform not to lose hope, even though military prospects looked dim.

> Ye suffrage ladies, don't despair,
> The time will shortly come,
> When Dorr in spite of martial law,
> Will call the exiles home.

The song invoked Biblical themes of liberation when it announced,

> The prison doors he'll open wide,
> The prisoners to set free,
> Then we will sing, in spite of King,
> And sound the jubilee.

Making direct reference to scriptural texts from Matthew and from Genesis, the suffrage song ranked Governor King's supporters as "pharisees and hypocrites" who had to answer for their "brother's blood" that "is crying from the ground." Condemning the sins of their political opponents, the song concluded ominously:

> Not all the waters, hard or soft,
> Our little State affords,
> Can wash the stains and bloody spots
> From your revengeful swords.

In unmistakable terms, the "Woonsocket Suffrage Song" framed the struggle between Dorr and King as a cosmic struggle between good and evil.

The suffrage ladies sharpened their political skills as the crisis deepened. Some gained fluency in the rhetoric of radicalism, writing to Dorr, as did the "Suffrage Ladies of Providence," of their dedication to "Equal Rights," or reminding him, as did one Mary Jane Campbell, of their shared passion

---

[34] "The Clam Bake and Pie Nie," *Woonsocket Weekly Patriot*, October 14, 1842.
[35] "Woonsocket Suffrage Song by a Suffrage Lady," Harris Collection of Broadsides, Brown University Library.

for "the caus of justice and humanity."[36] Catherine Williams reported that her group of suffrage ladies in Providence met weekly in her home to debate political issues.[37] On October 25, 1842, William H. Smith wrote to Dorr that "at a full meeting in the volunteers armory (half women) I commented at some length on the Algerine Constitution."[38] That fully one half of those in attendance at public suffrage meetings were women reveals just how powerful a presence they had become in the movement. On August 16, 1842, Mrs. Almira E. Howard of Pawtucket told Dorr that "the cause of justice which you have espoused is one that has my fervent prayers" and that she was planning to organize a committee to call on President Tyler when he visited the state.[39] In Providence, "a few Ladies of this City" expressed their solidarity with him by sending the sum of "one hundred dollars." Articulating a savvy appreciation of the class dimensions of Dorr's movement, the "Ladies" applauded the effort toward "establishing on a permanent basis the rights of the working man and mechanics of your native state."[40] By the summer and fall of 1842, the suffrage ladies had learned a good deal about Rhode Island politics.

Mrs. Ann Parlin, who served as secretary of the Providence suffrage women, took especially bold steps in advancing the Dorrite cause. In September 1842 she ventured from the city to take place in a clambake at Acote's Hill, the site where the suffrage men had made their last ragged stand. What made the occasion noteworthy, however, were the plans of the suffrage women to form "a regular military company, and turn out at stated times to drill and perfect themselves in military tactics." The *Woonsocket Daily Patriot* mocked the women, suggesting that "the flashes of their lustrous eyes, accompanied by Cupid's darts, would be more powerful in vanquishing a foe, than the flashes of their ammunition and the balls of their shooting-irons."[41] The Whiggish press in Providence battered them too, chiding that "Dorrites in petticoats will not show any less courage than was displayed by the Dorrites in pantaloons." Mrs. Parlin, whom they said had agreed to lead the company, "wisely made it a condition that they should not run away, as the men did."[42] In the weeks ahead, Ann Parlin paid dearly for

[36] "Suffrage Ladies of Providence" to Dorr, August 20, 1842; Mary Jane Campbell to Dorr, October 8, 1842, Dorr Correspondence, vol. 5.
[37] Catherine R. Williams to Dorr, October 9, 1842.
[38] William H. Smith to Dorr, October 25, 1842, Dorr Correspondence, vol. 5.
[39] Mrs. Almira E. Howard to Dorr, August 16, 1842, Dorr Correspondence, vol. 4.
[40] "Suffrage Ladies of Providence" to Dorr, August 20, 1842.
[41] "Ladies in Regimentals," *Woonsocket Weekly Patriot*, September 23, 1842.
[42] "Acote's Hill Clam-Bake," *Manufacturer's and Farmer's Journal, Providence and Pawtucket Advertiser*, September 26, 1842.

her role in the Acote's Hill clambake. Samuel Ashley wrote to Dorr that while she was "a woman of first rate abilities," he worried about the controversy she had stirred up. In cryptic terms he reported that Parlin and other suffrage women "have & are now withdrawing from the society of which they claim to be leaders—It is quite perplexing to us all—The fact is that they [are] accused by the algerines & we cannot vindicate them—what shall we do?"[43] Outside the Dorrite ranks, opponents kept up the pressure on her. Catherine Williams confided to Dorr that "the Algerines have torn Mrs. Parlin's character in fragments & several others so they boast & I expect every moment that they will take hold of mine."[44] Suffrage women who pressed against their domestic roles and projected themselves onto the political stage could expect savage abuse from their critics.

That Law and Order advocates felt compelled to tear Ann Parlin's character "in fragments" suggests that her actions touched a deep nerve. In some sense, she had reversed and rendered chaotic a whole range of prescribed social and gender relations. In the first place, she had boldly stepped into the manly territory of party politics. This was perilous ground for women. Calvin Whitney, a Dorrite supporter in Connecticut, somewhat humorously observed that women in his town were taking on more masculine roles when he wrote that "the *females* are unanimously suffrage to a *man.*"[45] Dorr himself had acknowledged this even as he complemented the women of Providence for their help in promoting his cause. "You have most nobly occupied the sphere," he wrote, "which is usually claimed by the other sex."[46] Second, she had taken a leading role in organizing a militia unit, clearly a traditional bastion of masculine authority and identity in New England.[47] She had done all of this on the actual site where Governor King's forces had broken the remains of Dorr's ragged insurgency, thus rehearsing in a kind of political theater the repression that the suffragists wanted their enemies to recall. And she had undertaken all of this on behalf of a man who was now wanted for treason against the state. On levels both personal and political, Ann Parlin threatened the foundations of the law and order that respectable Protestants held dear.

Catherine Williams knew well the risks of political activism but accepted them to become one of the most important female leaders in the Dorr

---

[43] Samuel Ashley to Dorr, October 12, 1842, Dorr Correspondence, vol. 5.

[44] Catherine R. Williams to Dorr, November 2, 1842, Dorr Correspondence, vol. 5.

[45] Calvin Whitney to Dorr, September 7, 1842, Dorr Correspondence, vol. 5.

[46] Thomas Wilson Dorr to "Suffrage Ladies of Providence," August 24, 1842, Dorr Correspondence, vol. 4.

[47] On the manly traditions and political significance of New England militia units, see especially David Hackett Fischer, *Paul Revere's Ride* (New York, 1994), 149–164.

insurgency. Born in Providence in 1787, she had already captured significant notoriety in Rhode Island prior to the Dorr Rebellion through her writing. "She was a warm politician," Sidney S. Rider noted, "Democratic to devotion, and in the Rhode Island troubles of 1842, espoused the cause of the suffrage party with all her might."[48] Her correspondence with Dorr, beginning at least as early as 1842 and stretching into the 1850s, reveals how important she was to the suffrage movement. As a well-known writer, Williams moved in elite social circles and took advantage of her contacts to boost the Dorrite cause. On September 6, 1842, she reported to Dorr that during June she had been in Washington and "had the pleasure of a conversation with Mr. Tyler, on the subject of Rhode Island affairs, in which I plead the cause of the Suffrage Party in R.I."[49] With Dorr on the run, she worked hard to improve the conditions of the prisoners held in Newport. So desperate was their plight that Seth Luther set fire to his own cell in order to get out. Never one to shrink from controversy, Williams marched off to see Governor King "to get something done to make them more comfortable."[50] She proved an able informant for Dorr while he was in hiding, keeping him apprised especially of the activities of the women who worked for the suffrage rebels. She gave him a detailed inventory of the female suffrage leaders in Providence, reported the earnings made from a clambake in Medbury, and served as a conduit of information from the front lines to Dorr's moving headquarters.[51]

Catherine Williams also provided Dorr with political counsel. On November 27, 1842, she wrote a blistering letter condemning the Thanksgiving celebration recently sponsored by Governor King and held in some of Providence's most respectable churches. She advised Dorr that "the good Ladies of our circle are sincerely desirous to have a day of appointment to hold public worship & should you be graciously disposed to grant their request, I hope it may be called a day of *fasting*." Williams was unwilling to abandon the religious high ground to her political opponents. She went on to "promise if no other dares to preach the sermon, I will go into the pulpit & preach it myself from the text 'Blessed are they that mourn.'" She had already thought about the logistics for such an event, informing Dorr that

[48] Sidney S. Rider, *Bibliographical Memoirs of Three Rhode Island Authors: Joseph K. Angell, Frances H. (Whipple) McDougall, Catherine R. Williams*, Rhode Island Historical Tracts, no. 11 (Providence, 1880), 57. See also Patricia Caldwell, ed., *Catherine Williams, Fall River: An Authentic Narrative* (New York, 1993).
[49] Williams to Dorr, September 6, 1842, Dorr Correspondence, vol. 5.
[50] Williams to Dorr, December 28, 1842, Dorr Correspondence, vol. 5.
[51] See Williams to Dorr, October 9 and November 2, 1842, Dorr Correspondence, vol. 5.

"the free Suffrage Universalists" had purchased "the little Christian Baptist Meeting-house & are about to move it to this side of the bridge so we hope to have a house we can borrow now and then." While Williams may not have been entirely serious about delivering a sermon, she was in earnest about her proposal. "Seriously," she explained, "I think we had better have a fast day or something of the kind." She believed that a gathering under religious auspices would "be immensely popular & an excuse to call all hands up & give our Enemies a start, it would not be like the lean & half-starved thanksgiving we have just had."[52] Given the religious rhetoric of the suffrage movement and the enthusiasm of its cadre of ministerial supporters, Williams's idea had real promise. But Dorr did not act upon it.

Despite Dorr's failure to move on her suggestion for a fast day, Catherine Williams continued to write to him in terms that explained the movement in religious language. On March 11, 1843, she sent Dorr wishes that the Lord would "direct you in all your counsels but remember he *resisteth the proud* & givith grace to the humble."[53] Three months later she wrote more consoling words, reminding him that "the Lord lifteth up & casteth down, and it is not the first time Usurpers have been permitted to triumph, but there is a fearful day of reckoning coming for some of them."[54] She warned Dorr not to harbor vengeful feelings himself, but to count on God's justice to bring his enemies to ruin. On September 17, 1843, she reported that the "Algerines are boasting that if they get hold of Gov. Dorr, they will put him in with two or three thieves or treat him in the same manner." She was quick to remind Dorr, however, that the Savior himself had suffered such a fate: "The Son of God was crucified between two Thieves."[55] Especially as their chances for temporal victory declined, Catherine Williams thought about the suffrage movement in ways that lifted it to a spiritual level. On October 12, 1850, she wrote to Dorr that the Lord would preserve them as part of a righteous "remnant who have not lowered the knee to the Image of Baal, or worshipped the golden Calf! There number is indeed small, but they are not extinct."[56] In such ways did Catherine Williams suffuse the Dorrite insurgency with divine purpose.

Given all of this, it is little wonder that Thomas Wilson Dorr and his rebels so horrified respectable and orderly Protestants. For in some sense, they

[52] Williams to Dorr, November 27, 1842, Dorr Correspondence, vol. 5.
[53] Williams to Dorr, March 11, 1843, Dorr Correspondence, vol. 7.
[54] Williams to Dorr, June 16, 1843, Dorr Correspondence, vol. 7.
[55] Williams to Dorr, September 17, 1843, Dorr Correspondence, vol. 7. Other letters from this period seem to suggest a level of intimacy between Williams and Dorr that transcends the world of politics. On March 16, 1844, Williams sent Dorr a slice of wedding cake from her daughter's "recent wedding." See Dorr Correspondence, vol. 8.
[56] Williams to Dorr, October 12, 1850, Dorr Correspondence, vol. 12.

fomented a triple revolution. First, they proposed to overturn Rhode Island's lawful constitution, thus throwing into chaos the government of the state. Dorr may well have been the only resident in the state who believed that he was not a revolutionary but the conservator of traditional American values. Second, that the rebels legitimated their cause in religious terms was also cause for concern, in part because the case they built had theological and historical merit. In pointing to the example of Roger Williams, for instance, who had challenged the authority of the Massachusetts Bay colony over the issue of "soul liberty," the Dorrites could claim considerable respectability. These claims for Christian legitimacy could not go unanswered. Third, the undeniable presence of women in the Dorrite ranks threatened the orderly principles of family government within bourgeois families. That many of the key female leaders in the movement were not plebeians, but women of property and accomplishment only made matters worse. They challenged directly the precepts offered by Francis Wayland in *The Elements of Moral Science*, in which he had insisted that women owed submission and obedience to men. In state, church, and family, the Dorrite insurgents represented the dark forces of chaos and social disorder.

Godly members of the Law and Order Party who supported Governor King's government countered the rebels by claiming the mantle of Christian legitimacy as their own. In response to a request from Governor King, congregations gathered throughout Rhode Island on July 21, 1842, for a solemn day of thanksgiving and reflection. Pulpits throughout the state rang with the voices of clergymen who denounced the rebellion and cast its proponents as agents of anarchy. As Francis Wayland's address earlier in May had made clear, respectable clergy needed little prodding from the government to weigh in on its behalf. "Nothing has filled the enemies of law and order with greater rage," gloated one Whig newspaper, "than the high and noble stand taken by the clergy against their insurrectionary doctrines."[57] Inspired by the gravity of the challenge to Rhode Island's established order, regular Baptist, Congregational, and Episcopal ministers rose in unison to defend it.

All of the ministers who held forth on July 21, 1842, knew that the Dorr Rebellion transcended the issue of suffrage rights in Rhode Island. For them, it represented nothing less than an opportunity for the dark and chaotic impulses inherent in humanity to be loosed upon law-abiding citizens. "The causes were much deeper than the limitations of elective franchise," explained Edward W. Peet of Grace Episcopal Church in Providence. "That was simply an occasion, an opportunity in which the monster of

---

[57] *Manufacturer's and Farmer's Journal, Providence and Pawtucket Advertiser*, July 4, 1842.

anarchy ventured to show his head and to test his energies."[58] Speaking from Newport, Peet's Episcopalian colleague, Francis Vinton, agreed. "The real issue in the late controversy in our State was the question of government, or anarchy," he said, "law, or the mere will of a numerical majority, informally and irregularly expressed."[59] Mark Tucker, of Beneficent Congregational Church, saw behind Dorr and his minions the work of a wider conspiracy designed to tear apart the social fabric. He worried that there were "men in New England who openly avow the destruction of all government, domestic and civil, of the Sabbath, and the ministry. Who can say then that the recent rebellion in this State is not the natural result of such horrible doctrines and has followed in the train of such efforts."[60] While he did not accord outside agitators the prominent role that Tucker did, Francis Wayland agreed that fundamental issues of governmental order were at stake in Rhode Island. "It is not to be concealed," he concluded, "that an attempt has been made to commit a revolting crime against the peace of this community. The lives and the property of this people have been put in peril." Even worse, he averred, "had this insurrection been successful, it must have been at the cost of wholesale pillage and murder."[61] Clearly, the ministers saw in Dorr a profound challenge to the underpinnings of orderly government and society.

These clergymen understood that the political passions aroused by the Dorrites had ripped families apart. "We have had to suffer the shame of household dissension," cried Edward Peet. "Contention, between different members of the same family is more distressing and humiliating than a contest between different families."[62] Mark Tucker thought that the decline of orderly family life was actually a cause rather than a result of the crisis. "This rebellion, in great measure, may be attributed to a want of *family government*," he said. "A man who has been trained to obey when he was young, will not rise up against the government when he is old."[63] In his May 22 address shortly after the arsenal attack, Francis Wayland had drawn a parallel between the destruction of the social compact Dorr had advocated and the

---

[58] Edward W. Peet, *A Sermon Preached on the Occasion of Public Thanksgiving, For the Happy Termination of the Late Civil Dissensions in Rhode Island; Delivered in Grace Church, Providence, July 21, 1842* (Providence, 1842), 11.

[59] Frances Vinton, *Loyalty and Piety; or, the Christians's Civil Obligations Defined* (Providence, 1842), 18–19.

[60] Mark Tucker, *A Discourse Preached on Thanksgiving Day, in the Beneficent Congregational Meeting-House, Providence, July 21, 1842* (Providence, 1842), 12.

[61] Francis Wayland, *A Discourse Delivered in the First Baptist Church, Providence, R.I. on the Day of Public Thanksgiving, July 21, 1842* (Providence, 1842), 27.

[62] Peet, *Sermon*, 11.

[63] Tucker, *Discourse*, 13.

possible demolition of marriage itself. "We have no more liberty to overturn the social compact when we will," he argued, "than the marriage compact."[64] If Dorr had succeeded, Wayland asked, where would the questioning of authority end? He feared that the forces unleashed by the rebels would push Rhode Islanders into what he called a "whirlwind of ceaseless revolution."[65] If the arrangements of orderly family life were the building blocks of stable government, then a threat to one spelled danger for the other.

The Law and Order ministers also worried that the Dorr Rebellion had inflamed relationships among the rich and the poor. Holding to the Whiggish notion of organic and harmonious class relationships, they found this prospect especially abhorrent. Mark Tucker, quite unfairly, charged the insurgents with wanting to destroy all banks and abolish all hereditary property.[66] Some months earlier, Francis Wayland, too had tarnished the Dorrites with the charge that they wanted to redistribute property in the state. "This division of property was to be effected as soon as the new government came into power," he had warned, "and that henceforward they would have no occasion to labor."[67] He came closer to the mark in pointing out that the rebellion had caused some to see the wealthy as villains in their own community rather than as leaders in dispensing benevolence.[68] Still, even in July, he held to the idea that the Dorrites were radical levelers. "Who does not see that the idea of equalization of property," he asked, "is as absurd as it is wicked?"[69] Edward Peet held out an even more chilling alternative. Had Dorr been successful, he said, then "thousands would have poured in from the festering sinks of our large cities, and rallied around the standard of revolution."[70] While Dorr had held rallies to gain support in New York, it is hardly likely that masses of immigrants would have descended upon Rhode Island to take a slice of the property that the rebels would be handing out. Indeed, the ministers seemed anxious to assign to Dorr and his followers ideas associated with Thomas Skidmore and other radicals in the New York workingmen's movement from the 1830s. Even if they knew that the Rhode Island Suffrage Association had never embraced such schemes, their comments on the potential for class warfare revealed their fears that the insurgents might have been tempted to take action against them as men of property, and therefore, political power.

---

[64] Wayland, *Affairs or Rhode Island*, 29.
[65] Ibid., 28.
[66] Tucker, *Discourse*, 11.
[67] Wayland, *Affairs of Rhode Island*, 18.
[68] Ibid., 24–25.
[69] Wayland, *Discourse*, 17.
[70] Peet, *Sermon*, 10.

The only way to stem the tide of rebellion, the ministers argued, was to insist that pious Christians tender their obedience to duly constituted governmental authorities. Following the lead set by Francis Wayland on May 22, virtually all of the ministers attributed the defeat of Dorrism to divine intervention. They also called for all Christians to heed the voice of God as it was revealed in human government. Their pleas on this point were direct and unambiguous. "Now is the time to impress upon the minds of all men of all parties," Mark Tucker maintained, "the necessity of unqualified submission to wholesome laws."[71] Edward Peet could not have agreed more. "Surely," he said, "there is not a Christian heart which does not vibrate in unison with the call of civil authority."[72] Frances Vinton pointed to the Biblical verse "render unto Caesar the things that are Caesar's, and to God the things that are God's" to make his point. "The Bible," he explained, "utters but one voice on this subject. It enjoins the duty of obedience to the regularly constituted authorities of the state, within the scope of their civil jurisdiction. It is not an uncertain sound. It repeats the declarations of Christ."[73] Francis Wayland, more simply, enjoined his fellow citizens "to maintain the righteous authority of law, and deliver this State from the miseries of anarchy."[74] Thus did these ministers see in civil ordinances the steadying hand of God's guidance.

The intensity of the constitutional crisis also pushed the Law and Order clergy to articulate openly the conservative political principles that had often remained latent in times of peace. Frances Vinton, for instance, insisted that the example of the American Revolution did not impart to citizens the right to stir up civil unrest for what he thought were frivolous ends. He argued that the Declaration of Independence itself testified that governments could not be overturned except for the most grievous of abuses. He noted, moreover, that Washington himself had advised "respect for the authority of the established government."[75] In no way did Vinton agree with the Dorrites who saw in the American Revolution an inspiration for their own insurrection. Mark Tucker, too, agreed that Christians ought to beware of those tempting them into the paths of radical reform. "This recent development should lead us to watch with more vigilance such men as *Garrison*, who is propagating errors of the worst character," he claimed, "openly assailing all government, the Holy Sabbath and the Christian ministry."[76] The ministers

---

[71] Tucker, *Discourse*, 15.
[72] Peet, *Sermon*, 3.
[73] Vinton, *Loyalty and Piety*, 12.
[74] Wayland, *Discourse*, 9.
[75] Vinton, *Loyalty and Piety*, 17; for his interpretation of the revolutionary heritage, see 15–17.
[76] Tucker, *Discourse*, 14.

worried especially about the ways in which the principles of democracy had been perverted by their opponents. Edward Peet thought that the principle of "government of the people" appealed to some of the worst passions of man. This political doctrine "receives an impulse which carries it towards a most perilous extreme, that extreme is insubordination, anarchy, and revolution."[77] Francis Wayland, too, feared that government by the many could subvert wholesome respect for the law and tradition. On August 22, 1842, he wrote to his uncle Daniel P. Wayland that "there is danger that the mere will of masses will come to be substituted for constitutional law."[78] Democracy itself held inherent dangers. "This doctrine of radical democracy," Frances Vinton explained, "you may clearly perceive, is subversive of all security."[79] In holding to the transcendent authority of law, in weaving a cautious interpretation of the American Revolution, in warning against the excesses of reform, and in harboring fears about the tyranny of the majority, Wayland and his companions announced themselves as political conservatives in the age of Jacksonian Democracy.[80]

In condemning the rebellion, the Law and Order clergymen acknowledged the seductive appeal of the Dorrite cause within their own congregations. From the outset of the crisis in May, Francis Wayland had known that suffrage rebels could be found among the ranks of respectable communicants. Edward Peet observed that even among Episcopalians the suffrage cause had found support. "And how happy would many a Christian minister now feel," he sighed, "if the church of God had not been called to take its full share of the public calamity. But alas the demon of dissension has stalked into the sanctuary! Brethren who have knelt at the same altars, have become suspicious of each other."[81] Mark Tucker knew that rifts had developed among the Congregationalists. He noted that "sad divisions had taken place" and called upon his members to "reclaim to reason and duty those who have sinned by countenancing opposition to the state."[82] Francis Vinton, too, observed that some believers had been lured into Dorr's movement. "That any professing Christian, whose sincerity I may not dispute, should uphold a doctrine so subversive of government," he maintained, "is possible and surprising."[83] As the issue of the rebellion had divided the

[77] Peet, *Sermon*, 6.
[78] Francis Wayland to Daniel P. Wayland, August 22, 1842, Wayland Papers, Brown University Archives.
[79] Vinton, *Loyalty and Piety*, 20–21.
[80] See especially Daniel Walker Howe's chapter on "Whig Conservatism," in *Political Culture of the American Whigs*, 210–237.
[81] Peet, *Sermon*, 12.
[82] Tucker, *Discourse*, 16.
[83] Vinton, *Loyalty and Piety*, 21.

ministers of Providence, so too did it throw individual congregations into turmoil.

The force of the insurrection threatened the peace and harmony of Providence congregations at a number of levels. Perhaps no group of communicants was placed at greater risk than those who inhabited Providence's black churches. As William J. Brown remembered it, Providence blacks, although few in number, occupied a pivotal position in the contest between the Suffrage Association and the Law and Order Party. Disfranchised since 1822, they realized that the Dorr's movement might offer them the opportunity to reclaim lost ground.[84] Alexander Crummell, the young pastor of Christ Episcopal Church, approached the suffrage reformers at their "People's Convention" in October, 1841, with a statement that called on them to embrace equal voting rights for black and white men. Crummell thought the exclusion of blacks from the suffrage movement to be "unrepublican" and championed their cause with a statement he read to the delegates. "Debarred as we have been of the advantages of learning, and denied participation in civil prerogatives," he said, "we unhesitatingly assert that we will not suffer by a comparison with our more privileged fellow-citizens of the same rank, in either religion, virtue, or industry."[85] His arguments failed to move a majority of the delegates. They voted forty-six to eighteen to abolish the property requirements for white men only, leaving black men in the same position as before.[86] Although Dorr was said to be sympathetic to Crummell's position, it was clear that a majority of the delegates were willing to sacrifice black political rights on the grounds of expediency.

The analysis proved, in part, to be correct. In late 1841 and early 1842 abolitionists visiting Rhode Island experienced a torrent of abuse virtually everywhere they went. From Woonsocket Falls to Providence, hecklers bombarded them with insults, broke up their meetings, and hurled snowballs at them. Frederick Douglass, an agent for the American Anti-Slavery Society, found himself confined to a "Jim Crow" train compartment during his brief visit. "In January 1842," writes Robert Cottrol, "the abolitionist speaker Abby Kelly was pelted with snowballs by a Suffrage party mob as she attempted to speak in Providence."[87] Alexander Crummell's congregation

[84] See J. Stanley Lemons and Michael A. McKenna, "Re-enfranchisement of Rhode Island Negroes," *Rhode Island History* 30 (1971): 3–13; Robert J. Cottrol, *The Afro-Yankees: Providence's Black Community in the Antebellum Era* (Westport, Conn., 1982), 77–90.

[85] The text for these remarks appears in Burke, *Interference of the Executive*, 111–113; see also Cottrol, *Afro-Yankees*, 73–74.

[86] Cottrol, *Afro-Yankees*, 74.

[87] Ibid., 75.

may have received a warning to stay clear of political entanglements. On the evening of May 24, 1842, less than a week after the arsenal attack, "some Person or Persons" set fire to the northwest corner of their church. Insurance covered the $500 of damage, but the culprits escaped into the night.[88] Although we cannot be sure who set the blaze, such an act fits the broader pattern of racial antagonism demonstrated by the suffrage reformers during the previous year.

In the troubling days following the church fire, Alexander Crummell and the Providence black community cast their fortunes with the forces of law and order. They sent two companies of black militiamen to Chepachet to assist in putting down Dorr's rebel forces. In return for their loyalty, black men received the vote. The reformed constitution created in the fall of 1842 inaugurated a period of cooperation between the Whigs and the black community that extended at least until 1848, when black voters could hardly stomach voting for Zachary Taylor, a Whig and a slaveholder, in the presidential contest. Democrats and suffrage advocates did not forgive Providence blacks their interest in claiming political rights. William J. Brown recalled, in understated fashion, that former suffrage activists "were not overburdened with love for the colored people," whom they blamed in part for their defeat. "They said if it were not for the colored people," reported Brown with pride, "they would have whipped the Algerines."[89] Navigating their way between two hostile camps each of which sought to use them to its own advantage, black political and religious leaders backed the winning side during the insurrection.

Alexander Crummell's church was not the only Rhode Island congregation to confront public acts of violence. In the mill village of Pawtucket, the violence sparked by the Dorr Rebellion proved an especially contentious problem for the churches. Pawtucket, a manufacturing center, contained landless operatives who took up Dorr's cause, occasionally hurling stones and insults at the state militiamen who guarded the Pawtucket Bridge. On June 27 these tense troops volleyed into a crowd, killing Alexander Kilby, "a peaceable and quiet citizen" of Massachusetts. Musket balls wounded two other men and "rattled upon the brick walls of the houses."[90] Although the attack was of minor military importance, the sight of militia forces firing

[88] Record Book, Christ Church, May 24, 1842, RIHS. See also the meeting of May 17, 1842, which noted the closing of the vestry meeting: "it being the Night which an attack was made on the 'Arsenal' by the Suffrage Constitutional Party by Thomas W. Dorr, Commander in Chief & Governor under Said Constitution." Such an inscription suggests that a measure of black support for Dorr endured until at least the night of the attack.
[89] William J. Brown, *The Life of William J. Brown, of Providence, R.I.* (1883; reprint, New York, 1971), 162.
[90] On the violence in Pawtucket see Burke, *Interference of the Executive*, 75–76.

into a crowd alarmed many residents. It also raised conflict among church members.

Following this disturbing spectacle, the Congregationalist pastor Constantine Blodgett sought to heal the wounds that violence had inflicted on Pawtucket residents. On July 10, 1842, he delivered a carefully crafted address titled "How to Win a Brother." Taking as his text Proverbs 18 ("A brother offended is harder to be won than a strong city: and their contentions are like the bars of a castle"), he aimed to calm the violent tempers of his communicants. Recalling the examples of Cain and Abel, Sarah and Hagar, and Absalom and Ammon, he observed that "animosities among brethren" could be "most rancorous, unrelenting, and cruel."[91] So, too, had the political turmoil of the present-day set church members and communicants against one another. Blodgett asked his listeners to give their attention to the true source of Christian unity. The Bible, he said, did not teach churches to gather around single political principles, such as "anti-slavery" or even "anti-intemperance." Rather, authentic fellowship should be "organized on the foundation of prophets and apostles, Jesus Christ himself being the chief corner-stone." He enjoined true Christians to sacrifice the interests of party and secular politics in order to pursue the more important ends of spiritual unity. He interpreted episodes of "strong party excitement" as character tests for the faithful.[92] Those with a pure love of Christ would learn to put politics behind them.

An anonymous "working man" published a pamphlet that indicted Blodgett's theology and the behavior of his communicants. Titled "Fighting Church Members," the treatise charged that "in the 'late war' in this State, some of Mr. Blodgett's leading members took guns, in order to shoot their neighbors if ordered to do so."[93] Its author also mocked Blodgett's calls for charity. "But we have seen that his charity gives license for church members to blow out their brethren and neighbor's brains," he chided, "and still be held in good fellowship." While shrill and overblown, the tract underscored the central point that Blodgett's argument had essentially described an ethic for the victorious. Calls for understanding and peace could easily be made by the forces of law and order now that they had gained the upper hand in the struggle. Such behavior, the "working man" claimed, did not warrant the term Christian. "That the late commotion in R.I. will tend to

[91] C. Blodgett, *How to Win a Brother, A Discourse Delivered in the Congregational Meeting House in Pawtucket, July 10, 1842* (Pawtucket, 1842), 4.
[92] Ibid., 11, 13.
[93] *Fighting Church Members, Brief Remarks on Mr. C. Blodgett's Discourse 'How to Win a Brother.' By a Working Man* (n.p., 1842), 4.

shew many of God's people," he cried, "that the church walls which surround them are but anti-Christian enclosures I doubt not."[94] Blodgett's sermon proved to be more prophetic than he had anticipated.

At Providence's Third Baptist Church, the communicants counseled peace not war. They urged all concerned to set aside partisan issues for the good of the church. On February 6, 1843, they passed a lengthy resolution designed to restore harmony among members in the congregation. With "females voting," the members acknowledged the damage that had been done to Christian fellowship as a result of "the political excitement which have agitated the inhabitants of our State during the past year." They promised that henceforth they would "take back, and bury in oblivion any unkind words and feelings which we have ever expressed or felt in regard to any member of the church touching the matters named in the above preamble." They pledged also "that we will not in time to come suffer the political opinions of our brethren to cause us to love them less, but will treat them as followers of christ, provided that such opinions are not repugnant to the laws of the land." Thus did the members implicitly acknowledge that political passions had set them against one another. But even in promising forbearance in the treatment of political differences, the members carefully included a provision that revealed their dedication to the principles of law and order. Christian tolerance had its limits.[95]

Other Rhode Island churches moved more directly against the Dorrite rebels in their midst. In a series of disciplinary cases, communicants around the state made it clear that an endorsement of Dorr marked not only treason against the state but heresy against the church. Never before in the antebellum period had communicants in Providence disciplined one another for their partisan political opinions. But the specter of rebellion pushed them to extraordinary measures. "No men have appeared to me so blood thirsty," complained Providence printer Benjamin T. Albro to Dorr, "as the deacons and church members."[96] Still, discipline cases against Dorrites served a largely symbolic function. Congregations did not institute wholesale inquisitions designed to purge all those with deviant political opinions. Had they taken this approach, it would have imperiled the principles of harmony and peace the churches sought to establish in the first place. Most cases, such as the one brought by First Baptist Church in Pawtucket against Henry Strange, were dispensed with quickly. On February 4, 1843, Strange "made his acknowledgment that he had been guilty of taking up arms to

[94] Ibid., 8, 10–11.

[95] Record Book, Third Baptist Church, February 6, 1843, RIHS.

[96] Benjamin T. Albro to Dorr, September 18, 1842, Dorr Correspondence, vol. 5.

escort Mr. Dorr last spring which he said was wrong and asked the forgiveness of the church."[97] Satisfied with his confession, the church took no further action against him. Rare cases, such as those that embroiled Second Baptist Church in Newport, stretched on for months and threatened to poison permanently the wellsprings of Christian harmony. But even though these cases were few in number, they laid out in clear terms the lengths to which respectable Protestants would go to insure obedience to state and church.

On July 7, 1842, the members of First Baptist Church in Providence ordered John B. Barton to appear before them. They charged him with pursuing "a general course of conduct, dishonorable to the cause of religion, particularly in sustaining the movement of Thomas W. Dorr in his late treasonable designs."[98] In taking action against him, the congregation confronted a man of proven responsibility and worth. He had joined the church in 1822 and purchased a pew worth $100 in the refurbished meetinghouse during the auction of 1832. A prosperous surveyor, Barton had demonstrated qualities of industry and steadiness over the period of his twenty-year association with the church. In pressing a discipline case against him, the congregation made it plain that previous loyalty to the church could not protect rebels from their scrutiny. John Barton reinforced his posture as a renegade member by refusing to meet with the congregation the following week. He must have known what was coming. The church expelled him. They also took the opportunity to announce a resolution that explained in depth their reasoning about his case and other instances of political deviance. They may have expected more problems and wanted to have a set of guidelines in hand for adjudicating other decisions. The members agreed that "many professors of religion of various denominations" had been implicated "in the late unlawful attempt to overturn the government of this state." They affirmed that "as a Church and as individuals we hold allegiance to the civil government to be a *Christian duty* enforced by many precepts." Anyone who had supported "insurrectionary movements" had "*grievously erred*" and would be required to confess this sin before the church.[99] In words that echoed the Law and Order sermons that followed only a week later, the members of First Baptist Church also provided a framework within which to reclaim repentant insurgents.

Stephen Basker accepted this offer. On July 22, 1842, he admitted that "he had acted in support of the suffrage cause" but denied that he had taken

[97] Record Book, First Baptist Church, Pawtucket, February 4, 1843, RIHS.
[98] Record Book, First Baptist Church, July 7, 1842.
[99] Record Book, First Baptist Church, July 14, 1842.

up arms against the state. In a letter he had sent to the congregation, he had also questioned its propriety in investigating the political opinions of its members. Upon prayerful reflection, he confessed that he had "changed his mind with regard to the authority of the Church to enquire into his conduct." Now chastened, he wished to withdraw his previous objections and submit to the lawful discipline of the church. With Francis Wayland himself making the motion, the members decided to accept his explanation and concluded "that the subject be dropped." By acknowledging the authority of both state and church, Basker won the approbation of his fellow communicants.[100]

At Beneficent Congregational Church, Peleg H. Seymour faced an array of more serious crimes. The congregation charged him with "taking up arms & proceeding to Armington on the Sabbath to escort Thomas W. Dorr from that place to this City on 15th May last." Seymour explained his behavior by asserting that "he believed said Dorr to be the rightful Governor of this State & that he was commanded by an officer under said Governor." He had, in his own way, only obeyed a recognized secular authority. The church found little of substance in Seymour's arguments. They accused him of "a gross violation of the Law of *God* in deserting his Holy Sabbath" and for "disobeying the Laws of the State & countenancing Rebellion against the Civil Government under which we live." An antinomian twice over, Seymour's behavior merited nothing but the condemnation of the congregation. On July 26, they withdrew their fellowship from him.[101]

The disciplinary cases of Sanford Bell and George C. Shaw offer perhaps the most compelling and detailed account of congregational strife during the Dorr Rebellion.[102] Members of Second Baptist Church of Newport, Bell and Shaw ranked among the congregation's old guard. They claimed a history of forty years with their fellow communicants, acknowledging that they had been "instructed from infancy to grey hairs" among people whom they considered with the tender affections of family. On September 29, 1842, they offered a four-page memorial, "To the Second Baptist Church in Newport, R.I.," that explained why they could no longer continue as members there. In painful and poignant terms, they explained how their political opinions had fractured the bonds of fellowship that had once united them with those they loved.

---

[100] Record Book, First Baptist Church, July 22, 1842.

[101] Record Book, Beneficent Congregational Church, July 15 and 26, 1842, Vestry, Beneficent Congregational Church, Providence, Rhode Island.

[102] All of the quotations that follow regarding the Bell and Shaw cases are from Record Book, Second Baptist Church, Newport, a memorial titled "To the Second Baptist Church in Newport, R.I.," dated September 29, 1842 and signed by Sanford Bell and George C. Shaw, RIHS.

Sanford Bell and George C. Shaw had never made a secret of their support of the suffrage cause and continued to champion it in their memorial. They pointed to two key sources—the Declaration of Independence and the Holy Bible—as the authorities that bolstered their belief in government based on the consent of the governed. On June 2, 1842, Bell and Shaw appeared before the church to answer questions from Deacon Abner Peckham "in relation to the agitations in the State." They admitted freely "our attachment to Equal rights and the People's Constitution, and more especially our decided disapproval of all military movements to sustain the same." Although the church found their explanations convincing, rumors continued to swirl around the two men. They learned that "false reports" alleged that they had "attended Caucusses of the Suffrage party on Sundays" as well as a host of other "foolish and ridiculous" charges. In response, they issued their own circular to the church; it reiterated their basic principles, including their dedication to a "pacific" approach toward resolving the suffrage question. They also signed a report for the Newport *Mercury* in which they announced their belief that for the People's Legislature to meet again would be "the height of folly." While they never retracted their dedication to the principle of government by the consent of the governed, Bell and Shaw struggled to take the revolutionary edge off their actions.

The members of Second Baptist Church took a dim view of such efforts. "The Pulpit and the Conference meetings, were vocal with censure of the suffrage cause, and Suffrage men," Bell and Shaw recalled, "to such a degree as to make our attendance in the house of God, an affliction rather than a blessing." On September 1, 1842, the church, by a narrow margin, voted to exclude them "for their unchristian conduct in relation to the late troubles in this State." A few days later the communicants had a change of heart. On September 5, 1842, at a special meeting they voted to repeal their earlier judgment against the two men. Both votes evidently took place without the charged men present to face the accusations brought against them. By handling the case in this way, the church offered Bell and Shaw a de facto repudiation of the principle of self-government in which they professed to believe. Indeed, Bell and Shaw complained that the church had first expelled them and later reinstated them "without our consent." They believed that "the summary course of action taken by the Church in this case" was "without precedent in any Baptist Church in America—certainly at variance in the practice of this Church, during our acquaintance, for forty years past." Adherents of democratic principles both within and outside their church, Bell and Shaw refused to accept the congregation's offer to restore them to full membership.

Individual congregations made it clear that they would not tolerate Dorrites in their midst. While early in the struggle the suffrage reformers had battled to gain the upper hand in casting their cause as a religious crusade, the forces of law and order eventually carried the day. Despite the efforts of stalwarts such as William S. Balch and James McKenzie, few religious figures could be found openly supporting Dorr or his cause after 1843. It may have been the religious flavor of the suffrage movement itself that prompted such a swift and decisive response on the part of orderly and respectable Protestants. From pulpits and in disciplinary meetings, they worked to ensure that true Christians supported the duly recognized civil authorities of the state.

By the middle of the 1840s bourgeois Protestants had defeated decisively the forces of religious and political radicalism in Rhode Island. In solidifying their victory, they did more than offer panegyrics on the themes of individual responsibility, moral improvement, or social order. They now made more expansive claims. For them, Christianity properly understood supplied the cornerstone of all human government. "It is on the religion of Jesus Christ alone," Francis Wayland explained, "that the freedom and security and permanence of every form of social organization must ultimately depend."[103] The Unitarian Samuel Osgood echoed Wayland's views. "Apart from the recognition of God and the obligation to observe divine law," he contended, "there can, or course, be very little assurance of private virtue or social order."[104] According to Mark Tucker, professors of religion should busy themselves "by strengthening & defending the foundations of civil liberty by promoting a spirit of subordination to the laws, by cherishing respect for rulers."[105] In almost Augustinian fashion, the clergymen preached that obedience to civic authorities would restrain the reckless and destructive capacities of man.

It would be a mistake to interpret the victory forged by Whigs and respectable Protestants as intentionally repressive or fundamentally coercive. Dedicated as they were to moral improvement and social harmony, they paused to reflect on why the Dorr Rebellion had taken place. In the concluding passages of his thanksgiving sermon, Francis Wayland wondered why "this chastisement has been inflicted upon us by our Heavenly Father?"[106] He answered his question with the assertion that pious citizens

---

[103] Wayland, *Discourse*, 19.
[104] Osgood's remarks quoted in an account of the meeting of the Rhode Island Sabbath Union, *Manufacturer's and Farmer's Journal, Providence and Pawtucket Advertiser*, May 29, 1845.
[105] Mark Tucker sermons and diaries, manuscript of a Thanksgiving Sermon Delivered on November 26, 1840, and November 30, 1848, RIHS.
[106] Wayland, *Discourse*, 14.

had strayed from dependence upon God and had allowed themselves to become selfish. "We have not been sufficiently aware," he argued, "of the duties which we owe to the community around us." Here Wayland's organic understanding of the social order afforded him the leverage to critique not only unruly Dorrites but complacent churchgoers as well. Now, Wayland insisted, was the time for all professors of religion to promote the spirit of forgiveness, reconciliation, and even self-denial. "Let us deny ourselves of ordinary conveniences," he directed, "that we may minister to other men's necessities."[107] In offering this view of Christian duty, Wayland refused to allow respectable Protestants to rest easy with their triumph over the forces of political chaos. By rededicating themselves to the principles of benevolence and charity, bourgeois communicants could rebuild an authentic religious community and also free themselves from the snares of greed. In the decades that followed the Dorr Rebellion, they determined to remake their religious community and, in the process, save their own souls.

[107] Ibid., 16, 29.

7

"The Pleasures and Vices of the City"
Church and Society, 1845–1860

On March 30, 1856, pastor Edward B. Hall of First Congregational Church captivated his communicants with an analysis of the spiritual crisis that gripped the Providence community. He spread before them the awful spectacle of the progress of frivolity, sensuality, and intemperance, an unholy trinity that threatened to undo them. Such sins preyed especially upon those who had given themselves over to the pursuit of worldly riches. "Excessive business," he declared, "when controlled by no religious principle, not only tends to consume the man, but tempts him to seek relaxation for his over-strained system in sensuous indulgence." Cravings for drink, the theater, dancing, and "infamous houses" could all be traced to a dangerous preoccupation with material success. These evils lurked everywhere in urban society. "I fear every city is corrupt," Hall proclaimed, "beyond the belief of any who do not look beneath the surface." While he averred that the dictates of good taste and Christian decorum prevented him from describing in detail the sins he had in mind, Hall's hair-raising acknowledgment of "the powers of the flesh, fashion, frivolity, ambition, avarice and lust" teased his audience with breathless references to the very sins he sought to eradicate.[1] His sermon resonates with what David S. Reynolds has called the "darkening of moral discourse" and the creation of a "subversive" reform literature that focused more on the horrors of sin than on its amelioration.[2]

Given the recent history of Providence's refined Christians, Edward Hall's

[1] Edward B. Hall, *A Lecture on the Pleasures and Vices of the City* (Providence, 1856), 7, 23, 6.
[2] David S. Reynolds, *Beneath the American Renaissance: The Subversive Imagination in the Age of Emerson and Melville* (Cambridge, Mass., 1988), 56; also 56–91 generally.

227

remarks to his members could well have been more sanguine. Rather than employing the rhetoric of sensational pessimism, he might have reveled in the strengthening of bourgeois religious culture. As we shall observe, bourgeois Protestants in Providence participated in the broader national process of cultural consolidation that John Higham identified nearly thirty years ago. In the decades between 1840 and 1860, he wrote, the "boundlessness" of the Jacksonian era gave way to "the formation of a more stable, more disciplined, less adventurous culture."[3] More recently, in his landmark study of Fourierism in the nineteenth century, Carl J. Guarneri has concluded that "increasing numbers of reform spokesmen evolved from the boundless optimism of the 1830s and 1840s to a new, more conservative orientation toward American life and institutions."[4] Certainly the decades following the upheaval of the Dorr Rebellion would have been tonic for those Christians weary of religious, social, and political upheaval. They had, after all, been victorious. If, in 1860, Providence's refined Protestants could have glanced back over the past two decades, they might have identified two special reasons for celebration.

In the first place, the threat of plebeian religious radicalism had sharply diminished. In part, this was a natural consequence of the successful offensive launched by respectable Protestants in the months following the collapse of the Dorr Rebellion. Protestant culture in Providence came to be identified, in stronger terms, with the values of personal discipline and social order. This particular political circumstance of Rhode Island history dovetailed with wider national trends in America's religious trajectory. As Nathan O. Hatch has argued, the religious "populists" of the early national era found it difficult to resist the "allure of respectability" in the decades before the Civil War.[5] Denominations such as the Methodists and Baptists, once "upstart sects" in America's religious culture, had now become central pillars of the Protestant establishment.[6] We have already glimpsed among Providence's Methodists and Freewill Baptists the beginnings of that familiar process by which religious radicals sought the trappings of respectability, including refined meetinghouses latticed with ranks of pews. That Francis Wayland, himself a Baptist and thus properly a member of an "upstart sect," had become the leading Northern moral philosopher of his generation reveals the degree to which denominations such as the Baptists and

---

[3] John Higham, *From Boundlessness to Consolidation: The Transformation of American Culture, 1848–1860* (Ann Arbor, Mich., 1969), 16.
[4] Carl J. Guarneri, *The Utopian Alternative: Fourierism in Nineteenth-Century America* (Ithaca, 1991), 335.
[5] Nathan O. Hatch, *The Democratization of American Christianity* (New Haven, 1989), 201–206.
[6] Roger Finke and Rodney Stark, *The Churching of America, 1776–1990: Winners and Losers in Our Religious Economy* (New Brunswick, N.J., 1992), 54–108.

Methodists had now become part of the Protestant mainstream.[7] Although plebeian religious culture did not disappear in Providence (Irish Catholics made the city's working class profoundly religious), the decades following the Dorr Rebellion were years of triumph for bourgeois Protestants.

A second element in the process of Protestant cultural consolidation involved closer cooperation between bourgeois women and bourgeois men in the cause of religious benevolence. Prior to the 1850s, elite women frequently offered stinging critiques of the economic and political structures crafted by bourgeois men. Beginning with the Providence Female Tract Society, continuing with the work of the Providence Employment Society, and culminating with the activities of "Dorrite Ladies" such as Catherine Williams, bourgeois women called bourgeois men to task for their moral failings. To be sure, many women stood by their men. For every Catherine Williams (an activist who sided with political radicals) there was an Emeline Barstow (wife of Mayor Amos C. Barstow, a supporter of the established order.) Still, it would be a mistake to overlook this vein of female opposition within bourgeois religious culture. So long as refined women chided their men about the treatment of factory operatives and needleworkers, so long as they championed radical political agendas, bourgeois religious culture would remain profoundly divided. This division healed in the decades following the Dorr Rebellion. Bourgeois women now joined their men in a series of institutional reform efforts that signaled a key change in the strategy of religious benevolence. The evidence from Providence confirms that "moral suasion" began to lose force as a justification for female reform and that this shift undercut more radical female demands for reform. Simultaneously, "more conservative benevolent activists sought to alleviate social and moral conditions by focusing more and more on benevolent institutions, often founded in close alliance with men."[8] It was this closing of the ranks, this new unity of purpose among bourgeois women and men, that laid the groundwork for the ultimate consolidation of Protestant culture in the 1850s.

There was thus considerable irony in Edward Hall's gloomy assessment of his city. At what might have been the moment of their greatest victory, bourgeois Protestants lapsed into a period of deep soul-searching. Their doubts were spawned, in part, by the success of the social ethic to which they had adhered over the course of three decades. Following their dedication to industry, personal discipline, and social order, they had become prosper-

[7] William G. McLoughlin, *New England Dissent, 1630–1833* (Cambridge, Mass., 1971), 2:1274.
[8] Lori D. Ginzburg, *Women and the Work of Benevolence: Morality, Politics, and Class in the Nineteenth-Century United States* (New Haven, 1990), 100. See also Carol Smith-Rosenberg, "The Cross and the Pedestal: Women, Anti-Ritualism, and the Emergence of the American Bourgeoisie," in *Disorderly Conduct: Visions of Gender in Victorian America* (New York, 1985), 129–164.

ous, comfortable, and content. And that was the problem. For now they worried about the spiritual consequences of their own material advancement. They pondered, too, the fate of the unchurched masses of workers who now floated beyond the compass of their fine and polished sanctuaries. The jeremiads offered by such ministers as Edward Hall were not, in the end, far removed from the agonies articulated by their Puritan ancestors. They "were professions of a society that knew it was doing wrong, but could not help itself, because the wrong thing was also the right thing."[9] For bourgeois Protestants of the 1850s, crisis and consolidation were two sides of the same coin.

The first dilemma faced by bourgeois Protestants grew from their intimate acquaintance with the fruits of free labor capitalism. They feared especially what they called the encroachments of "worldliness" into their souls and into their churches. Like Edward Hall, they feared the corrosive effects that absorption in business had on authentic Christian faith. In the 1840s and 1850s, these fears manifested themselves in a variety of different arenas: in church covenants and discipline cases, in the rise of a "Christian Socialist" movement in Providence, and in the pronouncements of pious residents during the economic panic and depression of 1857–58. While scholars have rightly pointed out that the key political controversy of the 1850s revolved around the debate between free labor and slave labor, this does not mean that all Northerners believed that free labor capitalism had created a society beyond reproach. Nor does it mean that the rise of the abolitionist movement necessarily prompted Northerners to accept, almost unquestioningly, the moral rectitude of their economic and social arrangements.[10] For even as the debate between the extension of slavery into the West polarized the American political system, some Northerners continued to acknowledge that the system of free labor could not be practiced without a profound cost to the Christian faith.[11]

---

[9] Perry Miller, *The New England Mind: From Colony to Province* (Cambridge, Mass., 1961), 51.

[10] The snug connection between the rise of capitalism and the antislavery movement has been illuminated brilliantly in the works of David Brion Davis, especially *The Problem of Slavery in the Age of Revolution, 1770–1823* (Ithaca, 1975). Christopher Clark, in *The Communitarian Moment: The Radical Challenge of the Northampton Association* (Ithaca, 1995), provides evidence that abolitionists did not eschew completely criticism of free labor capitalism. "The Northampton Association," he writes, "was one of many places in which discussions of capitalism and its faults took place in the early 1840s, and it crystalized an abolitionist vision critical of capitalism as well as of slavery" (99).

[11] Timothy L. Smith made this point long ago in his classic work, *Revivalism and Social Reform: American Protestantism on the Eve of the Civil War* (1957; reprint, Baltimore, 1980). He concluded that revivalists in the urban North "issued repeated warnings against the danger that the love of money would benumb social concern," even as they became increasingly interested in the evils of slavery (174).

The accumulation of capital in Providence in the years following the Dorr Rebellion rooted the fears of respectable Protestants in reality. By 1855 Providence had emerged as a bustling metropolis of forty-seven thousand residents that contained nearly as many banks (thirty-eight) as it did churches (forty-six).[12] "By the Civil War," writes Peter J. Coleman, "over two-fifths of the state's banks and almost three-quarters of its banking resources were located in the city."[13] Investors continued to channel money into the mill towns in neighboring Connecticut and Massachusetts and had funds to spare to pump into insurance companies, textile manufactories, jewelry businesses, and a host of other urban enterprises. Providence businessmen accumulated vast fortunes. In Alexander Duncan's case, the process took decades. Coming from a family in the older Providence trading elite, he joined forces with the manufacturing interests of Brown & Ives. By the outbreak of the Civil War, the firm operated mills in Rhode Island, Connecticut, and Massachusetts with a total of 275,000 spindles. Zachariah Allen, whose family could boast of significant manufacturing achievement, viewed Duncan with awe. In 1857, even as business prospects dimmed, Allen still considered Duncan to be a legitimate "millionare."[14] But Duncan would not stand alone as an entrepreneurial hero in his community. In this era Providence also launched the careers of the soon-to-be-famous Joseph R. Brown, a machine shop pioneer, and George H. Corlis, a steam engine innovator.[15] Moreover, we now have sufficient evidence from across the urban Northeast to conclude that during the antebellum era the income gap between the impoverished and the wealthy widened significantly.[16] If wealth corrupted faith, then the faithful of Providence had much to fear.

During the late 1830s and early 1840s, worries about the "worldliness" of members crept into church resolutions and covenants. In January 1839 the members of Beneficent Congregational Church agreed that "the joy of the Christian is such as the world knows not, and cannot result from those vain amusements which the world approve, and which give pleasure to the

---

[12] Edwin M. Snow, *Census of the City of Providence, Taken in July, 1855; with a brief account of the manufactures, trade, commerce, and other statistics of the city; and an appendix, giving an account of previous enumerations of the population of Providence* (Providence, 1856), 53. The reckoning of banks and churches appeared on the same page.

[13] Peter J. Coleman, *The Transformation of Rhode Island, 1790–1860* (Providence, 1963), 204.

[14] Ibid., 130, 201; Zachariah Allen diaries, November 8, 1857, Manuscript Collection, Rhode Island Historical Society, hereafter cited as RIHS.

[15] See Henry Dexter Sharpe, *Joseph R. Brown, Mechanic, and the Beginnings of Brown and Sharpe* (New York, 1949); Robert W. Kenny, "George H. Corliss: Engineer, Architect, Philanthropist," *Rhode Island History* 40 (1981): 49–61.

[16] Edward Pessen, "The Egalitarian Myth and the American Social Reality: Wealth, Mobility, and Equality in the 'Era of the Common Man,' " *American Historical Review* 76 (1971): 989–1034. See also Walter Licht, *Industrializing America: The Nineteenth Century* (Baltimore, 1995), 70.

natural heart." They also decided that any member attending "the Theatre, the Circus, Balls, and Dancing Parties" would be subject to disciplinary action. The resolution forbade travel on the Sabbath, even if for purposes of business.[17] In April 1843 the communicants of Richmond Street Congregational Church passed a nearly identical resolution.[18] In the same year, members at Third Baptist Church pledged themselves to abstain from "all unnecessary worldly conversation on the Lord's Day."[19] In 1852 members of the newly gathered Central Congregational Church, including George H. Corliss, voted to make "Christian usefulness the standard by which you decide the lawfulness of all your worldly business and amusements, abstaining from every practice and pursuit which shall interfere with these ends."[20] At Stewart Street Baptist Church, members promised to "live circumspectly in the world, 'denying ungodliness and worldly lusts.'" In the minds of these communicants, by clinging to the Sabbath and by rejecting secular amusements, Christians could follow St. Paul's injunction from Romans 12—"Do not be conformed to this world."[21]

Church discipline cases reveal that many members lost their battle with earthly encroachment. A survey of over a hundred cases in five congregations between 1840 and 1850 shows that slightly more than one-half of all the members disciplined faced charges that they had neglected their covenant obligations. (See Table 20.) Put simply, they failed to attend church. In contrast to discipline cases before 1820, when intemperance, sexual misconduct, doctrinal deviance, or disorderly walking constituted the major church crimes, now neglect of covenant clearly outdistanced other infractions. Congregations framed many of the cases against lapsing members in terms of a struggle between true faith and the ways of the world. In early 1843, the members of Beneficent Congregational Church accused George Taylor of attending "the Theatre & other places of worldly amusement."[22] High Street Congregational communicants admonished Crawford T. Angell for "absenting himself habitually from our communion and other stated meetings of the church and also of disorderly and unchristian con-

[17] Resolution in Mark Tucker, *The Centennial Sermon, preached before the Beneficent Congregational Church and Society in Providence, R.I., March 19, a.d., 1843* (Providence, 1845), 60–61.
[18] Record Book, Richmond Street Congregational Church, Resolution of April, 1843, RIHS.
[19] *A Sketch of the Third Baptist Church, Providence: With the Covenant and a list of Officers and Members* (n.p., 1843), 12.
[20] *Articles of Faith, and Covenant, and By-Laws of the Central Congregational Church, with a List of Members* (Providence, 1852), 7.
[21] *Articles of Faith, Covenant, Rules, Regulations, and a brief history, with a list of members of the Stewart Street Baptist Church, Providence, R.I. Constituted Feb. 3, 1851* (Boston, 1870), 21.
[22] Record Book, Beneficent Congregational Church, January 27, 1843, Vestry of Beneficent Congregational Church, Providence.

Table 20. Discipline cases in select churches, 1840–1850

Church crime	Number of charges
Neglect of covenant	58
Sexual misconduct	19
Doctrinal deviance	12
Intemperance	10
Disorderly walking	4
Others	19[a]
TOTAL	122[b]

Sources: Record Book, First Baptist Church, RIHS; Record Book, Third Baptist Church, RIHS: Record Book, Beneficent Congregational Church, Vestry, Beneficent Congregational Church; Record Book, High Street Congregational Church, RIHS; Record Book, Richmond Street Congregational Church, RIHS.
[a] These include cases brought against political dissenters during the Dorr Rebellion, cases involving personal disputes among members, cases of attending the theater or dancing parties, and the use of sinful or vile language.
[b] The total number of individuals charged in these discipline cases is 114. Since churches charged some members with more than one crime, I have included the total number of charges rather than the total number of persons charged.

duct with the world."[23] At the Richmond Street Congregational Church, Thomas C. Gladding faced a battery of similar charges. The members felt he had "willfully absented himself from the worship of God" and had "in its stead sought the pleasures of the world in sinful amusements with ungodly men."[24] In 1857, Baptist pastor James B. Simmons may have best summed up the problem when he complained to his congregation that "worldliness seems to be occupying us almost altogether."[25] The pull of earthly attachments was simply too strong for many Christians to resist.

Rather than submitting to the beguiling forces of the world, some Christians confronted them. The emergence of a substantial Fourierist movement in Providence in the late 1840s reveals that even respectable Protestants looked to substitute the ideas of "association" and cooperative labor for the individualism and competitiveness of free labor society. For thousands of Americans the doctrines of the Charles Fourier (as popu-

---

[23] Record Book, High Street Congregational Church, October 8, 1844, RIHS.
[24] Record Book, Richmond Street Congregational Church, July 8, 1845, RIHS.
[25] James B. Simmons, *A Pastor's Parting Counsel to His People* (Providence, 1857), 7.

larized by Albert Brisbane and others) held out an authentic "alternative" for the organization of society.[26] Feeding into the popularity of Fourier's communitarian ethic in America were its points of convergence with Christianity. Fourier's notion of universal human harmony achieved through cooperative labor and living arrangements seemed to embody the ideal of Christian brotherhood. Although Fourier himself had always made a place for self-interest in his theories, many Americans saw in his cooperative framework the promise of a society that embodied fundamental doctrines of Christianity.[27] In Providence especially, the Fourierist movement drew strength from these religious impulses.

The origins of Fourierism (or Associationism) in Providence can be traced to a series of lectures delivered by its leaders from Massachusetts in April and May 1847. The Fourierist luminaries Albert Brisbane, John Orvis, and George Ripley (of Brook Farm fame) stirred assemblies whose attentiveness and size they found gratifying. "The audiences were really the largest and best selected," reported the *Harbinger* (the chief Fourierist journal), "which it has been the lot of our Lecturers to address on a first visit to any city."[28] Fourierist leaders continued to praise the Providence community in the highest terms. "In no city in New England," the lecturers reported after their second trip, "have we had so numerous, select, intelligent, and interested audiences." As they looked out over eager listeners, the lecturers saw representatives "from all classes" and made special note of the presence of the "stolid conservative of 'law and order' " as well as the presence of reformers and even women.[29] Given that Fourier's new science of society placed a high premium on order and the intricate organization of people and their abilities, it is not surprising that law and order men from the Dorr War era would have found his ideas attractive. Conservatives and liberals alike could find in Fourierism elements of their own thinking. Among the Fourierist lecturers in Providence was the Unitarian minister William Henry Channing. During his discourses, he spoke "fervently of Fourierism as the perfect realization of Christian goals."[30] As they were prone to do, Channing and his fellow lecturers struck tones appropriate for a "Fourierist version of

[26] See Guarneri, *Utopian Alternative.*
[27] Ibid., 115–120.
[28] "Our Lectures," *Harbinger*, April 17, 1847, American Antiquarian Society Library, Worcester, Mass. On the Fourierist movement in Providence see especially Charles R. Crowe, "Utopian Socialism in Rhode Island, 1845–1850," *Rhode Island History* 18 (1959): 20–26; idem; "The Religious History of a Christian Socialist: Joseph J. Cooke's 'A Personal Relation,' " *Rhode Island History* 23 (1964): 81–89.
[29] "Lectures in Providence," *Harbinger*, May 1, 1847.
[30] Crowe, "Utopian Socialism," 23.

the jeremiad," calling their listeners to a fresh understanding of America's millennial mission.[31]

Following William Henry Channing's address Providence residents established their own Union of Associationists and elected a full slate of officers to give Fourierism an institutional presence in the city.[32] They worked closely with those in the Anti-Slavery Society, a constituency in which they found considerable support.[33] They successfully petitioned the state legislature to charter the Providence Benefit Union, "a new Fourierist inspired cooperative store."[34] They also took a hand in the creation of the Providence Workingmen's Protective Union, a cooperative labor union that owed much to Fourierist notions of community.[35] Once organized, the leaders of Fourierism in Providence also took a leading role in national policy in the American Union of Associationists. Joseph J. Cooke, who served as president of the Providence Association, played an especially active role in national affairs, helping to prepare resolutions on a whole range of topics from the plight of laborers to women's rights, pacifism, and the creation of a "Universal Church."[36] He also served on a special committee appointed by the Executive Committee "to inquire into and report upon the condition of the North American, Trumbull, and Wisconsin Phalanxes and other experimental efforts at Association now in progress."[37] At both the local and national levels, Providence Fourierists demonstrated by their deeds the zealous interest first identified by the visiting lecturers.

Providence Fourierists tinctured their work with an unmistakably religious dye. In its organization and structure the Workingmen's Protective Union took on functions that owed much not only to Fourierism but also to Christianity. The cooperative principles of Fourierism surfaced in one of the union's central missions: to overcome "the isolated way in which the laborer, as a man of small means, purchases the necessaries of life."[38] To combat this evil, workers created their own cooperative store. Like others who

---

[31] Guarneri, *Utopian Alternative*, 115.

[32] "Lectures in Providence."

[33] For references to abolitionists and Fourierists in Providence see "Providence Report to the American Union of Associationists," *Harbinger*, May 29, 1847; "Sayings and Doings in Providence," *Harbinger*, January 15, 1848.

[34] Crowe, "Utopian Socialism," 26.

[35] See *Constitution and By-Laws of the Workingmen's Protective Union, Division No. 52, Providence, R.I., Organized April, 1848* (Providence 1848). Although this document does not explicitly acknowledge Fourier or the American Associationists, reports from the *Harbinger* reveal that Fourierists had a key role in its organization and support.

[36] Crowe, "Utopian Socialism," 25.

[37] *Harbinger*, July 24, 1847.

[38] *Constitution and By-Laws of the Workingmen's Protective Union*, 7.

established mutual assistance groups in the 1840s, these workers pledged to provide one another with sick benefits, fuel, groceries, and employment information.[39] An initial fee of three dollars coupled with a twenty-dollar subscription to the trading store and monthly dues of twenty-five cents entitled members to these services. Joining the union, however, was also very much like joining a church.[40] Workers desiring to participate in the group, for instance, had to demonstrate "good moral character" and to refrain from the use or sale of "intoxicating drinks."[41] After endorsing these terms, members needed to keep their monthly assessments paid up or they would face disciplinary action. Monthly dues thus functioned as the equivalent of pew rents. In terms that echoed congregational covenants, workers could also be disciplined when found guilty of "gross immorality, intemperance, or other disorderly conduct." Like other churches, the union also established a "Visiting Committee" to call on any member struck with illness in order to "alleviate the brother's sufferings."[42] The religious character of the union reveals how workers created a blending of Christian and Fourierist themes.

Joseph J. Cooke, president of the Providence Associationists, sealed the connection between Fourierism and true Christianity as he comprehended it. In July 1847 he published in the *Harbinger* what amounted to a conversion narrative tracing his personal pilgrimage toward the doctrines of Charles Fourier.[43] Reversing the typical path of such narratives that followed the sinner from a life of evil neglect of religion to the promise of salvation, Cooke began his narrative with a description of his disenchantment with traditional Christianity. Although he had been "converted" to an evangelical church after doing time on an "anxious seat," he never felt quite settled among his fellow believers. Cooke wanted to live Christianity, not simply to profess it. He quit his dry goods business under the conviction that it was impossible to engage in "dry goods jobbing" and live in "accordance with the Golden Rule." Cooke became deeply vexed as well by the hypocrisy of the comfortable Christians with whom he sat on Sunday. "I could not

[39] See Sean Wilentz, *Chants Democratic: New York City and the Rise of the American Working Class, 1788–1850* (New York, 1984), 343–349; Bruce Laurie, *Working People of Philadelphia, 1800–1850* (Philadelphia, 1980), 174–175.

[40] For an analysis of how labor unions could provide a churchly environment see Ken Fones-Wolf, *Trade Union Gospel: Christianity and Labor in Industrial Philadelphia, 1865–1915* (Philadelphia, 1989), 77–84.

[41] *Constitution and By-Laws of the Workingmen's Protective Union*, 8.

[42] Ibid., 10, 13, 11.

[43] See Crowe, "Religious History of a Christian Socialist," for all quotations in Cooke's account. See also "A Personal Experience," *Harbinger*, July 10, 1847. (Crowe mistakenly, I think, dates the account to the July 19, 1847 issue.)

learn to *love* God," he confessed, "who had decreed that the largest portion of the human beings whom he had created should be eternally damned."[44] Living in the guise of a robust, evangelical Christian, Cooke felt ethically crippled.

Where traditional sinners often came to Christ via the medium of religious tracts or a simple story from Scripture, Joseph J. Cooke came to Fourierism by reading the columns of Albert Brisbane. Having "caught the idea of Universal Unity" Cooke's life changed dramatically. It seemed to him that the doctrines of Fourierism, not the strictures of evangelicalism, promised congruence with the true principles of the Bible. He made it clear that he made a distinction between "real Christianity and the common practice of it. The latter I condemn—the former I advocate." Cooke found especially appealing the "science" of Fourierism, its rationality, and its comprehensive demands on those who followed its teaching. Cooke held up the image of a man who made thousands of dollars each year and then siphoned off a few hundred to charity. "And is this *all* that Christianity calls for?" he asked indignantly, "We must answer no." In the end, only a dedication to the principles of Fourierism could bring about a Christian society. "It appears to me plain," he said, "that Association is the embodiment of the principles of Christianity."[45] For Joseph J. Cooke, the practice of Christianity and the ethics of free labor capitalism could not be reconciled.

Christians outside the circles of Associationism articulated sympathy with the broader contours of the Fourierist critique of capitalism. In 1848 Samuel Osgood, the Unitarian pastor of Westminster Congregational Church in Providence, reviewed the recent literature on socialism for the *Christian Examiner.*[46] He offered an impressive understanding of the works of thinkers from Blanqui and De Sismondi to Thomas Chalmers, John Stuart Mill, and Charles Fourier. Although Osgood recognized that the "great social problem of our age" was the "relation between man and wealth," Fourier's reasoning did not sweep him away.[47] He faulted the details of Fourier's thinking in three ways. Osgood rejected the idea that "the power of external arrangements," such as living in a phalanx or phalanstery, could alter "the dispositions of men." Such changes sprang only from the inner man. He also refused to take "any man to be our moral guide" who had

---

44 Ibid., 85, 87, 86.
45 Ibid., 88, 89.
46 S. O. [Samuel Osgood], "Christianity and Socialism," *Christian Examiner* 45 (1848): 194–217. That "S. O." was actually Samuel Osgood is suggested strongly by a review of the article in the *Harbinger* that attributed it to "an eminent Unitarian clergyman of Providence." Samuel Osgood is the only person that fits such a description. See "Christianity and Socialism," *Harbinger*, September 9, 1848.
47 S. O., "Christianity and Socialism," 194.

taken measures "to organize illicit love." Finally, Osgood had problems with the motivation for self-interest that Fourier claimed would be fully realized in communal living. "The whole doctrine of the desirableness of luxury," he scolded, "which lies at the basis of the phalanstery, seems to us very questionable." Where was the "self-denial of the cross" in all of this?[48] Still, for all his quibblings with Fourier's ideas, Osgood congratulated the Associationists for grappling with "the chief difficulty of our civilization. Its spirit is too earthly and sensual, too selfish and discordant."[49]

During the panic of 1857–58, religious interpretations of the economic collapse hinged on the notion that residents had become too hungry for material success. As he had during the depression of 1837, Francis Wayland again illuminated the evils of speculation. He contended that manipulating the value of currency or commodities did not add any true value to them. Rather, it produced a speculative "mania" that infected the entire community with a desire to accumulate ill-begotten wealth.[50] Merchants and bankers broken by the fluctuations of the market had only themselves to blame. "If you have made wealth your idol," he asked, "is it not just in God to take away the idol which you have worshipped?" Recalling the analysis he advanced twenty years earlier, Wayland warned that the "unhallowed passion for wealth is becoming too strong for the control of moral principle, nay, of religion itself." Christians should be grateful to God, he argued, for the collapse of business. For only when you were thus humbled would God "rescue you from a life of worldliness."[51] Christopher T. Keith, a grammar school principal, agreed with this interpretation. He confided in his diary that the crumbling of stock prices was "a proper punishment for our extravagance and sinfulness." Lessons could be learned from the failures of great businessmen. "It shows us that we should not put our trust in riches," he observed, "which may take to themselves wings and flee away."[52] Zachariah Allen, textile manufacturer, experienced directly the lessons learned by Christopher T. Keith. His journal for late 1857 and early 1858 describes the religious trials that eventually lead him to make a public profession of faith. In November 1857, with his mills at a standstill, Allen contemplated the sufferings of Christ. Although his own fortunes had deteriorated, he resisted the temptation of self-indulgence. "If men of modern times have embarrassments in business & other troubles," he reasoned,

---

[48] Ibid., 205, 206.

[49] Ibid., 200.

[50] Francis Wayland, *Thoughts on the Present Distress. Two Sermons Preached in the First Baptist Church, Providence, on the 11th and 25th of October, 1857* (Providence, 1857), 17.

[51] Ibid., 10, 24, 10.

[52] Christopher T. Keith diary, entries for September 18, 1857; January 24, 1858, RIHS.

"they are not buffetted & spit upon, scourged, & put to death." Still, Allen searched for meaning in the collapse of his affairs. "I am so impressively taught by this result the folly of devotion to worldly pursuits," he wrote, "that I cannot but look down upon them as unworthy."[53] Allen felt clearly the weight of his past sins.

The second dilemma identified by bourgeois Protestants lurked in the streets of the city, not in the recesses of their souls. They understood that thousands of unchurched workers could be found outside of their congregations. This was not an entirely new concern. Tract distributors and domestic missionaries had targeted laborers, operatives, and sailors for reform in the early nineteenth century. By the 1840s and 1850s, the need to create a more inclusive religious community assumed even greater urgency as the numbers of working-class residents swelled. By 1855 the city census tallied as many as eight thousand citizens who labored in the city's textile mills and machine or jewelry shops, worked in the building trades, or served as domestic servants and waiters. (See Table 21.) If such people received no training in piety, respectable Protestants argued, moral decay would destroy their city. Moreover, they came to a new understanding of the physical suffering and material needs of those in their midst. They saw that both material poverty and spiritual poverty would have to be addressed before religious community could be restored.

Careful observers of Providence's religious scene announced with alarm that thousands of workers lived beyond the reach of organized Christianity. In 1842, William Douglas, the city missionary employed by the Providence Female Domestic Missionary Society, discovered "not less than twelve hundred families who have no regular connection with any religious community." Such persons, he reported, lived and died "ignorant of even the first principles of our holy religion."[54] In his annual report for 1849, he explained that "ours is the city of moral plagues, & if something is not done to stay their deadly progress, if christian men & women do not come to our help to what source shall we look for aid."[55] By 1851, he announced that he had made some two thousand visits to city residents, "chiefly among a class of our population who has no religious connection with any society."[56] Edwin M. Stone, a Unitarian missionary, argued that masses of godless workers posed a threat to the entire community. In 1850 he reported flatly

[53] Zachariah Allen diaries, November 8 and 14, 1857, RIHS.
[54] *Annual Report of the Providence Female Domestic Missionary Society, presented by Rev. William Douglas, at First Baptist Meeting House, Monday evening, April 12, 1842* (Providence, 1842), 5.
[55] Report for November 5, 1849, Providence Female Domestic Missionary Society Manuscripts, RIHS (hereafter cited as PFDMS MSS).
[56] Report for November 1851, PFDMS MSS.

Table 21. Leading Providence occupations, 1855

Rank	Occupation	Number employed
1	Servants & waiters	2,240
2	Laborers	1,782
3	Factory operatives	968
4	Carpenters	852
5	Jewelers	773
6	Clerks	692
7	Machinists	552
8	Masons	364
9	Merchants	317
10	Grocers	308
11	Moulders	308
12	Teamsters	264
13	Mariners	257
14	Dressmakers	253
15	Painters and glaziers	246
16	Tailors	224
17	Blacksmiths	206
18	Boot and shoemakers	202
19	Tailoresses	202
20	Weavers	183

Source: Edwin M. Snow, *Census of the City of Providence, taken in July 1855; with a brief account of the manufactures, trade, commerce, and other statistics of the city; and an appendix giving the account of previous enumerations of the population of Providence* (Providence, 1856), 37–39.

that the "true prosperity of our city depends, in no small degree, upon the social and moral elevation of its laboring classes."[57] Critics charged that the poor had no recourse but to stay away from their social betters. Pointing to substantial pew rents, Jacob Frieze, a Universalist, maintained that a laborer "must place himself in a seat where he must be regarded as a pauper, or stay away altogether." Even if they took advantage of free seating, working people would be "mortified by the stare of contempt from all hands."[58] Finding adequate Sunday dress was another problem. The act of attending church, Frieze suggested, could be a humiliating experience for working people, reminding them of their own marginality and relative poverty.

The structure of pew costs in Providence churches sustains the analysis

[57] Edwin M. Stone, *Eighth Annual Report of the Ministry at Large in the City of Providence* (Providence, 1850), 21.

[58] Jacob Frieze, *The Elements of Social Disorder; a Plea for the Working Classes in the United States. By a Mechanic* (Providence, 1844), 31, 32.

Table 22. Pew valuations in select churches, 1850–1860

Church	Average value of Pew	Highest pew valuation	Lowest pew valuation	Number of pews
Saint Stephen's Episcopal Church, 1850s	$476.39	$1,100.00	$75.00	140
Grace Episcopal Church, 1851	375.38	700.00	40.00	170[a]
Brown Street Baptist Church, 1860	372.54	800.00	20.00	102
Saint John's Episcopal Church, 1850	345.65	430.00	200.00	76[b]
First Congregational Church, 1857	340.26	700.00	75.00	131
Beneficent Congregational Church, 1856	289.57	700.00	40.00	165[c]
First Baptist Church, 1855	282.91	800.00	30.00	144
High Street Congregational Church, 1850	210.00	350.00	70.00	74
First Universalist Church, 1850	209.95	380.00	50.00	119
Fourth Baptist Church, 1850	92.20	135.00	50.00	59

Sources: The values for Saint Stephen's Episcopal Church, Grace Episcopal Church, and Brown Street Baptist Church are from the pew plats held in the manuscript collections of the John Hay Library, Brown University; those for St. John's Episcopal Church are from box 14, folder 119, "Pew Rents, 1832–1864," University of Rhode Island Archives; First Congregational Church, from Benevolent Congregational Society Records, box 12, RIHS; Beneficent Congregational Church, from "Tax Assessments on Pews in Beneficent Church, 1857–1865," Vestry, Beneficent Congregational Church; First Baptist Church, from Charitable Baptist Society Records, box 2, "Report of Committee on new valuations of the Pews. April 2, 1855," RIHS; High Street Congregational Church Records, RIHS; First Universalist Church, Pew Volume for 1841–1863, RIHS; Fourth Baptist Church, Treasurer's Book, RIHS.
[a] Based on pews located on the ground floor; balcony valuations are not available.
[b] Based on those pews actually owned rather than the total valued.
[c] Based on ground pews and the thirty-one gallery pews listed.

that the working-class residents would have found the purchase of a good seat far beyond their slender means. (See Table 22.) By the 1850s, the top pews in respectable congregations often sold for as much as $800. This trend spanned denominational lines. In 1860, Brown Street Baptist pewholders actually paid more, on the average, for seats than did the Episcopalians at St. John's Church. By the 1850s, even Beneficent Congregational Church featured several ranks of $700 seats. The pew owners at Saint Stephen's Episcopal Church led the Providence community beyond the $1,000 mark, offering a few seats for $1,100 each. In an age in which a salary of about $600 per year would have sustained an urban family of four, these were princely sums indeed.[59] Even though a handful of pews continued to command prices as low as $20, purchasers of these seats would have been keenly aware of their inferior placement in the church. The gap between the most expensive and least expensive seats, like the gap between the wealthiest and poorest Americans, increased markedly during the 1850s.

[59] Licht, *Industrializing America*, 70.

But Protestant churches did not conspire to weed out their plebeian members. In 1855 the members of the Charitable Baptist Society (pewholders at First Baptist Church) showed special regard for those who held less expensive seats. While raising pew valuations (and thereby pew taxes) on the more expensive places, they held down the costs paid by holders of modest seats. Owners of $400 pews found their seats valued at $800, while the owners of $30 pews paid no new taxes. The members followed this policy owing to the "unusually large number of low priced pews, compared with other meeting-houses, which will hardly admit of any increase of valuation."[60] The affluent pewholders of the church agreed to shoulder a greater financial burden for the sake of those who held lesser seats. At First Congregational Church, too, regard for impoverished citizens and communicants endured. On November 3, 1857, the members of the Benevolent Congregational Society (pewholders at First Congregational) initiated a series of four special offerings. They directed these funds to the "laboring classes in this community" who had been suffering as a result of the economic panic. Some pewholders took pains to include the poor in worship services. On November 8, 1859, Alice Clark released her claim to her father's pew and returned it to the society "for the benefit of the Poor of the Church."[61] Her gesture underscores that even in one of the city's wealthiest congregations, less affluent worshippers could still be included.

The cost of pews in some meetinghouses remained reasonable. The valuations at High Street Congregational, First Universalist, and Fourth Baptist Church displayed remarkable consistency throughout the antebellum period. The practice of pew sharing, too, could reduce the taxes paid by worshippers. In 1850, at High Street Congregational Church forty-three out of a total of eighty-two pewholders pooled their resources. At Fourth Baptist Church, treasurer's records show that renters sometimes subdivided single pews into as many as five individual seats. On a pew valued at $60, for instance, the renter of one seat would be assessed for only about $2 in taxes each year. At Beneficent Congregational Church, where top pew values hit $700, at least thirty-six places in the gallery carried valuations of $125 or less. For those worshippers inclined to share or to rent seats, especially in the balcony, relatively inexpensive pews could still be found in Providence churches.[62]

---

[60] Committee report, April 2, 1855, folder marked "Pews 1805–1859," box 2, Charitable Baptist Society Records, RIHS.

[61] Benevolent Congregational Society Records, vol. 25, November 3, 1857 and November 8, 1859, RIHS.

[62] See sources for Table 22.

But a scattering of affordable seats did not necessarily solve the problem of bringing laborers, factory operatives, and sailors to church. At Beneficent Congregational Church, for instance, men of property held claim to most of the gallery pews. Even at Fourth Baptist Church, those who shared seats included artisans and skilled workers of means. Nathan Westcott and William D. Avery, both machinists who lived along North Main Street, rented a pew assessed at only sixty-five dollars. Yet, in 1850, each man found himself accountable for real estate taxes. It would be a mistake to assume that inexpensive seats perforce belonged to impoverished workers. Moreover, some congregations celebrated their exclusivity. In April 1844 the members of Grace Episcopal Church announced their pew auction with great fanfare. To attract buyers, they publicized their intention to "erect a new and elegant structure on the enlarged site." The newspaper reporting the coming sale crowed that the accommodations would be first-rate. "The many gentlemen of wealth and taste connected with the church," they observed, "furnish assurance that an edifice will be erected which will be one of the most conspicuous ornaments of the city."[63] Not aiming to attract worshippers of modest incomes, the building committee clearly crafted its appeal to enlist the support of wealthy residents.

Bourgeois Protestants thus confronted two seemingly intractable problems. When they looked inside themselves, they could perceive clearly that material success had blighted authentic spirituality. They had fallen victim to the very virtues of discipline and hard work that had promised to save them. When they looked outside themselves into the streets of their city, they saw threats of a different kind. Thousands of their fellow citizens lived, worked, and died outside the embrace of their congregations. These masses of unchurched workers spelled danger for the entire social order. "Scenes have transpired in the principal cities of our Union," announced the Unitarian missionary Edwin M. Stone, "which indicate a deterioration of morals, and a tendency to a condition of society truly alarming." He likened the depravity of the urban classes in modern America as rivaling those of "the demoralized state of Rome in the crowning period of her wealth and luxury."[64] Whether they turned inward or outward, respectable Protestants agreed that their city stood in dire need of redemption.

In response to these internal and external crises, the Providence bourgeoisie deployed a sweeping program of social and religious reform. On one front they initiated a series of institutional efforts designed to nourish

---

[63] "Sale at Grace Church," *Manufacturer's and Farmer's Journal, Providence and Pawtucket Advertiser*, April 25, 1844.
[64] Edwin M. Stone, *Fourteenth Annual Report of the Ministry at Large in the City of Providence* (Providence, 1856), 18.

workers' bodies as well as to feed their souls with Christian education and moral instruction. Women and men worked together to create a variety of homes for the physically and spiritually neglected. These efforts culminated in the creation of the Unitarian-sponsored Ministry at Large, a massive and multifaceted effort to combat the evils of poverty and immorality. In conjunction with these initiatives, respectable communicants launched a free church movement designed to recreate a sense of religious community. By jettisoning the sale and rental of pews, they aimed to reintroduce workers to the salutary influences of divine worship. The creation of reform institutions and the rise of the free church movement would provide a remedy to the problems that bedeviled them. A renewed dedication to charity would allow them to resolve ambivalence about increasing prosperity and simultaneously reforge religious community.

The creation of reform institutions and of free churches marked a critical point of departure from earlier patterns of religious benevolence. Trust in the power of social structures and in the construction of churches replaced the faith that tract distributors had once bestowed on the efficacy of religious print. In 1820s and 1830s, they had believed that tracts and Bibles possessed a quasi-magical quality. If tract distributors sowed the community with such seeds, they reasoned, religious and social reformation would inevitably blossom. But after making thousands of visits and handing out millions of pages of tracts, missionaries knew that sin still held sway. By the 1840s and 1850s, the forum of the free church represented a new technique for the spiritual improvement of the poor. Institutions, not tracts, might transform the evils of urban society. Reformers had not lost hope in converting the vicious, nor did they abandon religious literature. But now this process of spiritual reclamation would take place inside godly institutions and free churches rather than during the meeting of individual distributors and sinners in the streets.

Reform-minded women and men joined hands in the creation of these institutions of religious and social salvation. Together they established a network of organizations to minister to the needs of the dispossessed. The work of the Providence Female Domestic Missionary Society (PFDMS) and its missionary, William Douglas, pioneered this new era of harmony in bourgeois religious reform. The evangelical women of the PFDMS, led especially by Phebe Jackson, collaborated with Douglas to craft a ministry "peculiarly adopted to the poor."[65] William Douglas, whom the PFDMS hired in 1838, and Phebe Jackson seem to have been everywhere in the 1840s and 1850s, yoked in efforts to save impoverished workers, perishing sailors, "friendless

---

[65] Letter to Mr. Chester Pratt of the City Tract Society, June 11, 1838, PFDMS MSS.

females," and colored children. Douglas, along with Edwin Stone, proved to be one of Providence's most indefatigable urban missionaries. Phebe Jackson, a member of First Baptist Church, stood at the head of efforts to re-make the world of female reform. She joined First Baptist Church in 1843, evidently lived independently (she was assessed for taxes in her own right in 1850), and, like Douglas, made key contributions to the PFDMS and other reform ventures.[66] The intricate collaboration of William Douglas and women such as Phebe Jackson symbolizes in important ways the new bonds that drew together men and women in fresh networks of evangelical activism.

The remaking of evangelical reform took place gradually. In this endeavor, William Douglas blended the features of a traditional tract distributor with those of the new urban missionary. In many ways he retained the methods and attitudes typical of reformers of the 1820s and 1830s. He organized visiting committees to call upon the unchurched, and he kept scrupulous records of the number of tracts handed out. In 1842 he proudly calculated that there "have been distributed forty-eight Bibles and thirty-six New Testaments among families found destitute; and also about 41,280 pages of Tracts have been put in circulation."[67] He blamed intem-perance for most of the poverty and ruin he encountered. He continued to sort the poor into two groups—the worthy and the vicious. With respect to the latter, he warned reformers of the evils of "Misdirected Charity."[68] He worried about prostitution and the fate of "many girls in this city scarcely yet in their teens who are well versed in all the seductive wiles of the veteran courtesan."[69] The terrain of the streets remained a spiritual battlefield. And the task of the tract distributor was to confront the evil found there, to con-quer sin, and to remake this "city of moral plagues."[70]

William Douglas also brought new weapons to bear in this contest for a Christian community. Throughout the 1840s and 1850s, he gave the tem-poral needs of the poor increasing attention. In 1851 alone, he distributed 80 tons of coal, 10 cords of wood, 30 barrels of flour, 10 boxes of soap, 25 stoves, assorted clothing items, and 1,200 pairs of shoes. He initiated a loan system by which families could borrow money to purchase necessary items.

[66] On Phebe Jackson see *A List of Members with the General Rules and Regulations of the First Baptist Church in Providence, R.I.* (Providence, 1850), 18; *Providence City Tax* (Providence, 1850), 47; the 1850 Federal Manuscript Census reveals no spouse or children living with Jackson and states that she was forty years old in that year.

[67] *Annual Report of the Providence Female Domestic Missionary Society* (Providence, 1842), 18.

[68] *Annual Report of the Providence Female Domestic Missionary Society, presented by William Douglas at the Vestry of First Baptist Church, Monday, April 1, 1844* (Providence, 1844), 6.

[69] Report for November 5, 1849, PFDMS MSS.

[70] Ibid.

He searched out employment opportunities for those thrown out of work. He recognized that impoverished residents needed material support as well as spiritual nourishment.[71] His reports reveal, too, that Douglas worked to establish a more permanent footing for his ministry among the poor. During the early 1840s, he began to hold regular religious meetings on weekday evenings in "destitute neighborhoods." These gatherings took place in homes or in the streets. Some evidence suggests that Douglas began to think of these makeshift congregations as his regular flock. He tabulated the annual figures for conversions and deaths among these folk, just as established ministers put together their yearly reports. He preached regularly, too, in the Dexter Asylum and in the State Prison. As time progressed, Douglas began to throw more energy into these reform institutions.[72]

The work of William Douglas throws light on the emergence of professional missionary activism in antebellum America. Unlike tract and Bible distributors of an earlier age, who were typically volunteers from bourgeois congregations, Douglas labored as a paid employee of the PFDMS. In this capacity he was dependent on the contributions and subscriptions raised largely by female members for his comfortable salary, which reached one thousand dollars per year in 1843.[73] Phebe Jackson was among those who was constantly on the lookout for funds, serving in 1845 as the PFDMS "collector" for Third Baptist Church.[74] As Douglas prepared his annual reports for the "directresses" of the PFDMS, he had to demonstrate that he warranted their continuing approbation. Indeed, he sometimes referred to himself as "your Missionary" suggesting that he well understood the power relationship in which he was participating. Douglas, who was an ordained minister, may well have been the only clergyman in Providence who depended on the funds gathered by women rather than on the pew taxes paid by men for his living. Still, Douglas had leverage within the PFDMS. As a paid professional and therefore an expert of sorts, Douglas consistently offered advice about the initiatives the women should support. Since it was he who walked the avenues and visited and prayed with those whom he encountered, his word packed considerable authority. The "professionalization" of religious reform afforded women new sources of political power even as it began to extricate them from the travail of the city streets.

[71] On these activities see, reports for November 1851; November 6, 1848; November 1, 1847, PFDMS MSS.

[72] On these services see *Annual Report,* 1842, 18–19; *Annual Report of the Providence Female Domestic Missionary Society, presented by Rev. William Douglas at Beneficent Congregational Meeting-House, Tuesday evening, April 18, 1843* (Providence, 1843), 11–13; and *Annual Report,* 1844, 16–17.

[73] *Annual Report,* 1843, 23.

[74] Report for November, 3, 1845, PFDMS MSS.

When women in the 1840s and 1850s took a direct role in the work of benevolence, they favored more domestic forms of participation. They formed homes for wayward sailors, "friendless females," and colored children. They looked forward to establishing even more sheltering institutions, including an "Industrial House" and a "Home for Aged Women." In this way, the antebellum reformers of Providence set important precedents for the settlement house movement forged by Progressive reformers of the 1890s. Jane Addams and her colleagues need not have looked to the English example of "Toynbee Hall" for their inspiration.[75] They could have turned instead to the pioneering institutions created by antebellum reformers such as Phebe Jackson and William Douglas. Providence's own settlement movement of the turn of the century, manifest in the creation of Sprague House on Federal Hill, owed much to the bourgeois churches that had experimented with institutional reform well before the Civil War.[76]

But these antebellum homes differed from the Progressive settlement houses in at least three critical respects. First, the work of Jane Addams, Florence Kelley, and other Progressive women grew from their fundamental commitment to the unmarried life. The women of Hull House "had broken the most compelling social rule regulating the lives of women of their class—the compulsion to marry."[77] While some of Providence's domestic reformers, such as Phebe Jackson, were single women of independent means, most of the women who served as directresses of reform groups lived with husband and family. They included Mrs. Francis Wayland, Mrs. Edward Hall, Mrs. Amos Barstow, and Mrs. Stephen S. Wardwell, to name only a handful of prominent bourgeois women.[78] While Hull House depended largely on the collaboration of women with other women, Providence's antebellum homes rested on the collaboration of women and men. Second, the settlement house reformers actually lived in the homes they created, brushing shoulders with the impoverished members of society that they aspired to raise up. The homes created by antebellum reformers were different. Rather than bringing the dispossessed into their own parlors and dining rooms, bourgeois women and men set up alternative homes in which

[75] See Jane Addams, *Twenty Years at Hull-House* (1910; reprint New York, 1981), esp. 75.
[76] John S. Gilkeson Jr., *Middle-Class Providence, 1820–1940* (Princeton, 1986), 247–254.
[77] Kathryn Kish Sklar, *Florence Kelley and the Nation's Work: The Rise of Women's Political Culture, 1830–1900* (New Haven, 1995), 187.
[78] See the membership list of the PFDMS in 1838, PFDMS MSS. The list included 66 women from First Baptist Church, 43 women from Beneficent Congregational Church, 42 from St. John's Episcopal Church, 29 from Grace Episcopal Church, 26 from Richmond Street Church, 16 from Third Baptist Church, 15 from Fourth Baptist Church, and smaller numbers from Second Baptist, High Street Congregational Church, and the Methodist churches.

the impoverished and perishing might be tutored in the ways of refined and Christian domestic values but kept at a safe distance. Finally, while Progressive era reformers tapped the languages of the social sciences on behalf of civic reform, antebellum enthusiasts understood their duties in unmistakably religious terms.[79] Bourgeois women did not simply want to ease poverty, stamp out crime, banish intemperance, encourage industry, and cultivate refinement; they wanted to save souls as well.

The mission to rescue sailors from lives of immorality and consequent perdition reveals an important example of the cooperation of women and men in new efforts of evangelical reform. While seamen had always presented a compelling prospect for tract society colporteurs, by the 1840s Providence women sought a more systematic way to minister to their needs. In 1841 they established Seamen's Home on South Water Street. In establishing this home the women of the Ladies' Bethel Association blended their efforts with those of the local clergy. Ministers officiated at the dedication of the home, and Francis Wayland, Mark Tucker, and Francis Vinton served as an "examining committee" for the association's well-stocked lending library of books, tracts, and Bibles.[80] William Douglas, too, offered his talents. He conducted services in the Seamen's Home every Sunday for at least nine months each year. Here he found something of a regular congregation. Although drawing tiny assemblies, some fifteen to forty sailors, Douglas continued the tradition of ascribing to them a uniquely religious character. As if merely stating the obvious, he maintained that seamen "are more susceptible of religious impressions than landsmen." He looked forward to hearing "the weather-beaten sons of the ocean" relate "in their own forcible language" their conversion experiences. Like the women whom he served, Douglas sought to help the sailors by tending both to their "temporal and everlasting happiness."[81]

The women of the Ladies' Bethel Association believed that such bliss for seamen could be best nurtured in a domestic setting. They hoped that their Seamen's Home and its "domestic arrangements" would "soften and refine" the rough-hewn characters of the sailors it harbored.[82] If they could, even for a few moments, offer sailors a home, a fireside, and the routines and

---

[79] See here Ellen Fitzpatrick, *Endless Crusade: Women Social Scientists and Progressive Reform* (New York, 1990).

[80] *Report of the Ladies' Bethel Association, Providence, 1841* (Providence, 1841); *Constitution of the Providence Ladies' Bethel Association*, Broadsides, Brown University Library.

[81] On Douglas's work at the Seamen's Home see *Annual Report*, 1843, 12; Report for 1845, PFDMS MSS; *Annual Report*, 1842; *Constitution of the Providence Ladies' Bethel Association*.

[82] *Report of the Ladies' Bethel Association*, 6. For a wider treatment on the significance of the Christian home in this period see Colleen McDannell, *The Christian Home in Victorian America, 1840–1900* (Bloomington, Ind., 1986).

rituals of family life, moral and spiritual reformation would not be far behind. "In the bosom of a Christian family," reported the women, "[the sea-
men] have been welcomed to those domestic and social comforts which
contribute to the charm of *home*."[83] These comforts were especially important because they believed sailors to be an "overlooked" class of workers beyond the reach of more conventional reform efforts. "Isolated as he is from
the world at large," maintained the Bethel ladies, "he had been an outlaw
from their charities, so munificently bestowed on all besides." In the final
analysis, what the ladies wanted to do was to "mother" the sailors whom they
sheltered. They took pride in the fact that one sailor evidently addressed a
letter to them that began, "'Dear Madam, or rather Mother."[84] More than
anything else it was the idea of a powerful Christian home and its potential
for moral reformation that animated the Ladies' Bethel Association.

Faith in the transformative power of the home also animated the reformers who established the Providence Association for Friendless Females in
1851. This group brought together the efforts of Mrs. Francis Wayland and
Mrs. Edward Hall (who served as president and vice president respectively),
William Douglas, and Phebe Jackson (who served as treasurer and authored
the association's first annual report). Driven by the conviction that "the reformation of women is particularly the province of women," they sought to
provide a new home for those women who previously had walked the streets
in sin.[85] They wanted to "provide a 'home' in the truest sense of the word,
where those who were disposed to and become its inmates, should feel the
healthful influences of piety and love,—where habits of virtue, industry, and
order should be inculcated in their minds, taking the place of indolence
and vice."[86] To accomplish these ambitious ends, the women established a
"reform school" and set the "inmates" to work making dresses, pillow cases,
children's stockings, and other garments. Domestic work played an important role in the transformation of these sinners. "Accustomed as they have
been to a life of excitement," wrote Phebe Jackson, "and having no real love
of virtue to hold them, unless their attention is engrossed by constant, and
yet varied and agreeable occupation, it would not be strange if some of
them should weary of so monotonous a life."[87] The women also crafted an
extensive program of religious training for their "inmates," including "domestic devotion" conducted every morning and every evening. Careful reg-
ulation and the inculcation of steady habits were hallmarks of life in the

---

[83] *Report of the Ladies' Bethel Association*, 4.
[84] Ibid., 9, 6.
[85] *First Annual Report of the Providence Association for Friendless Females* (Providence, 1852), 6.
[86] Ibid., 7.
[87] Ibid., 11.

"home" created by the association. Eventually, hoped association members, its residents would be placed in respectable homes where they might begin a useful life of service.[88]

The Providence Association for the Benefit of Colored Children conceived of its mission in terms that would have been familiar to those who joined the Association for Friendless Females. Its founders aimed to establish a "shelter home" in response to "the cry of the friendless children in our community."[89] They also believed in the efficacy of hard work and tight discipline. "Industry and Order," wrote secretary Phebe Jackson in her 1859 report for the group, "are the two prominent aids of our care-takers in training the children for future usefulness, while Love rules the household." They wanted, as well, to place the children to whom they ministered in good Christian and, presumably, white homes. That the children were trained to serve is indicated by Jackson's note that the association was "cheered with good accounts from their employers, and from them assurances that they are pleased with their new homes."[90] The children in the "Shelter Home" were to be carefully educated, under the watchful eye of a Miss Vandoorn, who had served as matron since the association commenced its work in 1839. "Caring for the little flock under her charge with a mother's tenderness," Miss Vandoorn supervised the needs of some 240 children over a twenty-year period.[91] Like the Association for Friendless Females, the Association for the Benefit of Colored Children sought not only to transform sinners into Christians but to prepare able workers for the market economy.

The domestic politics of the 1840s and 1850s reveals an important shift in the way bourgeois women related to the economic activities of their men.[92] In the 1820s and 1830s groups such as the Providence Female Tract Society and the Providence Employment Society offered implicit critiques of the world of the market even as they sought to address its worst abuses. The Dorrite ladies of the early 1840s, too, represented a threat to a political economy that worked in the favor of men of property. In the decades after the Dorr Rebellion, however, Providence women turned the politics of domesticity to more conservative purposes. The homes they created now

---

[88] See *Constitution and By-Laws of the Providence Home for Friendless Females*, Brown University Library.

[89] *Twentieth Annual Report of the Providence Association for the Benefit of Colored Children* (Providence, 1859), 3.

[90] Ibid., 5, 6.

[91] Ibid., 4.

[92] For a wider discussion of domestic politics see Paula Baker, "The Domestication of Politics: Women and American Political Society 1780–1920," *American Historical Review* 89 (1984): 620–647.

functioned as institutions that provided salve for the worst abuses of the market economy but did not condemn the society that created those wounds in the first place. Missing from the reports of the Ladies' Bethel Association, the Association for Friendless Females, or the Association for the Benefit of Colored Children are even hints that Providence society (and especially its men) bore some fundamental responsibility for the presence of these ills. Unlike Providence women of earlier decades, who viewed the changes wrought by the market with some suspicion, female reformers of the 1850s closed ranks on this important issue. In limiting debate on the issue of the moral rectitude of the market economy, bourgeois women now aligned themselves more closely to their men. Ironically, at a time when bourgeois men seem to have been nearly obsessed with the moral failings of their economic system, bourgeois women stepped forward to seal the solidarity of their class.

Invigorated by the united efforts of women and men, bourgeois Protestants could think expansively about how to reach the dispossessed. In the winter of 1841, Unitarians from the First Congregational and Westminster Congregational churches gathered to establish "a Ministry to the poor in this place."[93] Over the next decades, they developed not only a free chapel but a program of evening schools, sewing schools, popular lectures, employment information, and material aid. Especially during the depression of 1857–58, these institutions touched the lives of thousands of working people. Under the guidance of the enthusiastic and perceptive Edwin M. Stone, the Ministry at Large became the city's premier missionary enterprise. Stone's annual reports to the trustees bristled with detail and demonstrated the effectiveness of the programs they funded. He tabulated with precision the numbers of worshippers and students who found shelter in the ministry's institutions. Stone proved himself an urban missionary of rare ability and keen insight, the perfect man to head up Providence's most extensive antebellum reform network.

In conducting services at the ministry's free chapel, Stone envisioned his potential congregation in the broadest possible terms. Since the "major portion" of his church was "composed of families dependent on day labor, or some mechanical occupation," he knew they could not be expected to remain in town for long.[94] He explained to the trustees that "our church is as an inn to the traveller, where he seeks refreshment for a brief space, and

---

[93] Minutes, December 8, 1841, Ministry at Large minutes, RIHS (hereafter cited as MAL). On the Unitarian reform impulse see Smith, *Revivalism and Social Reform*, 95–102; Daniel Walker Howe, *The Unitarian Conscience: Harvard Moral Philosophy, 1805–1861* (Cambridge, Mass., 1970), 244–255.
[94] *Thirteenth Annual Report of the Ministry at Large in the City of Providence* (Providence, 1855), 11.

then pursues his journey."[95] Despite the high turnover within his congregation, Stone argued that progress was being made in improving the morality and faith of the laboring classes. He observed that laborers retained a spark of the lessons they had learned in church and "that something has been done towards making a better population for Cranston, Olneyville, the Blackstone Valley, and Fall River."[96] He did not condemn these workers for failing to put down permanent roots in the community. "The very nature of operative labor," he reported in 1858, "and the fluctuations of demand and supply, render change almost inevitable." Even if workers had traveled "the circuit of manufacturing States," they still deserved "a religious home." In reflecting on his last eleven years of service, Stone noted that he had lost as many as four hundred families to other manufacturing districts. Such a volume, he reported with pride, would be "sufficient to make three respectable congregations."[97]

The schools operated by the Ministry at Large enjoyed a solid following. By 1855 the trustees estimated that at least 2,400 students had attended the Sunday school, 800 had attended the evening school, and 400 girls had attended the sewing school.[98] The evening school proved especially popular among children who worked in the mills by day. While bracketing their instruction with singing and scriptural readings, the teachers provided lessons on a wide variety of subjects. "Our system of instruction," reported Stone, "embraces reading, spelling, writing, arithmetic and geography."[99] The ministry also sponsored occasional evening lectures on various topics. In November 1849, for instance, a discourse on physiology drew a crowd of nearly four hundred persons to the chapel.[100] Like the schools set up by the Providence Female Tract Society nearly forty years earlier, the Ministry at Large classes provided instruction in both religious and secular topics.

Edwin M. Stone shared with the women of the Providence Female Tract Society the concern that factory labor undercut learning and training in morality. He fretted about the night shifts in which many of his younger pupils were engaged. "This inversion of the order of nature," he maintained, "must impair the physical condition of these juvenile operatives, and that it may prove detrimental to their manners and morals, there is great reason to fear."[101] But Stone did not simply wring his hands in despair. He

---

[95] *Eighth Annual Report of the Ministry at Large in the City of Providence* (Providence, 1850), 11.
[96] Ibid., 12.
[97] *Sixteenth Report of the Ministry at Large in the City of Providence* (Providence, 1858), 15–16.
[98] *Thirteenth Annual Report*, 28.
[99] *Eighth Annual Report*, 9.
[100] Minutes, November 26, 1849, MAL.
[101] *Ninth Annual Report of the Ministry at Large in the City of Providence* (Providence, 1851), 8–9.

made suggestions for even more comprehensive community improvement projects. He called for decent housing at rents that even women in the garment trades could afford. The conditions in some tenements, he concluded, convinced workers that they "cannot be decent even if they so wish."[102] He deplored the "starvation" wages that the merchant tailors set for their needlewomen.[103] He continued to insist on education as the key to moral elevation and material advancement. Free lectures must be "adapted to the operative and other laboring population hitherto unreached" to provide an edifying alternative to "demoralizing amusements." Stone proposed the creation of a new urban order, marked by adequate housing, fair wages, and a commitment to wholesome education.[104]

The depression of 1857–58 tested both Stone's idealism and the resources of the Ministry at Large. In his estimation, the Providence community beheld the "startling spectacle of not less than 4,000 persons thrown out of employ" during the gloomy winter months.[105] Stretching resources even thinner were substantial numbers of workers from nearby mill towns who came to the city seeking work or relief or both. Stone's chronicle of these hardships—beginning when the prestigious Eagle Screw Factory shifted to "short time" in October 1857—presents a detailed and compelling portrait of the panic.[106] Particularly perplexing to him was the obvious fact that unemployment rested "very heavily upon a worthy class of operatives and day laborers among us."[107] Decent, moral, and diligent workers now roamed the streets seeking to survive. In response the ministry opened a total of eight evening schools throughout the city. Five nights a week, an average of one thousand persons attended these classes, probably as much to shake off the cold as to learn. Stone also felt there was real value to civic order in keeping the unemployed out of trouble—"the most nicely adjusted police arrangements could not have effected so much for the quiet of our streets."[108] But the ministry left the task of providing material aid to the poor to the city government. In the six months between November 1857 and April 1858, the overseer of the poor dispensed over ten thousand dollars, most of it to persons of foreign birth.[109] While the Ministry at Large could provide shelter and instruction,

---

[102] *Twelfth Annual Report of the Ministry at Large in the City of Providence* (Providence, 1854), 27.
[103] *Fourteenth Annual Report of the Ministry at Large in the City of Providence* (Providence, 1856), 6.
[104] Ibid., 19–20.
[105] *Sixteenth Annual Report of the Ministry at Large in the City of Providence* (Providence, 1858), 6.
[106] Minutes, October 19, 1857, MAL.
[107] Minutes, December 21, 1857, MAL.
[108] *Sixteenth Annual Report*, 17.
[109] *Seventeenth Annual Report of the Ministry at Large in the City of Providence* (Providence, 1859), 16.

it did not possess the financial reserves to battle a major economic depression.

The initiatives undertaken by the Ministry at Large describe the outer limits of what bourgeois Protestants thought was possible in the 1840s and 1850s. The ministry proposed the most massive of private programs and created a complex network of interlocking institutions for worship, education, shelter, and material aid. Notwithstanding these prodigious efforts and Stone's deft insights, the ministry's aims were remarkably similar to the ones articulated by the women and men who established homes for Providence's dispossessed. For both the shelter homes and the programs of the Ministry at Large sought to reconstitute religious and moral community, but only in a limited sense. Like the Seamen's Home, the chapel and schools operated by the ministry quarantined workers into segregated institutions. Innovative as he was, Edwin Stone did not envision a more complete reincorporation of Providence's working people into the body of the faithful. Indeed, even as he illuminated the failings of the factory system and needlework, the schools conducted by the Ministry at Large trained workers to participate in the economic system that he so deplored.

If any reform initiative had the potential to restore more completely the ties of Christian fellowship among the social classes of Providence, it was the free church movement. The free church movement contained within it a revolutionary precept: church sanctuaries need not be subdivided with scrupulous attention to wealth and sheer economic power. "In a sense," Charles C. Cole Jr. wrote in his analysis of the free churches of New York, "the growth of a free church movement might be considered as marking the emergence of economic democracy in American churches."[110] Here was real potential for an even greater "democratization of American Christianity."[111] If pew auctions and pew rents could be abolished, then the old distinction between "society" and "church" would crumble, for there would be no mechanism to split the community of those who owned pews and from those who were members of congregations. The free church movement implied, too, that communicants themselves (including women) might attain more governance over issues of pastoral salaries, building projects, and other matters that had rested previously within the purview of the society of pewholders. The free church movement suggested, in short, a fundamental transformation in congregational polity. For with the power of the pewholders broken, average communicants would have a greater voice in governing their churches.

[110] Charles C. Cole Jr., "The Free Church Movement in New York City," *New York History* 34 (1953): 284.
[111] See Hatch, *Democratization of American Christianity*.

Since the free church movement posed a threat to the power of bourgeois men within their congregations, we might well ask why these men countenanced such an apparently drastic reform. In the first place, as we shall see, the free churches rarely delivered on their radical potential. Entrepreneurs took leading roles in establishing them and, once created, even the free churches quickly began to take on features of established congregations. Second, and perhaps more important, the mechanism of the free church allowed bourgeois culture to exorcise its spiritual demons, especially the nagging fear that material wealth corrupted authentic faith. Perhaps more than any other religious practice, pew auctioning symbolized the intrusion of commercial activity into the sanctuary of worship. Among those already touchy about the pervasive influence of "worldliness," the trade in pews looked especially suspicious. In 1856, pastor Benjamin Babbitt based his free church on the premise that "the Church of God shall in no way be made a house of merchandize." He deplored the fact that "to most men the Church is merely an instrument of collecting money to support a weekly lecture, by leasing seats and pews—a mere money speculation."[112] Moreover, respectable Protestants had come to recognize that a few seats "designated as places of poverty" would reinforce "the distinction between the rich and the poor in the very house of God."[113] Concern for the spiritual welfare of the poor blended with fears about the corrupting power of the market.

No single denomination or organizational style characterized the free church movement. Some churches, like the Mariner's Bethel Chapel, aimed to gather worshippers from a specific occupational group. Other efforts, such as the Unitarian-sponsored Ministry at Large, provided an array of services to their congregations. In contrast, the free churches launched by the Episcopalians, the Church of the Messiah, and the Church of the Redeemer focused more narrowly on the spiritual and sacramental needs of communicants. The Congregationalists, too, hoped that the Free Evangelical Congregational Society would assume the status of a permanent and respected church. Still other ventures owed more to individual reformers than to denominational planning. Perry Davis, the celebrated founder of Davis's Vegetable Pain Killer and a Baptist preacher, virtually owned the Stewart Street Baptist Church and allowed a congregation to meet there without paying rent. Providence ministers and laymen translated

[112] *The Charter, Constitution, and By-Laws, of the Church of the Messiah, Providence, R.I. with a statement and explanation of the Principles Involved in its organization, by the Rector* (Providence, 1856), 8, 28.
[113] "Free Churches," *Manufacturer's and Farmer's Journal, Providence and Pawtucket Advertiser,* February 21, 1844.

the conviction that the poor required salvation in vastly different ways.

What the free churches shared, however, was the unmistakable trajectory from mission outpost to respectable congregation. None of them remained for long, if they ever had been, true congregations for the outcast and the downtrodden. In the end, the very success of the free church movement (if measured in terms of the numbers who joined) betrayed the original hopes of the founders who saw in the abolition of pew rents the dawn of a new religious order. What the free church movement did do was to create congregations that bore the firm imprint of the refined congregations that had parented them. In taking this path, Providence's free churches mirrored developments that had taken place in New York in the 1830s and 1840s. There the mission churches created by the Episcopal City Mission Society "were behaving very much like the congregations of other respectable, if hardly fashionable, churches in and around Manhattan."[114] Try as they might, free church sponsors were consistently foiled by their own success.

The free churches maneuvered toward respectability in various ways. Created on December 26, 1844, the Mariner's Bethel Chapel intended to provide a place of public worship for sailors by reserving "all the Pews, slips, or seats in the centre of the house, or between the aisles thereof" as free places.[115] By 1858, church minutes reveal that the congregation began to seek its independence from the board of trustees that had created it. Unitarian influence over the chapel's Sunday school provided the point of conflict. During February, efforts to impose a Unitarian prayer book in its classes provoked a controversy between the trustees and the members. The members flatly rejected the book and resolved to select their own Sunday school superintendent. After initial protest, the Unitarians pulled their instructors out of the school. "I see no reason why the Bethel," commented one member, "may not now take a stand among her sister churches, and add her influence in promoting Christ's cause in this City."[116]

Under the guidance of the Church Missionary Union, the Episcopalians established two churches with more modest goals than the trustees of the Mariner's Bethel Chapel. Rather than reaching out to a specific occupational group, such as sailors, the Episcopalians appear to have simply wanted new members. In 1859, Daniel L. B. Goodwin, who led the initiative for the Church of the Redeemer, planned to collect "English families" who lived north of St. John's Church on the East Side. The pews at St. John's, he

---

[114] Carol Smith-Rosenberg, *Religion and the Rise of the American City: The New York City Mission Movement, 1812–1870* (Ithaca, 1971), 141.

[115] Minutes, December 26, 1844, Mariner's Bethel Chapel Records, RIHS.

[116] Minutes, February 15 and 25, 1858, Mariner's Bethel Chapel Records.

reasoned, "had long been held in the old families of the city" and left little space for newcomers.[117] Benjamin B. Babbitt, an ardent disciple of the free church philosophy, also sought to bring the Episcopalian presence to the manufacturing suburb of Olneyville. Both Babbitt and Goodwin expected their prospective communicants to contribute immediately to the financial health of these churches. Despite Babbitt's dedication to free seats, the Church of the Messiah included some pews appraised for leasing. He also announced the creation of a separate fund to finance the building of "a stone Church, which shall be an ornament to the city." Clearly Babbitt and the "liberal" contributors to the project envisioned the formation of a permanent and prosperous congregation.[118] Daniel Goodwin, too, required that worshippers pay for the church's carpet and provide seat cushions for the pews. By 1863 the church had instituted a system of regular offerings and, a few years later, paid the pastor's salary on their own.[119]

Judged in such terms, the Free Evangelical Congregational Society could boast of being the city's most successful free church venture, and thus, ironically, also its greatest failure. Between 1846 and 1860, it sustained a congregation of at least two hundred members. An 1853 list of its male members reveals a collection of small businessmen, artisans, and machinists.[120] Although the congregation included operatives and laborers during the 1840s, a more affluent sort of worker occupied the seats of this free church a decade after its formation. Like its sister churches in New York, the Free Evangelical Congregational Society found adherents among "the city's honest and industrious artisans and mechanics" rather than among its desperately poor.[121] By 1855 the society could afford to pay one "Mr. Payne" a six-hundred-dollar salary for running its "singing school."[122] Two years later they considered moving the church to a more prestigious location.[123] The very success of a free church could place it beyond the reach of the impoverished members it originally intended to serve.

Not all free churches drew inspiration from those who intoned high principles aimed at the restoration of religious community. The early history of the Stewart Street Baptist Church, founded in 1851, shows how the free

---

[117] *Brief History of the Church of the Redeemer, Providence, R.I., 1859–1889, together with the Constitution and By-Laws of the Parish* (Providence, 1890), 3.

[118] *Charter of the Church of the Messiah*, 27.

[119] *Brief History of the Church of the Redeemer*, 6–8.

[120] *Minutes of the Rhode-Island Congregational Conference, 1872* (Providence, 1872), "Tabular View of Church Members Since 1846," 37; and Minutes, January 11, 1853, Free Evangelical Society Records, RIHS.

[121] Smith-Rosenberg, *Religion and the Rise of the American City*, 143.

[122] Minutes, August 28, 1855, Free Evangelical Society Records.

[123] Minutes, May 11, 1857, Free Evangelical Society Records.

church idea mingled with sheer entrepreneurial savvy. Its members leaned heavily on the largesse of Perry Davis, a patent medicine manufacturer and Baptist preacher. Between 1852 and 1859, Davis virtually owned the church and regarded it as his own private domain. He pronounced sermons there and allowed the members to occupy the sanctuary free of charge.[124] Davis advanced a bizarre mixture of entrepreneurship and a commitment to free worship. He perceived no conflict of interest between his ministerial duties and his business ventures. Advertisements for Davis's Vegetable Pain Killer frequently contained hearty endorsements from local Baptist ministers.[125] In such ways did the creation of a free church coexist with the ethos of the market economy.

The creators of the free church movement could never liberate themselves from the tenacious grasp of the world. Even as they sought to establish safe havens for the poor and oppressed, their penchant for successful organization and promotion perforce ensured that the fledgling missions they formed would one day take their place as respectable congregations. One suspects, too, that the founders of the movement could never quite stomach the unsavory prospect of sitting hip-to-hip with the shabbiest and coarsest of their fellow citizens. Janus-faced, the free church advocates claimed to reach out to the least among their brethren but could not quite help seeking out members who were often not from the lowest ranks of city residents. Free church advocates, like those who established shelter homes and other reform institutions, sought a way to reform the poor while keeping them at arm's length. They might have invited the poor to sit with them in their own congregations. They might have abolished pew rents in their own churches. They might have reconfigured their own sanctuaries, shuffling the seats to obscure the clear demarcations of wealth and power. But they did not. Even in the face of crisis, bourgeois Protestants could not quite come to grips with the pervasiveness of a market culture that reached deep into their refined congregations.

The largest oversight among all of these Protestant efforts to remake religious community was the existence of a vibrant Irish Catholic community. The leaders of the free church movement appear to have ignored almost entirely a striking reality: precisely at the time they struggled to convert the laboring classes, Providence boasted the most self-consciously religious working-class in its history. Protestant reformers simply did not recognize the Irish Catholics as an authentic religious presence. They also doubted their ability to convert them. That they could speak of an unchurched

---

[124] *Articles of Faith of the Stewart Street Baptist Church,* 30–37.

[125] For an example of such advertisements see "The People's Pamphlet," Rider Collection, Brown University Library.

working-class during the 1850s exposes the most important lacuna in their overall vision for moral and religious reform.

The poverty and transiency of the famine Irish impressed native Rhode Islanders far more than their piety. In 1852 a committee reporting to the city council on relief of the outdoor poor claimed their resources "entirely inadequate when applied to the vast hordes of famishing paupers, thrown upon our shores from the almshouses and the prisons of Europe."[126] The marginal representation of Irish immigrants in the 1850 city directory and tax list testifies to their slender resources. Settling primarily in the city's First and Fifth Wards, residents of foreign parentage represented about 28 percent of the population there. But they seldom remained where they landed. One survey indicates that only 25 percent of Irish males remained in the Fifth Ward between 1850 and 1860.[127] Catholic church records, too, provide evidence of a mobile immigrant population. When Father Joseph Fitton married John O'Brien and Joanna Murphy at St. Patrick's Church, he described them as "both formerly of Ireland, of no particular residence at present."[128] An impoverished, transient, and Catholic population, the Irish transformed the Providence cityscape.

The level of religious intensity that the famine Irish brought with them to America remains a slippery question. Some scholars now judge that in Ireland before 1850 only about one-third of Irish Catholics attended Mass with any regularity. Marginal attention to sacraments and passing regard for clerical authority characterized this population. According to this line of argument, those who left Ireland between 1847 and 1860 "were part of the pre-famine generation of nonpracticing Catholics, if indeed they were Catholics at all."[129] Evidence from New York's Irish Catholic parishes in the 1860s seems to confirm this assessment. One survey suggests that church attendance had improved only slightly—to about 40 percent—during that decade.[130] Nevertheless, the Synod of Thurles in 1850 marked the beginning of a revival of Catholic piety. Over the next quarter of a century, the church hierarchy initiated a massive reform program. They increased dramatically the number of churches, schools, priests, and nuns and sought to

---

[126] *Report of the Select Committee Upon the Subject of Relief to the Out-Door Poor, Submitted to the City Council of Providence, May 10, 1852* (Providence, 1852), 3.
[127] Robert A. Wheeler, "Fifth Ward Irish—Immigrant Mobility in Providence 1850–1870," *Rhode Island History* 32 (1973): 57.
[128] St. Patrick's Church, Marriage Registers, May 6, 1846, Vestry of St. Patrick's Church, Providence, Rhode Island.
[129] Emmet Larkin, "The Devotional Revolution in Ireland, 1850–1875," *American Historical Review* 77 (1972): 651.
[130] Jay Dolan, *The Immigrant Church: New York's Irish and German Catholics, 1815–1865* (Baltimore, Md., 1975), 56.

exercise greater control over the devotional lives of their parishioners. The Irish Catholics who landed in Providence during the 1850s straddled two religious epochs, one characterized by loose attendance on official religion and the other distinguished by zealous attention to the Mass and other sacraments.

In the Diocese of Hartford, which included Rhode Island, devotion triumphed over indifference. Bishop Bernard O'Reilly presided over institutional gains that more than kept pace with the rapid influx of prospective church members. In 1850 his territory included 12 churches to serve an estimated population of 20,000 Catholic parishioners. By 1856, when his steamer disappeared at sea, O'Reilly supervised the devotions of 60,000 Catholics in 46 congregations. He nurtured the growth of 14 schools and 3 orphan asylums. He also trained new priests in a seminary he conducted in the basement of his house. If measured simply in terms of the ratio of churches to communicants, Rhode Island and Connecticut Catholics began to consolidate their own version of a "devotional revolution" in the 1850s.[131] In Providence four major parishes served the bulk of the Irish Catholic population. The Cathedral congregation and St. Patrick's stood ready to greet the famine immigrants when they arrived. Even by 1846, St. Patrick's church installed new galleries and increased its seating capacity to hold 1,250 worshippers, while another 450 persons could be accorded standing room. By 1853, O'Reilly was on hand to dedicate the newly completed St. Joseph's Church, which could accommodate some 1,600 worshippers. In 1858, Bishop McFarland blessed the Immaculate Conception Church, which served communicants living near the Corliss shops in the north end of town. Churches in nearby Pawtucket, Olneyville, and Cranston could also have drawn communicants from the city. Even a rough estimate suggests that by 1860 as many as 4,000 Catholics could simultaneously attend Mass in Providence's churches.[132]

Evidence from baptismal and marriage registers reveals that these parishes stayed busy. In 1852, probably a record year, over eight hundred children were baptized in the city's three churches. (See Table 23.) Marriage records, too, reveal that some communicants traveled for miles from mill villages without churches to participate in this sacrament. During the late 1840s, couples from the Lonsdale mills, the Blackstone valley, and Mendon, Massachusetts, made their way to St. Patrick's to be married. Catholic schools prospered as well. In 1851, Bishop O'Reilly had

---

[131] William Byrne, *History of the Catholic Church in the New England States* (Boston, 1899), 2:149. The best modern treatment is Robert W. Hayman, *Catholicism in Rhode Island and the Diocese of Providence, 1780–1886* (Providence, 1982).
[132] Byrne, *History of the Catholic Church*, 1:399–403.

Table 23. Baptisms in select Catholic parishes, 1841–1860

Year	Cathedral of SS. Peter & Paul	St. Patrick's Church	St. Joseph's Church
1841	—	68	—
1842	—	89	—
1843	160	143	—
1844	253	180	—
1845	285	191	—
1846	327	247	—
1847	341	276	—
1848	391	289	—
1849	404	279	—
1850	463	329	—
1851	397	276	65
1852	478	234	95
1853	428	185	81
1854	423	—	139
1855	436	—	91
1856	338	—	144
1857	305	—	136
1858	349	—	118
1859	365	—	178
1860	315	—	167

Sources: Baptismal registers of Cathedral of SS. Peter and Paul's; St. Patrick's Church; St. Joseph's Church, all in possession of the respective parishes in Providence.

Note: Data are not available for some years. St. Joseph's Church was formed in 1851. By 1858 the Church of the Immaculate Conception had been established in Providence, and more than 350 persons were baptized there between 1858 and 1860.

introduced the Sisters of Mercy in Providence, and the sisters set about conducting a "free school" in the basement of the Cathedral church. By 1855 the Bishop announced to the city census takers that 1,640 young Catholic scholars attended classes sponsored by the city's churches and the Sisters of Mercy. Given the limited resources of the city's Catholic community, these efforts illuminate another dimension of religious resolve. When coupled with the statistics on the sacrament of baptism, figures on school attendance reinforce the impression that adults wished to train their children in the faith.[133]

Protestant domestic missionaries, such as William Douglas and Edwin M. Stone, viewed these devout Catholics with grave suspicion. Normally men of

[133] Ibid., 1:395–396; Snow, *Census of Providence*, 33.

measured judgment and considerable street sense, they turned their harshest comments on the city's population of "foreigners." In 1845, Douglas reported that "the degraded population of our city are foreigners & most of them the votaries of a church whose vowed aims & tendencies are to establish & maintain ignorance among the common people."[134] So dim were the prospects for winning Catholics to Protestant churches that he announced that there was "little ostensible religious good he could ordinarily confer upon Irish immigrants."[135] Stone rarely even spoke of the Irish in religious terms. Instead, in his 1850 report to the Ministry at Large, he lumped the foreigners into three classes, based only on their ability to find work. The best Irish found "regular employment," the next step down the ladder included day laborers who sometimes found work, and below them could be found "regular leeches, beggars of the lowest quality."[136] To Stone and Douglas, the immigrants represented ignorance, immorality, and poverty— the triumvirate of evils they sought to eradicate.

The murder of the industrialist Amasa Sprague crystallized anti-Catholic sentiment, already primed by the Dorr Rebellion.[137] On December 31, 1843, a handyman discovered Amasa Sprague's body in a field near his home in Cranston. The immediate suspects included the Irish immigrants Nicholas, John, and William Gordon. Sprague had evidently blocked the renewal of a liquor license for Nicholas Gordon's small store—presumably because the employees of his print works regularly patronized the establishment. Nicholas Gordon placed himself at Mass in Providence on the day of the murder and thus escaped prosecution. His brothers were not as lucky. In March 1844, the Supreme Court of Rhode Island tried John and William Gordon for the murder Amasa Sprague. Thomas Carpenter, their attorney, presented evidence that the two suspects had been in church as well. Jeremiah Bagot testified that he "saw John Gordon in the Catholic Church at mass. He sat in No. 10 and I sat in No. 11, he on one side of the aisle and I on the other." Michael Holohan, too, explained that he had seen William Gordon "in the Catholic Church at mass." But this testimony did not prove convincing. Carpenter vainly tried to counter doubts by asking the court, "And are these witnesses to be disbelieved, because they happen to belong

---

134 Report for November 3, 1845, PFDMS MSS.
135 Report for October 2, 1848, PFDMS MSS.
136 Minutes, October 28, 1850, MAL.
137 See Charles Hoffman and Tess Hoffman, *Brotherly Love: Murder and the Politics of Prejudice in Nineteenth-Century Rhode Island* (Amherst, Mass., 1993). The Hoffmans speculate that it was not the Gordons but William Sprague, Amasa's brother, who plotted the murder. If that were the case, then it provides even more compelling evidence showing the degree to which the quest for wealth had corrupted ostensibly pious Protestants. See 137–146 for the Hoffmans' theory of the crime.

to the same church, and come from the same land?" Joseph Blake, the attorney general, pressed home the point that the Irish were known to possess "strong propensities; strong attachments and resentments." Among these, a powerful sense of "fraternal feeling" had provoked William and John to murder Sprague for trouble he had caused their brother.[138] The Gordon trial provided a forum for the debate on Irish Catholic character in general. And when John Gordon was found guilty and hanged in 1845, it signaled a verdict against the Irish Catholic community as well. Even pious Catholics could be dangerous murderers.

Concern with the Irish Catholic threat reached a crescendo in 1855, when the American Party captured an overwhelming majority of the seats in the Rhode Island General Assembly. But politics alone does not explain the success of Rhode Island nativism. To be sure, some Protestants worried that the Irish might seek political power. In 1851 the *Providence Daily Journal* held fast to the idea that the freehold requirement for naturalized citizens should be maintained. Otherwise, "our political rights and state institutions will be completely at the mercy of Irish Catholic voters, marshalled and drilled by Catholic Jesuits priests."[139] But such fears proved unfounded. The property requirement for immigrant citizens endured into the 1880s. Unlike the situation in Massachusetts or in New York, where the Irish emerged as an important political constituency, in Rhode Island they remained a marginal power.[140]

Even after the crumbling of the Know-Nothings as a political movement, Protestants and Catholics continued to view each other with suspicion and hostility. In March 1855, word surfaced that the Sisters of Mercy held a Protestant convert, Rebecca Newell, against her will. Although such reports proved false, a mob of nearly two thousand people assembled to menace the convent. Bishop O'Reilly's courage prevented the outbreak of large-scale violence. Placing himself between the crowd and the convent, he proclaimed, "The sisters are in their home, they shall not leave it even for an hour; I shall protect them while I have life, and, if needs be, register their safety with my

[138] Trial quotations are from *The Trial of John and William Gordon, charged with the murder of Amasa Sprague, before the Supreme Court of Rhode Island, March Term, 1844* (Providence, 1884), 56, 57, 116, 132.
[139] *Providence Daily Journal,* cited in John Michael Ray, "Anti-Catholicism and Know-Nothingism in Rhode Island," *American Ecclesiastical Review* 148 (1963): 31; see also Larry Anthony Rand, "The Know-Nothing Party in Rhode Island: Religious Bigotry and Political Success," *Rhode Island History* 23 (1964): 102–116; Charles Stickney, *Know-Nothingism in Rhode Island* (Providence, 1894).
[140] See John Mulkern, *The Know-Nothing Party in Massachusetts: The Rise and Fall of a People's Movement* (Boston, 1990); Robert Ernst, *Immigrant Life in New York City, 1825–1863* (Port Washington, N.Y., 1949), 162–171.

blood." But no blood was spilled and the mob retired.[141] During the 1858 prayer revival, one "Miss Carroll" found herself the target of harassment at her own baptism. In April, members of the Roger Williams Church, the Bethel Chapel, and Fourth Baptist Church gathered to immerse new members off India Point. Because Miss Carroll was a recent convert to the Protestant faith, her baptism had produced "great excitement among the Irish." Some of the crowd in attendance at the ritual greeted her with shouts of "kill her" and "drown her" as she dipped into the water.[142]

Edward Hall, then, may have been more accurate than he knew when he described his city in terms of a spiritual battleground. On the eve of the Civil War the faithful of Providence were a twice-divided people. Bourgeois Protestants found themselves at odds with the results of their own economic ethic, worried that their preoccupation with the world could lead them along the path toward sensual entertainment, frivolity, and dangerous self-indulgence. In combat with themselves, they sought to reach out to the unchurched in their midst, as much to solve their internal spiritual dilemmas as to recreate a more inclusive sense of religious community. But here they discovered fresh conundrums. Their free churches did not long sustain their status as missions among the poor. And, most important, their efforts to knit together the religious affections of city residents never included Irish Catholics. To say this is not to condemn bourgeois reformers for what they dared to do. Given the political climate and the nativist proclivities of Americans in the 1850s, it would have been nothing short of miraculous if Protestant missionaries such as Edwin Stone and William Douglas had sought to deal with Irish Catholics as people of authentic faith.[143] Even at its best, however, the moral perspective of bourgeois reformers could not comprehend that many of Providence's workers did not want the particular type of social salvation that they were being offered. In the moment of their greatest triumph, bourgeois Protestants could thus not restore the internal peace and the social harmony for which they so desperately longed.

---

[141] Hayman, *Catholicism in Rhode Island,* 137–140.

[142] *Providence Daily Journal,* April 15, 1858.

[143] See Tyler Anbinder, *Nativism and Slavery: The Northern Know-Nothings and the Politics of the 1850s* (New York, 1992).

Epilogue

The faithful of Providence traveled a considerable distance since the days when the members of First Baptist Church brought their case against Benjamin Knowles. A glance at two images of the city—one drawn by John Fitch in 1790 and the other a lithograph from 1858–59 titled *View from the West Bank of the River,* by John Perry Newall—suggests at least one important change that had transpired. In the 1790 sketch, included in Chapter 1, Providence's churches—First Congregational, First Baptist, and St. John's Episcopal—and the campus of Rhode-Island College loom as the only significant and individuated structures in the city. The other buildings, with a few exceptions, are strung along banks of the Providence River and clustered astride Weybosset Street as it stretches toward the sparsely settled West Side. There is a primitive, unrefined quality to the Fitch map that is part of its undeniable charm. No people are depicted. The perspective of the artist is nearly dizzying. Is it drawn from the point of view of someone walking down the streets, looking at the homes and businesses on either side? Or is it designed from a more lofty perspective, one that looks down on the city and its occupants? While ships are seen docked in the wharves and sailing in the river, they are rendered fantastically, some appearing even to sail upside-down out of the harbor. In the Fitch's hands, the only facades worthy of sustained attention are those of the churches. Piety commands the cityscape, triumphing over the portrayal of commerce.

The 1858 lithograph by John Perry Newall complicates this relationship. While church spires still punctuate the cityscape—the towers of First Congregational and First Baptist Church stand elegant and tall—what is most noticeable here is a city bristling with the pursuit of trade. A smokestack, a

View from the West Bank of the River, by J. P. Newall (1858–59). Newall's lithograph stresses the commercial activities of the city rather than its church spires. Courtesy of The Rhode Island Historical Society, RHi (×3) 339.

lumberyard, and warehouses fill the foreground. Vessels sail through the harbor. On some of them individual sailors can be made out. The lithograph looks toward the dense crowd of buildings on the East Side. While the casual observer would note a variety of churches tucked among the residences and businesses, the overall impression is one a bustling center of commerce and industry. The eye scans this busy image, sometimes resting on the steeple of First Congregational Church but landing more often, perhaps, on the ships in the harbor, on the American flag flying atop the state capitol, or on the high stacks of lumber at the bottom of the scene. While religion is still important, it must now compete, visually at least, with the other occupations of the city. Images of trade and commerce jostle with church spires for the attention of the viewer. Unlike the Fitch drawing of 1790, the Newall lithograph captures vividly the growing worldliness that so deeply vexed clergymen such as Edward Hall and Francis Wayland.

If viewers of Newall's lithograph could peer inside the churches that the artist depicted, they would glimpse other changes. They could not fail to see how city residents had reshaped in fundamental ways their comprehension of what it means to live in religious community. In the early national era, Providence's churches conceived of themselves in ways that approximated an extended civic family: these congregational families exhibited profoundly unequal relationships of power and prestige, for men clearly owned the church and its pews; but they were simultaneously inclusive, gathering residents of different races, social ranks, and gradations of wealth. In its wide social embrace, in its clear gradations of social hierarchy, and in its blurring of the public and private realms, this notion of religious community or "family" resonated with aspects of the Filmerian worldview that, according to Mary Beth Norton, typified New England's colonies in the seventeenth century.[1] By the 1850s, Providence churches had, in many ways, jettisoned this older, more organic understanding of religious community. Congregations now sorted themselves more neatly by race and ethnicity, status and wealth. To be sure, bourgeois Protestants shared with their early national counterparts conservative presumptions with respect to the ways in which religious institutions could mold and sustain social order. But by the 1850s, even the nature of this conservatism had changed. As George Frederickson has pointed out, by that time "the church-centered, organic view of society, with its stress on tradition and authority, was held by a small minority. It was clearly out of tune with the dominant trends of American thought."[2] For antebellum Northerners modern individualism prevailed over more conservative and community based ways of being in the world.[3]

This newer notion of religious community, one that recognized and validated the divides of ethnicity, class, and status, reflected the bifurcation of Providence religious culture. The process of religious bifurcation was first forged in the Rhode Island countryside; fueled by the revival of 1820, it crystallized in the 1830s and then shaped the struggle of the Dorr Rebellion during the 1840s. By the 1850s, the bifurcation of the city's religious culture, embodied in its bourgeois and plebeian manifestations, had become an accepted fact. Both plebeian and bourgeois members of the city's religious culture contributed to the creation of this new order. For their part, plebeian enthusiasts sought their own religious institutions outside the reach of the merchant and manufacturing elite. Their religious populism clashed with the more refined and respectable religion practiced by bourgeois Protestants. As for the refined Protestants, they established themselves in orderly and polished churches designed, in part, to keep the plebeian populists at bay. Even the reform institutions they created in the 1850s never intended to remake fully an organic and inclusive sense of religious

---

[1] See Mary Beth Norton, *Founding Mothers and Fathers: Gendered Power and the Forming of American Society* (New York, 1996).

[2] George M. Frederickson, *The Inner Civil War: Northern Intellectuals and the Crisis of the Union* (New York, 1968), 28.

[3] An intriguing explication that places individualism at the heart of American politics in the Jacksonian period is Lawrence Frederick Kohl, *The Politics of Individualism: Parties and the American Character in the Jacksonian Era* (New York, 1989).

community. Nor did Irish Catholic immigrants want to be part of such a renewed order. On the eve of the Civil War, religious culture within the city
had been irrevocably fractured.

The bifurcation of religious life in antebellum Providence—the story of
which has been told here—points toward a number of important conclu-
sions for students of American religion and society. First, it reminds us that
religious culture itself was a critical medium in which class relationships ma-
tured. Working people and their bourgeois social betters struggled to grasp
the mantle of Christian legitimacy as their own.[4] As is evident in the lives
and thought of Seth Luther and Francis Wayland, coarse populists and
refined Protestants forged the religious culture of antebellum Providence.
This is not to say that religion meant all things to all people in the early republic. But it is to argue that religion figured centrally in the process of class
formation in the Age of Jackson. This observation should lead us to a
healthy skepticism with respect to the explanatory leverage of sweepingly
consensual terms such as "the United Evangelical Front," or "the Benevolent Empire," or even "the Second Great Awakening," for they imply a fundamental unity of religious experience that escaped the residents of Providence, and quite possibly those living elsewhere in early America. The
evidence presented here shows that the chemistry of Christianity in this
period was too volatile and too complex to be reduced to such simple
compounds.

The process of religious bifurcation in Providence was a gendered one.
We have glimpsed how bourgeois religious culture, especially in the ways it
secured the economic power of churches in the hands of men, retained a
strikingly masculine character. Given the role bourgeois men such as
Stephen Wardwell played as pewholders and as leaders in religious benevolence, we need to question the extent to which "middle-class" religion in the
antebellum era had become "feminized." The story we have told here suggests that bourgeois women experienced subordination not only within
their homes but in the sanctuaries where they worshiped as well. Simultaneously, however, we have observed how benevolent and reform organizations laid a foundation for women's political culture in Providence. And we
have seen, especially in the activities of the "Dorrite ladies," that even before
they received voting rights, Rhode Island's women projected themselves
into the fray of partisan politics. In contrast to bourgeois religious culture,
the world of the plebeian enthusiasts exhibited, in its penchant for

---

[4] This was a point that Herbert G. Gutman made long ago for the late nineteenth century in
his classic essay, "Protestantism and the America Labor Movement: The Christian Spirit in the
Gilded Age," in *Work, Culture, and Society in Industrializing America* (New York, 1977), 79–117.
We are only beginning to appreciate the application of his insight for the antebellum period.

emotional expression and in its propensity for disorder and rebelliousness, qualities that were gendered female. Female preaching, too, particularly among Freewill Baptists and Methodists also played an important part in the creation of plebeian religious culture. And even in Providence proper, street preachers such as Seth Luther were targeted with church crimes, such as "disorderly walking," that carried a distinctly feminine connotation. To be sure, plebeian religion possessed its rough-and-tumble elements, clearly visible in a verbal combativeness that marked it as masculine. But in ways that we are only beginning to understand, the plebeian enthusiasts of the early republic look more "feminine" than their more "masculine" bourgeois counterparts.

The story we have traced here also informs our understanding of the complex relationship between evangelical Christianity and the rise of market culture in the antebellum era. The interpretation offered in this book suggests that good Christian people, both bourgeois and plebeian, regarded the rise of the market revolution with a profound sense of ambivalence. Churchmen in the early national era, men such as Jonathan Maxcy, James Wilson, and Asa Messer, promoted industry and commerce only within the compass of a moral world that stressed the obligations that merchants, farmers, and artisans owed to one another. Even in the pro-market pronouncements of Francis Wayland, concerns over sheer specula-tion lingered. The rise of the free church movement, too, signaled a level of discomfort with pew auctioning that tapped a deeper worry about the pen-etrating influences of worldliness. And bourgeois women, throughout the 1820s and 1830s, pointed out the corrosive effects of greed on the Chris-tian spirit of the city. Plebeians, as well, looked warily on the economic transformation of the early republic. They saw in factory labor, for instance, new patterns of work that would sap their spiritual and moral development by closing out opportunities for religious reading and prayer. They reached out for religious experiences that put them at odds with the good order and discipline of bourgeois congregations. In the writings of Seth Luther we find a religiously inspired assault on the presence of avarice in Jacksonian America as well as an attack on Rhode Island's restrictive suffrage requirements. It was, quite simply, not a forgone conclusion that the force of evangelical religion could be brought to bear on behalf of the market revolution. In many ways, evangelical Protestantism provided ballast against the rising tide of acquisitiveness and self-interest.[5]

Newall's lithograph suggests, perhaps, that the pious residents of

---

[5] See also Mark Y. Hanley, *Beyond a Christian Commonwealth: The Protestant Quarrel with the American Republic, 1830–1860* (Chapel Hill, N.C., 1994).

Providence had reached a happy accommodation with the pursuits of commerce and industry. The artist's churches seem so neatly interspersed with sites of trade as to present the viewer with a seamless urban web. But the ordering of life evident in the earlier sketch never quite disappeared. Even as they marched toward a new urban order, Providence residents could not quite turn their backs on another vision, an earlier and more primitive vision, one that told them that the interests of piety and commerce were not identical and that the goals of the former must always supplant the aims of the latter. It was a struggle they never fully reconciled. Perhaps it continues still.

Index

Numbers printed in italic denote illustrations.